Elementary Social Studies

Elementary Social Studies

Developing Reflective, Competent, and Concerned Citizens

Peter H. Martorella

Temple University

Little, Brown and Company   Boston   Toronto

Library of Congress Cataloging in Publication Data

Martorella, Peter H.
  Elementary social studies.

  Includes bibliographies and indexes.
  1. Social sciences — Study and teaching (Elementary) —
Teacher training. 2. Civics, American — Study and
teaching (Elementary) — Teacher training. I. Title.
LB1584.M343 1985   372.8'3044   84-10036
ISBN 0-316-54870-7

Library of Congress Catalog Card No. 84-10036

ISBN 0-316-54870-7

9   8   7   6   5   4   3   2   1

VB

Published simultaneously in Canada
by Little, Brown and Company (Canada) Limited

Printed in the United States of America

In memory of Constance Loomis Morgan

Preface

Children who enter elementary schools today will graduate from high school on the edge of the twenty-first century. In many respects the world they will face is likely to be much different from the one their parents encountered. They will be entering an era of lasers and computers, the possible colonization of space, increasing interdependence of nations, and new vocational opportunities, to sketch only a few characteristics of their future as adults.

In preparing for and assuming their roles as citizens of a democracy, children of today will need to acquire some of the same skills as did preceding generations of students. They must understand the basic principles and aspirations that undergird our democracy, and they must recognize the ties that bind us and the issues that can separate us as a pluralistic nation. They must understand, also, the need for competent participation in our society. The social studies curriculum must assume a major part of the societal responsibility for developing the knowledge, skills, and sense of commitment that make up effective citizenship. We thus are faced with the challenge of preparing children for the current world in which they live and for the future one that they will help build.

How will our schools in general and the social studies curriculum in particular help prepare children for this future world? How can the schools and the social studies curriculum in partnership help develop the knowledgeable, skillful, compassionate, and resourceful citizens that our democracy needs in order to survive and flourish? These are questions we attempt to answer in this text in ways that will be useful to prospective as well as experienced elementary and middle-school teachers. We begin with the contention that the fundamental purpose of the social studies curriculum should be to develop *reflective, competent,* and *concerned* citizens. This theme is carried throughout all chapters.

The book is divided into five parts. In Part I we explore the patterns and practice of teaching social studies. Because how we plan for and carry out our teaching must be influenced by how children develop cognitively and socially, we devote a chapter to the significance of developmental differences. Part II illustrates strategies for developing the *reflective* dimension of effective citizenship. Teaching concepts, facts, generalizations, hypotheses, problem-solving, and reflective thinking occupy our attention. Parts III and IV in turn concentrate on activities for developing *competency* and *concern* in young citizens. Skills — including social, research, and spatial skills — along with beliefs, attitudes, and values are key topics. In the final section of the text we examine some of the significant components of an *effective instructional climate* in elementary and middle schools. These include effective evaluation strategies; ways to improve communication, both in the classroom and outside; addressing special needs of all students, including the gifted and the handicapped; individualizing instruction; and discovering and implementing new resources and technologies.

Throughout each chapter boxed exercises are keyed to various points within the discussion. These have been designed to help you and your students:

1. reflect on a point discussed
2. go beyond the text to pursue a related subject of possible interest
3. test a strategy or principle through some experience in schools, in teaching children, or in developing instructional materials

Students and instructors may use these exercises in different ways and *adapt* them to special needs and situations. Some exercises may appropriately be completed in a course class. Others require access to resources typically found in instructional libraries or schools. Still others require work with elementary or middle-school students.

In writing this text our goal was to combine sound scholarship with a clear point of view. We hoped to create a comprehensive yet readable book, one that gives a feeling for children as well as a broad sense of the tasks and strategies in teaching social studies.

Brief Contents

Contents

Part Two Developing Citizens Who Think and Act Reflectively 67

PART ONE

Teaching Social Studies in America

1

The American Tradition of Social Studies

The Social Studies and Citizenship

It is traditional that of all the subjects children study in school, social studies has the most responsibility for preparing them to be citizens. What we now regard as social studies was seen early in America's history as that subject which would teach students about our nation's history, traditions, achievements, and aspirations. It also was to prepare them for responsibly exercising their rights and duties as citizens.

Social Studies as a Basic Subject in the Curriculum

Given these important charges by society, social studies has remained one of the "basics" of the curriculum, along with reading, writing, and arithmetic. The National Commission on Excellence in Education, reporting in 1983 that we were a "nation at risk" because of the declining quality of our schools, reaffirmed the importance of the social studies for citizenship education. In urging curricular reform the commission's report noted, "For our country to function, citizens must be able to reach some common understandings on complex issues, often on short notice and on the basis of conflicting or incomplete information."[1] Just as literacy and computation skills are essential in modern life, so also is a wide range of social information and skills associated with citizenship education.

The Social Studies and Democracy

For a democracy of over 225 million citizens to function effectively and to prosper it is essential, for example, that its members understand our political processes and how our leaders are chosen. Today parents, community members, the government, and society in general, expect the social studies curriculum to continue its historic mission of preparing young people for their roles as effective citizens.

3

The Nature of the Social Studies

In the early history of our nation what we now call the social studies curriculum drew heavily from three areas: history, civics (political science), and geography. The term "social studies" appears to have become popular after a curriculum committee's efforts appeared formally in a bulletin in 1916 entitled *The Social Studies in Secondary Education*.[2]

Debate within the Profession

Since the term came into popular use, social studies educators have continued to debate what the nature of their field should be. Commenting on the history of the social studies, Shirley Engle, a former president of the National Council for the Social Studies (NCSS), the professional organization representing the field, has written,

> We in the social studies have experienced, and experience to this very day, a struggle between contending and irreconcilable factions, one or another of which has, from time to time, depending upon the flow of civic affairs, enjoyed the ascendancy over the others, but none of which has ever given up the battle or emerged as total victor.[3]

Another NCSS president, Howard Mehlinger, put the matter more tersely: "Social studies has an identity crisis."[4]

Definitions of the Social Studies

Many different viewpoints regarding the nature of the social studies have been advanced over the years. Here is a cross section of some definitions of the field beginning with the first formal one, as included in the report of the 1916 committee mentioned earlier.

> The social studies are understood to be those whose subject matter relates directly to the organization and development of human society, and to man as a member of social groups.[5]

> The social studies are the social sciences simplified for pedagogical purposes.[6]

> The Social Studies is a broader field than that covered by the Social Sciences. It is more accurate to think of the Social Studies as an applied field which attempts to fuse scientific knowledge with ethical, philosophical, religious, and social considerations which arise in the process of decision-making as practiced by the citizen.[7]

> The social studies is an integration of experience and knowledge concerning human relations for the purpose of citizenship education.[8]

> Social studies is a kind of shorthand for the study of people by pupils in elementary and secondary schools.[9]

A Working Definition of the Social Studies. What does this continuing debate imply about the nature of the social studies today? Among other things it indicates that a consensus on the nature of the social studies is not likely to emerge in the near future. It also helps to explain why in recent years many social studies educators have been reluctant to propose new definitions of the field.

We will use the following working definition of the social studies in this text. The social studies are:

1. selected information and modes of investigation from the social sciences
2. selected information from any area that relates directly to the understanding and development of individuals, groups, and societies
3. applications of the selected information to citizens' decision-making

As you encounter discussions of the nature of the social studies in other readings, you may wish to compare those definitions to the one used here.

The Social Studies and the Social Sciences

A common thread weaves throughout social studies educators' perspectives of their field. It is their view of the relationship between the social studies and the academic disciplines of the social sciences. Most educators would concede that social studies gains some of its identity from the social sciences: history, political science, geography, economics, sociology, anthropology, and psychology.

The Social Sciences as Sources of Subject Matter
for the Social Studies

In teaching social studies we may draw primarily from one social science discipline, as when we look to history for an account of Columbus' trip to the new world. Or we may wish to use an interdisciplinary approach, tapping several of the social sciences to explain a topic. For example, we might use the insights of economists, sociologists, psychologists, and geographers to help explain why people in the United States today settle where they do.

The methods of inquiry used in the social sciences, such as the formulation and testing of hypotheses, also are important sources of subject matter. In their daily lives citizens often need the same skills as social scientists to function effectively. Figure 1.1 shows how the social studies curriculum draws on the social sciences for its subject matter.

The Social Sciences

The social sciences all use the scientific method, focus on understanding and explaining human behavior, and employ systematic collection and application of data. They also share an interest in predicting patterns and behavior, a concern for verification, a desire for objectivity, and interests in furthering knowledge and standards of scholarship. Each discipline, however, claims special insights that give it its distinct identification.

FIGURE 1.1   The contributions of the social sciences to the social studies curriculum

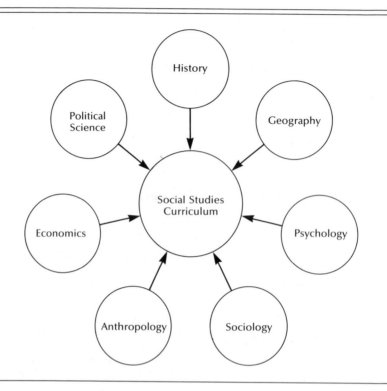

History

In its most fundamental sense, history is a chronicle or recollection of what occurred. Such chronicles may be oral or written, and they may relate to oneself, others, nations, social groups, or the like. As chroniclers, historians attempt to construct a coherent narrative of the sequence of events over time.

Since it is impossible to record everything about any event, and since all records are colored to some extent by our views and attitudes, history is also an *interpretation* of what occurred. Historians search for the *causes* of events, as well as the *effects,* and where the relationships are not obvious, they construct hypotheses (informed guesses) about what might have been.

Often the task of recording an event also involves investigating and reconciling alternative accounts and incorporating documents into a pattern of verified evidence. Hence, history is also a synthesis and explanation of many facts about the past. The fabric of history thus is woven with narratives, interpretations, and syntheses.

Political Science

Political science has its roots in philosophy and history. Plato's *Republic* and Aristotle's *Politics*, for example, are used today in college classes both in philosophy and political science. Above all, political science is concerned with the organization and governance of nations and social units.

More broadly, it is concerned with an analysis of *power*, and the processes by which individuals and groups control and manage one another. Power may be applied at the governmental level through the ballot box, but it is also exercised at board meetings and in many other social settings. Power, in some form, is exercised throughout society.

Political scientists are interested in the competing demands of various groups in our society as they affect governmental institutions. This has led to analyses of how different constituencies or interest groups influence and shape public policy. They are also interested in the relationships among nations, including how cooperation and ties develop and conflicts emerge and are resolved.

Geography

It is the concept of *place* that is central to the discipline of geography. Geographers are concerned with the location and character of places on the earth's surface. They attempt to relate these places; to explain how goods, events, and people pass from place to place; and to determine what factors have shaped these places. Maps and globes of all types often are their basic tools.

Geographers also attempt accurately to describe these locations on the earth's surface from many different perspectives. They examine what is below ground in the form of rocks and mineral deposits and what is above in the form of climate. Geographers have always been interested too in how the places affect the lives of people located there.

Economics

Economics is above all the study of production, consumption, and exchange. The object of these three activities is some set of goods, such as shoes, or some service, such as lawn cutting. Since these activities occur at all levels and on all scales — from an international conglomerate to a local newspaper carrier — they often are examined by economists according to the scope of their effect.

Within the framework of production, consumption, and exchange, economists study and document the patterns of human behavior and attempt to predict it. They also examine the surplus or scarcity of goods and services in relation to peoples' needs and wants. Since countries differ in their systems for organizing production, consumption, and exchange, economists also compare their applications. Similarly, they examine the international patterns of exchange or currencies to determine how these affect economic behavior among countries.

Sociology

Sociology is the study of human interactions within groups. Sociologists study people in social settings, sometimes called *social systems*. They focus on our behavior in basic social units such as the family, ethnic groupings, social classes, organizations and clubs, and in various community settings. Sociologists are interested in how all of the basic types of social institutions — for example, religious, economic, political, and legal institutions — affect our daily lives.

Sociologists also examine how individuals' activities preserve or change social systems. From the study of specific social systems, such as the various families within a small community, sociologists attempt to derive general principles that can be applied to all similar groups. Since sociology includes some analysis of behavior in every major institution within society, it often overlaps the other social sciences. The work of the sociologist studying the political behavior of various groups during a national election and that of a political scientist, for example, may intersect.

Anthropology

Closely aligned with sociology is anthropology. It is perhaps the most difficult discipline to define, since its scope is broad and it has several major subdivisions, including physical and cultural anthropology. Speaking broadly, anthropologists like to say that their discipline is the study of humankind.

Anthropologists are interested in both the biological and the environmental determinants of human behavior. How individuals use their genetic inheritance to adapt to and shape their environment makes up the major framework of what most anthropologists consider *culture*. Culture is a central concept in anthropology, as place is in geography. It refers to the entire way of life of a society, including not only behavior but shared ideas and language. Culture is unique to humans, and it is learned rather than inherited. In essence, anthropology is an attempt at greater understanding of the relationship between culture and people.

Psychology

Modern psychology derives from earlier religious and philosophical studies into the nature of humans and the reasons for their behavior. The question of whether an individual has a free will, for example, was merely shifted into a scientific arena as psychology developed. A discipline with many subdivisions, psychology focuses on individual mental processes and behavior.

Psychologists study animal as well as human behavior. Like anthropologists, they are interested in both the genetic and learned aspects of behavior. Much of the discipline concentrates on the process of learning, which psychologists regard as a major determinant of human behavior. The boundaries of psychology are often difficult to determine, since its investigations often spill over into biology, medicine, and physics, as well as into the other social sciences.

Psychology has both applied and experimental sides. Some branches, such as counseling psychology, apply knowledge directly to the solution of human problems in clinical settings. Other psychologists work in a laboratory, conducting controlled experiments that may not have any short-term applications to human behavior.

EXERCISE 1.1   Examining the Dimensions of the Social Sciences

There are several sources of information on the scope and sub-divisions of each of the social sciences. To examine one of the disciplines in more depth and to identify its areas of specialization consult the *International Encyclopedia of the Social Sciences* (17 vols. New York: Macmillan, 1968). Determine (1) the definition given for the social science discipline, and (2) its major subdivisions.

Other Sources of Subject Matter for the Social Studies

The social studies curriculum draws on many areas besides the social sciences for data. In the social studies one applies social knowledge to citizens' decision making. Teachers need to look to all sources of information that can help prepare students for this task.

The arts and sciences, the law, popular culture and music, data from students' daily lives, the social life within the school, and the mass media are but a sample of the possible sources of subject matter that are outside the framework of the social sciences, but that bear on the human condition. (See Figure 1.2.) Subject matter within these areas which relates to the organization, understanding, and development of individuals, groups and societies is relevant to the social studies curriculum.

Purposes of the Social Studies Curriculum

Why teach social studies? Closely related to the questions of the nature of the social studies and its relationship to the social sciences is the issue of its primary purpose in the curriculum. Debate over the purposes of the social studies curriculum essentially centers on which should be the *primary* or *dominant* one.

There is a general consensus that the fundamental purpose for the social studies should be *citizenship education*. Beyond this basic area of agreement, however, there are a variety of views on the purpose implied by citizenship education. These might be regarded as different notions of the primary purpose of the social studies or alternative views of how citizenship education can best be developed.

Alternative Views of Citizenship Education

For over a decade, Barr, Barth, and Shermis, have analyzed and attempted to categorize the sets of purposes that various social studies educators have advanced in the twentieth century.[10] Their work and that of Engle,[11] and Nelson and Michaelis[12]

FIGURE 1.2   Other contributions to the social studies curriculum

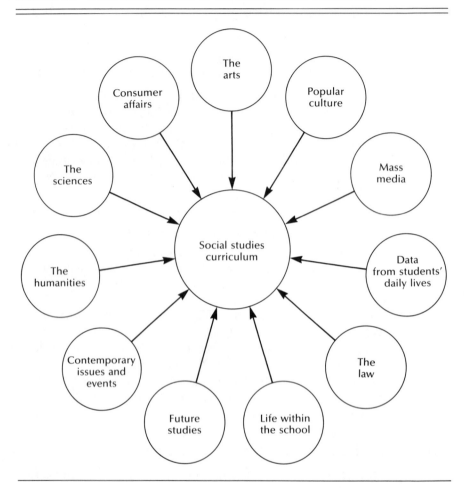

have identified five types of major purposes: social studies taught as *transmission of the cultural heritage, the social sciences, reflective inquiry, informed social criticism,* and *personal development.*

These five major purposes do not exhaust all of the possibilities. Furthermore, none of the alternative schemes that have been suggested, including the five summarized here, is completely distinct from the other categories. Often one category, when analyzed, appears in fact to include all other categories of purposes. Teaching social studies as reflective inquiry, for example, may at times include teaching for social criticism. Nevertheless, one can clarify one's own views by considering some of the emphases or dominant perspectives within the field that each statement of purpose reflects.

Major Purpose	*Description*
Social studies taught as transmission of the cultural heritage	Inculcate traditional knowledge and values as a framework for making decisions
Social studies taught as social science	Master social science concepts, generalizations, and processes to build a knowledge base for later learning.
Social studies taught as reflective inquiry	Employ a process of thinking and learning in which knowledge is derived from what citizens need to know to make decisions and solve problems
Social studies taught as informed social criticism	Provide opportunities for an examination, critique, and revision of past traditions, existing social practices, and modes of problem-solving
Social studies taught as personal development	Develop a positive self-concept, a strong sense of personal efficacy, and an understanding of one's relationship to others

---

EXERCISE 1.2   Identifying the Major Purpose of Teaching Social Studies

Consider each of the five major purposes proposed, and try to assess which you consider to be the most important. Further, try to decide how you would rank them in order of priority.

What are the reasons for your decisions? Is there a sixth purpose that you would prefer as your first choice? Could you create a synthesis position composed of parts of the five?

The Enduring Goal of the Social Studies: Reflective, Competent, and Concerned Citizens

As we indicated earlier, it is generally agreed that ultimately the social studies curriculum should in some way contribute to the development of the good citizen. This basic agreement endures while debate continues concerning the nature of the good citizen and how the social studies curriculum can best contribute to his or her development.

Developing Reflective, Competent, and Concerned Citizens

We believe that the basic purpose of the social studies is to *develop reflective, competent, and concerned citizens.* *Reflective* individuals are critical thinkers who make decisions and solve problems on the basis of the best evidence available.

Competent citizens possess a repertoire of skills to aid them in decision making and problem solving.

Concerned citizens investigate their social world, address issues they identify as significant, exercise their rights, and carry out their responsibilities as members of a social community. The reflective, competent, and concerned citizen is prepared to function effectively in today's world and that of the future.

Social Studies as a Matter of the Head, the Hand, and the Heart

We shall characterize social studies programs that seek to develop the three dimensions of the good citizen *as providing for matters of the head, the hand, and the heart.* The head represents reflection, the hand competencies, and the heart

TABLE 1.1   The reflective, competent, and concerned citizen

SOCIAL STUDIES AS A MATTER OF THE HEAD: REFLECTION

The *Reflective* citizen has:
> knowledge of a body of concepts, facts, and generalizations concerning the organization, understanding, and development of individuals, groups, and societies. Also the reflective citizen understands the processes of hypothesis formation and testing, problem solving, and decision making.

SOCIAL STUDIES AS A MATTER OF THE HAND: COMPETENCE

The *Competent* citizen has:
> skills to collect data systematically and accurately, identify and use reference sources, process and interpret data, and organize information chronologically and spatially. The competent citizen also has social skills related to group participation, communication, observation, and multicultural understanding.

SOCIAL STUDIES AS A MATTER OF THE HEART: CONCERN

The *Concerned* citizen has:
> an awareness of his/her rights and responsibilities, a sense of social consciousness, and a well-grounded framework for deciding what is right and what is wrong. In addition, the concerned citizen has learned how to identify and analyze issues and to suspend judgment concerning alternate beliefs, attitudes, values, customs, and cultures.

---

concern. The characteristics of the reflective, competent, and concerned citizen are summarized in Table 1.1.

The Interrelationship of the Head, the Hand, and the Heart. No dimension operates without the others. Thinking, skillful action, and feeling are intertwined. Reflective citizens consider what their heart tells them, and draw on their competencies to make a decision and act on it.

The relationship between head, hand, and heart is seldom so systematic or linear. We may read in the newspaper about an issue — unemployment, for example. As a result, we begin rationally to examine its dimensions more by employing our research skills. Our social concern then is aroused, and we are driven to investigate further. Finally, we are moved to social protest and action to help find solutions to the problem. This cycle of events, however, might as easily have begun more dramatically as a matter of the heart through our being fired unexpectedly.

Balance in the Curriculum. Social studies programs designed within this framework should offer students a balance of activities and subject matter for growth in reflection, competence, and concern. The attention or time paid to each may vary according to the level of the grade, the abilities and needs of the students, and the current needs of society, as Figure 1.3 suggests. The "hand," for example, may receive more weight in the social studies curriculum in the lower grades, and less in later years. However, some attention to all three dimensions is necessary for a balanced social studies program.

FIGURE 1.3 A social studies program that emphasizes reflection and competence

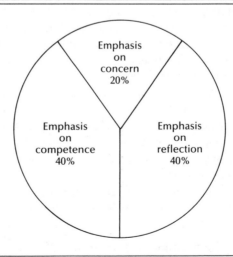

The American Tradition of Curricular Diversity

How does the diversity of views concerning the nature of the social studies and its purposes affect the typical curriculum in the elementary and middle schools across the United States? The answer is both simple and complicated. Since the framers of the Constitution rejected a national system of education, the matter of schools and curriculum fell to the individual states under the Tenth Amendment. The idea of eventually establishing across all states free and universal public schools was neither a national invention nor a concern.

Local School Districts

As a result, we have no national system of schooling, but rather a collection of thousands of local school districts. Although subject to general guidelines and standards for the social studies curriculum established by each of the states, a local school district has considerable autonomy in choosing its curriculum, materials, and teaching practices. This means that the potential for diversity in social studies programs across the United States is great.

Sample State Requirement for Social Studies

Elementary Grades: Each year a course in social studies must be taught. The social studies program must include anthropology, economics, geography, history, political science, and sociology.

— (Department of Public Instruction, State of Pennsylvania)

EXERCISE 1.3   Identifying State Guidelines for the Social Studies

Each state has a set of guidelines relating to the curriculum and teaching of social studies. Locate the set that applies to your state or the state in which you are planning to teach. Identify the regulations outlined for the elementary, middle, and secondary schools. Notice also whether the guidelines provide a definition of the social studies.

The Paradox of Curriculum Diversity and Homogeneity

Although the principle of local control promises diversity in curriculum offerings (theoretically, each local school board may create its own individual program) the social studies programs across the fifty states are actually quite similar. As we shall see, the social studies curriculum has retained its basic pattern across the United States for some time. In the absence of any national plan or federal role in prescribing curriculum, how can this be?

Factors Contributing to Curriculum Homogeneity. Much of the answer lies perhaps in five interrelated factors: tradition, accrediting agencies, teacher education programs, national organizations, and textbook adoption systems. Tradition bears heavily on those who would challenge the conventional scope and sequence of the social studies curriculum. Parents and community members tend to encourage preservation of the status quo, and teachers themselves are often most comfortable with what has become familiar.

Moreover, tradition influences the norms for accrediting agencies that examine the quality of our school districts across the country. It is also present in some of the objectives for teacher education programs, which must prepare teachers for the real world of schools before they can become innovators. Tradition is also an important consideration for national organizations, such as the National Council for the Social Studies and the National Council for Geographic Education, which provide curricular guidelines for programs.

The use of basal textbooks in most school systems, however, is perhaps the most significant factor in influencing the standardization of the curriculum. Not only are textbooks widely used, but they provide one of the standards by which schools are evaluated. The effect of textbooks in perpetuating the scope and sequence of the curriculum has been profound. We shall discuss this effect in the next section.

The National Pattern of the Social Studies Curriculum

It is much simpler to describe generally what the dominant national pattern of social studies for each grade level is than to report what it should be. A study in 1980, part of a major national survey of the condition of the social studies entitled Project SPAN, confirmed what earlier reports,[13] informal surveys, and anecdotal

TABLE 1.2 Basic social studies curricular pattern across the United States

Elementary	
Kindergarten–Grade 1	Self, Family, School
Grade 2	Neighborhoods
Grade 3	Communities
Grade 4	State History, Geographic Regions
Grade 5	United States History, Culture and Geography
Grade 6	World Cultures, History, and Geography
Secondary	
Grade 7	World Cultures, History, and Geography
Grade 8	American History
Grade 9	Civics
Grade 10	World History
Grade 11	American History
Grade 12	American Government/Problems of Democracy

data have indicated: the basic curricular pattern has remained essentially un-changed over the years.[14] It is shown in Table 1.2.

Scope and Sequence Patterns for the Social Studies Curriculum

The existing elementary curriculum has been called the "expanding communities" approach.[15] It is based on the notion that a child should be introduced in each year of school to an increasingly larger social environment. The curriculum moves from examining the self and the family in grades K–1 to the world at large in grade 6. The sequence of the curriculum for the middle and high school years is based primarily on tradition, on the pattern of courses that were set in 1916 by the Committee on Social Studies of the National Commission on the Reorganization of Secondary Education. Today there seems to be little reason for its order and repetition. Moreover, it does not appear to be well matched with the elementary curriculum.

There is no national consensus among social studies educators on the appropriate *scope* (list of topics) and *sequence* (order or grade level of topics) of the social studies curriculum. Nor is there agreement on the desirability of adopting a single scope-and-sequence model. Instead, many social studies educators have proposed alternative patterns for organizing the curriculum,[16] and some have even developed sample materials based on their models.[17]

The National Council for the Social Studies is reviewing a report from the Task Force on Scope and Sequence concerning a position statement on a recommended curricular sequence.[18] This report and its recommendations, if adopted by NCSS, should give teachers and schools a framework for initiating curriculum development across the grades. In the meantime the dominant scope and sequence pattern reflected both in basal text materials and school practices remains the one shown in Table 1.2.

EXERCISE 1.4   Identifying Local Curriculum Guidelines

Local school districts often produce a *curriculum guide* to indicate what is to be studied in each subject for each grade level. Sometimes a separate guide is prepared for each subject. At a minimum, the curriculum guide will indicate the scope and sequence of the social studies curriculum across grade levels.

Contact the administration office or the curriculum supervisor of several local school districts, and obtain a copy of the most recent curriculum guide that contains the sections relating to the social studies curriculum. Compare the list of topics and their sequence to the national pattern we have described. How are the districts similar to or different from the dominant pattern?

The Role of Basal Textbooks in the Social Studies Curriculum

One important way in which the social studies curriculum is shaped is through the basal textbooks we use in our schools. The best research evidence suggests that they are extensively used, and more often than other types of curricular materials.[19] A *basal* textbook represents the elements that the author or publisher regards as the basic material required to provide an appropriate social studies curriculum for one grade.

Teachers and schools often build on a basal text, using commercially produced and teacher-made materials. Some teachers use no text at all, creating their own programs from scratch and using general scope-and-sequence guidelines. Still others use a multibasal or multitext approach, picking those units or chapters from each text which best meet their specific curricular needs.

Generally the publisher of a basal social studies text will create an entire basal series covering grades K–6/7 or 1–6/7. Middle schools and middle grades present special problems, since publishers have not addressed their needs for basal series.[20] Each basal series is built around some model or notion of scope and sequence for the grades it covers. Adopting or purchasing a basal program, in effect, means adopting the curricular pattern on which the series is based.

Patterns in Basal Texts

Basal textbook series from major publishers usually incorporate surprisingly similar scope-and-sequence models. We might expect innovation and diversity from major corporations competing to provide products for over 40 million widely dis-

TABLE 1.3 Basal textbook scope-and-sequence patterns

	Series A	Series B	Series C	Series D
K	Understanding People's Needs	——	Looking At Me	Me
1	Understanding People	The Family	Meeting People	People
2	Understanding Families	The Neighborhood	Going Places	Neighborhoods
3	Understanding Communities	The Community	Communities	Communities
4	Understanding Regions of the Earth	The Earth	Earth's Regions	Our Regions
5	Understanding Our Country	The United States	United States	Our History
6	Understanding the World	The World	The World	Our World

tributed customers, but basal elementary texts reflect considerable homogeneity. Most basal series closely follow the expanding communities curricular model described earlier.

Samples of Basal Series. Table 1.3 lists a sample of recent basal social studies series and their major themes for each grade level. The series patterns may be compared to the expanding communities scope-and-sequence pattern summarized earlier.

Basal Series: Past and Present. Thomas and Brubaker found a similar pattern in basal texts over a decade ago.[21] The acceptance of these basic themes in major basal textbook series, their perpetuation over decades, and the heavy reliance of schools and teachers on basals have produced a *homogeneous* national curriculum pattern for the social studies.

Although our American system of curriculum adoption allows considerable diversity, the evidence suggests that this option is not often exercised with respect to the basic scope and sequence of topics, either by schools or publishers. However, basal texts may include very different types of activities and specific objectives. Series also vary considerably in their emphasis on each of the three dimensions of reflection, competence, and concern.

EXERCISE 1.5   Examining Basal Social Studies Textbook Series

Obtain several elementary basal social studies textbook series. Examine the titles and lists of topics included in each of the levels K–6, and compare them to the ones in Table 1.2. Determine whether the series you examined follow the same pattern and the expanding communities curriculum model.

Selection and Adoption of Basal Textbooks

How are textbooks selected for elementary classrooms? There are two basic ways: selection by local districts and state selection.

Local and State Adoption Policies. Currently, a majority of states permit local adoptions of basals, as shown in Table 1.4. However, twenty-three states, including two of the largest ones, California and Texas, use state adoption procedures. The implications of state adoption policies for states that permit local selection are considerable.

Since the twenty-seven states and the District of Columbia that permit local selection of texts can have as many sets of adoption criteria as there are school districts, they do not provide publishers with clear and unified guidelines as to what they desire. Often at both the local and state levels special interest groups attempt to influence the content and selection of texts. Group *A* may urge the removal of subject matter it considers offensive, whereas Group *B* may insist that some new material be inserted before a text is adopted. Other groups may lobby for or against the adoption of certain texts.

Effects of State Adoption Policies

The result of the state adoption pattern that has evolved is that the policies of states with centralized adoption policies have considerable effect on the type of texts which are produced for *all* of the states.[22] Publishers are reluctant to spend the money necessary to publish several versions of a new social studies series. They wish the product they market to be acceptable for potential adoption in all fifty states. To ensure this possibility, they look carefully to the adoption criteria of the twenty-three state boards, especially those representing the more populous states.

The trend in basal elementary social studies text publications seems to be toward even greater homogeneity in subject matter and scope-and-sequence patterns.

TABLE 1.4   State textbook adoption practices

Local option	*Some form of state adoption*
Alaska	Alabama
Colorado	Arizona
Connecticut	Arkansas
Delaware	California
District of Columbia	Florida
Illinois	Georgia
Iowa	Hawaii
Kansas	Idaho
Maine	Indiana
Maryland	Kentucky
Massachusetts	Louisiana
Michigan	Mississippi
Minnesota	Nevada
Missouri	New Mexico
Montana	North Carolina
Nebraska	Oklahoma
New Hampshire	Oregon
New Jersey	South Carolina
New York	Tennessee
North Dakota	Texas
Ohio	Utah
Pennsylvania	Virginia
Rhode Island	West Virginia
South Dakota	
Vermont	
Washington	
Wisconsin	
Wyoming	

Source: Educational Research Service, Inc. *Procedures for Textbook and Instructional Materials Selection.* Arlington, Va.: Educational Research Service, Inc., 1976.

Newer computer-based technologies in publishing, however, may allow publishers to provide schools with greater variety and more options.

Notes

1. National Commission on Excellence in Education, *A Nation at Risk: The Imperative for Educational Reform* (Washington, D.C.: United States Office of Education, 1983).
2. "Report of the Committee on Social Studies," in *Social Studies Strategies: Theory into Practice,* ed. Peter H. Martorella (New York: Harper and Row, 1976).
3. Shirley H. Engle, "Comments of Shirley H. Engle," in *Defining the Social Studies,* Bulletin 51, Robert D. Barr et al. (Washington, D.C.: National Council for the Social Studies, 1977), p. 104.
4. Howard Mehlinger, "Foreward," in *Defining the Social Studies,* Bulletin 51, Robert D. Barr et al. (Washington, D.C.: National Council for the Social Studies, 1977), p. iii.
5. "Report of the Committee," p. 9.
6. Edgar B. Wesley, *Teaching Social Studies in High Schools,* 3rd ed. (Boston: D. C. Heath, 1950), p. 34.
7. Shirley H. Engle, "Exploring the Meaning of the Social Studies," in *Social Studies Strategies: Theory into Practice,* ed. Peter H. Martorella (New York: Harper and Row, 1976), p. 234.
8. Robert D. Barr et al., *Defining the Social Studies,* Bulletin 51 (Washington, D.C.: National Council for the Social Studies, 1977), p. 69.
9. Leonard S. Kenworthy, *Social Studies for the Eighties in Elementary and Middle Schools,* 3rd ed. (New York: John Wiley and Sons, 1980), p. 6.
10. Barr et al., *Defining the Social Studies,* p. 67.
11. Engle, "Comments of Shirley H. Engle," in *Social Studies Strategies,* pp. 103–104.
12. Jack L. Nelson and John U. Michaelis, *Secondary Social Studies* (Englewood Cliffs, N.J.: Prentice-Hall, 1980), Chap. 1.
13. Douglas P. Superka et al., "The Current and Future Status of the Social Studies," *Social Education* 44 (May 1980): 362–369.
14. See, for example, the discussion in R. Murray Thomas and Dale L. Brubaker, *Decisions in Teaching Elementary Social Studies* (Belmont, Calif.: Wadsworth, 1971), p. 125.
15. Paul R. Hanna, "Revising the Social Studies: What is Needed?," *Social Education* 27 (April 1963): 190–196.
16. See, for example, Bruce R. Joyce, *New Strategies for Social Education* (Chicago: SRA, 1972), pp. 266–284; Edwin Fenton, *The New Social Studies* (New York: Holt, Rinehart, and Winston, 1967); and David A. Welton and John T. Mallan, *Children and Their World: Strategies for Teaching Social Studies,* 2nd ed. (Boston: Houghton Mifflin, 1981), Chap. 4.
17. For a sampling of curricular materials that deviate from the expanding communities model, consult *Social Studies Materials and Resources Data Book,* ed. Judith Hedstrom and Frances Haley (Boulder, Colo.: Social Science Education Consortium, annual volumes).
18. John Jarolimek et al., *In Search of a Scope and Sequence for Social Studies, Social Education* 48 (April 1984): 249–264; 273.

19. James P. Shaver et al., "The Status of Social Studies Education: Impressions from Three NSF Studies," *Social Education* 43 (February 1979): 150–153.
20. Peter H. Martorella, "Social Studies Goals in the Middle Grades," *Journal of Research and Development in Education* 13 (Winter 1980): 47–59.
21. Thomas and Brubaker, *Decisions in Teaching,* p. 125.
22. Sherry Keith, *Politics of Textbook Adoption,* Project Report No. 81-A7 (Palo Alto, Calif.: Stanford University, Institute for Research on Educational Finance and Governance, April 1981).

Suggested Readings

Barr, Robert D., et al. *Defining the Social Studies.* Bulletin 51. Washington, D.C.: National Council for the Social Studies, 1977.

Berelson, Bernard, et al. *The Social Studies and the Social Sciences.* New York: Harcourt Brace Jovanovich, 1962.

Berelson, Bernard, and Steiner, Gary A. *Human Behavior: An Inventory of Scientific Findings.* New York: Harcourt Brace Jovanovich, 1964.

Chase, Stuart. *The Proper Study of Mankind: An Inquiry into the Science of Human Relations.* New York: Harper and Row, 1963.

Goodlad, John I. *A Place Called School: Prospects for the Future.* New York: McGraw-Hill, 1984, Chapter 7.

Gross, Richard E., et al. *Social Studies for Our Times.* New York: John Wiley and Sons, 1978, Section 2.

Hedstrom, Judith, and Haley, Frances, eds. *Social Studies Materials and Resources Data Book.* Boulder, Colo.: Social Science Education Consortium, annual volumes.

Keith, Sherry. *Politics of Textbook Adoption,* Project Report No. 81-A7. Palo Alto, Calif.: Stanford University, Institute for Research on Educational Finance and Governance, April 1981.

Lawton, Denis. "Foundations for the Social Studies," in *UNESCO Handbook for the Teaching of Social Studies,* ed. Howard Mehlinger. Paris: UNESCO, 1981.

Mehlinger, Howard, and Davis, O. L., eds. *Social Studies,* 80th Yearbook of the National Society for the Study of Education, Part II. Chicago: University of Chicago Press, 1981.

Morrissett, Irving, ed. *Social Studies in the 1980s.* Alexandria, Va.: Association for Supervision and Curriculum Development, 1982.

Nelson, Murry R. "Social Studies: Something Old, Something New, and All Borrowed," *Theory and Research in Social Education* 8 (Fall 1980): 51–64.

Shaver, James P., et al. "The Status of Social Studies Education: Impressions from Three NSF Studies," *Social Education* 43 (February 1979): 150–153.

Social Education, 48 (April 1984), special issue with reactions to preliminary report of Task Force on Scope and Sequence.

Superka, Douglas P., et al. "The Current and Future Status of the Social Studies," *Social Education* 44 (May 1980): 362–369.

Wehlage, Gary, and Anderson, Eugene M. *Social Studies Curriculum in Perspective.* Englewood Cliffs, N.J.: Prentice-Hall, 1972.

2

Teaching Social Studies Across the Grades: The Significance of Developmental Differences

One of the exciting aspects of being a teacher or a parent is the opportunity to see youngsters develop and change. The enjoyment we all get from pouring over snapshots from our childhood or seeing what someone we know looked like as a child reflects human interest in development. Sometimes it is difficult to fathom how a person we remember at one stage of development has changed so radically in physical appearance, social demeanor, and mental ability.

A person's cycle of life is characterized by many changes and developments, some biological in origin and some environmental. Each developing individual has a unique pattern and rhythm of physical, social, and mental growth. Researchers, however, have attempted to generalize about processes of development, especially in children and adolescents. Many of their insights provide guidelines for making social studies instruction more effective.

The Nature of Development

Educators frequently use the term *development* to refer to three basic types of changes — physical, social, and mental — in children. (See Figure 2.1.) *Developmental readiness* refers to children's physical, social, and mental ability to carry out an instructional task.

FIGURE 2.1   Three basic dimensions of human development

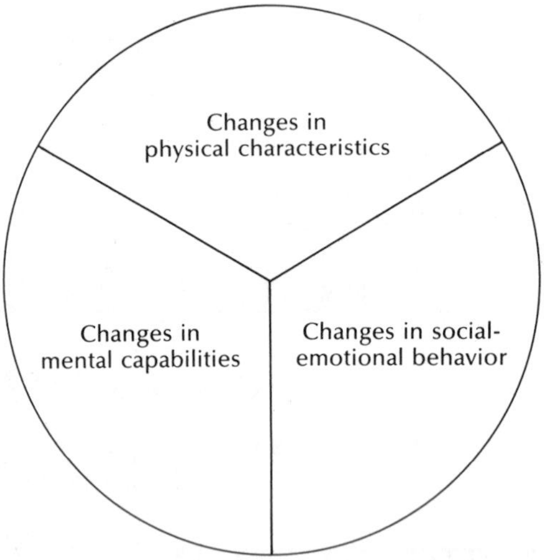

Physical Development

Physical developmental changes over time include variations in height and weight, in the size of various parts of the body, in the onset of puberty, and in general motor ability. For example, children often do poorly in printing and writing as they enter school until their motor coordination improves.

Social Development

Differences in social development are often more subtle. As a child learns which patterns of social behavior are considered acceptable, social development progresses. This process requires learning to function effectively in social settings within both child and adult cultures. It includes learning what is considered to be appropriate dress, language, customs, courtesies, and other behavior in social situations.

Mental Development

In recent years perhaps attention has been focused more on mental developmental than on any other area. As children grow older, they typically interpret and respond to intellectual tasks in qualitatively different ways. Their processes of reasoning and problem solving and their understanding of the physical and social world change significantly. Among other things, they alter their views of space, time, quantity, morality, and causality.

By the time they have reached the first or second grade, for example, children can generally perform mental operations in trial-and-error fashion in their heads without having to act them out in each case, as they did when they were younger. David Elkind illustrates this point in relation to social studies as follows:

> A five year old whom I asked, "Can you be an American and a Protestant at the same time? . . . replied, "Only if you move!" To this young man "Protestant" and "American" were clearly places that you could not occupy at the same time. For the child of six or seven, however, a class of things is no longer regarded as a kind of place where all of the elements sit. He recognizes that the same element can be in two classes at once.[1]

Development Through Stages

Pronounced developmental changes in individuals' physical maturation, social characteristics, or quality of thinking are often called *stages*. Puberty, for example, refers to a period of dramatic physical change in children. Children's social behavior shifts from predominantly *egocentric* behavior to *empathic* behavior (the ability to view an issue from another's perspective).

We also use stages to mark major developmental shifts in *intellectual capacities*. When a shift to a higher level of thinking is discerned, as Elkind noted, a student is said to have moved to a more advanced stage of mental growth. Stages are relatively arbitrary signposts indicating that children have arrived at a certain point in their physical, social, or mental development.

The Relationship of Stages to Chronological Age

The stage of development that a child has reached may be correlated approximately with chronological age. That is, most seven year olds — or more accurately, those between ages six to eight — may be presumed to be roughly at the same stage of development. They thus are likely to possess certain physical, social, or intellectual capabilities and to be lacking others, which will be acquired at the next developmental stage.

This correlational relationship of chronological age and stage tells teachers approximately what student characteristics to expect. At the same time, teachers should realize that given individuals will deviate from the expected *average* pattern. Some students will be only entering a predicted stage and still others will have moved beyond it. Although most children in the United States begin school at age five or six, they typically will differ greatly during their kindergarten and first-grade years in their physical, social, and mental abilities.

Jean Piaget's Stage Theory

Jean Piaget's theories about developmental stages have been reported in detail, and several interpretations of his works exist. Since he began to report his findings over a half-century ago, other researchers have attempted to document, refine, and challenge his theories. Even today, his views are controversial.[2]

Piaget stated that four basic periods of mental development exist, as shown in Table 2.1. One must move sequentially through the stages without skipping any.

TABLE 2.1 Piaget's theory of stages

Stage of development	Approximate chronological age
Sensorimotor	Birth to 2 Years
Preoperational	2 Years to 7 Years
Concrete Operational	7 Years to 11 Years
Formal Operational	11 Years and Older

Each stage involves more complex thought processes and builds on patterns of thinking acquired in the previous stage.

For example, a child in the preoperational phase is capable of more complex thought than a child in the sensorimotor phase. It may be useful to think of Piaget's stages as descriptions of the thinking *capability* of an individual.[3] At a particular point in development, the potential for a qualitatively different type of thinking emerges.

Preoperational Period. The early childhood years are preoperational. A major characteristic of children's behavior at this stage, Piaget suggests, is *egocentrism.* Children are incapable of taking into account the point of view of others. In a discussion, for example, of how best to eliminate litter on the playground, considering a perspective other than their own on the issue is beyond the understanding of preoperational children. They find it difficult to weigh the relative merits of alternative solutions to a problem.

The logic of children's reasoning at this stage is also limited and is called *transduction.* That is, children reason that because two events are associated, one causes the other. For example, a child might reason that the playing of the national anthem at a sports event *causes* it to begin.

Concepts of time, space, quantity, and relations are still ill formed during this period. Past, present, and future, for example, are difficult to understand in any meaningful way. Similarly, problems exist with putting objects in correct sequences, such as from first to last or from smallest to largest.

Concrete Operational Period. The concrete operational period is the first developmental phase that completely falls within the elementary school years. During this period a child normally acquires the ability to organize and relate experiences into an ordered pattern. Among the capabilities germane to social studies activities that Piaget's theory suggests are acquired during this period are *reversibility,* and *multiple classification.*

Reversibility. Reversibility involves an understanding that an object's or event's essential properties remain even when it is transformed. When a dollar, for example, is changed into one hundred cents in coins and then back to a dollar the amount of money never changes.[4] Altering shape, form, size, color, and the like does not cause an item to change its basic properties.

Multiple Classification. Multiple classification is the ability to classify items according to more than one attribute simultaneously. A child has acquired this ability when he or she can understand that a woman can be at the same time a mother and a judge or that a political figure can be a senator while also being a Republican or a Democrat. Applied to events, multiple classification is the ability to compare, contrast, and draw conclusions. The capacity for multiple classification is required, for example, to handle a social studies question such as, ''How are the American Revolution, the Russian Revolution, and the Civil War similar and different, and what can we conclude from our study of all of them?''

Formal Operational Period. Formal operations typically begin in the middle-grade years. According to Piaget's studies, a new form of thinking emerges. Children begin to manipulate symbols and ideas, and to think abstractly rather than concretely. They can develop and test hypotheses, make inferences, deduce logical conclusions, and engage in problem solving.

Formal operational children, unlike their concrete operational counterparts, can go beyond the immediate information available. They can draw further conclusions through reasoning by implication. Those areas of the social studies which require hypothesis development and testing, problem solving, developing generalizations, and abstract thinking generally, presume some formal operational capabilities.

Consider a situation similar to the one used by J. McV. Hunt in experiments with children.[5] Two children, one of whom has reached the stage of formal operations and one who is still in the stage of concrete operations, are assigned this classification task:

> *Classification Task.* A new planet has just been discovered. As on earth, humans on this planet are classified as male (M), female (F), and also as adults (A) and children (C). It is not known which combinations of these classes exist on the planet. Name *all* of the possible combinations of humans that might exist on the planet.[6]

The concrete operational child is likely to give four possible conditions: male adults, female adults, male children, and female children. In contrast, the formal operational child is likely to be able to reason by implication that these additional classifications are possible:

Other Possible Conditions

Male adults and female adults, but no male children or female children

Male adults and male children, but no female adults or female children

Male adults and female children, but no female adults or male children

Male adults, female adults, and male children, but no female children

Male adults, female adults, and female children, but no male children

Male adults, male children, and female children, but no female adults

Female adults and male children, but no male adults or female children

Female adults and female children, but no male adults or male children

Female adults, male children, and female children, but no male adults

Male children and female children, but no female adults or male adults

Male children, female children, male adults, and female adults

No humans at all

Onset of the Formal Operational Period. It is not surprising that the age at which children reach the stage of formal operations often varies widely. Similarly, considerable debate exists concerning when the *majority* of contemporary children reach it. Hallam's research in Great Britain with students' study of history, for example, led him to conclude that a majority of children do not reach the stage of formal operations until *after sixteen* years of age.[7] Other investigators have suggested that only about half of all adult Americans *ever* achieve full formal operational thought.[8]

EXERCISE 2.1   Preliminary Assessment of Piagetian Stages

Select a group of four children in grades 3–6 and a group of four in grades 7–9, and administer the classification task in the text. Record the grade level and chronological age of each student and his or her list of possible classes. If students are uncertain as to what is meant by a class, offer the example, "adult males."

Compare your findings with what might be expected by the stage theory of Piaget, and discuss your conclusions.

Jerome Bruner's Cognitive Development Theory

Jerome Bruner, whose theories draw heavily on the work of Piaget, offers a somewhat different view of development as it relates to intellectual growth. He has suggested a three-fold schema for cognitive development. His research indicates that children and adults learn through the *enactive* mode (doing), the *iconic* mode (imagery), or the *symbolic* mode (words).[9]

Enactive, Iconic, and Symbolic Modes of Learning. During each cognitive stage learning occurs predominantly through doing, through images, or through symbols such as spoken or written words. Any subject matter that can be presented in a form that matches the child's dominant mode of thinking is appropriate. Learning activities that capitalize on children's current mode of thinking allows them to deal with a subject at their level of understanding.

Developmental growth, Bruner contends, involves mastering each of the increasingly more difficult modes of representation, enactive to iconic to symbolic. It also includes developing the ability to translate each form into the other. For instance, translation might occur through a discussion of what had been observed and learned from a picture.[10]

Young children acquire much of their early learning through the enactive mode, by acting on and interacting with their environment. Iconic representation normally becomes dominant roughly during the early childhood years. Thereafter, the symbolic mode of learning gradually becomes the most common.

Lawrence Kohlberg's Cognitive Developmental Theory

Piaget's stage theories were also applied to children's moral reasoning. His investigations revealed that children exhibit qualitatively different types of moral reasoning. Younger children are more likely to refer to authority figures in making judgments about right or wrong. What a parent says is right, for example, is accepted by the child as the norm. Older children, on the other hand, are more likely to take into account the principles of reciprocity and cooperativeness.[11] As they mature, children begin to understand that they must take the needs of others into account in making moral judgments.

Moral Development. For over a quarter of a century Lawrence Kohlberg and his associates have developed, refined, and tested a theory of *moral development* based on Piaget's notion of hierarchical stages. Kohlberg's early work on the development of moral reasoning in children in the United States and abroad led to the identification of six stages through which all individuals may move.[12] His theory is characterized as *cognitive* developmental because of its focus on reasoning processes as they normally mature over time.

Stages of Moral Development. In extending the work of Piaget, Kohlberg identified six closely related stages of moral development. They are summarized in Table 2.2. Kohlberg contends that each stage builds on the others and that no stage may be skipped. Moral development can be retarded at any stage, however.

Moral development, according to Kohlberg's theory, is stimulated by confronting students with moral dilemmas.[13] These consist of brief episodes involving matters of right and wrong in which only two courses of action are available. An individual must take a position on one side of the argument or the other, offer reasons for the choice, and entertain the competing position and alternative rationale.

Neither of the two possible positions is considered to be morally preferable or to indicate a more advanced stage of moral reasoning. Rather, it is the *type* or *quality* of reasoning that indicates the dominant stage of moral development one has reached.

For example, two small children are asked whether it is right to take a dollar from the billfold of a rich person if he or she is out of the room and cannot see a child taking the money. One child says no, because a promise was made to a parent never to take something that belonged to someone else. The other child says yes, because the rich person will never know, and no punishment will result. *Both*

TABLE 2.2   Kohlberg's stages of moral development

Stage 1. *Orientation to Punishment and Obedience.* The physical consequences of an action determine whether it is good or bad. Avoidance of punishment and unquestioning deference to power are valued in their own right.

Stage 2. *Instrumental Relativist Orientation.* Right action consists of that which serves to satisfy one's own needs and occasionally the needs of others. Human relations are viewed in a pragmatic perspective. Reciprocity is seen in terms of "you scratch my back and I'll scratch yours."

Stage 3. *Good Boy–Nice Girl Orientation.* One seeks approval of others and attempts to avoid disapproval. Behavior is guided by conforming to some stereotype of what the behavior of the majority is. One earns approval by behaving in a "nice" way.

Stage 4. *Law and Order Orientation.* An individual adheres to established rules for their own sake. "Doing one's duty," showing respect for authority, and maintaining the existing social order for its own sake constitute right behavior.

Stage 5. *Contractual Legalistic Orientation.* An individual recognizes arbitrary rules for the sake of agreement. Personal opinions and values are considered to be relative. Right tends to be determined in terms of what has been agreed on by the whole society or more general principles such as "the greatest good for the greatest number." This represents the morality implicit in the Constitution and in many of the policies and documents of the American government.

Stage 6. *Conscience or Principle Orientation.* One looks to his or her own conscience and to the principle of mutual respect and trust for moral guidance. Right is defined by a decision of conscience in accord with self-chosen logically derived principles. These are abstract universal principles of justice, of the reciprocity and equality of human rights, and of respect for the dignity of human beings as individuals.

Source: Adapted from Lawrence Kohlberg, "The Cognitive-Developmental Approach to Moral Education," in *Social Studies Strategies: Theory into Practice,* ed. Peter H. Martorella (New York: Harper and Row, 1976), pp. 127–142.

children reflect only stage 1 reasoning, as described in Table 2.2. Neither child reasons beyond the point of obeying an authority or avoiding punishment.

Onset of Stages of Moral Development. In Kohlberg's theory, just as in Piaget's, stages may be related roughly to chronological age. Most children in the primary grades are likely to be at stages 1 and 2 and those in the intermediate grades at 2 and 3. Most secondary students are likely to be at stages 3 and 4, with some at 2 and a few at 5. Kohlberg maintains that the majority of all individuals, youngsters and adults, never advance beyond the third or fourth stages of development.

Some of the same criticisms that have been voiced about Piaget's stage theory have been directed toward the work of Kohlberg and his associates.[14] In addition researchers have questioned whether reasoning related to classroom-based dilemmas indicates how individuals will respond to real moral crises. Much of Kohlberg's research is more recent than the early studies of Piaget, and investigations are continuing to refine, advance, and challenge his theories.

Erik Erikson's Theory of Developmental Stages

Erik Erikson's developmental stages differ from those of Piaget and Kohlberg in several basic respects. His work emphasized the crucial emotional or affective, rather than the cognitive or thinking, transformations that people undergo as they develop.[15] Society places demands on children as they grow up, and these create *emotional crises*.

Stages of Development. Erikson identified eight, rather than six or four, developmental shifts that occur in response to the crises. They are summarized in Table 2.3.

Stages as Emotional Crises. Each of the stages, according to Erikson, represents an emotional watershed for an individual. Once one passes through the crisis, both one's self and the way one relates to others changes. Erikson maintains that at each crucial period in one's development, as shown in Table 2.2, two key emotional polarities exist together in a state of tension. These are the emotional forces that tug at individuals and ultimately must be resolved, if one is to advance developmentally.

Onset of Developmental Stages. The developmental periods that most closely parallel the preschool, elementary, and middle school years are those dealing with initiative vs. guilt, industry vs. inferiority, and identity vs. role confusion. During these periods, Erikson contends, children confront a basic crisis. The outcome will determine the direction their boundless energy will take. They may become autonomous individuals who are allowed by adults to take the initiative in learning or they may be made to feel guilty about their high activity level and continuous curiosity.

At the next stage, children struggle with learning to gain recognition in an

TABLE 2.3 Erikson's developmental stages

Infancy and preschool	Basic trust vs. mistrust
	Autonomy vs. shame, doubt
	Initiative vs. guilt
School years	Industry vs. inferiority
	Identity vs. role confusion
	Intimacy vs. isolation
Adulthood	Generativity vs. stagnation
	Ego integrity vs. despair

Source: Erik Erikson, *Childhood and Society*, 2nd ed.
(New York: Norton, 1963), pp. 247–274.

academic environment, thus becoming industrious and avoiding being branded in-ferior. Students are trying to cope with society's demands of productivity and competence.

With the onset of adolescence, children confront the crisis of ending their childhood and meeting new demands. They attempt to gain a new postchildhood identity and a clear sense of their role in life.

Implications of Developmental Differences for Teaching Social Studies

Theories of developmental stages offer important perspectives from which to es-timate student capabilities and limitations for learning. They can serve as a mon-itor of the reasonableness of teachers' expectations for students or as a guide to facilitate development. Since developmental theories focus on both cognitive and affective growth, they incline us toward a balanced social studies program of the head, the hand, and the heart, as described in Chapter 1. The developing child is growing socially, emotionally, and mentally, and continually is testing his or her growth through action.

Children should be given social studies materials and activities that capitalize on their growing capabilities. Moreover, since children in any given class are likely to be at different developmental levels, some provisions for individualized instruc-tion will be necessary. Above all, instruction — particularly for younger chil-dren — should emphasize *concrete learning activities* and afford frequent oppor-tunities for *social interaction*. Developmental theories also offer some guidelines for those areas of the social studies curriculum where many children are likely to need special assistance, such as concepts of *causality, time, space,* and *morality*.

A brief overview of some of these implications follows in this chapter. In Chapters 5 through 9, we will examine in some detail a variety of basic strategies for selecting and constructing social studies activities and experiences appropriate for primary, intermediate-grade, and middle-school students.

Concrete Learning Activities

One of the clearest instructional implications of developmental psychology is the need for concrete learning activities and materials during the early years of social studies instruction. One researcher has summed up the matter bluntly: "It is use-less to present abstract material to students before they are ready to assimilate it."[16]

Nature of Concrete Social Studies Activities. Although "concrete" has many meanings in education, generally it refers to that which can be perceived directly through one or more of the senses: seeing, hearing, tasting, touching, or smelling. Thus, a teacher who wishes to provide a *concrete* learning experience on how a civil trial is conducted may take the class on a field trip to observe a trial in action.

Once concrete learning has occurred, the lessons of the trip can be augmented with an *abstract* follow-up discussion of the operations of the court.

Enactive, Iconic, and Symbolic Social Studies Activities. The three modes of thinking identified by Jerome Bruner and described earlier also suggest some strategies for providing concrete learning experiences for children. Subject matter can be presented through the *enactive* mode, by having students do or act on something, such as building a shelter. Concrete experiences also could be provided through the *iconic* mode, through the use of pictures, visual material, or imagery that the learner creates. These strategies may be contrasted with those which use the *symbolic* mode, an *abstract* form of learning that involves hearing or reading about something. In most activities, the instructional choices seldom are between only concrete and only abstract learning. A mixture usually occurs.

A teacher might provide children with contrasting experiences representing *each* of the three modes, on the concept of the assembly line as follows. Students could be asked to participate in a simulated assembly line for producing some simple product (enactive); or they might be shown a filmstrip describing an assembly line or a field trip to a local plant (iconic); or they could be asked to read their texts and then discuss the subject (symbolic).

Children and Abstract Learning

Children, of course, use many abstract social studies concepts, such as *love, fairness,* and *democracy,* in all stages of development. However, they often use them in speaking or writing without understanding their basic meanings. They quickly learn at home and even more in schools that the mere use of certain words in a situation will pass for learning and understanding. Students very early observe that repeating the correct words in the proper context will gain approval or rewards from the teacher and other adults in the school.

We may regard these abstractions, which are not developed spontaneously and internalized by children but are learned through imitation or rote, as "phony concepts." Children often become quite proficient in using phony concepts in situationally correct ways without any real understanding of their conceptual meaning. Little Clara, for example, has learned from shrewd observation both how to ease her conceptual burden and gain teacher approval when asked a question in class such as, "What do you like best about our country?" Clara has learned that responding with the words, "democracy" and "freedom of speech," whatever they mean, will more than satisfy the teacher.

Regarding children's use of phony concepts, psychologist David Ausubel has pointed out,

> One reason pupils commonly develop a rote learning set in relation to potentially meaningful subject matter is because they learn from sad experience that substantively correct answers lacking in verbatim correspondence to what they have been taught receive no credit whatsoever from certain teachers.[17]

EXERCISE 2.2   Translating Learning Modes

Select any elementary basal social studies textbook, grades 1–3.
Pick a topic or a sample of subject matter that is presented within
the text narrative (symbolic mode). Develop a sample activity to
illustrate how the same material could be taught to a child through
the *enactive* mode.

Social Interaction

Social interaction in the social studies involves children sharing experiences, taking roles, discussing, disputing, and listening in small- and large-group activities.
The view that social interaction should be a major component of social studies
instruction derives from developmental theorists' observations that through this
process children begin to move away from egocentrism. As a child increasingly
interacts with others, he or she begins to internalize the existence and significance
of alternative points of view.

Oral Participation. Oral participation in social studies instruction, whether in small
groups or in class discussions, can be instrumental in refining and improving children's thinking. Defending and explaining one's own ideas, as well as learning to
listen to others, help to clarify thinking. As children engage in verbal give-and-
take, they not only share their thoughts, but they test them out as well. In short,
when children's conversations in groups have purpose and guidelines, they promote both social and cognitive growth.

Concepts of Causality

An understanding of causal relationships involves a grasp of how one set of events
is caused by another, whether it be a physical or psychological cause. A child
comes to realize, for example, that the physical phenomenon of rain causes the
ground to be wet. Similarly, he or she realizes that psychological events, such as
father's bad mood, causes a party to be an unpleasant affair.[18]

Understanding Cause-Effect Relationships. Irving Sigel provides an excellent
detailed description of an activity that involves children with various levels of understanding of cause-effect relationships, as well as with principles of classification.

> Let us take a unit of study which is common in our public schools, namely,
> the pioneers. . . . Consider first the tepee. What attributes of the tepee can be
> identified? We can talk about its function as a domicile, its portability, the ma-
> terials from which it is made, and its shape. We can show the child how each of
> these attributes applies to this particular tepee. Consider next the log cabin of the
> pioneer. What attributes does the log cabin possess? We can use the same kind
> of criteria, i.e., the function, portability, the materials, and shape. . . .

The teacher can ask the children to examine these objects and explain or think about the significance of each of the attributes that are listed. Let us take, for example, the issue of shape. Why is a tepee conical? What function does this shape serve? It is related to fire; a simple way to make smoke escape is to leave a hole in the top of a conical structure. Why is a log cabin rectangular? This is a simple way to build with logs.[19]

Concepts of Time

Time and temporal concepts are often difficult for young children to grasp. "To the young child," Elkind observes, "there is little difference between 'later,' 'in a few minutes,' or 'next week,' which are all understood primarily as 'not now.' . . . Only late into middle childhood does he begin to appreciate years and dates."[20] The understanding of calendar or historical time does not normally occur until third or fourth grade, and a sense of being able to plan for the future probably does not arise until adolescence.[21] Although youngsters may be able to remember and recite dates and events well into the past or ahead in the future even in the early grades, they have no conceptual sense of the temporal spans involved.

Organizing Events in Chronological Order. Activities such as time charts and timelines, which require students to arrange events in chronological order, help to establish the perspective of one action preceding or following another. Allowing children to arrange series of pictures of events, such as those shown in Figure 2.2, in the correct sequence works toward the same objective.

Some other ways of helping children to grasp concepts related to time are the use of time visits, identification with some figure in the past, and imaginary dialogs between famous historical figures. Time visits require children to pick some point in the past, and then to compare conditions that existed then with those in their own lives. A child might be asked to compare what it would be like to grow up during the colonial period with the experience of today.

In identifying with a historical character a student must try to imagine the world of the past that the historical character experienced. Creating a make-believe diary of the character is one way of building such identification. What would the individual observe and record; what would seem important and interesting?

A third approach involves students in creating imaginary dialogs. Using real historical data and selecting from different time periods famous historical figures such as George Washington and Abraham Lincoln, students attempt to create a discussion that might have taken place between the personalities. In this way they compare both periods and individuals.

Spatial Concepts

Spatial concepts are fundamental to understanding one's relationship to another individual or a place. They most often appear in social studies in the discipline of geography, but they are distributed throughout the social sciences. Political

FIGURE 2.2   Series of six events to be arranged in correct chronological order

Source: Peter H. Martorella et al., *Looking at Me: Teacher's Manual, Level K* (New York: McGraw-Hill, 1983), p. 81. Reprinted by permission.

boundaries, locations of cities, landmarks, land masses, and the relationship of objects in space are all part of spatial understanding.

Using Abstract Models. The teacher must be careful not to overburden youngsters with learning abstract spatial tools for which they can have no conceptual understanding or immediate practical use. Spatial concepts frequently introduced in the early grades — such as earth and state — are highly abstract and difficult for children to understand, since they cannot be directly observed or easily related to concrete experiences. The fact that *another abstraction,* a map or a globe, may be used to represent them is not necessarily helpful to a child. Young children may learn the names of capitals or the list of countries within a continent, and even be able to do some primitive mapping of objects in their environment.[22] However, an understanding of their relationship in space and their social significance is not likely to emerge until the end of the elementary grades.

Locating the Child in Space. Spatial understanding in the social studies can begin with children's awareness of their own place in space through the creation of body maps. Later it can be extended to identifying and mapping objects and people familiar to them. These are concrete phenomena that can be located and verified within their immediate environment, such as the classroom, school, neighborhood, or home.

Concepts of Morality

Moral development theory and the teaching strategies based on it allow the school to participate in an important area of a child's self-growth without moralizing. Children can be helped to improve their moral reasoning without being conditioned to subscribe to one particular moral course of action. Moreover, society is served to the extent that its young citizens develop a heightened moral consciousness.

Moral Dilemmas. A basic instructional strategy devised and refined by Kohlberg and his associates to stimulate moral development was described earlier. As suggested, it involves presenting students with moral dilemmas centering on real or hypothetical issues, which are to be discussed in small groups. Typical dilemmas are brief case studies relevant to the students' age levels and interests. They involve fundamental issues such as rights, justice or fairness, and rules. In the discussions, probe questions are raised by the teacher to force students to consider the motives behind actions and to consider the effect of a moral decision on all of the parties concerned.

Alternative Views of Learning

Not all researchers and theorists view learning and development in terms of stages. Stage theorists consider biological maturation to be a key determinant in individual development. Some investigators, however, have emphasized the influence of environment.

Reinforcement Theory

In this tradition prominent figures in psychology such as Ivan Pavlov, James B. Watson, Edward Thorndike, and B. F. Skinner have viewed the process of development as the accumulation of learned responses. As new responses to some stimulus (such as receiving a present) are learned and reinforced, individuals develop a collection of behaviors over time. Instruction involves reinforcing those behaviors which children are to learn, and discouraging others.

Social Learning Theory

Closely related to this school of thought is the view that development is primarily the gradual accumulation of patterns of behavior from imitation and modeling. Proponents of this perspective include Albert Bandura, Clark Hull, and Robert Sears. They argue that as models (parents and others) are observed and imitated, we continually develop and refine our own emotional and cognitive behavior. As we present students with models in instruction, curriculum materials, and teacher behavior, they have an opportunity to imitate and acquire patterns of behavior.

The Broad Perspective

In teaching the social studies to develop reflective, competent, and concerned citizens, teachers should look broadly to the insights that researchers and theorists with different perspectives have provided on the physical, social, and mental processes of development. No single perspective adequately addresses all aspects of changes that children undergo or the wide variety of learning differences that they typically exhibit during their school years. Stage theories explain some changes in students, reinforcement theory others, and social modeling theory still others. Collectively, however, the different views of development offer teachers useful guidelines for selecting subject matter and devising instructional strategies.

Notes

1. David Elkind, *A Sympathetic Understanding of the Child: Birth to Sixteen,* 2nd ed. (Boston: Allyn and Bacon, 1978), p. 108.
2. See, for example, K. Riegel, "Dialectical Operations: The Final Period of Cognitive Development," *Human Development* 16 (1973):346–370; and E. Sullivan, *Piaget and the School Curriculum: A Critical Appraisal* (Toronto: Ontario Institute for Studies in Education, 1967).
3. Mary C. Day, "Thinking at Piaget's Stage of Formal Operations," *Educational Leadership* 39 (October 1981): 44–47.
4. Irving E. Sigel, "Social Studies Strategies Derived from Some Piagetian Theories," in *Social Studies Strategies: Theory into Practice,* ed. Peter H. Martorella (New York: Harper and Row, 1976), p. 78.
5. J. McV. Hunt, *Intelligence and Experience* (New York: Ronald Press, 1969), pp. 231–32.
6. Peter H. Martorella, "Social Studies Goals in the Middle Grades," *Journal of Research and Development in Education* 13 (Winter 1980): 51.
7. Roy Hallam, "Piaget and the Teaching of History," in *Social Studies Strategies: Theory into Practice,* ed. Peter H. Martorella (New York: Harper and Row, 1976), p. 87.
8. Lawrence Kohlberg and Carol Gilligan, "The Adolescent as a Philosopher: The Discovery of Self in a Post-Conventional World," *Daedalus* (Fall 1971): 1051–1086.
9. Jerome S. Bruner, *Beyond the Information Given* (New York: Norton, 1973), pp. 327–328.
10. Ibid., p. 317.
11. Jean Piaget, *The Moral Judgment of the Child,* trans. M. Gabain (New York: Free Press, 1965), Chaps. 2 and 3.
12. Lawrence Kohlberg, "Educating for a Just Society: An Updated and Revised Statement," in *Moral Development, Moral Education, and Kohlberg,* ed. Brenda Munsey (Birmingham, Al.: Religious Education Press, 1980), pp. 455–570.
13. Lawrence Kohlberg, "The Cognitive-Developmental Approach to Moral Education," in *Social Studies Strategies: Theory into Practice,* ed. Peter H. Martorella (New York: Harper and Row, 1976), pp. 129–130.
14. See, for example, John Gibbs, "Kohlberg's Stages of Moral Development: A Constructive Critique," *Harvard Educational Review* 47 (February 1977): 43–61; and William Kurtines and Esther B. Grief, "The Development of Moral Thought: Review

and Evaluation of Kohlberg's Approach,'' *Psychological Bulletin* 81 (August 1974): 453–470.

15. Erik Erikson, *Childhood and Society,* 2nd ed. (New York: Norton, 1963).

16. Hallam, "Piaget and the Teaching of History," p. 87.

17. David P. Ausubel, *Educational Psychology: A Cognitive View,* (New York: Holt, Rinehart and Winston, 1968), pp. 37–38.

18. Elkind, *A Sympathetic Understanding,* p. 117.

19. Sigel, "Social Studies Strategies," pp. 79–80.

20. Elkind, *A Sympathetic Understanding,* p. 115.

21. Ibid., pp. 116–117.

22. James M. Blaut and David Stea, "Mapping at the Age of Three," *Journal of Geography* 73 (October 1974): 5.

Suggested Readings

Ambron, Sueann R. *Child Development,* 3rd ed. New York: Holt, Rinehart and Winston, 1981.

Bruner, Jerome S. *Beyond the Information Given.* New York: Norton, 1973.

Elkind, David. *A Sympathetic Understanding of the Child: Birth to Sixteen,* 2nd ed. Boston: Allyn and Bacon, 1978.

Erikson, Erik. *Childhood and Society,* 2nd ed. New York: Norton, 1963.

Ginsburg, Herbert, and Opper, Sylvia. *Piaget's Theory of Intellectual Development,* 2nd ed. Englewood Cliffs, N.J.: Prentice-Hall, 1979.

Hallam, Roy. "Piaget and the Teaching of History," in *Social Studies Strategies: Theory into Practice,* ed. Peter H. Martorella. New York: Harper and Row, 1976.

Helms, Donald B., and Turner, Jeffrey S. *Exploring Child Behavior,* 2nd ed. New York: Holt, Rinehart and Winston, 1981.

Hersh, Richard, et al. *Promoting Moral Growth: From Piaget to Kohlberg,* 2nd ed. New York: Longman, 1983.

Kohlberg, Lawrence. "Educating for a Just Society: An Updated and Revised Statement," in *Moral Development, Moral Education, and Kohlberg,* ed. Brenda Munsey. Birmingham, Al.: Religious Education Press, 1980, pp. 455–470.

Lickona, Thomas, ed. *Moral Development and Behavior: Theory, Research and Social Issues.* New York: Holt, Rinehart and Winston, 1976.

Pagano, Alice L., ed. *Social Studies in Early Childhood: An Interactionist Point of View.* Washington, D.C.: National Council for the Social Studies, 1978.

Piaget, Jean. *The Language and Thought of the Child.* New York: Harcourt Brace Jovanovich, 1926.

Piaget, Jean, and Inhelder, Barbel. *The Growth of Logical Thinking from Childhood to Adolescence.* New York: Basic Books, 1958.

Rosenzweig, Linda W., ed. *Developmental Perspectives on the Social Studies.* Washington, D.C.: National Council for the Social Studies, 1982.

Sigel, Irving E., and Cocking, Rodney R. *Cognitive Development from Childhood to Adolescence: A Constructivist Perspective.* New York: Holt, Rinehart and Winston, 1977.

3

A Planning Model for Teaching Social Studies

One of the earliest and most difficult roles a beginning elementary teacher has to master is instructional planning. For new teachers especially, the challenge of providing quality learning experiences for twenty-five to thirty-five youngsters for over four hours a day, five days a week in at least four, and often six, subjects is an awesome one.

Effective teachers can assume this responsibility in part by becoming proficient in planning. Thorough, thoughtful, and systematic planning is a key ingredient in successful teaching at any grade level. Although there is much more to a "good" teacher than being a competent planner, it is one of the fundamental characteristics.

Experienced teachers who have invested years in planning often seem to belie this fact. They make effective teaching look easy to a neophyte. When asked, they even may profess to have done no immediate planning. In fact, through trial and error over the years, teachers gradually build on their successful planning experiences. They learn to reduce their planning tasks considerably without sacrificing the quality of the learning experiences they provide. Effective teachers far removed from the early years of their own teaching frequently have forgotten how much time they initially spent in planning. Some even express surprise at the amount of time and detail that teachers in training must devote to becoming good instructional planners.

Basic Issues in Planning for Social Studies Teaching

In this chapter we will explore the major elements of effective planning in social studies instruction. In functional instructional planning this involves fundamental questions such as: Why teach social studies? and What subject matter should be taught at each grade level, and in which order? These questions touch on the major dimensions of planning for social studies instruction. They include both practical and theoretical issues. A third fundamental question in planning, How should one teach social studies?, and others relating to instructional strategies will be addressed in Parts II, III, and IV.

Why Teach Social Studies?

To answer the question ''Why teach social studies?'' a teacher must decide what the overriding purpose of the social studies curriculum should be. The answer to the ''why'' question provides a conceptual framework for what is to be planned for the curriculum and a basic direction for what it is to accomplish.

Purpose, Goals, and Objectives. Determining why social studies should be taught requires a teacher to identify the major *purpose* of social studies teaching, as we discussed in Chapter 1. It also involves stating and justifying some important general *goals* that will guide the course of study for a given grade. Further it leads to spelling out some specific *objectives* for short-term and long-term planning.

What Subject Matter Should Be Taught and in Which Order?

Which knowledge is most valuable? Selecting from the vast reservoir of potentially useful information that children should learn has been a perennial challenge for curriculum planners. The question of what subject matter and in which order involves what educational planners call scope and sequence.

Scope and Sequence. When teachers ask, ''What am I supposed to teach?'' they wish to have some sense of the *scope* or list of the topics they are to teach. The *sequence* or order of the topics answers the question How are they to be logically related in the learning process? The sequencing of subject matter taught has implications for, among other things, the preparation of materials and the organization of time. In Chapter 1 we discussed the scope-and-sequence pattern typically followed across the United States.

Determining the Purpose, Goals, and Objectives of Long-Term and Short-Term Instruction

All social studies planning begins with some explicit (conscious or stated) or implicit (unconscious or unstated) notion of the purpose of the social studies. In Chapter 1 we suggested that most social studies educators would agree that the basic purpose of the social studies is citizenship education.

Identifying the Major Purpose of Teaching the Social Studies

Beyond this area of general agreement however, we saw five positions on the best way to promote citizenship education. These positions are that the major purpose of teaching social studies should be:

1. to transmit the cultural heritage of our society
2. to teach the knowledge and skills of the social sciences
3. to develop reflective inquiry
4. to encourage informed social criticism
5. to promote personal development

Planning begins when the teacher adopts some variation of these five or some sixth position as a statement of purpose. A statement of purpose will guide the teacher through the other planning decisions.

Social Studies Goals

Educators' general plans for the year or a shorter unit of time are their curricular goals. They express broadly what is to result from an instructional program in terms that are clear and represent a teacher's intentions. Although there is one statement of purpose for the year's program, there typically will be several goals that it is designed to satisfy. Goal statements may be different for each level of the social studies curriculum or they may remain the same across the grades.

Sample Goals. One school district, for instance, established these six goals for each grade, K–6.

1. To prepare each student to be a responsible and effective citizen in a changing society.
2. To help each student acquire an understanding and appreciation of cultural heritage and human achievement.
3. To help each student acquire an understanding of himself/herself and an appreciation of his/her worth as a member of society.
4. To help each student develop respect for the worth, rights, and beliefs of others.
5. To help each student understand the need for the conservation and preservation of the natural environment.
6. To help each student understand and take advantage of the opportunities open to him/her to prepare for a productive life.[1]

Goals also may be related to a particular discipline, such as history: "to develop an appreciation of the struggle of the minority in different historical periods to exercise its rights of freedom of speech and of religion." Establishing goals is an important step toward creating a basic framework for a course of study, and for leading to more specific curriculum expectations.

Social Studies Objectives

Related to goals are the curriculum objectives for the school year, one lesson, or some other unit of time. Objectives state specifically and clearly what students are expected to learn as the outcome of some instruction. Whereas goals communicate the framework for the curriculum, objectives translate them into specific statements of what students are to achieve.

Sample Objectives. Consider the following sample objectives, and then contrast them with the goals given earlier.

To identify correctly on the first trial at least five of the continents on a globe or a map.

On completing the text reading, the student will be able to present in writing or orally three causes of the Civil War.

To score at least 75 percent on a multiple-choice test covering the subject matter studied in the first unit.

After this unit, students should be able briefly to describe the economic systems and the relative standards of living in all of the countries studied.

As a result of the field trip pupils should understand some of the ways that other families differ from their own with respect to customs, foods, types of shelter, and the use of leisure time.

After completing the group assignment students will better understand how to listen to one another and to work cooperatively.

Objectives and Student Learning Outcomes. All of those objectives indicate some clear student learning outcomes, but some are more specific than others. The first three are very specific, since they give criteria or standards (e.g., number of items expected) and the conditions for demonstrating achievement of the objective (e.g., writing). Objectives that are stated with this specificity and describe clearly the expected behavior of the student are called *behavioral objectives.*

Both behavioral and nonbehavioral objectives can be used in the social studies to plan instruction and to clarify the expected outcomes of student learning. Some topics lend themselves more to the use of behavioral objectives (e.g., locate the states and list their corresponding capitals). Objectives may be stated for individual lessons, for a unit of study, or for the year. An objective may be included in more than one lesson.

Writing Statements of Objectives. Often statements of objectives begin as did some in our list, "As a result of this lesson, the pupil will be able . . ." At other times, as in the first example, the introductory phrase is assumed, and the objective begins instead with "write," "draw," "point to," etc. Many lists of verbs have been developed for use in writing objectives, and they suggest the range of possibilities that can be considered for students to demonstrate learning. A sample list is provided here.

The student will be able to:

rank	identify
assemble	sort
predict	match
rate	point to
select	summarize
role play	organize in order
classify	locate
construct	define
draw	write
diagram	state in his/her own words

EXERCISE 3.1   Identifying Goals and Objectives

Using aids such as curriculum guides and basal texts, identify examples of social studies goals and objectives that have been developed for various grade levels. Organize the list by grades, K–8, and locate at least two goals and two objectives for each level.

Balancing Goals and Objectives in the Curriculum

In Chapter 1 we suggested that the social studies curriculum should incorporate at each grade level some balance among reflection (matters of the head), competence (matters of the hand), and concern (matters of the heart). The reflective citizen was characterized as having knowledge of a body of concepts, facts, and generalizations about the organization, understanding, and development of individuals, groups, and societies. This citizen was also viewed as knowing about the processes of hypothesis formation and testing, problem solving, and decision making.

The competent citizen was seen as having skills such as collecting data systematically and accurately, identifying and using reference sources, processing and interpreting data, and organizing information chronologically and spatially. Competent citizens also were described as having skills in group participation, communication, observation, and multicultural understanding.

The concerned citizen was characterized as having an awareness of his or her rights and responsibilities, social consciousness, and a well-grounded framework for deciding what is right and wrong. He or she also knows how to identify and analyze issues and to suspend judgment on alternate beliefs, attitudes, values, customs, and cultures.

Balance in the social studies curriculum begins with identifying goals and objectives that address to some extent each of these three dimensions of the good citizen. For each grade planning should include goals and objectives that emphasize in some degree reflection, competence, and concern as they relate to effective citizenship.

The Cognitive and Affective Domains. Curriculum planners usually classify goals and objectives that address reflection, competence, and concern as being within either the cognitive or the affective domain. The *cognitive* domain is concerned primarily with thinking processes and the *affective* domain with feelings and emotions. Systems for creating and classifying goals and objectives within these domains were developed by Benjamin Bloom and his associates over two decades ago. Their efforts are reported in two major works, one for each domain, entitled "taxonomies of educational objectives."[2] These works have greatly influenced educational planners.

Some goals and objectives indicate directly which of the two domains they emphasize. Goal 4 in the preceding section, for instance, pertains primarily to the affective domain. Many goals and objectives, however, relate to both domains. *In reality, the head, the hand, and the heart are intertwined to some extent in all learning outcomes.* Curriculum planners emphasize one domain over another at some points in instruction and attempt to ensure that the curriculum offers some balance between the two.

Ordering Subject Matter into Units and Lessons

With a purpose, goals, and objectives in hand, the educator can now select and order subject matter to achieve them. Several guidelines have been developed for social studies programs at the local, state, and national levels. Most states have some requirements or legal codes, such as these two, which pertain to the social studies curriculum:

> Each teacher shall endeavor to impress upon the mind of the pupils the principles of morality, truth, justice, patriotism, and a true comprehension of the rights, duties, and dignity of American citizenship, to teach them to avoid idleness, profanity, and falsehood, and to instruct them in manners and morals and the principles of a free government.[3]
>
> The State Board has ordered that every course in U.S. History and Pennsylvania History taught in the elementary and secondary schools shall include the major contributions made by Negroes and other social and ethnic groups in the development of the United States and the Commonwealth [Pennsylvania].[4]

Local Planning Guidelines

At the local level a teacher is often assigned a general framework, such as ''American history,'' even before planning begins. In other cases, as when a basal text has been adopted, teachers are given a course of study for the entire year. However, even in these cases, there is generally some latitude for deciding the final scope and sequence of the curriculum. The teacher can usually supplement the general course outline periodically with extra lessons on timely topics, such as local elections or current events, or topics of special interest to students.

Professional Organization Planning Guidelines

Organizations such as the National Council for the Social Studies (NCSS) periodically issue general guidelines for curriculum planning in schools across the nation such as the *Revision of the NCSS Social Studies Curriculum Guidelines*. These often cover a range of issues related to planning and provide checklists of practical considerations and suggestions.

Unit Planning

The subject matter to be studied during the year may be divided arbitrarily into logical *units* of study. A unit is a series of sequenced and related lessons organized around some theme, along with resources for learning and procedures for evaluation. Resources frequently include, textbooks, readings, posters, work sheets,

---

EXERCISE 3.2 Applying Curriculum Guidelines

Locate the *Revision of the NCSS Social Studies Curriculum Guidelines*, found in the April 1979 issue of the periodical, *Social Education*. Also, select a copy of a recent basal social studies text for any grade and the related teacher's guide/manual. Using the sections of the curriculum guidelines that are relevant to text analysis, identify the strengths and shortcomings of the text.

---

simulation games, transparencies, drawings, guest speakers, field trips, films, videotapes, recordings, and assorted other media.

Units may extend for any length of time, but typically they require three to six weeks to complete. They may be organized around any theme that has some clear meaning for the teacher and the students.

Sample Unit Topics. Some illustrations of unit titles follow:

"Communities and How They Change"

"Shelters Around the World"

"The Plains Indians"

"Poverty in America"

"Understanding Our Behavior"

"The Causes of the Civil War"

"Rules We Live By"

"The Bill of Rights"

Sources of Units. Units are found in many places. Teachers, themselves, are major developers of individual units. Many of these units are shared within a school or district and often are published in curriculum guides and professional journals. In creating their own units, teachers build on their special interests, expertise, or unusual experiences, such as travels. A teacher-created unit often begins with general ideas on some subject a teacher feels students should learn about. To this base of ideas the teacher adds details to give the unit shape and reality.

Teacher-Made Units. Consider the teacher who has visited the People's Republic of China over the summer. He or she wishes to share the excitement and insights with next year's sixth-grade class. The idea for a unit on "The China of Today" begins to take shape.

"Why should my students be asked to learn about China?" the teacher asks himself or herself. From this question goals emerge that suggest an important rationale for the study, other than merely sharing the teacher's interesting experiences. How much time can be spared for such a unit? Time is often difficult to estimate accurately, especially for a beginning teacher. Answering the time question helps the teacher to organize the list of subtopics. Objectives, related teaching strategies, resource materials, and some plan for evaluation follow, and a new unit unfolds.

Commercially Produced Units. Commercial publishers and professional organizations also publish collections of units for different grade levels, and they organize textbooks into units. An example of how a year's course of study can be organized into units can be found in the sixth-grade text entitled *Our World: Lands and Cultures.*[5] It is divided into seven units (See Figure 3.1), which normally would be spread over the thirty-six weeks of the school year. Each unit is organized into three to five subtopics. These, in turn, are organized into two to five related lessons, along with resource materials found in the basal text. A test is also included in each unit. A given lesson may take more than one class period to complete, depending on the topic and the grade level.

Teachers often augment the school district's basic curriculum with commercially prepared units on some special need or interest of students. Many such units can be easily incorporated into a classroom program and are found in instructional materials centers, local school district curriculum guides, books such as some of the suggested readings at the end of this chapter, and teacher journals and publications. The organization, elements, and terminology in such units vary considerably.

The Elements of Basic Unit Planning

In sum, the general elements of basic unit planning can be viewed as follows.

1. Develop an idea for a special topic of study arises, and convert it into some theme or subject-matter focus with a title. (Unit Title)
2. Break the big idea or theme for the unit into more specific ideas and smaller subtopics. (List of Topics)
3. Indicate for which group of children or grade levels the unit is intended and include them in the planning if possible. (Target Student Population)
4. Approximate the time that can be spent on the unit. (Time Required)
5. Construct a brief overview of the unit, and determine its importance and use for the intended class. (Overview and Rationale)
6. Identify basic goals for the unit. (Goals)
7. Outline the specific objectives to be accomplished with the unit, and arrange them in sequential order. (Objectives)
8. Match objectives and subtopics, and begin to identify and develop related teaching strategies and activities. (Teaching Strategies and Activities)
9. Identify, locate, and organize the available individuals and instructional resources that will be needed. (List of Resources)
10. Develop a plan to evaluate the effectiveness of the unit. (Evaluation Procedures)

FIGURE 3.1   A year's course of study organized into units

UNIT 1

How Societies Are Similar and Different

Chapter 1 The Land and the People

Lesson 1   The Island Country of Japan
Lesson 2   The Deserts of Egypt
Lesson 3   France, The Crossroads of Europe
Environment: Energy
Lesson 4   The High Lands of Peru
Time Out for Map and Globe

Chapter 2 Social Groups

Lesson 1   Social Groups in Japan
Citizenship: Elections in Japan
Lesson 2   Social Groups Among the Bedouin
Lesson 3   Social Groups in France
Lesson 4   Social Groups Among the Quechua

Chapter 3 Religion

Lesson 1   Religion in Japan
Lesson 2   Religion Among the Bedouin
Lesson 3   Religion in France
Lesson 4   Inca Beliefs of Yesterday, Quechua
Beliefs Today
Building Social Studies Skills: Landforms Under the Ocean

Chapter 4 Technology

Lesson 1   A Way to Study Technology
Lesson 2   Technology in Japan
Lesson 3   Technology Among the Bedouin
Lesson 4   Technology in France
Lesson 5   Technology Among the Quechua
Careers: In the Great Outdoors

Chapter 5 Art

Lesson 1   Art in Japan
Lesson 2   Art Among the Bedouin
Someone You Should Know: Anwar Sadat
Lesson 3   Art in France
Lesson 4   Inca Art of Yesterday, Quechua Art
Today
Unit Test

UNIT 2

How People Learn to Live Together

Chapter 6 Working and Playing Together in Groups

Lesson 1   What Is Expected Behavior?
Lesson 2   Learning Expected Behavior

Chapter 7 Learning from Parents

Lesson 1   The Rajputs of India
Citizenship: Republic Day in India
Lesson 2   The Gusii of Kenya
Lesson 3   The Italians

Chapter 8 Learning from Play and Stories

Lesson 1   Rajput Children at Play
Lesson 2   Stories from Mexico's Past
Building Social Studies Skills: Causes of Climate

Chapter 9 Learning in School and Out

Lesson 1   On an Israeli Kibbutz
Lesson 2   In the Eternal City of Rome
Consumer Concerns: Television Advertising

Chapter 10 When Different Cultures Meet

Lesson 1   Nairobi
Lesson 2   Jerusalem
Someone You Should Know: Golda Meir
Lesson 3   Juxtalahuaca
Unit Test

UNIT 3

Who We Are

Chapter 11 The Norwegians

Lesson 1   The Norwegians and Their Environment
Lesson 2   The Norwegians and Their Nation
Someone You Should Know: Thor Heyerdahl

Chapter 12 The Zaireans

Lesson 1   What It Means to Be Zairean
Lesson 2   What It Means to Be Luba
Environment: Pollution

Chapter 13 The Balinese

Lesson 1   A Woman of a Village Family
Lesson 2   Villagers Honor What Is Important
Lesson 3   First a Villager, Then an Indonesian
Citizenship: Decision-Making in Indonesia

Chapter 14 The Chinese of the People's Republic

Lesson 1   Raising Food Together
Lesson 2   A Neighborhood Committee
Lesson 3   Student Life
Building Social Studies Skills: Reading the Newspaper

(Figure continues on following page.)

FIGURE 3.1. Continued

Chapter 15 The French-Canadians of Quebec
Lesson 1 The French-Canadian Heritage
Lesson 2 Living in the French Manner
Lesson 3 French and English Together
Unit Test

UNIT 4

How People Use their Resources

Chapter 16 The Australians
Lesson 1 The Australian Past
Lesson 2 Resources in Australia Today
Lesson 3 How Australians Use Their Resources
Consumer Concerns: Money and You

Chapter 17 The Costa Ricans
Lesson 1 The Costa Ricans Past
Building Social Studies Skills: Circle Graphs
Lesson 2 Resources in Costa Rica Today
Lesson 3 How Costa Ricans Use Their Resources

Chapter 18 The West Germans
Lesson 1 The West German Past
Lesson 2 Resources in West Germany Today
Lesson 3 How West Germans Use Their Resources
Someone You Should Know: Kathe Kollwitz

Chapter 19 The Guineans
Lesson 1 The Guinean Past
Lesson 2 Resources in Guinea Today
Lesson 3 How Guineans Use Their Resources

Chapter 20 The Yugoslavs
Lesson 1 The Yugoslav Past
Lesson 2 Resources in Yugoslavia Today
Lesson 3 How Yugoslavs Use Their Resources
Careers: In Music
Time Out for Testing
Unit Test

UNIT 5

Leadership in Government

Chapter 21 Why People Form Governments
Lesson 1 What Governments Do
Lesson 2 Kinds of Governments
Lesson 3 Governments Change
Citizenship: Freedom of the Press

Chapter 22 Leaders Within Nations
Lesson 1 Tribal Leadership in Nigeria
Someone You Should Know: Nnamdi Azikiwe
Lesson 2 Village Leadership in Malaya
Lesson 3 Leadership in a Swiss Canton

Chapter 23 Leaders of Nations
Lesson 1 A King Who Does Not Rule
Lesson 2 A Leader With Great Power
Lesson 3 Leaders Sharing Power
Building Social Studies Skills: Map Projections
Unit Test

UNIT 6

International Interdependence

Chapter 24 People Depend Upon Each Other
Lesson 1 The People of a Nation Are Interdependent
Lesson 2 The Nations of the World Are Interdependent
Lesson 3 International Interdependence Is Growing
Building Social Studies Skills: Writing a Report

Chapter 25 International Trade and Business
Lesson 1 Laws Affect Trade
Lesson 2 Common Markets
Lesson 3 Commodity Organizations
Consumer Concerns: Consumers' Rights

Chapter 26 Meeting Crises and Seeking Peace
Lesson 1 Earthquake!
Lesson 2 WHO Cares About Health
Lesson 3 Causes of War
Citizenship: Treaties
Lesson 4 The United Nations
Someone You Should Know: Dag Hammarskjold
Unit Test

UNIT 7

Cultures Change

Chapter 27 Ireland
Lesson 1 The Celts of Antiquity
Lesson 2 The Coming of Christianity
Lesson 3 A Blend of Old and New in Ireland Today
Building Social Studies Skills: Time Lines

FIGURE 3.1.   Continued

Chapter 28 Brazil

Lesson 1   The Traditional Ways
Lesson 2   The Coming of Modernization
Someone You Should Know:
Carolina M. de Jesus

Chapter 29 The Union of Soviet Socialist Republics

Lesson 1   Revolution
Lesson 2   Collectivization and Manufacturing

Lesson 3   Two Families
Environment: Oceans

Chapter 30 The Republic of the Philippines

Lesson 1   Before Independence
Lesson 2   The Philippines Today
Careers: In Sports
Unit Test

Source: Our World: Lands and Cultures (Glenview, Ill.: Scott, Foresman, 1983). Reprinted by permission.

---

11. Organize all of the material into a series of sequenced lessons for the amount of instructional time allotted. (Lesson Plans)
12. Assess whether the lessons and activities are developmentally appropriate for the specific group of students to be taught or whether some modifications will be necessary for individual students. (Developmental Appropriateness)

Resource Units and Teaching Units

Units are sometimes classified as *resource* units and *teaching* units. Although they share many elements, resource units are generally more extensive and detailed than teaching units, and often are designed to be used by many teachers for a variety of students. They are structured to help a teacher with each phase of planning a teaching unit. A resource unit typically would list more subtopics, objectives, teaching strategies and activities, resources, and evaluation procedures than one teacher needs to use.

Working with a resource unit, a teacher can create a unit for a specific population of students and for a given length of time. The creation of a new teacher-made unit often merges planning for a resource unit with planning for a teaching unit. Typical resource units incorporate the first ten steps in the sequence just summarized. Teaching units include steps 11 and 12.

Sample Resource Units. An American history resource unit taken from the University of Minnesota's Project Social Studies is shown in Table 3.1. Since the original unit is long, only the initial sections have been included. Also, the lists of materials have been omitted to save space.

Formats for Unit Planning. A variety of unit *formats* or ways of organizing and presenting information exist. Table 3.1 shows a multicolumn format to organize the elements of the unit. A sequential organizational pattern is shown in Table 3.2. The choice of format in unit planning is largely a matter of personal preference.

TABLE 3.1 A resource unit sample

Objectives for unit

GENERALIZATIONS

1. Although culture is always changing, certain parts or elements may persist over long periods of time.

2. Most political communication depends on the use of symbols, stereotypes, and other communication short-cuts; effective communication depends on the effective manipulation of these symbolic tools.

3. Whether an increase in centralization accompanies the increase in cohesion that accompanies or follows group conflict depends upon both the character of the conflict and the type of the group.

SKILLS

1. *Attacks problems in a rational manner.*
   a. Uses sub-questions to guide him in collecting relevant data.

2. *Gathers information effectively.*
   a. Reads for details which support or contradict generalizations and main ideas.
   b. Listens to discussion for main ideas, supporting detail, and to evaluate what he hears.
      1) Listens for details.
   c. Gains information by studying films.

3. *Evaluates information and sources of information.*
   a. Checks facts against his own background of information and collects additional information when he needs to check the facts.
   b. Looks for points of agreement and disagreement among authors.
   c. Chooses the most reliable source of information in terms of bias and competency of authors.
   d. Checks on the completeness of data and is wary of generalizations based on insufficient evidence.

4. *Has a well-developed sense of time.*
   a. Has a sense of the passage of time.

5. *Organizes and analyzes data and draws conclusions.*
   a. Classifies data.
   b. Organizes his materials to fit the theme and follow his organization.
   c. Generalizes from data.

Objectives for activities	Teaching procedures	Materials
Generalization: Although culture is always changing, certain parts or elements may persist over long periods of time.	1. Construct bulletin boards, contrasting life in 18th century Boston, Williamsburg and Philadelphia with that of 17th century Plymouth and Jamestown. (Pictures of the 18th century cities are available from the Chamber of Commerce. Pictures of Jamestown and Plymouth should have already been acquired in Unit III.) Be certain to show the size of the town, housing available, shops available, farming, etc. Have the class discuss the bulletin boards, considering such items as: physical layout, house size, probably population, economic activities, wealth, etc.	Write: Chamber of Commerce for Williamsburg, Boston, Philadelphia Write: Plymouth Plantation Inc., Jamestown Festival Park

Objectives for activities	Teaching procedures	Materials
Skill: *Reads for details which support or contradict generalizations and main ideas.*	2. Introduce the pupils to the many biographies and novels which have been written about the revolutionary figures of Boston, Williamsburg, and Philadelphia. Have each pupil choose one.	See bibliography for books. Any of the standard biographies, chosen to fit the reading level of the child, will work.
	The stories of these figures make exciting reading in themselves so be certain to discuss carefully with the students what you want them to look for as they read. Give them a study guide of questions. Have them use the questions to take notes as they read. These questions should be framed to obtain data from these works on: (1) the occupations and wealth (in land and/or goods) of these men, (2) living conditions of these cities, (3) the trade of the cities, (4) the religion of the people of these cities, (5) the pre-Revolutionary experiences of these men, (6) the activities of the legislative assemblies and other colonial organizations such as Sons of Liberty, Committees of Correspondence. Continental Congress, (7) the changing attitudes of these men toward their respective states and toward a central government, (8) the changing attitudes of these men toward England 1763–1774, (9) the national symbols which become important to these men, (10) the attitudes of the heroes of these books to other important revolutionary figures.	
	Have pupils begin their reading in class and supervise their note-taking. Make certain they understand that they will be responsible for these people in class discussions.	
Skill: *Listens for details.*	3. Using available maps, give an informal, illustrated lecture on the extent and size of the colonial settlement in 1763. Show the areas settled, the population of the chief cities, the national and religious makeup of the population, the crops grown, the trade products and routes. Show also some scenes of America at that time.	Lord and Lord, *Historical Atlas of the U.S.*

(Table continues on following page.)

TABLE 3.1   Continued

Objectives for activities	Teaching procedures	Materials
	Have the students compare this data with similar data on the colonies in the 17th century.	
Skill: *Has a sense of the passage of time.*	4. Have each pupil read a text book to gain an overview of the unit. Using the text, each pupil should construct for himself a timeline of chief events of this period. Have him keep and use the timeline as the unit progresses.	Read texts geared to reading level.
	5. Read to the class travelers' descriptions of life in these American cities prior to the Revolution. Have them discuss the reliability of these descriptions.	
Skill: *Uses subquestions to guide him in collecting relevant data.*	6. Have each pupil choose one of the three towns to study as the unit progresses. Make certain he understands that he is responsible for collecting data about the city as the unit progresses and that he will write a paper at the end of the unit in which he discusses the role his city played in the Revolution. He should also prepare a map of the city, indicating locations important to the revolutionary movement. He will obtain information on his own about the city, but he should also be alert to various class activities in which his city is featured, such as in discussion of inhabitants of these cities, movies, pictures and other descriptions of events in these cities.	Consult library resources.
Skill: *Chooses the most reliable source of information in terms of bias and competency of authors.* Generalization: Although culture is always changing, certain parts or elements may persist over long periods of time. Skill: *Chooses the most reliable source of information in terms of bias and competency of authors.*	7. Have each pupil choose one of the classic events of the Revolution, i.e., Boston Massacre, Boston Tea Party, Paul Revere's Ride, Patrick Henry's Resolve, Battle of Yorktown, Benedict Arnold's Treason, etc. (excluding the Battle of Lexington which will be done in detail in developmental activities). Have him check a variety of sources on these topics such as texts, encyclopedia, biographies of people involved, collections of first-hand accounts such as *The Spirit of '76*, histories of the Revolution, etc. Have each	Use: texts, encyclopedia, biographies, Commager and Nevins, eds., *Spirit of '76*, Sheer and Rankin, *Rebels and Redcoats.* Consult library resources.

Objectives for activities	Teaching procedures	Materials
Skill: *Checks on the completeness of data and is wary of generalizations based on insufficient evidence.*	pupil prepare a paper in which he discusses the ways in which the sources differed in their descriptions and interpretations of these events. He should give his own version of the events, based on the readings. Make certain pupils understand that they will be responsible in class discussions for the expert knowledge of these events.	

Source: University of Minnesota, Project Social Studies, 1967

EXERCISE 3.3   Analysis of Resource Units

Examine several resource units, either commercially prepared or teacher-made ones, and notice the various formats used, amount of detail, types of materials included, and the like. Notice also how they were similar and how they differed.

TABLE 3.2   Sample format for unit planning

UNIT PLAN

I. Descriptive Characteristics
    Title:
    Student Target Population/Grade Level:
    Estimated Time Required:
    Rationale and Overview:

II. Goals and Objectives (Number each to save time and for easy referral in constructing lesson plans.)
    Goals:
    Specific Objectives:

III. Teaching Strategies and Activities (Briefly describe the list of possibilities, and number them for later reference.)

IV. List of Resources (List each item and subdivide by type: e.g., textbooks, speakers, field trips, reference works, various media. Number each for easy reference.)

V. Evaluation Procedures (Relate each item to the goals and objectives stated earlier.)

VI. Lesson Plans (Sequence of plans to achieve the goals and objectives of the unit.)

Lesson Planning

As we have suggested, individual lesson plans are the final stage of planning for a teaching unit. They are also used by teachers for short-term objectives. Ms. Wolman, for instance, may decide that a lesson on the nature of money in our society would help her third-grade students to understand the economic unit on "Goods and Services" that they have been studying.

A lesson may last for one class period or extend over several days. Lesson plans in essence show what is to be accomplished and with which procedures and resources on Monday through Friday in daily teaching. They also help the teacher at some points to determine whether learning is occurring.

Unlike initial planning, which answers Why should students study a topic? lesson planning answers How is learning to occur? To develop effective lessons teachers must give careful thought to the details of initiating and carrying through instruction in an interesting and meaningful way for a particular group of students. They must take into account what has come before the lesson and what is to follow it, as well as what happens during it.

Formats for Lesson Planning. A quick review of lesson plans found in curricular guides, teacher's manuals for basal texts, and teacher's publications and periodicals will reveal that, as there are many units, there are also many notions on what they should include and which format should be used to construct them. Examples vary in structure, terminology, degree of detail, and number of elements. The plans in Figures 3.2 and 3.3, on pages 57–59, illustrate this point.

As for unit planning, selecting a format for lesson planning is largely a matter of teacher preference. Many schools, however, request that teachers use a format that has been standardized in the school or district. One reason for this standardization is to simplify communication between teachers and supervisors, administrators, and other teachers, such as substitutes. For some teachers, this requirement presents a problem, since they feel more comfortable and function more effectively with their own format. These teachers may want to "keep two sets of books," one in a personalized format for actual use, and the other with the same information in a standardized format requested by the school.

The Elements of Basic Lesson Planning. A lesson plan in any format will have the following elements:

1. *Title*. Each lesson should be given a title that communicates its focus. Assigning a number as well can make reference to materials easier when you are doing other planning.
2. *Goals and objectives*. The lesson objectives should be stated clearly and as specifically as possible. They should indicate which aspects of reflection, competence, and concern (for example, concept formation, communication skills, value analysis) are to be addressed. Although the lesson itself may not list the goals it helps achieve, it should be clearly related to them during planning.

3. *Initiatory activity.* A lesson plan begins with some brief interesting activity that arouses curiosity and focuses attention on what is to be learned. An initiatory activity says to the student, ''This is something you might like to learn about.''

4. *Teaching strategies and activities.* In general, teaching strategies and activities are procedures for achieving the instructional objectives. Different types of strategies exist for different objectives. Strategies include questions, statements, directions, actions, and even the sequence of those elements. They also deal with how the teacher organizes and presents subject matter. Activities include a broader variety of student tasks, only some of which are directed by the teacher. Teacher and student roles in the lesson should be spelled out, as well as major questions to be asked or key instructions to be given.

5. *Resources.* Somewhere within the lesson the resources that will be used should be listed for easy reference. The order in which the materials are to be used also should be clearly indicated.

6. *Transition.* Each lesson should include some transition to the next one. This may consist merely of a summary of the day's activities, with some indication of what is to follow and how the two lessons are related. It also might consist of some *evaluation* of a phase of learning that has just been completed.

EXERCISE 3.4   Lesson Planning

Select a topic, a grade level, and a lesson plan format (from Figures 3.2 and 3.3 or another source), and develop a sample social studies lesson.

FIGURE 3.2   Sample format for lesson plan.

CLOTHES TELL STORIES

PURPOSE OF THE LESSON

To demonstrate to the pupils that clothes may tell us something about those who are wearing them.

EXPECTATIONS

Upon completion of this lesson, pupils should be able to:

Identify three uniforms and tell what people wear them.

Recognize and tell some information that uniforms suggest about the wearers.

RESOURCES

Webstermasters, pp. 39, 40

drawing paper and crayons

magazines, newspapers, catalogues (optional)

children's clothing — see Evaluation (optional)

BACKGROUND

Clothes are tangible expresss of our culture and play an important role in children's experiences. Sometimes, clothes even become a *(Figure continues on following page.)*

FIGURE 3.2   Sample format for lesson plan

source of conflict between children and their parents.

The lesson helps pupils discover that what we wear, when we wear it, and even how we wear it may tell others something about us.

Note: The lesson may require two sessions. Plan the Ending the Lesson experience for the second session.

STRATEGIES
Arousing Interest

Ask four children to stand in front of the class. Then tell the class: "Look at their clothes. How are their clothes alike?" (Wearing pants, sneakers, sweaters; colors.) Say: "Think about other clothes that you have, and tell why you are not wearing them today." As they tell you why, emphasize the fact that for every choice there is a reason. "Do you have special clothes you wear on special days?" Indicate to the class your clothes tell a story about you. Repeat comments made by two or three of the pupils to illustrate the point. For instance, "Arthur wore sneakers to school because they are good for playing and running at lunch time. Mary is wearing a short-sleeve top because it is very warm today, and she wants to be as cool and as comfortable as possible." Then say: "I'm going to try to see if I can tell some things about you by looking at your clothes." I'll try to think of some things that have not been mentioned yet." By now, you know the children well and may have a lot of fun surprising the children with what you have to say. For example, "Margaret, you are wearing blue. Because you often wear blue clothes, I think blue is one of your favorite colors."

The Lesson

Distribute Webstermasters, pp. 39 and 40. Read the titles. Help the pupils identify each picture. Guide the pupils in recognizing the story the clothes in each picture tell about the person. Spend some time discussing each picture. This will help pupils to group pictures later.

As you discuss the pictures, ask: "Have you ever seen anyone dressed like this?" If pupils have, encourage them to tell about it. Ask: "Why is this person dressed this way? What does this clothing tell us? What do you think this person is doing? What do you think this person is about to do?"

Say: "Suppose you wanted to put some of the clothes these people are wearing into a group. Look at the pictures on both pages. Which pictures would you choose for a group? Circle the pictures that have the clothes you chose to group together."

Have pupils share their responses and tell why the pictures were chosen for the groups.

Ending the Lesson

Ask the pupils: "How are clothes on pages 39 and 40 alike? How are they different from each other?" Compare all the clothes on one page at a time.

Distribute drawing paper. Have the pupils draw pictures of clothes they wear that tell a story about them. Say: "It could be a bathing suit that tells you like to swim. It could be a cap that says you like baseball, but be sure it tells something about you. It could be your favorite clothes." Or, pupils may find and cut out magazine pictures of such clothes to paste on the page. At the bottom of the page, you may wish to write the pupils' comments about their pictures.

EVALUATION

Display pictures on a bulletin board of people wearing uniforms similar to those that pupils identified during the lessons. You may also use the Webstermasters pictures again or the pupils' drawings. Ask pupils to relate stories the clothes suggest about the people wearing them by telling why or for what occasions the clothes are being worn. Each child should be able to relate at least two "stories." On a second bulletin board, display children's bedclothes, children's playclothes, and children's party clothes. If you cannot get children's clothing, use pictures instead. Ask the pupils to identify the types of clothing displayed. Each child should identify two types.

Source: Peter H. Martorella et al., *Looking at Me, Teacher's Manual, Level K* (New York: McGraw-Hill, 1983), pp. 79–80. Reprinted by permission.

FIGURE 3.3   Sample format for lesson plan

CONSUMER CONCERNS: THEN AND NOW
(pp. 132–133)

Suggested Teaching Time
1 day

Objectives
Students will learn how to:

list advantages and disadvantages of modern means of preserving foods.

compare the past and present forms of packaging products.

tell how buyers can be influenced by the packaging of a product.

Teaching Suggestions
Say: *We have been talking about things that change. When the parents of your great-grandparents went to a store to buy groceries, they went to a store that was very different from our modern supermarkets. Grocery stores have changed.*

Turn to page 132 and you will see what it would be like to visit an old grocery store, one the parents of your grandparents might have visited. Have students try to identify the foods in the picture of the old-fashioned store pictured on pp. 132–133. Read page 132 aloud. Then say: *Now let's look at the small picture on page 133. What changes do you see?* Read page 133 aloud. After reading, have ready to show the class an array of foods or food labels that carry the words, "No Preservatives" or "No Artificial Color or Flavor Added." After explaining the meaning of these labels, ask the class why they think these foods have these labels. Point out that some studies have shown that these things can be harmful to people. (Point out also that in the days before preservatives were added to foods, people sometimes got sick from eating spoiled food.)

As children mention the differences in the ways food is packaged today, ask: *Why do you think these changes in packaging came about?*

What might happen to cookies that are sold in a bag instead of a box? What can happen if fruits like tomatoes or peaches aren't packaged? Help the class to conclude that packaging helps to keep foods fresh, clean, and in good condition.

Say to the class: *Some foods are packaged in glass. What do you sometimes buy in glass containers? Some foods are packaged in metal cans. What are some foods you buy in metal cans? Some foods are packaged in boxes. What are some that come in boxes? Other foods come in sacks or bags. What are some things you buy in bags? Why do you suppose some foods are in glass bottles or jars? Metal cans? Boxes with see-through tops? Is the packaging important to people who want to buy the food? Why?*

Many people are concerned about the large amount of paper, glass, metal, and plastic that is being used. These people think we should use packaging only when it is absolutely necessary. Let's stop and think about this: Which of these things need to be put in packages?

1. milk
2. toy cars
3. eggs
4. combs
5. pencils
6. writing tablets

What are some things that do not need to be packaged? Then, why are they sometimes in a package? Have you ever wanted something because of the picture on the packaging? What was it? How important is the color of packaging? Does the printing on packaging ever influence you to want something?

Source: Scott, Foresman and Company, *Families and Friends, Teacher's Edition* (Glenview, Ill.: Scott, Foresman, 1983), pp. 132–133. Reprinted by permission.

Scheduling Social Studies Lessons

Part of an elementary teacher's planning is deciding each day's schedule of instruction. A typical school day will begin around 8:45 and end about 2:45. If an hour is taken for lunch, this leaves about five hours each day. Of the five hours approximately one hour is likely to be taken up with recess, restroom breaks, announcements, preparation for lunch and leaving, settling in after various breaks, and other noninstructional tasks. This leaves roughly *four hours for instruction* each day.

During the four hours teachers must plan to schedule instruction in language arts, mathematics, and science, as well as social studies. At some points during the week, room in the schedule probably also will have to be made for music, physical education, art, and possibly other subjects, such as foreign languages. Specialty teachers will provide some of this instruction in many school districts, and classroom teachers often have to build their schedules around those of the specialists.

Guidelines for Scheduling

The time to be spent on each subject may be left to the individual teacher, or the school district may establish guidelines. Chicago's Department of Curriculum, for example, suggests the weekly time distribution for elementary schools shown in Table 3.3.

In any school, elementary teachers need to count on scheduling twenty hours of instruction for each week, as well as planning to provide most of it. The scheduling of instruction thus is yet another dimension of effective planning. Experienced teachers realize that not all time during the day has equal value for instruction, and so they often try to ensure that "premium" time is used for especially important instructional objectives. The period just before lunch and just before dismissal, for instance, is generally regarded as poor instructional time, whereas that shortly after arrival is considered to be premium time.

Some teachers prefer to set a basic schedule for each day and to maintain most of the instructional slots throughout the week. Others construct the schedule to fit the time requirements of the lessons they will be doing during the week. Consider a lesson that involves a simulation game likely to take sixty minutes to complete and discuss. Rather than rush the lesson or divide it into two days, the teacher would want to build the schedule around it.

Still other teachers prefer to study certain subjects in a concentrated fashion for a certain period of time. For example, instead of studying social studies for forty minutes a day, five days a week, for thirty-six weeks a year, a fifth-grade teacher might spend eighty minutes daily for half of the school year. There is no best pattern for scheduling, but it is important to recognize the amount of time that is actually spent in social studies instruction, and allocate an equal share of premium time to that instruction.

TABLE 3.3 Weekly time distribution

Subject areas	Weekly time distribution in minutes							
	Gr.1	*Gr.2*	*Gr.3*	*Gr.4*	*Gr.5*	*Gr.6*	*Gr.7*	*Gr.8*
Language arts (listening, speaking, writing, reading, spelling, handwriting)	820	800	625	500	460	400	300	300
Mathematics	125	125	150	200	200	225	225	225
Social studies	80	100	140	175	175	200	200	200
Science	75	75	120	120	160	170	200	200
Art	60	60	60	60	60	60	60	60
Music	60	60	60	60	60	60	60	60
Physical education	60	60	60	80	80	80	80	80
Health and safety education	80	80	80	80	80	80	80	80
Library science	60	60	60	80	80	80	80	80
Foreign language or other subject areas	80	80	145	145	145	145	145	145
Home economics and/or industrial arts	—	—	—	—	—	—	70	70

Source: "Overview of the Instructional Program of the Chicago Public Schools, Kindergarten-Grade 8." Board of Education of the City of Chicago, Ill., 1982. Reprinted by permission.

Sample Schedules for Social Studies Instruction

Four general ways to approach scheduling are shown below; they are based on the assumption that approximately 200 minutes a week has been allocated to social studies instruction. The actual time to be allotted for each week, of course, will vary with the grade level.

Schedule 1: Social Studies, Monday through Friday, 40 minutes each day

Schedule 2: Social Studies, Monday, Wednesday, and Friday, 60–70 minutes each day

Schedule 3: Social Studies, Monday through Friday, every other week, 80 minutes each day

Schedule 4: Social Studies, sometime during Monday through Friday complete at least five activities in the Social Studies Center

Here is a sample *fixed* daily schedule for a sixth-grade class:

8:45–9:00 Taking attendance, collecting milk money, discussing the day's schedule, miscellaneous housekeeping chores

9:00–10:00	Language arts, handwriting, reading
10:00–10:15	Recess
10:15–10:55	Social Studies
10:55–11:30	Science
11:30–12:10	Library or physical education or art or music or health education
12:10–12:15	Prepare for lunch
12:15–1:15	Lunch
1:15–1:25	Settle in, discuss afternoon activities
1:25–2:10	Mathematics
2:10–2:35	Reading
2:35–2:45	Wrap-up, reminders, clean-up, prepare for dismissal

Planning Across the Grades

To this point we have been discussing planning for a single grade or a year's course of study. Schools and districts, however, often attempt to plan *across the grades* to ensure continuity from year to year in the curriculum. This is usually done on a K–6, K–8, or K–12 basis, as we discussed in Chapter 1, and may involve teachers from each grade level. Such planning establishes the basic scope and sequence of the curriculum for all the grades involved and for all of the teachers in a school or district.

Sequencing Goals and Objectives

Planning across the grades involves many of the issues involved in planning for a single year. The sequencing of goals, objectives, and subject matter is extended over a much larger time frame, however. Instead of developing them for a single year and a single grade, a school or district may attempt to lay out all the goals and objectives a student is to achieve over grades K–6 or K–8, for example.

Although some of these may be assigned to each grade level, there may be provisions for students to progress at their own rates. By the end of the kindergarten year, for example, some students already may have achieved the initial objectives of the first-grade social studies program. Other students may still be working toward important kindergarten objectives when they enter the first grade. This approach to planning across the grades views instruction as a continuous strand. The strand is broken when significant learning objectives in a sequence are ignored or left behind, just because a school year has ended and students move on to a new grade.

The city of Chicago has published a sequenced list of recommended social studies objectives, K–8. These are intended to guide the social studies program throughout the city's schools. The district's recommendations are shown in Table 3.4.

TABLE 3.4 Scope and sequence, K–8, for major social studies objectives.

K

- Tells about self, including name, address, and city.
- Describes interests, such as pets, games, and toys.
- Identifies new friends at school.
- Describes the many ways of being a friend.
- Describes the physical appearance and characteristics of the schoolroom.
- Tells what the schoolroom rules and regulations are.
- Explains the purpose of a family and the roles of family members.
- Describes some interests and activities of family life.
- Explains what is involved in caring for a home.
- Explains how leisure time is used.
- Recognizes the importance of responsibility at home and in school.
- Participates in room and school activities in accordance with rules and regulations.
- Tells what is happening in a picture portraying an urban area.
- Uses the globe to learn the shape of the earth.

1

- Identifies rules and reasons for proper behavior at school.
- Develops a respect for individuals of ethnic and racial groups.
- Tells ways of becoming a good friend.
- Identifies school workers.
- Recognizes the need for love, cooperation, and understanding in a family.
- Identifies neighborhood areas of homes, businesses, and recreation.
- Recognizes examples of cooperation in the neighborhood.
- Identifies different ways of travel.
- Compares an urban community with a farm community.
- Identifies animals that are seen at the zoo.
- Compares people in the neighborhood with people in neighborhoods in other urban areas.
- Distinguishes between a map and a globe.
- Recognizes land and water areas on a map and on a globe.

- Identifies *north* and *south* on maps and on a globe.
- Identifies pictorial symbols on maps.

2

- Describes the people and customs of the community.
- Explains available community public services.
- Names types of foods, clothing, and homes that are available in the community.
- Identifies community workers.
- Explains the importance of respecting school property.
- Describes places and types of recreation in the community.
- Explains how weather and climate affect the community.
- Explains the benefits of modern transportation.
- Identifies various kinds of communication.
- Describes the differences between a Chicago community and another urban community.
- Describes the differences between a Chicago community and an overseas community.
- Reads information on charts.
- Uses picture maps.
- Locates information on a globe.
- Computes distance in blocks from home to parks and playgrounds.
- Locates the equator on a globe and maps.

3

- Lists factors that make Chicago a great city.
- Explains how Chicago functions as the "heart" of the metropolitan area.
- Explains why Chicago is a famous city.
- Identifies symbols on the flag of Chicago.
- Recognizes famous names in Chicago history.
- Identifies three important events in the early history of Chicago.
- Explains some of the duties of a citizen of Chicago.
- Compares Chicago with another metropolitan area in the United States.

(Table continues on following page.)

TABLE 3.4 Continued

- Compares Chicago with an overseas metropolitan area.
- Obtains information from simple line and bar graphs.
- Locates Chicago on a map and globe in relation to Illinois and other states in the region.
- Locates main streets of Chicago on a city map.
- Locates home and school on a map of Chicago.
- Identifies major bodies of water and land on maps and on a globe.

4

- Describes the physical features of the regions of the United States.
- Explains how natural resources have contributed to the growth and development of Illinois.
- Explains how natural resources have contributed to the growth and development of the various regions of the United States.
- Explains how the people in the various regions of the United States meet their basic needs.
- Compares and contrasts regions of the United States with similar regions in other parts of the world.
- Identifies on maps such surface features as mountains, plains, lands, and water.
- Locates land and water boundaries of the continental United States.
- Groups states within the United States according to regional locations.
- Recognizes natural and political boundaries on maps.
- Uses map symbols to find the capitals and the population of cities.

5

- Identifies the routes used by the people who discovered the New World.
- Lists reasons why people came to the New World.
- Describes some of the problems encountered in building the new nation.
- Explains some of the causes of the westward movement.
- Compares and contrasts the government of Canada with that of the United States.

- Explains the current relationship between Mexico and the United States.
- Describes the ways of life in Central and South America.
- Explains the relationship of Puerto Rico to the United States.
- Exhibits a knowledge of the geography of Latin America.
- Uses a scale of miles in computing distances.
- Uses parallels of latitude and meridians of longitude to locate places on a map and a globe.
- Compares flat maps with a global representation of the world.
- Uses maps to relate natural factors to the economic development of a region.

6

- Explains how the land and climate influence cultural patterns in the Eastern Hemisphere.
- Describes how the historical development of countries in the Eastern Hemisphere has influenced present conditions.
- Compares and contrasts the people and their ways of living in countries of the Eastern Hemisphere.
- Compares and contrasts the political systems of the Union of Soviet Socialist Republics and the United States.
- Describes present conditions in countries of the Eastern Hemisphere.
- Recognizes the interdependence of the United States and the regions of the Eastern Hemisphere.
- Uses the globe and maps to locate areas of the world discussed in current events.
- Develops the ability to use a map scale for measuring distance.
- Locates time zones and the International Date Line on a map and on a globe.

7

- Describes life in primitive times.
- Lists contributions of early civilizations.
- Compares and contrasts Greek and Roman civilizations.
- Identifies the contributions of African cultures.

TABLE 3.4   Continued

- Describes changes in the ways of living during the Middle Ages.
- Describes the problems the English colonists encountered when settling the new nation.
- Compares and contrasts the viewpoints of the Loyalists and Tories.
- Lists some of the problems encountered by the political leaders when trying to unite the nation.
- Explains how the acquisition and development of western lands strengthened the nation.
- Explains the conflicting interests that resulted in the Civil War.
- Relates how the physical features of a region influence its history.

8

- Lists the characteristics of a modern industrial nation.

- Lists several reasons that explain the emergence of the United States as a world power.
- Identifies the major conflicts in which the United States has been involved since the 1930s.
- Explains the role of the United States in an interdependent world.
- Reads and interprets historical documents.
- Demonstrates knowledge of the national and state governments by fulfilling requirements of Public Law 195.
- Compares and contrasts the functions of state and local governments.
- Identifies the future needs of the city of Chicago and the state of Illinois.
- Develops effective skills in the interpretation of current events.
- Uses maps to discover patterns of land use.
- Uses the globe to demonstrate the importance of geographic positions in the world

Source: "Overview of the Instructional Program of the Chicago Public Schools, Kindergarten-Grade 8." Board of Education of the City of Chicago, Ill., 1982. Reprinted by permission.

Still another way to approach planning across the grades is to determine basic objectives that should be emphasized continually throughout the elementary/middle-school years. In each grade they are to be reemphasized and reinforced through increasingly difficult activities and learning experiences.

Planning for Effective Instruction

As we have seen, planning for social studies instruction occurs at the level of the classroom or the school district, for a day, year, or series of years. Apart from the important practical considerations we have discussed, thoughtful consideration of the specific nature of what students are to learn and why they are to learn it is essential for effective instruction.

To plan we must have clear reasons for what we will do and a sense of our specific goals and objectives. We must also make prudent use of the limited instructional time available to us during the school day. As a teacher becomes more skilled in organizing time, schedules, and resources and in planning lessons and units, he or she will have more time to focus on the actual instructional process and how it can be made more effective. Perhaps most important, he or she will have more opportunities to focus on the needs, interests, and progress of individual students.

Notes

1. Hatboro-Horsham School District, *Social Studies Program for Hatboro-Horsham (PA)* (Horsham, Pa.: Hatboro-Horsham School District, 1981).
2. See Benjamin S. Bloom et al., *Taxonomy of Educational Objectives. The Classification of Educational Goals. Handbook I: The Cognitive Domain* (New York: David McKay, 1956); and David R. Krathwohl et al., *Taxonomy of Educational Objectives. Handbook II: Affective Domain* (New York: David McKay, 1969).
3. *Education Code*. Sacramento, Calif.: State of California, 1963. Vol. 1, p. 356.
4. Herbert E. Bryan [ed.], *A Handbook of Information on Pennsylvania Law and Legal Opinions Relating to Education*. Harrisburg, Pa.: Pennsylvania School Board Association, 1973, p. 125.
5. Scott, Foresman Social Studies Program, *Our World: Land and Cultures, Teacher's Guide* (Glenview, Ill.: Scott, Foresman, 1983).

Suggested Readings

Allen, Jack, et al. *Social Studies for the 80's*. Washington, D.C.: National Education Association, 1980.

Cooper, James B., et al. *Classroom Teaching Skills*. Lexington, Mass.: D. C. Heath, 1982.

"Goals for the Social Studies: Toward the Twenty-First Century," *Journal of Research and Development in Education* 13 (Winter 1980): special issue containing twelve articles on the topic of goals in social studies by a group of leading social studies educators.

Jarolimek, John. *Social Studies in Elementary Education*. 6th ed. New York: Macmillan, 1982, Chapter 2.

Joyce, William W., and Alleman-Brooks, Janet E. *Teaching Social Studies in the Elementary and Middle Schools*. New York: Holt, Rinehart and Winston, 1979, Part II, Section A.

Kenworth, Leonard S. *Social Studies for the Eighties in Elementary and Middle Schools*, 3rd ed. New York: John Wiley and Sons, 1981, Chapter 10.

National Council for the Social Studies. *Revision of NCSS Social Studies Curriculum Guidelines*. Washington, D.C.: National Council for the Social Studies, April, 1979.

Welton, David A., and Mallan, John T. *Children and Their World: Strategies for Teaching Social Studies*. 2nd ed. Boston: Houghton Mifflin, 1981, Chapter 3.

PART TWO

Developing Citizens Who Think and Act Reflectively

4

Teaching Concepts, the Foundation of Reflection

Developing citizens who think and act reflectively is one of the major responsibilities of any social studies program. A democratic society depends on citizens who have a well-grounded body of concepts, facts, and generalizations about human behavior, their country, and the world. In applying such knowledge rationally to practical affairs, citizens need to be able to raise and test hypotheses and to engage in problem solving. These abilities are acquired cumulatively, beginning early in the home, becoming more formalized with the onset of kindergarten and schooling, and developing continuously throughout life.

The Components of Reflection and Rational Action

Reflection is a complex process, involving the brain and the different functions of its hemispheres, the nervous system, body chemistry, and other factors not yet completely understood by scientists. The outcomes of this often mysterious process are classified in several ways by psychologists and educators.

Concepts, Facts, Generalizations, Hypotheses, and Problem Solving

In establishing curriculum objectives and learning activities for children, one often identifies these elements of reflection: *concepts, facts, generalizations,* and *hypotheses.* The systematic pattern of thinking and action in which the elements of reflection are involved to find solutions to problems is called *problem solving.* In problem solving students develop hypotheses; they also use concepts, facts, and generalizations already acquired and, as a result, often learn new ones.

Knowledge. What we regard as an individual's knowledge consists of a complex network of the elements of reflection. The fact of our date of birth, for example, is linked in some way to our concept of *birthday*. As further reflection occurs, we incorporate the new information into our network and it becomes related with the old knowledge.

The Foundation of Reflection: Concepts. Within this chapter we will focus on the learning and teaching of the building blocks of all reflection, concepts. We will examine their nature, the types that exist within the social studies curriculum, and some strategies for helping children develop and apply them in reflection. In the following chapter, we will explore the distinctions among concepts, facts, generalizations, and hypotheses, as well as the dimensions of problem solving.

The Nature of Concepts

All thinking and action involve concepts. They broaden and enrich our lives and allow us to communicate easily with others. When individuals share a concept, they can use concept words as shorthand to communicate a large body of information. Because you and I share many concepts, we can communicate more rapidly and efficiently and I do not need to explain in detail each item I discuss. A communication breakdown often occurs because one of the parties lacks the concepts necessary to the conversation. This frequently happens in social studies textbooks when the author assumes knowledge that the student does not have.

Concepts also make it easier to sort out large numbers of living beings, objects, and events into a smaller number of categories such as males, turtles, mountains, and battles. Concepts are *hooks* on which we can hang new information. When we encounter new subject matter that does not fit neatly on any existing conceptual hook, we may broaden our idea of what some existing hook can hold or we create a new one. These conceptual hooks tidy up our knowledge structure and make it easier to learn and to remember information.

Test of Concept Knowledge

Before we examine the nature of concepts, let us establish what you already know about them. Consider the following statements, and mark a ''T'' for true and an ''F'' for false statements.

Concept Test

_____ 1. This page is covered with concept names.

_____ 2. Although concepts appear in many different forms, all of them are basically alike.

_____ 3. Every discipline of the social sciences is built around concepts.

_____ 4. It is the subject matter to which a concept belongs that makes it easy or difficult to learn.

_____ 5. Learning about what a concept is *not* helps us to learn what it is.

_____ 6. Learning a concept occurs in the same way as learning a fact.

_____ 7. The more information a student has about a concept, the easier it will be to learn it.

_____ 8. Subject matter to teach a concept is presented in the same way as that for other objectives.

_____ 9. Unless you can explain what a concept is in your own words, you have not really learned it.

_____10. The longer a concept name is, the more difficult the concept is to learn.

Compare your answers with the Answer Key at the end of the chapter before the Suggested Readings. The rest of the chapter explains the reasons for the answers. When you have finished reading the chapter, retake the test and check your answers again to see if you have understood all of the major points.

Definition of a Concept

In their simplest form, concepts may be regarded as *categories into which we group all phenomena within our experience.* Phenomena may be emotions, people, living organisms, thoughts, objects, or events; in short, they are anything of which we are aware.

Concept Names. Categories usually have single or multiword labels associated with them, such as *fear, leader, mammals, the weekly accomplishments, flags,* and *school assemblies.* People can, however, form concepts without any name. This, in fact, occurs for a new discovery, insight, or creation. A new concept comes into being, and as it is shared and communicated to others it passes from the status of "whatchamacallit" or "thingamajig" to having a concept name. The discovery of subatomic particles in physics, which eventually were labeled *quarks,* is an example. Names for new significant concepts are usually attached quickly because they simplify communication.

Concept Associations. We group our experiences by more than names and mental images. We use all of the personal associations we have accumulated in relation to the concept. One's concept of money, for example, includes more than checks, bank drafts, currency, and credit cards. It is also attached to one's economic goals and many other personal associations with money that make one's concept unique.

Personal and Public Dimensions of Concepts. These rich individual associations, which are part of every concept, we will call the *personal dimension* of concepts. Because each person's concept of even basic items, such as *chair,* are shaped by his or her special experiences over time and by the culture, it is often difficult to share many of the personal dimensions of a concept. Two people who find they "have a lot in common" often mean they have discovered similar personal associations with certain concepts.

In contrast, the *public dimensions* of concepts are those characteristics which we learn in common, and which permit the sharing of concepts. Although we may not be able to share the professional banker's personal concept of *money,* with all of its nuances and detail, we can easily communicate the fundamental public properties of the concept. It is on the public dimension of concepts that the school's curriculum focuses.

Concepts in Social Studies Programs

By the time they finish high school, students will have encountered thousands of concept words in their social studies classes and textbooks. Only a fraction of those words actually will be learned as concepts, and become more than a familiar word. Some of the concepts that are found in social studies instruction follow.

city	ocean	mountain
nation	colony	boundary
delta	river	family
culture	norm	democracy
news	war	peace
revolution	flag	assembly line
island	suburbs	earth
map	power	group
custom	prejudice	nationality
poverty	transportation	law
future	money	north
equator	desert	neighborhood
holiday	community	conflict
waste	citizen	love
causality	supply	demand
year	freedom	shelter

EXERCISE 4.1   Identifying Concepts in Social Studies Basal Texts

Select a basal social studies textbook for any grade. Identify the text title, the grade level, the author and publisher, and the copyright date. List all of the concepts that are included in twenty-five pages of the text, beginning with the first page of the first chapter. (For this exercise include only those concepts which are *nouns* or *adjectives*.)

Concepts in Texts and Other Reading Materials

The typical basal text includes many concepts, some of which it attempts to teach the students, and many of which it assumes they already know. Here are some concepts used in a first-grade basal social studies textbook.[1]

address	alike	atlas
bar graph	change	choosing
continent	dependence	different
earth	fairness	family
feelings	friends	globe
holiday	map	moving
museum	need	ocean
rule	safe	want

If the concepts in texts and instructional materials are to be more than words for students, they must be taught before or with lessons that assume their understanding. Often texts and reading materials for young children are heavily loaded with abstract concepts, which then are explained with other abstract concepts. Consider both the logic of the instruction as well as the number of abstract concepts packed into the following sentences in a basal social studies text for second graders. Beside a picture of a globe with an equator drawn around it, these statements appear: ''The globe also shows the equator. The equator is an imaginary line. It goes all around the globe.''

Types of Concepts

Concepts have been classified in many ways for students. Each system of classification offers different insights for balancing curriculum and lesson planning. Three major ways of grouping concepts for social studies instruction are according to: the social science discipline in which they most frequently appear, their concreteness or abstractness, and the nature of their attributes.

Social Science Concepts

One way to group concepts is by social science discipline. Although all concepts are really interdisciplinary (that is, they belong to no one discipline and are used by many), some concepts appear more frequently in one discipline than in another. For example, *power* occurs throughout political science and *map* is used continuously throughout geography. Some concepts, such as *year* or *love,* however, cannot be neatly grouped under any single discipline.

Concrete and Abstract Concepts

Concepts may also be sorted into *concrete* and *abstract* classes. *Flag* and *shelter* are concrete, whereas *fear* and *prejudice* are abstract. Concrete concepts can be perceived directly through one of the senses. Abstract concepts are those which cannot be directly perceived.

In reality, the line between what is concrete and what is abstract seldom is so clearly drawn. Consider the list of concepts on page 72. Although some (such as *democracy*) clearly cannot be directly perceived, and some (such as *map*) clearly can, many of them, (*neighborhood* and *family,* for example), lie somewhere in between. Some aspects of neighborhood and family are (people and dwellings) visible, but other important characteristics (the relationships of individuals to one another) are abstract.

EXERCISE 4.2   Assessing the Levels of Concreteness and Abstractness in Concepts

Place the sample list of forty-eight concepts found on page 72 along the concrete–abstract continuum shown below. Two examples from the list are given. Use a dictionary if you need help.

flag   democracy

Concrete   Abstract

Concept Attributes

Some concepts are more complex than others. What makes some complex is their properties. Notice the basic properties in this dictionary definition of *chair:* "A piece of furniture consisting of a seat, legs and back, and often arms, designed for one person." In contrast, the concept *near* has far more complex attributes. Philadelphia may or may not be considered to be near Baltimore. It depends on whether one is dealing with city blocks or planets. Learning the concept *near* involves more than identifying a single, simple set of attributes.

Conjunctive, Relational, and Disjunctive Concepts.   Concepts may be classified according to their types of attributes as conjunctive, relational, or disjunctive.[2] The least complex concepts, such as *chair,* are *conjunctive.* A conjunctive concept has a single fixed set of characteristics that define it. For example, there may be many different chairs, but all of them share an essential set of characteristics.

The most complex type of concept, such as *near,* is classified as *relational.* Unlike conjunctive concepts, relational ones have no fixed set of characteristics. They can be defined only by comparison or in relation to other objects or events. One cannot tell whether a person, place, or thing is "near," only whether it is near to something else. One must then use some criterion to make a judgment of nearness.

Waste, resources, and *safe,* are examples of relational concepts in the social studies. These concepts require students to focus on the characteristics of items being compared and also on some rule. A resource, for example, may be "anything people can use to satisfy some need." To determine whether an empty plastic bottle is an example of resource or of waste, however, requires one to determine its relation to a user or a use.

Between the least complex and the most complex concepts are *disjunctive* ones. Disjunctive concepts are similar to conjunctive ones, except that they have *two or more* sets of alternative characteristics that define them, rather than a single one. *Citizen* is such a concept. Citizens of the United States are those born in the country *or* those who fulfill some test of citizenship *or* those who are born in another country of parents who are citizens.

Learning a Concept

Everyone learns thousands of new concepts during a lifetime without ever giving much thought to the matter. Over time these concepts are reinforced, revised, and refined. This process continues naturally and often unconsciously. We become aware of what is involved in acquiring a concept when someone tries to teach us or we try to learn a new one.

Learning a New Concept

It would be difficult for you to recall vividly the experiences involved in learning many of the concepts you already have. Instead, we intend to have you learn some *new* concepts. In learning them, you will be putting yourself in the shoes of a youngster who is confronted with this task continually in a classroom situation. Everything about the concepts will be new, including their names.

As you learn, reflect on your strategies, your successes and mistakes, and your feelings about the tasks. Consider the four concept instruction sheets in Figures 4.1–4.4 on pages 76–79, and then answer the questions. When you feel you have learned a concept, check your responses with the Answer Key at the end of the chapter before the Suggested Readings.

Children's Problems in Learning Concepts. The experience of learning these new concepts should have sensitized you to some of the problems that children experience, beginning with trying to remember (and spell correctly) what appear as strange names. It should also suggest why students sometimes have thoughtful reasons for wrong answers. Also, it should indicate how learner problems can be caused by the instruction rather than by student inadequacies.

Sources of Difficulty in Concept Learning

The four examples in Figures 4.1–4.4 represented different levels of difficulty in concept learning. Several elements were included to make some of them deliberately more difficult than others. There was a disjunctive concept, *zrapple,* and a relational one, *rimple,* as well as two conjunctive concepts. As we discussed ear-

FIGURE 4.1   The concept of *figural*

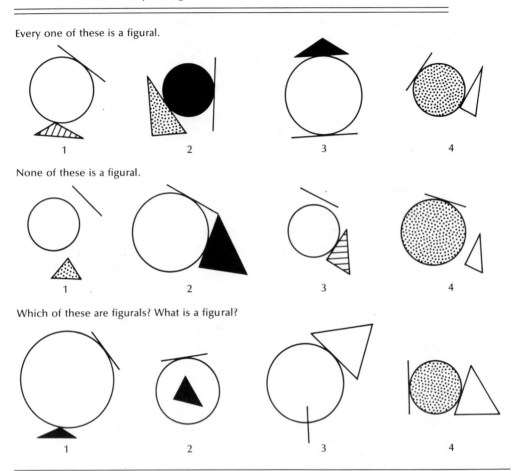

Every one of these is a figural.

1   2   3   4

None of these is a figural.

1   2   3   4

Which of these are figurals? What is a figural?

1   2   3   4

lier, relational and disjunctive concepts are typically more difficult to grasp than conjunctive ones.

Another element of difficulty was an increase in the number of characteristics that defined the concept. These are called *criterial attributes*. *Squarp*, for instance, had four criterial attributes, and *zrapple* had two.

More difficulty was added by asking you to state the concept definition or rule. This is a different, and for young children usually a much more difficult, task than identifying examples of the concept. To be said to have learned a concept, one need only discriminate examples from nonexamples. Telling what the concept is in your own words or even selecting a correct definition among incorrect ones is a more advanced level of learning. This point will be developed in Chapter 10, which deals with evaluation.

FIGURE 4.2   The concept of *squarp*

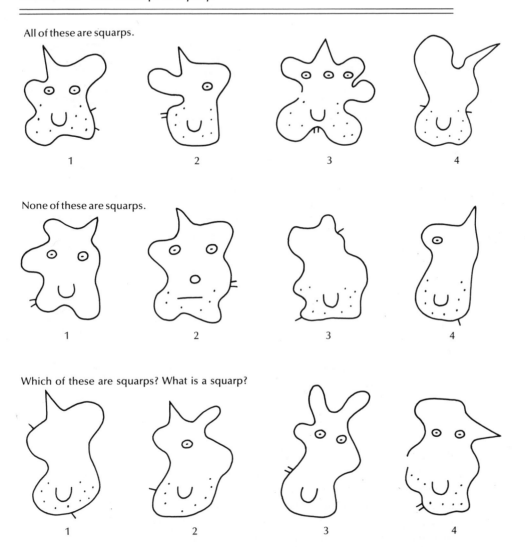

All of these are squarps.

1   2   3   4

None of these are squarps.

1   2   3   4

Which of these are squarps? What is a squarp?

1   2   3   4

Correcting Misconceptions

The formal learning of concepts in schools often consists of correcting *misconceptions* (incorrect or incomplete concepts), as well as attaining new ones. Many students, for example, have the misconception that all deserts are hot places. Although they may have noted correctly that lack of precipitation and vegetation are common to all deserts, they mistakenly also associated the intense heat of the deserts with which they were familiar, such as the Gobi and the Sahara.

FIGURE 4.3   The concept of *zrapple*

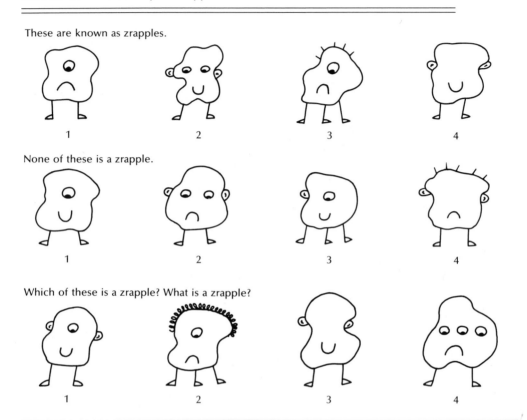

These are known as zrapples.

1   2   3   4

None of these is a zrapple.

1   2   3   4

Which of these is a zrapple? What is a zrapple?

1   2   3   4

Stereotypes. When we attend too closely to the *noncriterial* properties of concepts and begin to treat them as criterial ones, we often develop *stereotypes.* As an illustration, on the basis of a limited range of experiences with people classified as *Italians,* a child learns incorrectly the stereotype that Italians are "people who have dark hair, use their hands when talking, and like spaghetti." From these limited and isolated cases, the child begins to form a concept of *all* Italians.

Much of the instruction students receive confuses criterial and noncriterial attributes, and contributes to the development of stereotypes. It is only when students are made to examine the limitations of their experiences, usually through exposure to different examples, that they begin to revise their misconceptions.

Concept Hierarchies

Often it is helpful in both teaching and learning concepts to order a series of concepts into a *hierarchy.* This consists of identifying the most encompassing of the concepts, and then relating all of the others to those in a logical sequence or dia-

FIGURE 4.4 The concept of *rimple*

All of these are rimples.

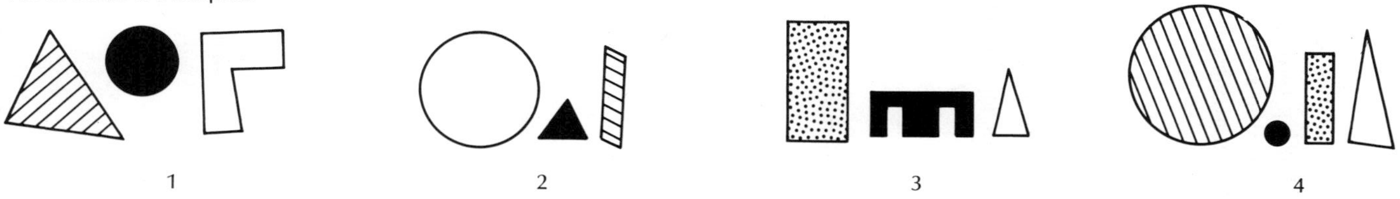

None of these is a rimple.

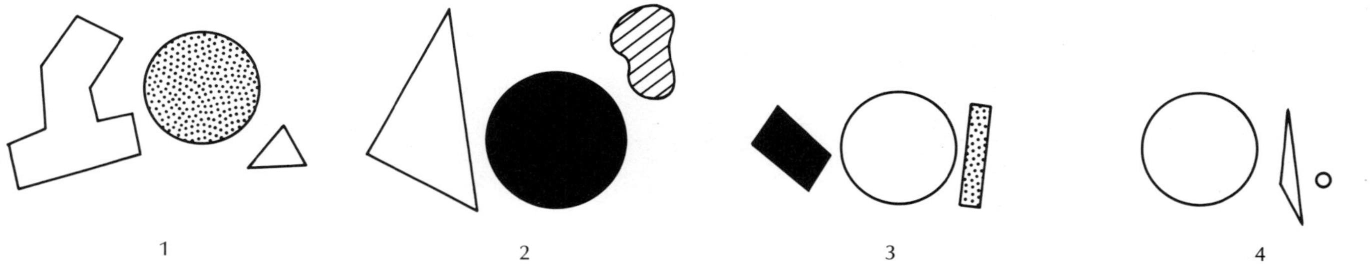

Which of these is a rimple? What is a rimple?

gram. Consider the following set of concepts: *harbor, valley, lake, gulf, ocean, plateau, water body, mountain, ocean, land mass, isthmus, river, delta,* and *peninsula.*

They could be taught and learned in a random order, or they could be organized in some logical sequence according to their relationship to one another, as illustrated in Figure 4.5. Even when concepts are not learned in some hierarchical fashion, ordering them in this way at some point makes remembering them and their relationship to one another much easier.

Teaching a Concept

Among all of the concepts that we learn, only some are appropriate to teach formally in schools. Hundreds of common concepts, such as *pencil, shoe, shirt, fork,* generally are learned informally by students. Once a list of significant concepts has been identified as appropriate for teaching, each concept can be analyzed to determine the major elements that the teacher will require to teach it.

Concept Analysis

In analyzing a concept to be taught, it is necessary to identify: the *name* most commonly associated with the concept; the concept *rule,* which defines what the concept is; the *criterial attributes* that make up the essential characteristics of the concept; some *noncriterial attributes* that are nonessential characteristics, but nevertheless are frequently associated with the concept; some *examples* of the concept; and some related *nonexamples* of the concept, which show what the concept is not.[3]

Name. Which name is most commonly associated with the concept? (Example: ''island'')

FIGURE 4.5 A concept hierarchy

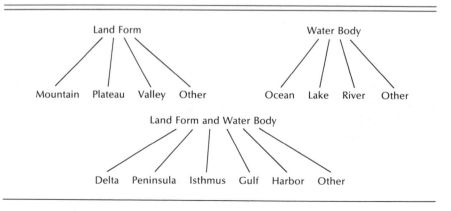

Rule. What clear and simplified definition explains what the concept is? (Example: "island is a body of land surrounded by water") The concept rule specifies the list and relationship of the criterial attributes and the sequence in which they occur, if this is an important feature of the concept. Concept rules are obtained from general or specialized dictionaries (such as the *Dictionary of Political Science*), encyclopedias, textbooks, and the mass media.

Often one must synthesize information from several sources to create a brief and uncomplicated rule. The concept rule is used to clarify the teacher's thinking about which materials will be needed. It will also be used to communicate a formal description of the concept to students at some point.

Criterial Attributes. Using the concept rule, give the distinct, essential characteristics that make up the concept. (Example: land, water, surrounding)

Noncriterial Attributes. What are some nonessential characteristics that one often finds present with the concept but are not part of it? (Example: size — large, small) Noncriterial attributes occur in many different forms, as Table 4.1 illustrates, and are present with virtually any concept. There are some details in nearly all illustrations of concepts that mislead some viewers into believing they are part of the concept.

Examples. What are some interesting, different, and learner-relevant illustrations of the concept? (Example: islands with people, islands with no vegetation, islands in different bodies of water) Figure 4.6 indicates the examples that one teacher planned to use in teaching the concept of *power*.

Because of the diversity of concepts, there is no specific number of examples that are required to teach the concept. The examples you provide, however, should represent the range of cases that appear commonly. For example, in teaching the concept of *transportation*, the set of examples should include land, sea, and air, motorized and nonmotorized, large-scale and small-scale cases.

TABLE 4.1   Analysis of concept criterial and noncriterial attributes

Concept name	Criterial attributes	Typical noncriterial attributes
desert	region, limited precipitation, lack of vegetation	location, habitation, topography
delta	river mouth, land formation, deposited soil	size, type of soil, time when formed
organization	group, doing things, common interests or problems, rules	age of members, sex of members, nature of interests or problems
transportation	carrier, moving, place-to-place, objects or people	distance moved, size of carrier, number of objects or people

FIGURE 4.6   Outline of examples used by a teacher to teach the concept of *power*

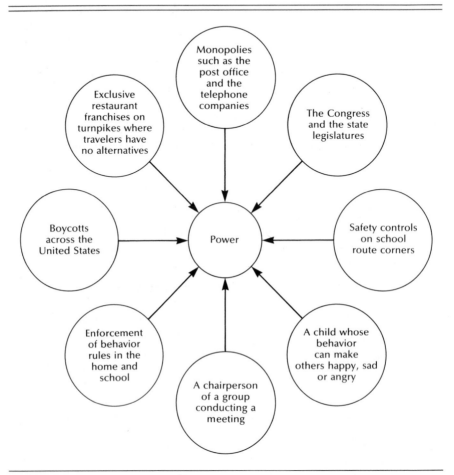

Nonexamples. What contrasting examples (what the concept is *not*) will help highlight its significant features? (Example: As a nonexample of island a teacher might use *isthmus,* a body of land which has water on only three sides) Each concept is a nonexample for every other one: *book* is a nonexample of a *chair.* In teaching concepts, however, it is most helpful to a learner if the nonexamples are closely related to the concept being learned in one or more respects. Through comparing and contrasting similar examples and nonexamples, such as the *island* of Cuba and the *isthmus* of Panama, students can begin to identify what is essential to the concept of *island.* A sample concept analysis in Figure 4.7.

FIGURE 4.7   Analysis of the concept *globe*

CONCEPT ANALYSIS

Name: Globe

Rule: A round object that has a map of the earth drawn on it.

Criterial attributes: Roundness, map, earth, drawn on

Noncriterial attributes: Size, color, weight

Examples: Transparent globes, inflatable globes, relief globes, globes showing cities, globes made of different materials, globes of different colors, globes of different sizes

Nonexamples: Maps of the earth, maps of a place on the earth, on round objects, drawings on round objects

---

EXERCISE 4.3   Concept Analysis

Select a concept from the list on page 72, and complete a concept analysis similar to the one shown in Figure 4.7.

Teaching Strategies

Once the elements of a concept have been identified, a teaching strategy can be developed. A model based on research relating to the teaching of concepts that have clearly defined characteristics follows.[4]

Basic Teaching Model. The basic steps in teaching a concept are listed below.

1. Prepare the set of examples and nonexamples identified and place them in some logical order for presentation.
2. Prepare cues, directions, questions, and student activities for the materials to draw attention to the criterial attributes and the similarities and differences in examples and nonexamples. In written materials, cues may be arrows, notes in the margins, underlining, and the like.
3. Present the examples, nonexamples, and instructions as close together as possible so that students can easily compare all the cases. For young children, use visual, three-dimensional materials or hands-on activities wherever possible.
4. Encourage students to volunteer their observations and to ask questions.
5. At some point, present or elicit from the group the concept rule in terms that are easily understood by all students.
6. Assess whether the concept has been learned by asking students to identify

new examples of the concept. Learning also may be assessed at more advanced levels.

In implementing the basic model, teachers may elect to use a *discovery* approach or an *expository* approach.

Discovery and Expository Approaches. In a discovery approach students are expected to determine which characteristics are unique to the concept and to infer its rule. By contrast, expository approaches make explicit these elements of the concept. Both discovery and expository approaches have merit in teaching concepts.

For the concept of *globe* and the analysis of the concept found in Figure 4.7, examples of the two approaches follow.

Discovery Approach. A sample lesson might include the following sequence of steps:

1. *Focusing attention.* "[Showing globe] Which of you boys and girls have ever seen one of these before?"
2. *Selecting a name for the concept.* "What could we call this?" (Tentatively decide on a name to call the concept or else introduce the actual name, *globe.*)
3. *Identifying criterial attributes.* "What does its shape remind you of? How would you describe the shape to someone? What is this drawing [pointing to map or globe]? Have you ever seen anything like this before [pointing to map]? How is this map like others you have seen? In which ways is it different?"
4. *Identifying noncriterial attributes.* "Notice these things which are different in all of the examples [size, colors, materials]. These are not important differences. Globes often come in different sizes. They also have different colors, and are made of many different materials."
5. *Presenting further examples and nonexamples.* The series of examples and nonexamples outlined in Figure 4.9 is introduced, and attention is called to the criterial and noncriterial attributes. In each case, students are asked "How is this [example] similar to the first one? How is this [nonexample] different from the first one?"
6. *Relating the criterial attributes.* "Can anyone summarize all the things that all globes [or other name used] have?"
7. *Verbalizing the concept rule.* "Who can complete the sentence I have just written on the board. 'Globes are things which are _____ _____.?' "
8. *Assessing learning.* "Here is a set of pictures of some objects. I would like you to come up and point to the examples of the globes. The rest of the class can see if they agree with the choices."

Expository Approach. An expository approach follows the same basic steps as discovery approaches, but it achieves learning objectives more directly and explicitly. For example, a teacher would point out the criterial attributes and note their occurrence among all examples, rather than depend on students themselves to infer these conclusions. The teacher would then present examples and nonexamples and discuss with the students the ways in which these did and did not illustrate the concepts.

At some point the concept rule would be stated verbally, and possibly written on the board. Children would be encouraged to discuss confusing points, and at the conclusion, the teacher would assess whether the concept had been learned.

Effective discovery and expository teaching strategies stimulate student curiosity and involvement. Both also use thought-provoking questions and are sensitive to the developmental level of students.

EXERCISE 4.4   Developing a Lesson to Teach a Concept

Pick any grade level and develop a strategy to teach a social studies concept. Use the lesson plan elements given in Chapter 3, page 56 and the basic teaching model outlined earlier in this chapter. You may use either a discovery or an expository approach.

Teaching Materials and Activities

There are several ways teachers can create special materials or activities related to concept development. These include the use of concept sheets, minitexts, folders, bulletin boards, and games.

Concept Sheets. A basic concept sheet consists of a set of brief narrative examples and nonexamples, along with questions to assess whether the concept has been learned. The narratives include a statement of the concept rule. A sample concept sheet is provided in Figure 4.8.

EXERCISE 4.5   Developing a Concept Sheet

Using the data from the concept analysis which you completed in Exercise 4.3, create a concept sheet similar to the one illustrated for the concept *organization* (Figure 4.8).

Concept Minitexts. Related to a concept sheet, a minitext is a short self-instructional text designed by a teacher to teach a single concept to a specified student group. Minitexts include *all* of the instruction a child will require to learn a new concept, including an assessment at the end. They may use pictures from magazines, photos, drawings, and the like, as well as narrative material, integrated into an interesting format. For interest appeal and durability, they also usually have an attractive cover and are sturdily constructed. Some sample pages from a minitext designed to teach the concept of family to a young child are shown in Figure 4.9.

Constructing a minitext requires the completion of a concept analysis and the application of the basic teaching model. Unlike informational texts and other books,

FIGURE 4.8   A concept sheet

ORGANIZATIONS

Sue is a member of the Explorers and Steve is a member of the Boy Scouts. Explorers and Boy Scouts are *organizations*. The members of these groups have certain rules. They also enjoy playing games and going on camping trips together.

Some of the girls and boys in one fourth-grade class started a Magic Club. It is an *organization*. The children all were interested in magic tricks and illusions. They agreed that they needed some rules for the club, such as how often they should meet and how officers were to be chosen.

People in the stands at a football game are *not* an organization. They all are interested in football. But they all do not belong to any special group. They also do not have any rules that they all have agreed to.

Sarah and her parents belong to the church near her home. William and his father belong to the temple across town. Both the church and the temple are *organizations*. Members of both organizations come together to worship and learn about God. They all agree to observe certain customs and believe certain teachings of the church and the temple.

Ms. Wilcox owns a small welding company. She is the only one in the company. She takes care of the entire business, and does all of the work. Her company is *not* an organization. Ms. Wilcox is very interested in the company, and she does follow certain rules in doing business. Since her company is only one person and not a group, it is not an organization.

All the neighbors in a local community have a problem they wish to solve. There is too much trash on the streets. They form an *organization* called the Community Council. The members agree to keep a careful record of all trash observed and to report it each day to the city. They also each agree to spend three hours a week working together to pick up trash in the community.

The House of Representatives of the United States is an *organization*. Representatives must observe certain rules to remain members of the House. They have many different interests, but they also share some. One common interest is to pass laws for the country. In order to accomplish anything, a majority of the members must be in agreement.

A dozen people who were on a boat cruise suddenly become shipwrecked on an island. They are *not* an organization. They do all have the same interest — saving their lives. But no one is able to come up with a set of rules that everyone can agree to.

Do you think you now know what an organization is? Try answering the following questions.

1. Which of these is an organization?

   a. five strangers at a party
   b. the principal of a school
   c. two friends
   d. the United States Army

2. Which is true about *all* organizations?

   a. They must have at least five members.
   b. They have rules and common interests.
   c. Members must pay dues.
   d. There is always an elected leader.

3. Which is true about *all* organizations?

   a. They must have at least one adult.
   b. Members must meet at least once a week.
   c. They always include both males and females.
   d. There must be at least two people.

4. An organization is a kind of

   a. government
   b. group
   c. meeting
   d. place

5. An organization is a

   a. collection of people in one place who are interested in having a good time or in stating their opinions in public
   b. group of people who vote the same
   c. way of doing things
   d. group of people with accepted rules who do things together because they have the same interests or problems

Source: Adapted from Peter H. Martorella, "Teaching Concepts," in *Classroom Teaching Skills,* James M. Cooper et al. (Lexington, Mass.: D. C. Heath, 1982), pp. 213–216.

a minitext teaches *one* important concept effectively. A successful minitext will help a child for whom it is designed to learn the target concept. A sample self-evaluation form for determining how well a minitext has been designed is shown in Table 4.2.

Concept Folders. A concept learning activity that can be used at all grade levels is concept folders. Older students can use file folders or ones constructed with art paper. Younger children can even use shoe boxes to store data on individual concepts. A concept is identified for each folder, and after its attributes and rule have

---

EXERCISE 4.6   Creating a Concept Minitext

Select a concept and a grade level at which it might be taught. Create a minitext to teach the concept, following the criteria in this text. After completing the minitext, evaluate it using the form in Table 4.2. Once the minitext has been revised and completed, field test it with a student for whom it was designed and who has not yet learned the concept.

TABLE 4.2   Minitext evaluation form

Minitext Evaluation

Rate each of the following criteria from 1 to 5.

Instructional component	Rating
1. Is the concept a significant one to learn?	_____
2. Do the materials clearly and adequately represent the concept definition?	_____
3. Are all of the concept attributes clearly illustrated in the materials?	_____
4. Do the materials draw attention to the noncriterial attributes?	_____
5. Is there an adequate number of examples and nonexamples used?	_____
6. Do the materials follow the basic model of concept teaching?	_____
7. Is the material self-instructional and appropriate for the students intended?	_____
8. Is the material clear and the language used appropriate for students?	_____
9. Are evaluation items included which adequately assess concept learning?	_____
10. How interesting is the design of the minitext?	_____
Total Rating	_____

FIGURE 4.9 Section of a minitext to teach the concept of *family*

Look at this word:

family

Do you know what it means? Do you have a family? Mostly everyone we know has a family, but sometimes they are different. My family is my mother and father, my brother and sister, and me. Maybe your family has no sisters and 3 brothers. Families come in all sizes and colors but they have many things that are the same.

A family is a group of 2 or more people. It can have 2 people or 50 people. One person is not a family.

The people in a family must live together for at least part of the time. When you get older and move out of your house, you will still be in the family because you have lived with them for at least part of the time.

The last thing to know about a family is that the people must be related by blood, marriage, or adoption. You are related to your grandparents, parents, aunts, uncles, cousins, and brothers and sisters by blood. When a man and a woman get married, they are a family. When a child is adopted by a family, he or she becomes part of that family.

(Figure 4.9 continues on following page.)

FIGURE 4.9. Continued

Let's look at different groups of people and decide if they are families. Remember what a family is and what it must have.

Meet Susie, her mother and father, and her little sister. This group is a family. There are more than 2 people. These people live together. The children are related to their parents by blood. The mother and father are related by marriage. This group has all the things to be a family.

Now we know what a family is.

1) A family has 2 or more people.

2) The people must live together for at least part of the time.

3) The people must be related by blood, marriage, or adoption.

A group of people must have all 3 parts to be a family.

Mrs. Franklin is an old woman who lives all alone in her house. Her husband died a few years ago and she has no children. Mrs. Franklin is _not_ a family. She is only one person and a family must be a group of 2 or more people.

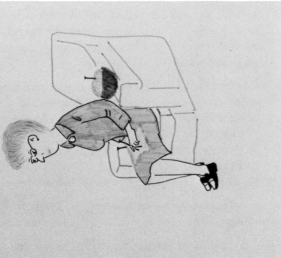

Mr. and Mrs. Harris live with their daughter Nancy and her husband, Mike. Nancy and Mike have a son. These people are a family. They are more than 2 people who live together and are related by either blood or marriage.

been identified and clarified and some examples and nonexamples are provided, students are asked to collect data over some period of time. Data may be pictures, cases, stories, or observations. When the projects are completed, students can share the contents of the folders in small-group discussions or by placing their materials on poster board.

Concept Bulletin Boards. A bulletin board prepared by either the teacher or students can be used to highlight examples and nonexamples of a concept. As with concept folders, bulletin boards can contain pictorial or written materials.

Examples and nonexamples should be close to each other and should be appropriately labeled. Once the initial bulletin board is developed, students can be encouraged to look for further examples and similar nonexamples, and to add to the display. Here is a sample of a bulletin board display for *transportation:*

These Are Transportation   These Are Not Transportation
(Attach pictures of the following items under the appropriate columns.)

These Are Transportation	These Are Not Transportation
Bus full of people	Room full of people
Subway	
Airplanes	Kite
Train	
Golfcart	Ferris wheel
Ships	
Submarine	Fish in water
Raft	
Rocket	Telegraph wires
Truck	
Bicycle	Stationary exercise bicycle
Hovercraft	
Balloon	Cloud
Car	
Blimp	Park bench
Motorcycle	
Horse	Cat
Wagon	
Stagecoach	Rocking horse
Tractor	
Oxen and cart	Windmill
Rickshaw	
Dog sled	Arrow being shot

Concept Games. Games of all types that have clear objectives and guidelines can be powerful and enjoyable learning activities. Teachers may create many gamelike activities that can encourage students to consider (1) the criterial attributes of concepts, (2) how concepts are related, and (3) ways concepts are similar and different.

One illustration of such an activity is the game, "Would You Like To Be . . . ?"[5] It consists of a set of questions in the form of "Would you like to be a(n) . . . ?" There are two basic rules: all questions must be answered in the form of "Yes, I *would* like to be a(n) . . ." or "No, I would *not* like to be a(n) . . ."; and all answers must include a word that is different from the last one in the question. For example: Question, "Would you like to be a *tomato?*"; answer, "No, I would not like to be a red thing." Any list of concepts may be used, although the game should begin with some concrete items and progress to abstractions.

Another illustration is the "How Are Things Alike?" game. It is an adaptation of a game developed by Wallach and Kogan in their studies of thinking in young children.[6] Sets of related objects, events, or people are presented to students, and they are asked to indicate how the items are related to one another.

Sets of items and statements and questions similar to the following may be used: "Tell me all the ways that a river and an ocean are alike." or "In what ways are maps and globes alike?" or "How are socialism and capitalism alike?" A similar activity based on a structured set of questions and developed by Hilda Taba and her associates is illustrated in Chapter 11 in the discussion of questioning strategies.

Answer Key: Concept Test

1. True	6. False
2. False	7. False
3. True	8. False
4. False	9. False
5. True	10. False

Answer Key — Concept Learning Activity

The numbers of the *figurals* are 1 and 4. Figurals are a triangle and a line segment that border a circle but never touch each other.

The numbers of the *squarps* are 1 and 4. Squarps are figures that have a smile (up-turned mouth), freckles, two whiskers, and a point on their head.

The numbers of the *zrapples* are 2 and 3. Zrapples are figures that have *either* one eye and a frown (down-turned mouth) *or* two ears and a smile (up-turned mouth).

The number of the *rimple* is 1. Rimples are any series of three or more figures in which the second figure (counting from left to right) is shorter than the rest when all figures are placed on the same plane.

Notes

1. Scott, Foresman Social Studies, *Families and Friends* (Glenview, Ill.: Scott, Foresman, 1983).
2. Jerome S. Bruner et al., *A Study of Thinking* (New York: Science Editions, 1962), p. 41.
3. Peter H. Martorella, "Research on Social Studies Learning and Instruction: Cognition," in *Review of Research in Social Studies: 1970–1975,* F. Hunkins et al. (Washington, D.C.: National Council for the Social Studies, 1977), pp. 25–26.
4. Ibid. See also Beverly J. Armento, "Teacher Behaviors Related to Student Achievement on a Social Science Concept Test," *Research in Teacher Education* 28 (March–April 1977): 46–52 and C. Warren McKinney et al., "The Effectiveness of Three Methods of Teaching Social Studies Concepts to Fourth-Grade Students: An Aptitude-Treatment Interaction Study," *American Educational Research Journal* 20 (Winter 1983): 663–670.
5. For sample lists of sequenced concepts and a transcript of a class session using the game, see Peter H. Martorella, *Concept Learning in the Social Studies: Models for Structuring Curriculum.* (Scranton, Pa.: INTEXT, 1971), pp. 112–113; 145–149.
6. Michael A. Wallach and Nathan Kogan, *Modes of Thinking in Young Children* (New York: Holt, Rinehart and Winston, 1965), p. 32.

Suggested Readings

Bank, Adrienne, et al. *A Practical Guide to Program Planning: A Teaching Models Approach.* New York: Teachers College Press, 1981.

Brown, Roger. *Words and Things.* New York: Free Press, 1958.

Bruner, Jerome S., et al. *A Study of Thinking.* New York: Science Editions, 1962.

Carroll, John B. "Words, Meanings and Concepts," *Harvard Educational Review* 24 (Spring 1964): 178–202.

Eisner, Elliot W. *Cognition and Curriculum: A Basis for Deciding What to Teach.* New York: Longman, 1982, Chapter 2.

Fancett, Verna, et al. *Social Science Concepts in the Classroom.* Syracuse, N.Y.: Social Studies Curriculum Center, 1968.

Gagné, Robert M. *The Conditions of Learning.* 3rd ed. New York: Holt, Rinehart and Winston, 1977.

Martorella, Peter H. *Concept Learning in the Social Studies: Models for Structuring Curriculum.* Scranton, Pa.: INTEXT, 1971.

Martorella, Peter H. "Teaching Concepts," in *Classroom Teaching Skills,* James M. Cooper et al. Lexington, Mass.: D. C. Heath, 1982.

Ribivich, Jerilyn K. "A Methodology for Teaching Concepts," *The Reading Teacher* 33 (December 1979): 285–289.

Tennyson, Robert, and Park, O. "The Teaching of Concepts: A Review of Instructional Design Research Literature," *Review of Educational Research* 50 (1980): 53–70.

Vygotsky, L. S. *Thought and Language,* ed. and trans. Eugenia Hanfmann and Gertrude Vakar. Cambridge, Mass.: MIT Press, 1962.

5

Teaching Students to Hypothesize, Generalize, and Solve Problems in the Social Studies

How do facts, generalizations, and hypotheses differ, and how are they distinguished from concepts?

As we have seen, concepts are essentially categories of experience into which we group phenomena. The building blocks of all knowledge, concepts are a part of every fact, generalization, and hypothesis. If our concepts are ill formed or incomplete, the ideas we build from them will be improperly shaped. When we think, make a decision, or act, we draw on a network of concepts, facts, generalizations, and hypotheses — the elements of reflection.

Facts, Generalizations, and Hypotheses in the Social Sciences

Facts

Citizens are bombarded daily with facts and with assertions that appear to be facts. Facts appear in many forms and relate to trivial as well as significant matters: "Washington was our first President." "I just got a freckle on my nose."

In our society facts are valued, and individuals often will go to great lengths, spending much time and even money, to get them. People who have knowledge of facts or have access to such knowledge often have considerable power and status, witness heads of countries, inventors, and gossip columnists.

Facts are statements about concepts that are *true* or verified for a particular case on the basis of the best evidence available. From a concept cluster that includes *island, ocean, group,* and *state,* this fact statement arises: "There is a group of islands located in the Pacific Ocean that makes up one of our states."

Often a person will accept an assertion as a fact even though it may not be supported by evidence or may be considered by most people to be false. Many people accept as a fact, for example, that Columbus was the first European to reach America, even though considerable evidence to the contrary exists. Other assertions are accepted as facts on the basis of the best evidence available at the time, only to be proven false later. The supposed *fact* that the sun revolved about the earth was only grudgingly discarded by the world in favor of the newly verified *fact* that the moving body was actually the earth.

Generalizations

Generalizations are similar to facts in that they are also statements about relationships among concepts. Compare this *fact* from a text, "Multimillionaire Nelson Rockefeller was a member of many organizations," with this *generalization,* "Organizational memberships are more frequent among the upper classes."

Generalizations summarize and organize a great deal of information obtained from analyses of many sets of data. The summary results in a single, broad statement that applies to the past and the present. Generalizations may apply to all cases everywhere ("All known human societies have religions") or to some more limited context ("In the United States, marriages most frequently are determined by the mates themselves").

Generalizations can also *predict,* or pose conditions in the form of "If . . . then" statements: "*If* there is a national election, *then* the turnout of white-collar, professional, and business people is likely to be greater than that of semiskilled and unskilled workers." The statement presents an opportunity to make a prediction that if one set of conditions is present (national elections), a second set will follow (a pattern of voter turnout).

Through the understanding of a single generalization, students can draw further conclusions about many specific cases not yet encountered. From the generalizations about voting behavior, for example, students can make some predictions about future national elections.

Examine the following list of statements, and assess whether each seems to be a generalization or a fact.

1. New York has a population of over 6 million people.
2. What people regard as *shelter* takes many different forms around the world.
3. The Navaho and Iroquois are Indian tribes.
4. Human beings live in groups.
5. There are letters on this page.

If you identified numbers 2 and 4 as generalizations, and the rest as facts, you have a basic grasp of the distinction between these two elements of reflection.

Hypotheses

Like facts and generalizations, hypotheses are statements about concepts. Hypotheses are ideas or guesses that attempt to explain why some condition exists or has existed. They occur when we confront something we wish to understand or make sense of: ''What makes someone become a criminal?'' ''Why does the price of computers continue to drop while that of automobiles increases?'' ''How was a small group of colonists able to gain independence from a nation as powerful as England?''

Hypothesis Formation. Hypothesis formation begins when we attempt to resolve or answer such questions. The hypotheses we propose may be based on a great deal of experience or background, or they may be ''off the top of our head.'' In either case, hypotheses developed are then *tested* by gathering and comparing evidence that supports or refutes them. Since some types of evidence are often conflicting and inconclusive, many hypotheses never advance beyond the status of a guess. The hypotheses to explain why Lee Oswald assassinated President Kennedy are examples.

Other hypotheses can be verified if one is able or willing to do all that a conclusive test requires. Society or researchers, however, may decide the costs of the tests are greater than the benefits to be derived. To prove the hypothesis that certain conditions or chemicals *cause* cancer, rather than to suggest only that a significant *relationship* between them exists, for example, would require humans to be randomly assigned to dangerous conditions, whether they wished to assume the risk or not.

Still other hypotheses can never be verified or refuted, since the necessary evidence is impossible to obtain. Speculations about ''what might have happened'' had certain events in history been altered fall into this category. An example is the hypothesis that ''Germany would have won World War II and altered the course of history profoundly'' in response to the question, ''What would have happened if Hitler had not waged a two-front war or had perfected the V-2 rocket just a bit sooner?''

Many hypotheses, however, can be tested by gathering and comparing data. When a hypothesis seems to be true as evidence is gathered, it can tentatively be regarded as either a fact or a generalization, depending on its characteristics. Frequently, through further testing, the original hypothesis is revised to some extent.

Using Facts, Generalizations, and Hypotheses in the Social Sciences

Social scientists are continually discovering facts, developing and testing hypotheses, and producing generalizations about social phenomena. Generalizations allow social scientists to summarize large sets of data obtained from many investigations and to predict the results of investigations. They also are economical in the sense that once established and verified, they make it unnecessary to test evidence in each new case.

For the social scientist, every generalization begins as a hypothesis about some social phenomenon. Once tested and found to be valid and to apply to a broad range of cases, a hypothesis begins to evolve into a generalization. At every stage of their work, social scientists require carefully verified facts organized in some easily retrieved fashion.

Retrieving Facts. Having facts *in memory* is one system of retrieval, but it is a limited one in an era of rapidly proliferating data. All scientists rely on a variety of data retrieval systems for quickly accessing information. Most notably, however, thousands of individuals across the United States who have personal computers routinely access at any hour of the day commercial data bases for a small fee. They retrieve many types of information, ranging from encyclopedia entries to airline schedules.

Even miniaturized computer-based systems for quickly accessing "facts" on a topic already exist. They are likely to increase in number and scope, to become easy to use — even for a child — and to be less and less expensive within the next decade. As this phenomenon increasingly occurs, the significance of and need for large numbers of specialized "facts in memory" is likely to diminish for both scientists and citizens.

EXERCISE 5.1 Identifying Generalizations From the Social Sciences

Identify two generalizations from each of the social sciences, other than those found in this textbook. As references you may wish to consult introductory textbooks, specialized reference works, and encyclopedia. Select only those generalizations which would be suitable for developing activities with elementary classes.

Developing and Verifying Facts, Generalizations, and Hypotheses

Classroom instruction that has as its objective the learning of facts, generalizations, and hypotheses should concentrate on subject matter that is likely to be functional in the life of citizens. The ageless curriculum question of "Which knowledge is of most worth?" is important in selecting from the welter of social studies subject matter.

Selecting Subject Matter of Worth

Although basal textbooks and curriculum guides provide some suggested answers to the question, in the final analysis of the needs of each class, they are only partly satisfactory. No answer shaped for all students across the United States or for a region or district can adequately address what is most appropriate for a given class.

Each teacher ultimately must determine which knowledge is most worthwhile to his or her students. In identifying subject matter, a teacher must search for that which can best address the purpose and goals of the curriculum. Moreover, the subject matter selected should provide students with knowledge that will be useful to them in both their present and future roles as citizens. A simple final test to apply to the subject matter selected, no matter what the age of the students, is to ask the question, "Do I find this material in any way to be interesting, relevant to daily living, of real value, or essential to functioning in our society?"

Learning Significant Facts

All students need to have experience in locating, identifying, organizing, and verifying significant facts, and in distinguishing them from opinions and hypotheses. They also need to understand that isolated facts do not have meaning. A child can learn two lists of fifty pairs of names — one with capitals and states and the other with nonsense words — in the same way. Neither list has any real, immediate functional value beyond pleasing a teacher or gaining recognition.

Learning Facts in Meaningful Contexts

Facts learned outside some meaningful context as "nonsense words" are often quickly forgotten, long before they can be used. More important, students do not relate them to previously learned facts, concepts, and generalizations. This last point is illustrated by a child who has learned all of the states and capitals without error on Monday, but yet cannot answer the question on Friday, "Can you name one city in every part of the United States?"

Memory Techniques. As we suggested, instruction that emphasizes memorization, without purpose is intellectually bankrupt. However, that which ignores the value of quick retrieval in some situations is impractical. Several techniques are designed specifically to improve memory and the recall of meaningful factual material. These are called *mnemonic* devices.

Use of Imagery. Several investigators have pointed to the value of systematically using *imagery* to remember subject matter.[1] Students who wished to remember the various battles of the Civil War, for example, might visually imagine Bull Run as a bull, Gettysburg as a Getty gasoline station, and so on.

Keyword Method. Another mnemonic device that has been shown to be effective with elementary students is known as the *keyword method*.[2] It relies on images and a simple system for linking them. Using this technique, students might learn such items as the names of states and capitals by first forming images of each and then creating some linkage between the images. For example, "apple" might stand for Annapolis and "marry" for Maryland. The images might be linked with a new image of "apples getting married."

First-Letter Technique. A more traditional mnemonic device is the *first-letter* technique. With this mnemonic, words are remembered either by arranging their final letters in some form of alphabetical order, or by creating a new word with the list of first letters. Often several mnemonic devices may be combined in one technique. For example, to remember the list of American presidents in correct chronological order, one may remember a sentence that begins, *"Watch a jolly man make . . ."* (*W*ashington, *A*dams, *J*efferson, *M*adison, *M*onroe).

EXERCISE 5.2   Testing Memory Techniques

Locate and consult the references cited in the discussion under memory techniques. Then select some sample of social studies subject matter that you are interested in trying to remember, such as a list of items or sequence of events. Apply and test the memory techniques.

Once you have committed the material to memory, briefly describe the process. Identify the material you selected to memorize, the techniques you used, the approximate amount of time the process took, and the degree of success you experienced.

Learning Significant Generalizations

Students need experiences in examining and analyzing data for patterns, summarizing their conclusions, and then deriving significant generalizations. From the learner's perspective, it is the *understanding that results from the analysis and that is represented by the statement of a generalization* that is significant. For instance, children who have examined and discussed pictures of families from many different countries, socioeconomic settings, and racial groups have a basis for developing a generalization. They now can be guided to find an organizing principle for their experiences, for remembering data, and for fitting new related data into a pattern under a generalization such as, "Families everywhere take many different forms."

Contrast this example with one in which a child has only been taught the statement. Merely learning the verbal statement of a generalization without developing the understanding that results from comparing sets of information is not the same as learning a generalization.

Developing and Testing Hypotheses

Students developing and testing hypotheses employ many of the skills discussed in Chapters 6 and 7. They need practice and assistance at each grade level, both to generate plausible hypotheses to explain and answer simple but interesting problems and questions, and to gather and compare data to test those hypotheses.

Children in the primary grades can begin their experiences through practice in developing basic hypotheses for simple issues. Activities such as this take into account students' developmental needs, as well as their lack of experience with hypotheses: "Using this kit of blocks and materials, what are some different ways that we could organize a neighborhood? You can either tell me a way or show it with the materials."

Learning about Multiple Causality. Gradually, children can be introduced to the concept of *multiple causality,* which is crucial to many issues in the social studies. To undersand multiple causality students must realize that there may often be several causes to explain or account for something. To answer the question, "How can people who are good friends fight and even physically hurt one another?" students need to consider that several hypotheses are likely to be correct.

EXERCISE 5.3   Teaching Children to Develop Hypotheses

Select any social studies topic and any grade in K–3. Develop an activity to encourage and teach young children how to develop hypotheses.

Basic Teaching Strategies

As with the teaching concepts, strategies to aid students in developing and testing hypotheses and generalizations, may include either an *expository* or *discovery* approach. In an expository approach a generalization derived fom the social sciences is first presented to students as *a hypothesis to be tested.* The general approach is to assist students in locating and examining relevant evidence that supports or refutes the generalization. By contrast, discovery approaches withhold the generalization from students. Materials and procedures are structured in such a way that students will infer or deduce a generalization from their investigations.

Expository Approaches. There are many forms of expository approaches, ranging from simply calling attention to statements in texts and helping students find supporting evidence, to having students themselves offer generalizations, which the class then tests. The basic steps in an expository approach might be summarized as follows:

1. State, write, or call attention to some generalization that is a learning objective for the lesson.
2. Review major concepts that are part of the generalization.
3. Provide instructions, questions, cases, relevant materials, and assistance to illustrate and verify the generalization.
4. Have students identify, find, or create new cases of the generalization.

Consider a class in which the objective is to have the students learn the generalization, "The environment influences the type of shelter that people have." Ms. Olski, the teacher, begins the lesson by first writing the generalization on the chalk board. Next she reviews the major concepts in the generalization — *environment, influences,* and *shelter* — by asking the class to refer to the text glossary. She then summarizes the meanings on the board.

Once the concepts have been clarified, the class is divided into five groups, each of which is given one of the following questions to answer.

What are the parts of your house?

What different types of shelters do people in this area have?

How are these different shelters constructed?

What different kinds of weather conditions do we have in this area?

What are some things that all shelters in this area have?

Each group shares its conclusions with the class, and the major points are outlined on the board under the headings *Area, Types of Shelters,* and *Type of Environment.*

At this point Ms. Olski introduces pictures of many types of shelters used around the world, including boat houses, caves, tree houses, yurts, thatched huts, stilt houses over water, and solar houses. Along with each type she provides a short explanation of the environments in which the shelter is found. Each example is also summarized under the three headings on the board.

The students are redirected to the generalization written on the board at the beginning of the class. Then, in a brief question-and-answer session, they discuss the relationship of the various examples of the generalization.

At the conclusion each of the five groups is asked to identify some new cases of shelters and how their environment influenced their design. The children are encouraged to use the library, and some relevant resource materials are identified. The group's findings are then shared with the class.

Discovery Approaches. There are no specific procedures for discovery approaches to teach generalizations, although all share some properties. They all engage and assist students in: examining sets of data and materials; identifying and explaining through questioning and discussion similarities and differences, patterns, and trends in the data analyzed; summarizing their conclusions; and discovering or inferring the unstated generalization.

Let us reconsider Ms. Olski's class and the generalization she wished to teach, this time using a discovery approach. Instead of revealing the generalization at the outset by writing it on the board, she begins by reviewing the significant concepts in the generalization. She proceeds with step 3 of the expository approach, stopping after the illustrations and discussions of the various shelters.

At this point, however, she asks the students to sum up what they have learned about shelters and environment. Toward the end of this discussion Ms. Olski might ask, ''How could we put into one sentence what we have learned about the relationship of environment to people's shelters all over the world?''

The concluding activity could be the one used in the expository approach for step 4. Students would be asked to find new cases to validate their discovery. Since they have already developed the generalization by discovering it on their own, they are now trying to apply or test it further.

Comparing Discovery and Expository Approaches. In the illustrations of the two approaches, they differed chiefly in the amount of *responsibility placed on students to identify relationships between cases and the actual generalization.* Both involved students in thinking, doing, and learning, and both led students to understand the necessary relationships. In a discovery approach, the puzzle of what is to be discovered motivates many students to continue self-directed learning. To provide variety, instruction should include both approaches.

EXERCISE 5.4   Teaching Generalizations

Select one of the generalizations in Exercise 5.1 and a grade level, K–8. Develop a lesson plan to teach the generalization using either a basic expository or a discovery strategy.

Reflective Thinking and Problem Solving

The terms inquiry, critical thinking, the scientific method, reflective thinking, and problem solving all have been used at one time or another to refer to the process by which individuals solve problems through reflection. They all refer to the general sequence of actions in analyzing a body of data, bringing meaning to it, and drawing conclusions from it. This sequence involves students in learning to raise and answer "how, where, when, and why" questions.

Most discussions of reflective thinking or problem solving derive from the work and writings of the American philosopher and educator, John Dewey. His ideas are outlined in detail in two books, *How We Think* and *Democracy and Education.* In these works, especially the first, Dewey develops clearly what a problem is and how it relates to reflective thinking.

The Nature of Problems

The term *problem,* as it is used in discussions of problem solving, generally refers to three different types. It refers to *personal* problems, such as how to become more popular, how to get along with others, or what to do when you lose your job. It may refer to significant *social* problems faced by one society or the world, such as poverty, inequality of opportunity, crime, or unemployment. The third type is a *psychological* state of doubt. When a woman, for example, passes a store window in which two signs are placed, one which reads "Yes, we are open," and another which says "Sorry, we are closed," she is faced with a problem in this third sense.

Problem-solving approaches may intersect with two or all of these types. This would be the case when students who are personally experiencing a great deal of anxiety because of their poverty are asked in class to address the international problem of the poor. The broadest application of problem solving, however, involves the third type. Problem solving in this sense involves a teacher in creating a psychological state of disequilibrium in students that causes them to attend to the subject matter being taught, regardless of its topical content.

Problems as Psychological States. In a psychological problem a student perceives that something is peculiar, frustrating, irritating, puzzling, disturbing, contrary to what is expected, or incongruous. Students are asked to answer the question of "Why is this so?" or "How can this be?" or "What is the cause of this?"

Creating Problems Using Subject Matter. A psychological problem is created when the teacher succeeds in structuring and sequencing subject matter in a special way. It is not the subject matter itself, but the way in which it is presented that makes it psychologically problematical. The power of the problem-solving approach in this sense derives from students' natural tendency to want to relieve the psychological disequilibrium they experience by solving the problem or finding explanations or data to account for it.

Any subject matter can be used for problem solving in this sense, if a teacher can frame it in such a way as to pose an interesting and intriguing question. Problem solving situations often appear in popular periodicals and are psychologically perplexing and intriguing even though the reader has little interest in the actual subject matter. Consider the following example:

The Missionary and Cannibal Problem.

Three missionaries and three cannibals must cross a river in a rowboat that can hold only two people. Each of the six can row, and the goal is to get all safely across the river. Under no circumstances, however, should there ever be more cannibals than missionaries present in any location, or else the missionaries will be eaten. How can it be done?[3]

Can you solve this problem, and, if so, how did you do it? What makes this a psychologically frustrating, perplexing, or interesting problem? (The solution can be found at the end of the chapter before the Suggested Readings.)

Concepts, Facts, Hypotheses, and Generalizations in Problem Solving

The psychological notion of problem solving focuses on defining the problem. It also involves proposing alternative hypotheses to explain the problem. Further, it includes gathering and applying data to test the hypotheses, and settling on tentative conclusions that solve the problem for the moment. As students engage in problem solving in this sense, they apply concepts, facts, hypotheses, and generalizations to a solution, and they learn new ones in the bargain. Problem solving thus is a way both to organize and interrelate existing knowledge better and to acquire new information.

Students do not first learn facts, for example, then engage in problem solving. They use facts already learned and acquire new ones as they engage in problem solving. In problem solving the elements of reflection are learned not as isolated bits of information but as part of a pattern of psychologically meaningful knowledge.

Problem-Solving Techniques

Several suggestions have been summarized from research findings and individuals' experiences to aid students in improving their problem solving capabilities. These include ways to clarify and interpret problems, break them into smaller parts, and develop solutions. A list of basic suggestions follows.[4]

1. *Get the big picture.* Before tackling the problem, go over it several times to be sure that you clearly understand the entire problem.
2. *Develop some model to express the problem.* Express the problem in your own terms by saying it aloud, writing it out, diagramming it, drawing a picture, or using a mathematical symbol or equation.
3. *Break the problem into parts.* Once the big picture is developed, try breaking the problem into subproblems.
4. *Use analogies and metaphors.* Analogies and metaphors, especially familiar ones, are like models in helping to simplify a problem.
5. *Discuss the problem with others.* Often just talking about the problem with someone else helps to clarify it and to suggest a solution.
6. *Withhold judgment on a solution.* Search for several different solutions simultaneously, rather than commit yourself to one course of action.

Strategies for Problem-Solving Activities

Teacher-created psychological problems can motivate students to learn facts and develop hypotheses and generalizations. Not every lesson or topic, however, lends itself to the development of problem-solving strategies, since it is often difficult to create a sharp, relevant problem focus for students. Part of the teacher's major responsibility in creating problem-solving activities is to ascertain what in the subject matter is likely to appear problematical to students. If students do not perceive a psychological problem that requires a solution, no real problem solving will occur.

Reflective Thinking Model

A five-step model for problem solving, adapted from John Dewey's *How We Think,* follows.[5] It gives the teacher a sequence of activities to use in engaging students in problem solving.

1. Structure some aspect of the subject matter students are to learn to create a puzzle, dilemma, discrepancy, or doubt.
2. Have the students internalize the problem by asking them to verbalize it. Clarify the problem if necessary.

3. Solicit some hypotheses from the students that might explain or account for the problem. Clarify terminology where necessary, and allow sufficient time for student reflection.

4. Help students to test the validity of their hypotheses and to examine the implications of the results. When necessary, help by providing reference materials and background and by keeping students on the topic.

5. Help students to decide on a tentative conclusion that seems best to explain the problem. Stress the tentative nature of the conclusion, since future studies and further evidence may lead to a different conclusion.

Using the Problem-Solving Model. The most crucial step in the model is the first. Unless a teacher has aroused students' curiosity about the problem, students are not likely to participate actively in problem solving. In general the type of material that will be perceived as puzzling or will disturb students' equilibrium will be a function of the class's age and background.

The model outlined is at best a general road map for developing problem-solving strategies. Dewey himself suggested that problem solving as it occurs in natural settings does not always follow steps in order. Individuals often ''jump ahead,'' temporarily skipping steps, or return to a step already passed.

> The five phases . . . of thought that we have noted do not follow one another in a set order. On the contrary, each step in genuine thinking does something to perfect the formation of a suggestion and promote its change into a leading idea or directive hypothesis. It does something to promote the location and definition of the problem. Each improvement in the idea leads to new observations that yield facts or data and help the mind judge more accurately the relevancy of facts already at hand. The elaboration of the hypothesis does not wait until the problem has been defined and an adequate hypothesis has been arrived at; it may come at any intermediate time.[6]

Teaching for Problem Solving. Figure 5.1 shows how the problem-solving model can be used as a general guideline for a teaching strategy, with movement back and forth between the steps. It gives a teacher's summary of a class session involving a group of ten- and eleven-year-old children. The session, which lasted ninety minutes, was videotaped, and the summary was abstracted from the tape. The subject under consideration was political elections and political institutions. Since the lesson occurred in February a few days before Abraham Lincoln's birthday, which was a legal holiday at the school, the teacher used Lincoln as the springboard for developing the initial problem focus.

Problem Solving as a Dynamic Process

As we suggested earlier, problem solving is generally a more complex process than proceeding step by step to a solution. To try to grasp the dynamic character of true problem-solving strategies, let us review the basic problem-solving model and the lesson just described.

The sequence of actions in the model is illustrated in Figure 5.2. To the right

FIGURE 5.1 Summary of a problem-solving activity involving a class of fifth- and sixth-grade students.

Initially the students were asked to respond to the question, "What comes to mind when you think of Abraham Lincoln?" The function of this question was to settle the class, review their prior associations with Lincoln, and alert them to the problematic episode that was forthcoming. After approximately 10 minutes of free exploration without challenges, the class was told that the teacher wished to share a problem with them.

"Listen to these two statements made by Abraham Lincoln, and then tell me if you can see what my problem is. The first statement, let's call it A, is taken from the works of Abraham Lincoln":

Statement A

Let us discard all this quibbling about this man and the other man, this race, and that race and the other race being inferior, and therefore they must be placed in an inferior position. Let us discard all these things, and unite as one people throughout this land, until we shall once more stand up declaring that all men are created equal.[a]

"Is there anything in this statement that seems odd or out of order?" The students thought not, and we proceeded to the second statement, B. "Listen to this second statement, let's call it B, also taken from the works of Lincoln":

Statement B

I will say, then, that I am not, nor ever have been, in favor of bringing about in any way the social and political equality of the white and black races: that I am not, nor ever have been, in favor of making voters or jurors of negroes, nor of qualifying them to hold office, nor to intermarry with white people. . . .

   And inasmuch as they cannot so live, while they do remain together there must be the position of superior and inferior, and I as much as any other man am in favor of having the superior position assigned to the white race.[b]

"Do you notice anything wrong now? What is the problem here?" At this point, students were given some time to reflect upon the statements, verbalize the discrepancy in various ways, and generally to clarify the specific problematic issue. After the problem was restated in several ways, the statements were both repeated to the class.

To implement the third step of the model, the question was raised, "How do you account for these two statements, both made by Lincoln?" The students had many immediate hypotheses, which were clarified and recorded on the board. Four basic hypotheses were suggested as follows:

1. He changed his mind.

2. He was speaking to different groups with each of the statements, and he told each group what he thought they wanted to hear.

3. One statement was what he thought to himself (e.g., as in a diary), and the other one was the one he told people.

4. He was misunderstood (i.e., his words were taken out of context).

After exhausting the many responses, some of which were simply variations on the same theme, the point was emphasized that several possibilities existed concerning our guesses (hypotheses). Only *one* might be correct, *several* answers might be true, or *none* of our explanations might be correct.

"What kind of information," the students were asked, "would we need to have in order to check out our guesses and see if they might be correct?" Responses were clarified and listed on the board under the label "Initial Facts Needed." They fell into four categories: (1) when the statements were made, (2) to whom they were made, (3) what the rest of the statements (context) were like, and (4) where they were made.

At this point several possibilities were open to the teacher: have the students themselves initiate a search for relevant facts, either individually or in groups; ask certain students to volunteer or appoint volunteers to research the facts; or provide certain facts for the students to test the hypotheses. The third option was exercised due to time and other constraints and to focus attention on the testing rather than on the data-

(Figure continues on following page.)

FIGURE 5.1.   Continued

gathering process. In effect the teacher acted as a research resource for the students. Such a role is both legitimate and often efficient, depending on the objectives of a lesson. The amount and sequencing of factual information provided by the teacher, however, are important variables.

Consider the procedures employed by the teacher. With respect to the first fact needed, the students were informed that statement A was made on July 10, 1858, and that statement B was made on September 18, 1858. These dates were read aloud and then written on the board. The class expressed surprise.

"What do these facts do to any of our guesses?" the class was asked. The students suggested that the facts eliminated the first hypothesis. After soliciting their rationale, the teacher qualified their conclusion with the observation that "Lincoln *might* have changed his mind on this point in just two months, but it *was* a short period of time for such an important issue."

As to the second fact required, the students were briefly instructed on how the quotes and their sources could be authenticated. "In this case," they were told, "we are placing some faith in the reliability of the historian who gave us the information that it is correct." It was noted that we often have to do this but that sometimes the historian proves to be in error, as later research reveals. In indicating that our best immediate evidence was that the statements were *not* taken out of context, it was also indicated that the statements were parts of speeches.

While the teacher had no information concerning to whom the speeches were made, the class was told that statement A was made in Chicago while statement B was given in Charleston. These facts were written on the board alongside the respective dates:

Statement A: July 10, 1858, Chicago.

Statement B: September 18, 1858, Charleston.

These new facts were greeted with "oohs" and "aahs."

Again the question was raised, "What do these facts do to our guesses?" The students suggested that the third and fourth hypotheses were rejected and the second was strengthened. When

pressed for an explanation of how hypothesis 2 was strengthened by the facts, they indicated that the audience for statement A was northern while that for B was southern. When pressed for further clarification of this point, they indicated that the Chicago group, being northern, would be *against* slavery while the Charleston group, being southern, would favor it.

Psychologically speaking the class was ready to stop at this point. It had struggled with a problem and had reached what appeared to be an obvious conclusion supported by facts. Many of the children were smiling with some satisfaction, and all the hands had gone down.

The problem was regenerated quickly, however, with the following sequence of instructions: "By the way, what was Lincoln's purpose in making speeches in 1858?" Some were not sure; most said he was running for President. In a 2–3-minute lecture, the group was briefed concerning Lincoln's remote presidential possibilities in 1858, the conditions that made his nomination actually possible, and how presidents campaigned and were elected in that period. This new information clearly presented some confusion within the class.

Someone then contributed a vague recollection of the Lincoln-Douglas debates and suggested that the statements might have been part of them. No one knew the context of the debates. This information was provided for the class and followed by the question, "In what state did Lincoln's Senate campaign take place?" After some discussion this question was resolved in favor of Illinois.

Then the students were asked, "What would Lincoln be doing campaigning in the *South* for a Senate seat in Illinois?" This question caused considerable consternation and generated a great deal of discussion but was never answered to anyone's satisfaction. I then added two bits of new information to the facts already listed on the board:

Statement A: July 10, 1858. Chicago, *Illinois*.

Statement B: September 18, 1858, Charleston, *Illinois*.

Amid the noisy reactions, the teacher raised in succession the issues of why the class had

FIGURE 5.1.   Continued

seemed so sure of its earlier conclusion, how the new facts affected their list of hypotheses, and how Lincoln could make such contradictory public statements in the same state. They acknowledged that their stereotypes of northern and southern behavior colored their interpretation of the earlier facts, that they now required more facts, and that communication systems in 1858 were much different than those we have today.

A wall map of the United States was used to illustrate the next set of facts. Chicago was located and the general characteristics of its population in 1858 noted. Similarly the city of Charleston in the southern part of Illinois was identified on the map. From this discussion it emerged that Illinois in Lincoln's day, much like today, represented sharp divisions in political opinion in the northern and southern sections. The location of Charleston, Illinois suggested the possible kinship with the proslavery stands of the bordering

southern states as well as physical separation from Chicago.

The students had renewed confidence in hypothesis 2, after their momentary loss of faith. The final challenge to their tentative conclusion took the form of the question, "How did senators get elected in those days?" No one knew. It was explained that people didn't get to vote for senators until the twentieth century, about the same time that women were given the right to vote. This explanation was followed by the question, "What would Lincoln be doing *campaigning* for the Senate?" A final brief explanation sufficed: Lincoln campaigned for state legislators pledged to vote for him as senator if they were elected to the state legislature.

[a]Quoted in Richard Hofstadter, *The American Political Tradition* (New York: Alfred A. Knopf, 1948), p. 116.
[b]Ibid.

FIGURE 5.2   Diagram of a problem-solving strategy in action

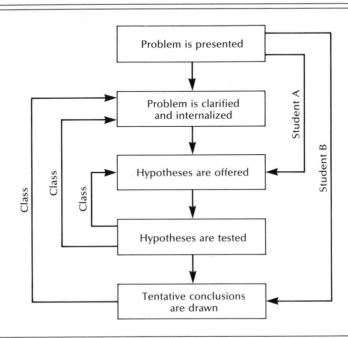

and left of the steps are some examples of the actual sequence of events. As shown with the lines to the right of the model, students *A* and *B* moved immediately after the presentation of the problem to offer respectively, a hypothesis and a conclusion.

The lines on the left of the model show the times the teacher and the class were cycled back to steps to refocus on the problem or to add a new hypothesis while examining evidence. In Figure 5.2 we observe dynamic movement back and forth within the five steps.

Problem Scenarios

In the lesson just analyzed, two brief quotations from the same individual served as the problem springboard. A problem springboard can take many forms: charts, tables, graphs, pictures, cartoons, drawing, maps, recordings, films, videotapes, field trips, observations, and different types of print material. More than the form of the material, it is how and when the teacher introduces it, as well as the questions, comments, and cues he or she uses that will determine whether students perceive a psychological problem. As students express surprise or disbelief, look perplexed, or shake their heads, for example, they offer signs that a teacher has succeeded.

Two additional scenarios that could be used as springboards for problem-solving lessons follow. The first is appropriate for the primary grades and the second for the intermediate grades.

Learning about Holidays. Divide the class into groups and have them list as many holidays as they can. When they are finished, make a composite list on the board or a large sheet of paper. Give each group a calendar listing major holidays. Ask the groups to determine when the holidays occur throughout the year. Also have them list any new holidays they find. Add all new holidays to the composite list.

At this point raise the basic question "Why do we have holidays?" Encourage the class to develop hypotheses, and list them on the board without evaluating them. Have each group evaluate and discuss the hypotheses over several days. This can involve some library research and some interviews with adults about the advantages and purposes of common holidays. When the investigations have concluded, each group should discuss its findings and settle on a collective conclusion.

Call each group's attention to the distribution of major holidays throughout the calendar, and provide background information on them as needed. Point out any major holidays that groups or the class might have missed. Let all groups share their conclusions and discuss them as a class. As a followup ask the class, "Can you think of any group that might be interested in getting a new national holiday? Why?"

Learning the Names of the Presidents. Place a large poster showing all of the presidents of the United States on a bulletin board. It should include their pictures, their order of succession, and some brief biographical information about each of them. (Such posters are commonly available inexpensively or free from commercial publishers or supply houses.)

In some fashion, allow each student to examine the poster and answer the questions placed under the poster: "Who are your favorites? Why?" When every student has done this, repeat the process using a new set of questions: "Which presidents are your least favorite? Why?"

When the students have completed the assignments, discuss their choices and reasons as a group. Construct a class list of favorites and nonfavorites. In the discussion provide some background on each of the presidents, as necessary, relating each to some historical event during his tenure. Ask why some presidents are better known than others and how our views of the presidents have been influenced. Provide some in-class or library research time for students to learn more about their favorites and nonfavorites.

Finally, remove the poster. Give each group a long sheet of paper with a timeline on it representing the presidency from its inception to the present. Ask each group to place its favorites somewhere on the timeline (dates may be included, but are not necessary). Follow with the list of least favored, and last, try to fill in the remaining presidents. Each group can check its results against the poster, and fill in or revise data as needed. As a culminating activity, discuss whether anyone changed his or her choices and why.

Problem-Solving Charts

One way to organize and record the discussion and sequence of analysis in problem-solving activities is by using a problem-solving chart such as Figure 5.3. Either

FIGURE 5.3　Problem-solving chart

Statement of the problem:		
Hypotheses	*Data required for testing*	*Possible sources*
_____	_____	_____
_____	_____	_____
_____	_____	_____
_____	_____	_____
_____	_____	_____

Tentative conclusions	*Supporting facts*
_____	_____
_____	_____
_____	_____
_____	_____
_____	_____

the chalk board or a large sheet of paper may be used to record the data and the details of the activity.

EXERCISE 5.5   Creating Problem Scenarios

Create two problem scenarios similar to the ones described in the text. One should be suitable for primary children and the other for intermediate students. Field test one of them with a class of students, and use the problem-solving chart in Figure 5.3 to organize the discussion. Identify the grade level, number, and type of students used, and briefly describe and evaluate the results.

Case Studies as Springboards for Reflection

Case studies are brief sets of data that present a single idea, issue, event, document, or problem in some detail. In other words, they present in-depth coverage of a narrow subject. Teachers may draw on a wide variety of materials for case studies and present them in many media formats: transparencies, hand-out sheets, records, teacher-made video and audio cassettes, films, field trips, observations, and written materials. Material may be as near as the community newspaper.

Types of Case Studies

Case studies take many forms. Four basic types follow.[7]

Stories and Vignettes. These are dramatized accounts of either authentic or fictitious events to focus attention on an issue. Example: a story of a group of neighbors who through community action made municipal government more responsive to its needs.

Journalistic Historical Events. These include original newspaper accounts, recordings or video records of historical events, eyewitness accounts, and the like. Example: copies of the front pages of major dailies announcing the stock market crash of 1929.

Research Reports. Materials such as the results of studies, statistical tables, census reports, and the like, may be organized and summarized to form a case study. Example: a table showing the population of the twenty-five largest cities in the United States according to the 1980 census.

Documents. This category includes a range of items: speeches, diaries, laws, records, and generally primary source materials. Example: some excerpts from the diaries of immigrants who came to the United States at the turn of the twentieth century.

TABLE 5.1 Case study of the shifts in racial composition over a decade in the five largest cities in the United States

City		White	Black	*Hispanic descent*	Other
		Racial composition of the population			
New York	1970	6,091,503	1,665,470	1,104,327	177,906
	1980	4,293,695	1,784,124	1,405,957	993,211
Chicago	1970	2,207,767	1,102,620	—	56,570
	1980	1,490,217	1,197,000	442,061	317,855
Los Angeles	1970	2,173,600	503,606	—	138,855
	1980	1,816,683	505,208	815,989	644,872
Philadelphia	1970	1,278,717	653,791	—	16,101
	1980	963,084	638,878	63,570	66,248
Houston	1970	904,889	316,551	—	11,362
	1980	799,530	440,257	281,224	176,299

Source: Census Bureau

Sample Case Study

A research-report case study is shown in Table 5.1. It attempts to summarize and dramatize the racial composition of major American cities. Questions and comments could be added to the case, if the teacher wishes.

EXERCISE 5.6   Creating a Case Study

Select one of the four types of case studies described in the text. Identify a grade level or student population with whom you would use the materials and develop a case study. Show specifically how you would use the case as a springboard to a problem-solving activity.

Solution: Cannibals and Missionaries Problem

There are several ways to solve the problem (see page 106). This one describes each trip from one bank to the opposite shore and back as one round trip.

First Round Trip: The boat carries one missionary and one cannibal to the opposite shore. The boat returns with one missionary in it.

Second Round Trip: The boat carries two cannibals to the opposite shore. The boat returns with one cannibal in it.

Third Round Trip: The boat carries two missionaries to the opposite shore. The boat returns with one cannibal and one missionary.

Fourth Round Trip: The boat carries two missionaries to the opposite shore. The boat returns with one cannibal.

Fifth Round Trip: The boat carries two cannibals to the opposite shore. The boat returns with one cannibal.

Sixth Trip (one way): The boat carries two cannibals to the opposite shore.[8]

Notes

1. See, for example, F. S. Bellezza, "Mnemomic Devices: Classification, Characteristics and Criteria," *Review of Educational Research* 51 (1981): 247–275 and Robert Somer, *The Mind's Eye* (New York: Dell, 1978).
2. See, for example, J. R. Levin, "The Keyword Method in the Classroom. How to Remember the States and Their Capitals," *Elementary School Journal* 80 (1980): 185–191 and M. Pressley et al., "The Mnemonic Keyword Method," *Review of Educational Research* 52 (1982): 61–91.
3. Adapted from Moshe F. Rubinstein, *Patterns of Problem Solving* (Englewood-Cliffs, N.J.: Prentice-Hall, 1975).
4. Richard M. Cyert, "Problem Solving and Educational Policy," in *Problem Solving and Education: Issues in Teaching and Research,* ed. D. T. Tuma and F. Reif (Hillsdale, N.J.: Lawrence Erlbaum, 1980), pp. 6–7.
5. John Dewey, *How We Think* (Boston: D. C. Heath, 1933), pp. 106–115.
6. Ibid., p. 115.
7. Fred. M. Newman, *Clarifying Public Controversy: An Approach to Teaching Social Studies* (Boston: Little, Brown, 1970), pp. 238–239.
8. Rubinstein, *Patterns of Problem Solving.*

Suggested Readings

Beyer, Barry K. *Teaching Thinking in Social Studies,* 2nd ed. Columbus, Ohio: Charles E. Merrill, 1979.

Dewey, John. *How We Think.* Boston: D. C. Heath, 1933.

Dewey, John. *Democracy and Education.* New York: Macmillan, 1944.

Fair, Jean, and Shaftel, Fannie R., eds. *Effective Thinking in Social Studies.* Thirty-Seventh Yearbook. Washington, D.C.: National Council for the Social Studies, 1967.

Gross, Richard E., and Muessig, Raymond H., eds. *Problem-Centered Social Studies Instruction: Approaches to Reflective Thinking.* Washington, D.C.: National Council for the Social Studies, 1971.

Hullfish, H. Gorden, and Smith, Philip G. *Reflective Thinking: The Method of Thinking.* New York: Dodd, Mead, 1961.

Hunt, Maurice P., and Metcalf, Lawrence E. *Teaching High School Social Studies.* 2nd ed. New York: Harper and Row, 1968, Chapters 2, 3, and 5.

Massialas, Byron G., and Hurst, Joseph B. *Social Studies in a New Era*. New York: Longman, 1978, Chapter 2.

Ryan, Frank L. *Exemplars for the New Social Studies*. Englewood Cliffs, N.J.: Prentice-Hall, 1971.

Rubinstein, Moshe F. *Patterns of Problem Solving*. Englewood Cliffs, N.J.: Prentice-Hall, 1975.

Smith, James A., *Creative Teaching of the Social Studies in the Elementary School,* 2nd ed. Boston: Allyn and Bacon, 1979, Chapter 1.

Smullyan, Raymond. *The Lady or the Tiger?* New York: Alfred A. Knopf, 1982.

Welton, David A., and Mallan, John T. *Children and Their World: Strategies for Teaching Social Studies*. Boston: Houghton Mifflin, 1981, Chapter 6.

Wickelgren, W. A. *How To Solve Problems*. San Francisco: W. Freeman, 1973.

PART THREE

Developing Competent Citizens

6

Social Skills

Whether at home, at school, on the job, or at a party, having good relationships with others or "getting along" requires social skills. These skills are the glue that binds groups and society as a whole together harmoniously and productively. In whatever we hope to accomplish cooperatively social skills are instrumental in achieving our goals. Some children seem to learn this fact early in life and continue to add to their repertoire of social skills into adulthood.

Social Skills as Competencies

We regard individuals who have acquired the skills to work and communicate effectively with a variety of people in many situations as being *socially competent*. Such competency often is learned, at least in part, informally and naturally through family training and peer imitation. Children, for example, usually learn not to interrupt a conversation when another is speaking or to listen as well as to talk.

If our social environment is rich in lessons as we mature, we continuously acquire and integrate sets of social skills. Once we have acquired them, we begin to apply them to settings different from the ones in which they were learned. In this fashion over time many people manage to assimilate naturally the basic social competencies necessary to navigate successfully through life.

Social Skills in Childhood

In the normal course of growing up some children do not acquire the fundamental social competencies essential for effective living and positive relationships with others. As any kindergarten teacher can testify, children appear at the school door for the first time with varying levels of proficiency in social skills. Unless the teacher gives the children assistance or training, these differences in levels of social skills are likely to remain and even increase, much like the differences in reading abilities.

Socially Competent Children. From a study of more than 100 children over two years, Burton White has concluded that the socially competent six year old is characterized by behaviors that include the following:

Can get and maintain the attention of adults in socially acceptable ways.

Uses adults as resources in socially acceptable ways.

Can express both affection and hostility to adults.

Can both lead and follow peers, can compete with them, and can express both affection and hostility to them.[1]

Social Skills for Survival

The technological, mobile, and interdependent society in which today's students live has most of its over 225 million members concentrated in fewer than fifty geographical centers. If these citizens are to interact harmoniously and to lead rich and productive lives, they will require a core of social skills. We will call these basic social competencies *survival skills*.

Survival Skills

No consensus currently exists on what the survival skills should be. Four clusters of skills are suggested as a starting point for constructing such a list:

group participation skills

communication skills

observation skills

multicultural understanding skills

Although one cluster may be emphasized at one grade level — communication skills in the primary grades, for example — all of the clusters merit some attention and reinforcement at each grade level. Besides the social studies, the other subjects in the formal curriculum can contribute to the development of these skills. The development of social skills also may be encouraged through informal actions in the playground, the cafeteria, and other school areas.

Group Participation Skills

In our society the role played by groups such as committees, teams, and social organizations is a dominant one. There are several reasons why individuals agree to join and work within a group for short or long periods of time. Whether we are in school or out, we expect that a group to which we belong will fulfill some social objective. Working within a group, for example, may help us complete a task we might not otherwise be able to do or to do as well.

Using Groups in the Classroom

Similarly, if the use of group work can enable a teacher to achieve some instructional objective, it is an appropriate tool. Also, group activities are desirable when they enable a student group to accomplish a task more efficiently or more effectively than an individual can. Group work per se is neither a good nor a bad instructional tool, and it should be used only as appropriate to curricular objectives.

Since organized group work often is outside the range of students' natural experiences, it may be helpful to provide them with models or case studies of structured group activities. One might use a field trip to accomplish this. Viewing videotapes of groups such as school board or city council meetings can also be helpful.

If a community cable television channel exists, it may offer a more convenient way to make observations. Video excerpts from popular television programs that show organized group activities also may be used. Younger children are especially likely to benefit from seeing films or firsthand cases of other children working in groups. Besides observing and analyzing examples of different groups at work, all children will need to practice and experiment with different group forms and alternate roles within groups.

Organizing Group Work

There are several basic considerations in organizing groups to work effectively. These include providing adequate space, controlling noise, and avoiding distractions. The membership of a group also often determines whether its objectives are likely to be realized. There is no magic number for a group, although five to seven students is generally a good size. Both the size and the membership of a group should be related to its task or objective.

Identifying Group Members. Among the many ways of identifying the members for a group, five are suggested here:

> student self-selection
>
> assignment by general background characteristics (e.g., interests or experiences)
>
> assignment by abilities or skills
>
> random assignment
>
> assignment by behavioral characteristics

The last four procedures require the teacher to assess how certain student characteristics are related to the task and effective operation of the group. Although there is no best way to choose group members, there are better ways for different objectives.

For instance, consider an activity in which the objective is to improve the multicultural understanding within a classroom. Assignment by general background to include a mix of racial or ethnic representatives within each group is likely to be a better choice than student self-selection. Similarly, in a class with several behavioral problems at the beginning of a school year an important consideration for some tasks may be to ensure that potentially disruptive students are not grouped together.

Using Sociograms. One way to gather data on student group preferences and other information for assigning students to groups is to construct a *sociogram*. A sociogram is a diagram of children's social choices among their classmates. Students are first asked to answer privately and in writing two oral or written questions: "With which three children in this class would you most like to work?" and "With which three children in this class would you prefer not to work?"

Tabulating Students' Preferences. The student responses then are collected and tabulated, as shown in Table 6.1. Positive choices are given a +1 and negative choices a −1. For the class shown, the results indicate several popular children and a range of students who are less popular. They also reveal isolated students who attracted neither positive nor negative reactions. They show further that a few children, such as Student 16, were rejected by many classmates.

In several cases feelings were reciprocated; that is, some students who preferred to work with someone were in turn preferred by that person. More complex patterns also emerged. For example, some students preferred to work with students who preferred *not* to be in the same group.

Summarizing Students' Preferences. The data in Table 6.1 may be summarized in a figure similar to Figure 6.1. In the smallest circle (labeled *A*) are placed the numbers of all the children who received *no* negative ratings and *more than* three positive ratings. In the outermost ring *(D)*, are placed the numbers of students who received *more than* three negative choices and *less than* two positive choices. Of the remaining students, those who received more positive choices than negative choices or an equal number go in circle *B*. Those who received more negative ratings than positive ones go in circle *C*. Students who were not chosen at all are placed on the outside of the circles. To permit easy identification of sexes, different colors of pencils/pens should be used for boys and for girls.

EXERCISE 6.1   Developing a Sociogram

Find a class at any grade level in which the teacher is willing to let you develop a sociogram. Explain the purpose of the activity, and indicate the nature of the questions you will be asking students. Indicate the grade level and size of the class.

Complete the sociogram using the procedures discussed in the text, and analyze the results. Share the findings with the teacher, and compare your analyses. At the end, summarize the data as in Table 6.1 and Figure 6.1.

TABLE 6.1 Tabulation of class preferences

Student number	1	2	3	4	5	6	7	8	9	10	11	12	13	14	15	16	17	18	19	20	21	22	23	24	25
1								−1								−1	+1	−1		+1		+1			
2																−1	+1	−1		−1		+1		−1	
3	+1			+1																		+1			
4			+1					−1					−1	−1		−1	+1	−1							
5	+1							−1								−1	+1					+1			
6					+1			−1																	
7					−1						−1			−1						−1					
8			+1					−1	+1				−1	+1		−1	+1	−1		−1		+1			
9			+1					−1						+1		−1	+1				−1	+1			
10			+1					−1								−1	+1					+1			
11			+1	−1				−1					−1	+1		−1	+1	−1				+1			
12	+1		+1					−1								−1	+1								
13			+1					−1	+1			+1	−1	+1		−1	+1	−1			−1				
14	+1		+1					−1			+1			+1		−1	+1				−1	+1			
15								−1							−1										+1
16	−1			−1				−1						+1	−1	−1	+1				−1	+1			
17	−1		+1						+1		+1			+1	−1	−1	+1	−1				+1			+1
18		−1	+1					−1							−1							+1		−1	+1
19															−1										
20			+1	+1					−1		−1			+1	−1	−1	+1			+1		+1			
21				−1				−1						+1								+1			
22			+1					−1			−1			+1								+1			
23			+1					−1						+1						−1		+1			
24		+1	+1													−1					−1	+1			
25	+1		+1					−1						+1		−1	+1					−1			−1
Total+	5	1	15	2	1	0	0	0	3	0	1	1	0	12	0	0	14	0	0	1	0	17	0	0	2
Total−	2	1	0	3	1	0	0	18	1	0	3	0	4	2	3	17	0	6	0	4	5	1	0	2	0

FIGURE 6.1   Summary of tabulation data

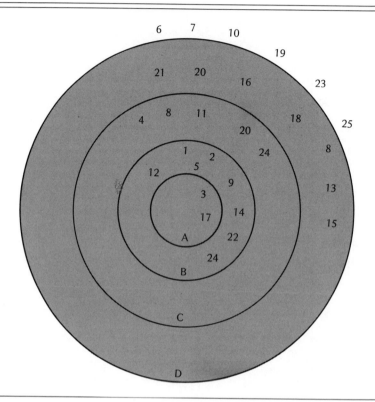

Group Techniques

There are limitless ways for groups to accomplish a task, depending on the size and ages of the membership. Youngsters placed within a group, however, must be capable of assuming or experimenting with the *roles* they are assigned or select in order for the group to function effectively. Different techniques require different responsibilities or roles of group members. A simple example is the role of recorder in a group, which requires some basic writing, organizing, and reading skills.

Some group techniques that may be used effectively in social studies instruction are

> brainstorming
>
> majority-rule decision making
>
> consensus decision making
>
> decision making by ratings
>
> composite reports
>
> agenda use
>
> the jigsaw puzzle

Whichever group techniques are employed, it is important for teachers to provide some variety. A steady diet of any one technique is likely to reduce its effectiveness or produce boredom.

Brainstorming. When a group's objective is to get as many solutions for a problem as possible on the table for consideration, *brainstorming* is an excellent technique. One of its foremost proponents is Alex Osborn.[2] The main ingredient for a brainstorming session is a problem that the group members wish to solve, such as "How can America reduce its energy consumption?" To conduct a session, the group will require a leader, a recorder to list the possible solutions, and the agreement of members that all ideas will be accepted and recorded without evaluation.

All ideas offered should be listed without discussion. They should be listed as quickly as possible without indicating the names of the authors. Once all ideas have been listed they can be discussed. Finally, the group members can reach some agreement on the most useful solutions.

Majority-Rule Decision Making. The technique perhaps most widely associated with groups and decision making is *majority rule*. For issues that involve such things as taking a stand, selecting individuals for a task, or reconciling different points of view, it is an effective technique. Moreover, many students are already familiar with this technique when they enter school. In fact, what many students most need to learn is that it is not appropriate for all group objectives.

Majority rule involves discussion, and compromise if necessary, to reach an agreement. Arriving at a group decision requires a formal or informal vote to determine the wishes of the majority. Where appropriate to protect group members from peer pressure or intimidation, votes may be recorded secretly. An example might be a group attempting to decide class officers.

Consensus Decision Making. Unlike majority rule, *consensus decision making* requires all members of a group to agree on the final solution. Majority rule encourages building coalitions, and produces temporary subgroups of "winners" and "losers." In contrast decisions by consensus require *all* members' views to be taken into account, since all must agree on the final results. Jury decisions are an example of consensus decision making. All twelve members of a jury must agree on the final verdict.

Decision Making by Ratings. Decision making by ratings requires that various choices of individuals within a group be weighted and averaged. This technique is a mathematically based compromise between the majority-rule and consensus techniques. It commits a group to the decision or decisions that receive the best average rating from all members.

Consider a group of seven students trying to decide which actions various levels of government should take to resolve the energy crisis. The rating technique proceeds as illustrated in Table 6.2. Once students through research have identified the major types of actions to be taken by government, they rate each possibility.

Their first choice is given a 1, the second a 2, and so on to their last choice.

TABLE 6.2   Decision making by ratings

Possible actions identified from research	Individual ratings of group members							
	Tom	*Tammy*	*Ann*	*Bill*	*Sam*	*Lea*	*Ron*	*Total*
Action 1	4	1	2	5	1	5	2	20
Action 2	1	5	1	4	3	2	5	21
Action 3	2	4	4	3	5	3	1	22
Action 4	3	3	3	2	2	2	3	18
Action 5	5	2	5	1	4	4	4	25

Issue: How government can help solve the energy crisis

The individual ratings then are totaled, and the action with the *lowest* total rating becomes the group's choice. An optional final step in the rating technique is to permit the members to discuss their ratings further, and then to conduct a second round of rating to arrive at the final decision.

Table 6.2 also indicates how the rating technique can produce a *group* position that represents a compromise for each member. Action 4, the group's selection through rating, was *not* the first choice of any member. Further, it was only the third choice of a majority of the members.

Composite Reports.   A composite report is one that synthesizes and summarizes all the information the members of a group have collected on a subject. Rather than presenting a series of individual reports, students in the intermediate grades are often organized into groups for research on a topic. The collective findings of the group then are presented to the class or the teacher in a single systematic report.

Composite reports take many forms and often employ different types of media. Skits, debates, collages, dioramas, bulletin boards, mobiles, and student-made films, filmstrips, and videotapes are but a few of the formats that have been used for composite reports. When students have limited opportunities to meet as a group to construct their composite reports, they may use *data charts*.

Data charts such as Figure 6.2 require the group to have a *division of topics* among all members and a *set of common properties* that each member will research within a topic. Group members also must decide on the *questions* they will use to compare, contrast, interpret, and generalize from the data collected and summarized. The chart itself may be constructed on the chalk board, kraft paper, posterboard, or another medium. It may be organized by the group as a whole or completed in sections by individual members and then spliced together when the group assembles.

Agendas.   Many adult organizations conduct meetings using an agenda or an ordered list of topics to be discussed when the group is in session. An agenda is a

FIGURE 6.2 Data chart for composite report

Mayoral candidates	Education and experience	Positions on minority rights	Positions on taxes	Positions on education	Positions on crime	Plans for improving the city	Major campaign themes
Polonski							
Eyre							
Goldstein							
Wilson							

more formal way of organizing a group for a task. It often keeps a group progressing efficiently toward its objectives when it might otherwise stray from its tasks. Even younger students can gain some experience in using agendas, if a simplified format is used (see Figure 6.3).

The teacher, the students, or both can construct the agenda. Some of the basic elements for agenda are:

a list of topics or questions to be addressed by a group during one meeting and the order in which they are to be considered

a time period when the meeting is to begin and, optionally, when it is to end

a leader to hold the group to the topics and order listed on the agenda

the name of the student responsible for providing information concerning a topic (optional)

a time limit for each agenda item (optional)

Jigsaw Puzzle. The jigsaw puzzle technique differs in several ways from the preceding ones. It involves each group participant in sharing parts of a solution to a common problem. The problem generally is a quiz or assignment given by the teacher. Each member is given only some of the "pieces of the puzzle" (the answers to the quiz or assignment). No member of the group has enough information to solve the problem alone. Only by sharing and relying on all the others in the group can any member succeed.

The technique's basic objective is to encourage children to cooperate, share, and work together effectively. Getting children to view one another as allies rather than competitors in achieving common learning goals can often be a difficult task for a teacher. Many children's activities both in and outside of school reward competition and discourage cooperative behavior.

FIGURE 6.3 Simplified group agenda

AGENDA

Fieldtrip Commmittee

    June 5, 1984

    Library 10

    9:30–10:15

1. Review of last meeting's (Paul: 3 minutes)
2. Plans and group assignments for field trip (Ms. Craven: 10 minutes)
3. Ways to complete assignments (25 minutes)
4. Individual assignments (Sarah: 5 minutes)
5. Next meeting date and time (Deb: 2 minutes)

Educators and psychologists working in the Austin, Texas, elementary schools to improve relationships between white and nonwhite children devised the technique to encourage cooperative learning among interracial groups of intermediate grade children. In *The Jigsaw Classroom,* Aronson and his colleagues describe the results of their research, as well as examples of the technique applied to social studies classes.[3] They offer a brief example of how the technique works:

> For example, in the first classroom we studied, the next lesson happened to be on Joseph Pulitzer. We wrote a six-paragraph biography of the man, such that each paragraph contained a major aspect of Pulitzer's life. . . . Next we cut up the biography into sections and gave each child in the learning group one paragraph. Thus every learning group had within it the entire life story of Joseph Pulitzer, but each child had no more than one sixth of the story and was dependent on all the others to complete the big picture.[4]

After completing an experimental program that employed the technique, the investigators reported that in integrated schools Anglos learned equally well in both jigsaw and competitive classes, but that blacks and Mexican-Americans performed better in jigsaw than in competitive classes.[5] In addition they reported that at the conclusion of the study the students liked both groupmates and others in their class better than when the study began. The technique is reported to have worked with students in grade 4 through high school.

Communication Skills

What are commonly called communications breakdowns abound in American society. Countries go to war, spouses separate, children fight, and individuals of all ages and types cut themselves off from potentially meaningful relationships, often largely because of basic communication failures.

Communication minimally requires a sender, a receiver, and a message. Three types of communication skills closely related to the social studies are *listening, conflict resolution,* and *negotiation.* These are central to productive and mutually satisfying discussions among citizens in a democratic society. In the home, in the marketplace, at work, or at play, all of us are called on to employ these skills to achieve some of our most fundamental goals and to live in harmony with others.

Listening

Some students, as they enter school, appear to be good listeners; they have already learned to wait quietly until another finishes speaking. Becoming a good listener, like becoming a good speaker, requires skill. The basic characteristics of good listeners seem to be allowing senders to complete their messages without interruption and interpreting the senders' main points without error. Both conditions are necessary for effective listening, and both require practice.

In the classroom helping students become good listeners includes teaching them to take turns in talking and to wait for acknowledgement before speaking. It also

FIGURE 6.4   Sample rules for teacher-led group discussions

GROUP DISCUSSION RULES

Rule 1. Everyone must sit quietly and pay attention when another person is speaking.

Rule 2. Only one person may speak at a time.

Rule 3. In order to speak each person must raise his or her hand and be recognized by the teacher or group leader.

Rule 4. Everyone has a right to speak, but we must take turns.

requires that the teacher delay calling on impulsive speakers. Often posting a simple set of rules to encourage listening in structured teacher-led discussions can be a helpful reminder to children. An example is shown in Figure 6.4. Some other techniques that help build listening skills are:

requiring all students periodically to restate or review what another said earlier

creating gamelike rules to provide practice in letting everyone speak and listen

asking students periodically to take notes when others give reports or short presentations

having students listen to public speakers or media figures and then quizzing them on what was said

A brief self-evaluation form to examine discussion habits in groups is shown in Table 6.3.

TABLE 6.3   Self-evaluation form for discussions

What do I do in discussions?			
	Sometimes	*Always*	*Never*
1. Do I do most of the talking?	_____	_____	_____
2. Do I usually talk only a little?	_____	_____	_____
3. Can I follow the suggestions of others?	_____	_____	_____
4. Do I get angry when others do not agree with me?	_____	_____	_____
5. Do I interrupt others?	_____	_____	_____
6. Do I take turns talking?	_____	_____	_____
7. Do I stay on the subject?	_____	_____	_____
8. Am I a good listener?	_____	_____	_____

Conflict Resolution

Even very young children in our society have to resolve conflicts. On farms, in the suburbs, and in the cities, children from every socioeconomic stratum are exposed to conflict in a variety of forms. They see conflict among nations on television and film. And they may be directly exposed to conflict between parents and among other adults, within gangs in some neighborhoods, and between siblings and other children. The alarming national statistics on child abuse also suggest that children themselves are often the victims of conflict and misplaced aggression.

Students' Personal Conflicts. Many of children's personal conflicts deal with access to desired concrete objects, such as candy and toys, rather than with abstractions, such as different points of view. Approaches to teaching conflict resolution skills should communicate to children that conflict is a normal, everyday occurrence in a complex, interdependent society.

Sources of Conflict. Conflicts arise when the goals of individuals or groups clash. The resolution of conflict can be destructive (a fight or battle) or constructive (a compromise or a treaty). Classroom activities that encourage children to experiment with alternative ways of resolving conflicts, to better understand the sources of conflicts, and to work out constructive solutions to their own conflicts can help students develop the skills they will need to be effective citizens.

Conflict Resolution Strategies. In a set of multimedia materials, *Focus on Self Development: Involvement,* Anderson and Henner offer many activities to help students become more aware of the sources of conflicts and to explore alternate ways of resolving them.[6] They outline thirteen types of activities, six of which are summarized here.[7]

1. *Open-ended sentences* for completing or initiating a paragraph, such as "One reason that countries have wars is _____."
2. *Tense situations* or scenarios in which the class is given a question or premise involving a conflict. Students then are asked to role play the characters in the scene. Anderson and Henner provide several examples of tense situations:

    Students unjustly accused of breaking windows try to decide how to make the people they know are guilty confess. . . . Tenants meet to decide what to do about a landlord who has failed repeatedly to satisfy their demands for needed building improvements. . . . Someone pushes in line ahead of others who have been waiting for an hour.[8]

3. *Propaganda materials* in which some students find articles on both sides of an issue to demonstrate how conflict often is generated by propaganda.
4. *Conflict within situations* wherein class members try to identify with students who are experiencing inner conflict. For example, they might consider the student who is very good in academic areas but does not try because of fear of embarrassment.

5. *No-conflict settings,* which demonstrate the positive as well as the negative possibilities of conflict. For example, students could be asked, ''Show us what a sport would be like if all conflict disappeared from it.''[9]

6. *Fighting words* that individuals often insert into an argument to anger another. Students could be asked to consider words, phrases, or actions they and others they know use to provoke a member of their family or a friend, the occasion on which the words or actions might be used, and the responses they would produce.

EXERCISE 6.2   Field-testing a Conflict-resolution Activity

Select a grade level and a class, and field test one of the six strategies for conflict-resolution. Adapt the examples as needed for the group of students with whom you are working. At the conclusion assess the activity's effectiveness. Note which modifications would be desirable if the activity were repeated with another group.

Negotiating

Closely related to the skills of conflict resolution are those of negotiating. Negotiating involves knowing how to come to terms with someone over an issue. This skill is central to success in our society and to living in harmony with others. It oils our governmental, business, and social machinery and keeps the world operating. Each citizen eventually has to use negotiating skills to get another person to do something they want.

The Process of Negotiating. Facility in negotiating often involves patience, self-confidence, and the ability to present your position understandably and acceptably. It also includes highlighting your strengths and minimizing your weaknesses, using influence, being willing to compromise, and framing an issue in your terms. This is a sizable set of qualities, and hence difficulties are associated with developing the skill of negotiating. No simple collection of activities will train children in this skill, but a beginning can be made at any grade level.

Strategies for Developing Negotiating Skills. One useful technique is to engage students in open-ended role-playing scenarios that involve negotiating. These situations should require students to devise stratagems and use persuasion to achieve a goal that is within reach but requires another's assent. A simple example might be a child's attempts to convince parents to extend the hour of bedtime.

Case studies of successful negotiators can help in demonstrating negotiating skills to intermediate-grade and middle-school children. These can be presented through visual media such as films and videotapes, as well as through articles. Many popular televisions shows are sprinkled with clear, albeit overdrawn, models of successful negotiators.

One of the most visible, ongoing examples of negotiations for the social studies class is the daily drama between and within the executive and the legislative branches of our federal government. When the president, for example, invites selected representatives of the Congress and the Senate to Camp David for lunch to gain support on a key bill, students are provided with a case study of a skillful negotiator in action. Such cases can provide clear models and a springboard for discussing those qualities which make negotiations succeed.

An example of commercial materials suitable for use with students in grades 4–8 are the *Social Science Laboratory Units* created by Lippitt, Fox, and Schaible. Within the series they developed a unit with activities and materials to help students understand how the processes of negotiation and influence occur.[10] Figure 6.5 illustrates a sample student activity from the unit.

EXERCISE 6.3   Creating Cases of Successful Negotiating

Identify two cases of success negotiators at work, suitable for discussion with elementary or middle-school children. Consult newspapers, television shows, and periodicals for examples. Indicate how individuals or groups were able to negotiate with another party in a way that both sides found satisfactory.

Note the specific actions the negotiators took to achieve their ends. After analyzing the cases translate them into a set of materials that could be understood easily by students.

Observation Skills

During a normal day we are confronted with more visual and other stimuli than we can notice and process. A commuter driving to work through midtown Manhattan at 8:00 A.M. would never arrive safely at work if he or she tried to observe all the elements in the environment. On an average day a motorist confronts hundreds of assorted motorized vehicles, flashing signs, displays, pedestrians of every description, sounds of all sorts, and traffic signals, to name but a few of the stimuli.

To survive in our culture we must often fragment our observations, learn to screen out many items, and focus on small, manageable segments of our environment. "It is impossible to observe everything," anthropologists Spradley and McCurdy remind us.[11] Therefore, all citizens learn to become selective in their observations.

Developing Observation Skills

Helping students develop observation skills involves aiding them in becoming more astute observers of slices of their environment such as their homes, their neighborhoods, and their society. Observational skills include the ability to obtain as

FIGURE 6.5   Student activity dealing with negotiating and influence

---

REASONS FOR ACCEPTING INFLUENCE

Classroom Questionnaire

Directions: Do you always do what your classmates ask you to do? Probably not. But aren't there certain students who are usually able to influence you? What are these persons like? What special qualities do they have? Listed below are 17 items that children say are important reasons for influence. First read all of them, then rank them in order of their importance to you. Place a 1 in the space before the statement you think is the most important quality, a 2 in the space before the statement you think is the second most important, and so forth. You would put a 17 in front of the least important quality.

___*a)* Smart in school

___*b)* Has good ideas about how to have fun

___*c)* Good at making things

___*d)* Good at games with running and throwing

___*e)* Knows how to fight

___*f)* Strong

___*g)* Acts friendly

___*h)* A good person to do things with

___*i)* Asks you to do things in a nice way

___*j)* Doesn't start fights and doesn't tease

___*k)* Knows how to act so people will like him

___*l)* Plays with you a lot

___*m)* Likes to do the same things you like to do

___*n)* Nice-looking

___*o)* Has things you'd like to have

___*p)* Gives you things

___*q)* Does things for you

Source: From *Social Science Laboratory Units: Influencing Each Other* by R. Lippitt, R. Fox and L. Schaible. © 1969, Science Research Associates, Inc. Reprinted by permission of the publisher.

---

much information as can be used about an object, event, or area and to distinguish among our own objective descriptions, inferences, and opinions or value judgments.

Using Media to Develop Observational Skills. Training children in observational skills can include activities as fundamental as examining and discussing open-ended pictures. Students can be asked first to describe what they see. Then they can be encouraged to hypothesize about how the situation might have occurred and about what may happen next. Finally, they might be asked to offer their subjective reactions to the situation. The class's discussion could be summarized on the chalkboard as here:

What I saw	How I think it happened	My reactions

Students in the intermediate grades may be shown a two- to four-minute clip of a filmstrip, 8mm film loop, or 16mm film, without sound or with the sound turned off, which illustrates people engaged in some activity. Films of people from other cultures engaged in typical daily tasks or in special celebrations are fine visual materials for developing observational skills. Initially the media should be shown without instructions. After the viewing, ask the students simply, "What did you see?" The class's responses should be recorded on a sheet, and then *covered* with another sheet of paper.

The class now should be divided into three groups. Ask the first group to observe how *time* is used in the film. Ask a second group to focus on the *people* and what each person is doing. Ask group 3 to observe which *things* are used and how.

Show the same film clip a second time. Each group should summarize its members' individual observations and report its findings to the class. Again the observations may be recorded on a sheet and then covered. Viewings may be repeated, more observations may be recorded, and finally, all of the different sets of observations compared.

Usually, each new viewing will reveal observations that were missed in earlier sessions. The simple observational framework of time, people, and things, corresponds to that used by anthropologists in ethnographic field work. In the social studies class it is an interesting way both to view traditional media and to develop observational skills as they are practiced by social scientists.

Multicultural Understanding Skills

We all share in the broad cultural framework that characterizes our country and allows us to call ourselves "American." In addition, we have a point of cultural reference, should we care to use it, which allows us to distinguish ourselves from the larger cultural framework. "A particular culture, in distinction to 'culture' in general," anthropologists inform us, "is made up of certain ways of acting, thinking, feeling, and communicating that are used by the people of a group and that distinguish them from other groups.'' [12]

Cultural and Ethnic Groups

Because our many groups prize those distinguishing characteristics which give them individuality, we regard our nation as being ''culturally pluralistic'' or ''multicultural.'' Similar to cultural groups are *ethnic* groups. These are made up of people who identify themselves on the basis of ancestry, real or imagined, and some common customs, traditions, or experiences, such as language, history, or nationality.

There is often little distinction made between cultural and ethnic groups. Individuals often use the terms interchangeably in referring to themselves and others.

Developing Multicultural Understanding Skills

Banks, who has written widely on the subject, observes, ''The major goal of multicultural education is to change the total educational environment so that it promotes a repect for the wide range of cultural groups and enables all cultural groups to experience equal educational opportunity.'' [13] In the broadest and most fundamental sense, skills for multicultural understanding are those which enable children to identify, respect, and suspend judgment concerning the characteristics of a cultural group different from their own. Developing multicultural understanding skills requires an ongoing commitment on the part of teachers, parents, and all those within the school.

Many skills are developed slowly over time. Some, such as empathy, are acquired only when children reach an appropriate developmental stage. And all are affected by the training a child receives in the home. Even preschoolers learn from their home and neighborhood environment to imitate and promote attitudes of tolerance or intolerance, and to appreciate or reject groups that are culturally different.

Guidelines. Progress toward multicultural understanding can be made if children are provided with experiences where they can:

1. Learn how and where to obtain objective, accurate information about other cultural groups.
2. Identify and examine positive accounts of other cultural groups or individuals from such groups.
3. Learn tolerance for diversity through experimentation in the school and classroom with alternate customs and practices.
4. Encourage, where possible, first-hand positive experiences with different cultural groups.
5. Practice empathic behavior (trying to put themselves in the shoes of a person from a different cultural group) through puppetry, role playing, and simulations.

6. Practice using "perspective glasses"; that is, try to look at an event, historical period, or issue through the perspective of another cultural group.

EXERCISE 6.4   Literary Materials that Contribute to Multicultural Understanding

Identify a collection of children's books that have as their objective promoting multicultural understanding. Organize the books into three basic levels — primary, intermediate, and middle-school. List the author, title, publisher, and copyright date of each book. Alongside each work, indicate in a sentence or two that aspect of multicultural understanding which the book is designed to further.

Materials for Developing Multicultural Understanding

Fortunately, a fine assortment of instructional materials is available to aid teachers in developing multicultural understanding skills. A sample is included here. Other texts are listed in the Suggested Readings at the end of the chapter. These texts, in turn, list many other materials for promoting multicultural understanding.

Instructional Materials

Building Ethnic Collections: An Annotated Guide for School Media Centers and Public Libraries, Libraries Unlimited, P.O. Box 263, Littleton, CO 80160.

Ethnic American Minorities: A Guide to Media and Materials, R. R. Bowker, P.O. Box 1807, Ann Arbor, MI 48106.

Materials and Resources for Teaching Ethnic Studies: An Annotated Bibliography, Social Science Education Consortium, 855 Broadway, Boulder, CO 80302.

Organizations.   Several organizations provide collections of written materials and media, which are periodically updated. Most will provide a materials list free of charge. Here are some of those organizations:

The Anti-Defamation League of B'nai B'rith, 823 United Nations Plaza, New York, NY 10017.

The Council on Interracial Books for Children, 1841 Broadway, New York, NY 10023.

Multicultural Resources, Box 2945, Stanford, CA 94305.

Notes

1. Herbert Yahraes, *Developing a Sense of Competence in Young Children* (Washington, D.C.: National Institute of Mental Health, 1978), p. 1.
2. Alex Osborn, *Applied Imagination*, 3rd ed. (New York: Charles Scribner, 1963).
3. Elliot Aronson et al., *The Jigsaw Classroom* (Beverly Hills, Calif.: Sage, 1978).
4. Elliot Aronson, "Busing and Racial Tension: The Jigsaw Route to Learning and Liking," *Psychology Today* (February 1975): 47.
5. Aronson, et al., *The Jigsaw Classroom*, p. 117.
6. Judith L. Anderson and Melody Henner, *Focus on Self-Development: Involvement* (Chicago: SRA, 1972).
7. Ibid., pp. 159–163.
8. Ibid., p. 159.
9. Ibid., p. 162.
10. Ronald Lippitt, Robert Fox, and Lucille Schaible, *Teacher's Guide: Social Science Laboratory Units* (Chicago: SRA, 1969).
11. James P. Spradley and David W. McCurdy, *The Cultural Experience: Ethnography in Complex Society* (Chicago: SRA, 1972), p. 16.
12. *Cultural Anthropology Today* (Del Mar, Calif.: CRM, 1971), p. 53.
13. James A. Banks, *Teaching Strategies for Ethnic Studies*, 2nd ed. (Boston: Allyn and Bacon, 1979), p. 23.

Suggested Readings

Anderson, Judith L., and Henner, Melody. *Focus on Self-Development: Involvement*. Chicago: SRA, 1972.

Aronson, Elliot, et al. *The Jigsaw Classroom*. Beverly Hills, Calif.: Sage, 1978.

Baker, Gwendolyn C. *Planning and Organizing for Multicultural Instruction*. Reading, Mass.: Addison-Wesley, 1983.

Banks, James A. *Teaching Strategies for Ethnic Studies*. 3rd ed. Boston: Allyn and Bacon, 1983.

Chapin, June R., and Gross, Richard E. *Teaching Social Studies Skills*. Boston: Little, Brown, 1973, Chapter 3.

Chesler, Mark, and Fox, Robert. *Role-Playing Methods in the Classroom*. Chicago: SRA, 1966.

Grant, Carl A., ed. *Multicultural Education: Commitments, Issues, and Applications*. Washington, D.C.: Association for Supervision and Curriculum Development, 1977.

Johnson, David W., and Johnson, Roger T. *Learning Together and Alone*. Englewood Cliffs, N.J.: Prentice-Hall, 1975.

Kenworthy, Leonard S. *Social Studies for the Eighties in Elementary and Middle Schools*. 3rd ed. New York: John Wiley, 1981, Chapter 15.

Kurfman, Dana G., ed. *Developing Decision-Making Skills*. Forty-Seventh Yearbook. Washington, D.C.: National Council for the Social Studies, 1977, Chapter 5.

Schmuck, Richard A., and Schmuck, Patricia. *Group Processes in the Classroom*. 4th ed. Dubuque, Iowa: W. C. Brown, 1983.

Shaftel, Fannie, and Shaftel, George. *Role Playing in the Curriculum.* 2nd ed. Englewood Cliffs, N.J.: Prentice-Hall, 1982.

Welton, David A., and Mallan, John T. *Children and Their World: Strategies for Teaching Social Studies.* 2nd ed. Boston: Houghton Mifflin, 1981, Chapter 11.

7

Research, Chronological, and Spatial Skills

In addition to a repertoire of social skills, the competent citizen requires a range of *research, chronological,* and *spatial* skills to function effectively in our society. As our lives become more complex, our society more mobile, and information sources more abundant, this cluster of skills will become increasingly important to citizens of all ages. What we have come to call the knowledge explosion places special burdens on citizens to sort through the mass of available materials and separate the meaningful from the trivial.

Mr. and Ms. Everyperson make use of research, chronological, and spatial skills in handling their shopping, planning their budgets, and projecting their futures. They also use these skills in making intelligent choices at the ballot boxes or the theater and in understanding what they have done or seen there. Such skills also help them keep accurate records of their affairs, locate places, give and follow directions, and attend to similar practical matters.

Research Skills

At its most basic level, research can be viewed as seeking a satisfactory answer to a question. When we do research, we are looking for and finding information in response to some query. We also must compare, contrast, and evaluate the information once it has been collected to determine whether it is satisfactory.

Research involves clusters of skills related to *collecting data systematically and accurately, identifying and using reference sources,* and *processing and interpreting data.* These are prerequisite skills for success in many social studies and other subject matter activities. They are also central for functioning as effective citizens in a modern technological society.

143

Collecting Data Systematically and Accurately

The ability to record information accurately and to organize it in some logical or easily usable fashion is one of the social scientist's most important skills. It is also vital for the average citizen. On occasion we all need to have a correct account of some event and to secure this information in a form that can be easily accessed. Accurate data and good records often allow us to make informed judgments and form the basis for modifying our behavior when desirable.

As an example, my local utility company recently began to provide its customers with some new information on their monthly bill. Each bill now includes data on the electricity consumption over the past thirteen months, including that of the month of the billing and that of the same month one year ago. The data are recorded (or stored) in an easy-to-read bar graph, which allows the customer to compare each month's electricity use. One can compare consumption during the current month with that during the same month last year.

Since the temperature during the month may influence the consumption rate as much as one's behavior, it is also included in the record (Figure 7.1). This information and the manner in which it has been stored for easy retrieval and examination allows a customer to make some informed decisions. For example, a

FIGURE 7.1   Chart of electricity use

AVG KWH PER DAY

THIS IS YOUR ELECTRIC USE PROFILE

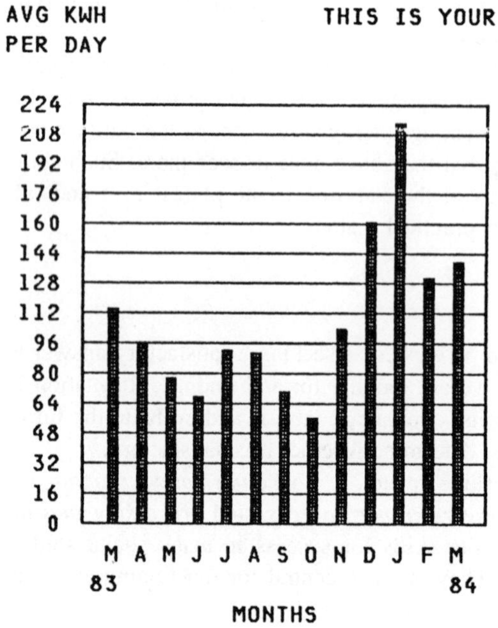

BILLING PERIOD	AVG DAILY TEMPERATURE	AVG KWH PER DAY
MAR 1984	35° F	139.6
MAR 1983	42° F	114.3

MONTHS

customer can decide whether increased conservation is warranted or can estimate a future electrical budget.

Activities Involving Students in Collecting Data. At any grade level, students can be encouraged through simple or complex activities dealing with everyday phenomena to:

> make observations over time carefully, objectively, and in an organized manner
>
> store, file or summarize such observations in some form which is clear and easily used

To make objective observations students must separate their evaluations of or opinions about an event from behavioral descriptions that focus on "who, what, where, and when." It is the difference between reporting that you saw "a terrible game," and observing that you saw two teams of football players each fumble at least five times, throw a combined total of eight interceptions, together produce only 106 yards of offense, and play to a scoreless tie.

Consider a kindergarten youngster who records each day on a class feelings chart how he or she felt that day with a "smiley," "frowning," or "neutral" face. He or she is engaged in the same basic task as the older student who is asked to watch local newscasts for two weeks and record the following sort of information:

> number and type of commercials
>
> amount of time spent on sports
>
> amount of time spent on weather
>
> amount of time spent on news
>
> amount of time spent on *each* news story (length)
>
> number of live commentators used (newscaster, weatherperson, etc.)
>
> number of commentators who are female or members of a minority group

Natural, after-school activities often provide similar opportunities to practice and apply data collection skills. Many youngsters enjoy keeping score at a baseball game on a program scorecard, which is an elaborate and initially complicated exercise in recording details and later permits an objective summary of the game. Tabulating the types of cars or the states on their license plates or the numbers of people in each while traveling, can be both a game and a data-collecting exercise.

Ways of Organizing Data Collected. The forms used to record and file observations and data may vary. Students should have opportunities to experiment with different forms, as long as they are clear and functional. Each of us develops his or her own style of filing and saving information. However, if ten individuals organize their information in different ways, sharing and summarizing the information often becomes tedious or impossible.

For this reason social scientists and others often develop common systems for categorizing and reporting information. Some of these are quite complicated. Others such as the conventions for footnoting and bibliographic references, seem strange to students initially. Some typical ways in which data are stored are personal filing systems, formal filing systems such as the Dewey Decimal or the Library of Congress book categorizing systems, and folders with a simple keyword system (e.g., "animals," "people," "machines"). Still other forms are charts, tables, graphs, tapes, and computer diskettes. Additional ways include note cards organized in some order, notebooks organized into sections, and oral histories (some cultures and subcultures use no written or technologically-based systems for recording or retrieving information, relying instead on memory, tradition, and oral accounts).

Identifying and Using Reference Sources

Part of the problem in using reference sources effectively is identifying just what a "reference" might be. Virtually any item, including an individual, may serve as a reference for a particular question or problem. The telephone book and the Yellow Pages are reference sources that most people have around their homes.

Similarly, when we wish to consult a reference source to decide whether a particular film is worth seeing, we may call a friend who has seen it. Or we may locate a recent review of the film in a newspaper or magazine. When we wish to discover the meaning or the correct spelling of a word, we consult a dictionary. To decide which television programs we wish to watch at 8:00 P.M., we may examine a television guide or program listing.

The notion that many sources are appropriate reference possibilities is an important one for students to learn. What determines whether the source is legitimate or appropriate is how useful and authoritative it is in solving a problem or answering a question. Extending the scope of reference sources beyond those readily available in homes and textbooks is also an important part of using references effectively. This involves learning about some of the most common sources in many libraries (usually found in a section entitled "Reference Materials"). It also includes discovering which ones are suitable for which audience, what sorts of material they contain, and how information is actually accessed from them.

Identifying Appropriate Student Reference Materials. There are several reference books for teachers that list formal reference sources appropriate for students at different grade levels. Two examples are Carolyn Sue Peterson, *Reference Books for Children* (Metuchen, N.J.: Scarecrow, 1981) and Christine L. Wynar, *Guide to Reference Books for School Media Centers,* (Littleton, Colo.: Libraries Unlimited, 1981; supplements to update the collection have been added periodically).

Several books on how to use libraries and reference works in them have been written especially for youngsters. Two are Florence Damon Cleary, *Discovering Books and Libraries: A Handbook for Students in the Middle and Upper Grades,* 2nd ed. (New York: H. W. Wilson, 1977) and Margaret G. Cook, *The New Library Key,* 3rd ed. (New York: H. W. Wilson, 1975).

Activities for Introducing Reference Materials. One way to introduce reference materials is to use them to create interesting, puzzling, or intriguing questions for students that require them to use such sources. The difficulty of the questions may be varied for different age and ability groups by providing more or fewer clues. The actual materials to be used in answering the questions may be made available within the classroom. As alternatives, students may be given a list of helpful reference materials or just allowed to use the school library and identify resources on their own.

Problem Sheets. Consider the following activity, presented in the form of a problem sheet.[1]

PROBLEM SHEET

Problem: You are to discover the identity of Country *X*, a real country, described below. Use any reference sources that you wish. The ones that have been identified for you may be especially helpful. After you have discovered which country it is, list all of the references you consulted. Then tell whether the reference helped you learn the identity of the country and in which way.

Country *X*

Country *X* differs from many other nations in several ways. It covers an area of 600,000 square miles and has approximately 1 million people. It is one huge plateau, with the eastern half consisting mainly of plains with some mountains and the western half largely of mountains with some plains. Hundreds of lakes exist throughout the country, especially in the mountains, and in the hilly and mountainous regions, there are forests.

In climate Country *X* suffers from cold winds that sweep across the treeless plains and from great temperature extremes. For example, the temperature has risen to 105° (Fahrenheit) in the summer and to −50° in the winter. Although there are many fish, the people have not really cultivated a taste for them, and exist chiefly on their livestock products and game.

Identity of Country *X*:

Reference sources used to determine identity:

Which were useful and in which way:

The problem sheet could have contained additional information that would make the solution somewhat easier. For example, the following data could be inserted into the paragraphs of the original description to give students more clues. These additions would make it easier to limit the list of countries that could match the description.

1. There are fewer than two people per square mile in the country.
2. One-third of the country is a desert, but only a small part of it is sandy. There is enough vegetation in the desert to support the feeding of camels and horses.
3. The lack of abundant raw materials and suitable transportation systems restricts industrial growth.

4. The major occupation of the country is herding, although some small-scale industries have been started.

5. The people of the country are largely nomadic, customarily dress in long flowing robes called *dels,* and live in canvas huts called *yurts.*

EXERCISE 7.1   Creating a Problem Sheet

Select a topic and a grade level and create a problem sheet, using a real country as the subject. Also create a list of clues, similar to those in the text, which could be used to help students identify the country.

The country, by the way, is the Mongolian People's Republic, sometimes called Outer Mongolia. Any similar material that presents a puzzle or problem of identification, whether it deals with a country, a city, an event, an individual, or any other unit can satisfy the same objective. The aim is to have students discover the functional value of reference sources through an interesting activity.

Question Springboards. Even a basic set of questions can be used to introduce reference materials. Simple lists of questions may be developed from questions posed by students themselves or from interests the teacher has identified. Consider the following sample activity, which contains a question sheet and list of reference sources. All of the questions in the ten-item sheet can be answered by consulting the appropriate book in the reference sources.

QUESTION SHEET

1. Who was the founder of the Girl Scouts of America?

2. What are some of the customs and dress of the people of Chad?

3. What are the main functions of the Federal Reserve Board?

4. How does the per capita income of Saudi Arabia compare to that of other countries in the Middle East?

5. Locate a picture of a Model T Ford. When did the Model T appear, and what was unusual about it?

6. What do you consider to have been the most important contribution of Charles Ives?

7. What are the major industries in the Mongolian People's Republic?

8. What are some of the major events that happened in the year your mother (or your father) was born?

9. Locate Butte in the index for the state of Montana. What major park is southeast of it?

10. Locate and copy a recipe from a foreign country.

REFERENCE SOURCES[2]

Album of American History. This multivolume history of the United States is composed of pictures arranged chronologically.

Dictionary of American History. This multivolume work is arranged in alphabetical order, and includes articles on a variety of historical topics, some famous and some not so well known.

The Illustrated History of the World and Its People. In thirty volumes a wealth of information is presented on the geography, people, history, arts, culture, and literature of individual countries of the world. There is also information on foods, religions, dress, holidays, festivals, customs, and educational systems of the countries, as well as many other aspects.

Statesman's Yearbook. In one volume a succinct thumbnail sketch of each country is provided.

Worldmark Encyclopedia of the Nations. This multivolume guide to nations is arranged alphabetically by the name of the country, and provides basic information on the social, political, historical, economical, and geographical features of a country.

United States Government Organization Manual. This is an official federal publication that gives an overview of federal agencies, including their history and functions.

Dictionary of American Biography. This is a multivolume source of information on nonliving Americans who have made some significant contribution to American life. Included are politicians, artists, musicians, writers, scientists, educators, and many other types.

Encyclopedia of American Facts and Dates. In a chronologically organized single volume a wide variety of important dates are included, covering all facets of American life.

School and Library Atlas of the World. This work contains an assortment of maps, statistics, and assorted data. Each state and country is shown on a map, along with an index.

EXERCISE 7.2   Identifying Social Studies Reference Materials

Identify ten additional social studies reference materials, similar to the ones discussed in the text. Provide a brief description of each reference, and create a question sheet with sample questions that your references could answer.

Processing and Interpreting Data

Processing and interpreting data accurately requires careful attention to what is heard, seen, felt, and even tasted or smelled. Data are encountered through all of our senses, and we may process these data firsthand through personal encounters, such as attending a concert or a meeting, or eating a meal. We may also experience them indirectly, as when we read a book that describes a place, watch a television report of an event, or hear a recording of a concert. Often several of our senses are involved in processing data, as when we savor and consume a piece of apple pie or a charcoal broiled steak.

We all are familiar with the phenomenon that different individuals processing the very same data often will focus on different aspects and, as a result, give different accounts of what was experienced. Five people from a rural area, for example, who visit the same section of the Bowery in New York for the same length of time are likely to come away with different accounts of what each observed. One may focus on the despair in the faces of the derelicts encountered. Another may talk about the noise and traffic. Still another will emphasize the drab visual landscape, the scattered debris on the sidewalks and streets, and the decaying areas. A fourth will remember the melange of smells, which seemed offensive but distinct. The last member may have little clear recollection of any of those aspects, but instead vividly recall the assortment of little shops and vendors in some detail.

Each of the accounts may be reasonably accurate reports of what the individual experienced. However, all of the accounts are clearly different. Taken as a whole, they may present a more adequate account of the Bowery than any single report.

Interpreting Written Material. As data are processed, we begin to interpret them and to draw conclusions. As citizens and as students we are often called on to process and interpret information from texts and books, articles, charts, graphs, tables, and pictures. Written material often presents students with special problems of interpretation, because they often have difficulties with reading in general, an issue that we will discuss in Chapter 12.

In the social studies it is especially important that students begin early to develop the skills to analyze and interpret written materials. Students need to learn to distinguish fact from opinion, bias from objectivity, reality from fiction, extraneous from essential information, and neutral words from those which arouse emotions, and to consider what is excluded, as well as included, in written material.

Comparing Sources and Biographies. Often in interpreting written material it is necessary to compare two or more sources, and then draw conclusions. A starting point for introducing the comparison of sources can be the study of biographies. Biographies typically interest children a great deal, and many high-interest books at various reading levels exist. Any school librarian can show you some of these books. Like their adult counterparts, biographies written for children sometimes suffer from distortions, idealized portrayals, inaccuracies, misconceptions, and poor scholarship.

Stereotypes, Myths, and Legends in Biographies. Occasionally the deficiencies of some biographies persist and eventually lead to the creation of stereotypes and myths that are difficult to destroy. Witness the story many of us learned about George Washington and the cherry tree he allegedly chopped down. Apparently the story first appeared in a biography of Washington published in 1806.

As one reads today this third-hand account constructed from heresay, it is difficult to take it very seriously. Nevertheless, it launched a legend.

> Some idea of Mr. Washington's plan of education . . . may be collected from the following anecdote, *related to me twenty years ago by an aged lady, who was a distant relative, and, when a girl, spent much of her time in the family* [italics added]. ``. . . One day, in the garden, . . . he [George] unluckily tried the edge

of his hatchet on the body of a beautiful young English cherry-tree. The next morning the old gentleman, finding out what had befallen his tree, which, by the by, was a great favorite, came into the house, and with much warmth, asked for the mischievous author. . . . Presently George and his hatchet make their appearance. 'George,' said his father, 'do you know who killed that beautiful little cherry tree yonder in the garden?' This was a *tough question;* and George staggered under it for a moment; but quickly recovered himself: and looking at his father, with the sweet face of youth brightened with the inexpressive charm of all-conquering truth, he bravely cried out, 'I can't tell a lie, Pa; you know I can't tell a lie. I did cut it with my hatchet.' '— Run to my arms, you dearest boy, cried his father in transports, run to my arms; glad am I, George, that you killed my tree; for you have paid me for it a thousand fold. Such an act of heroism in my son is worth more than a thousand trees, though blossomed with silver, and their fruits of purest gold.' "[3]

Students cannot possibly be kept from reading all biographies that suffer from such flaws, nor should they be. To attempt to "shield" students completely from all of these types of written material would be both undesirable and unrealistic. Doing so would not help them begin to deal with the same kind of deficiencies that abound in the mass media and the everyday world of experience. Rather than attempt to avoid such materials completely, teachers need to help students to interpret and evaluate them.

Biography Activities. One approach is to have children read several books on the same subject and then compare the findings. Unlike most adults, children, particularly younger ones, do not seem to find this task repetitive. In fact, they often may read the same book several times.

A series of questions similar to the following biography exercise may be used to help students develop their processing and interpretive skills. The activity also helps children acquire a more balanced insight into an individual's life. Not all of the questions would be appropriate for younger children, but at least some of them could be used at any level.

BIOGRAPHY EXERCISE

1. What things were the *same* in the books you read?
2. What things were *different* in the books you read?
3. What did each of the books say about _____ when he/she was small?
4. What did each of the books say were the most important things that _____ did in his/her life?
5. Whom did each of the books say were the most important people in _____'s life?
6. How would you sum up what you have learned from reading all of the books about _____'s life?
7. If a friend asked you to tell him or her which *one* book he or she should read, which one would you choose? Why?
8. After you finish answering the other questions, use one of the encyclopedias in the

classroom or the library, and see what *it* says about _____. What kind of things did the encyclopedia say that were also in the books you read?

9. What kind of things did the encyclopedia *leave out* that were in the books you read? Why do you suppose this happened?

Encyclopedias as References. Children should discover the inevitable shortcomings of otherwise useful general reference works such as encyclopedias. All encyclopedias, because of their attempt to be comprehensive, are severely limited in the space they can devote to any topic. No matter how authoritatively and carefully a topic has been researched and written, an encyclopedia entry must omit much material that students often need to get a balanced understanding of an individual or group.

Consider, for example, if you were asked to sum up your life in an essay. The only restrictions are that it must be no more than 250 words, all of the information must be accurate and objective, the reading level must be no higher than the fourth grade, and that you must include everything the reader needs to know. He or she will have no other information about you.

If you feel at all uncomfortable about having to record your life's history for all to see under these limiting conditions, keep in mind that entire *groups* or *nations* are often described in encyclopedias in even fewer words. Students need to understand the necessary constraints under which encyclopedias operate. Moreover, they need to regard an encyclopedia as a *starting point* for a serious investigation, rather than a one-stop comprehensive reference library.

Interpreting Charts, Graphs, and Tables. In our society much of the information we share with one another is communicated through charts, graphs, and tables. Each edition of a local paper will carry many of these and citizens similarly use them to summarize information or to simplify communication. When we ask our neighbors what their vacation was like, much of their answer may be in the form of snapshots. If an economist wishes to cut through reams of statistical data and complex discussions to present the magnitude and distribution of unemployment in the United States he or she may use a graph, such as the one shown in Figure 7.2. Figures such as that one summarize and communicate quickly a great deal of otherwise complex data.

Extracting facts, generalizations, and hypotheses from such summaries through interpretation, however, is often not easy for either adults or children without some experience and training. This is especially true when the picture, table, chart or graph contains many details or quantitative data or when the terms used and the way in which information is organized are not familiar. Students need assistance in experimenting both with creating and analyzing different types of figures.

Guidelines for Discussing Charts, Graphs, and Tables. Many kinds of meaningful questions may be asked to help students become more skilled at processing and interpreting data from charts, graphs, and tables. Some guidelines for discussing figures follow, along with sample questions and an appropriate sequence.

FIGURE 7.2   Unemployment in the United States, 1947–1976

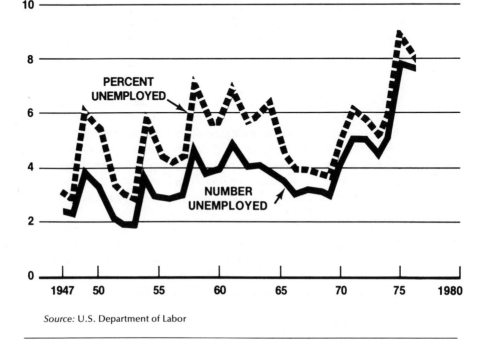

Unemployment in the United States
1947 - 1976
MILLIONS OF PERSONS/PERCENT OF WORKERS UNEMPLOYED

Source: U.S. Department of Labor

1. What does the figure show? (Ask a series of questions that relate to the caption or title, the facts presented, and each major set of data in the figure.)
2. What is similar and what is different in the figure? (Ask a series of questions that require students to compare and contrast sets of data.)
3. What conclusions can you draw or how would you sum up this figure in a sentence? (Ask a series of questions that call for students to raise hypotheses, make generalizations, or organize the facts.)

Chart, Graph, and Table Activities. Even young children may be introduced to the use and interpretation of tables, charts, and graphs through natural or practical examples and activities. In class a graph similar to the one shown in Figure 7.3 may be constructed and analyzed using simple materials and a basic set of questions. The materials necessary are a marking pen, a jar of paste, a sheet of paper approximately 2′ x 4′, and twelve sets of different colored paper measuring 1½″ x 3″, each set with seven pieces.

FIGURE 7.3   Birthday graph

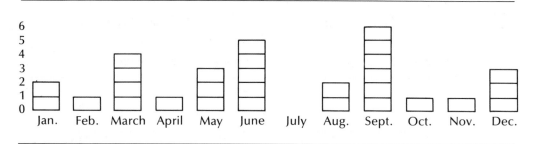

Children are asked to name the months of the year, which are recorded along the bottom of the graph. Each child can identify or be given the month of his or her birthday, and then can paste one of the colored pieces at the base of the graph above the appropriate month. A different colored piece should be used for each month, and pieces should be pasted one atop the other. When the children are finished, the units of pieces for each month may be counted and listed at the left of the graph, and the results can be analyzed and discussed. A similar graph could be made with fabric pieces and a flannel board.

Some figures that could be used for analysis with older children are shown in Figures 7.4 and 7.5. Other than those figures which students themselves create, useful tables, charts, and graphs often can be found in newspapers and periodicals, such as *The New York Times, USA Today,* and *Newsweek.* Figures in popular publications such as these usually deal with current events and generally are sim-

FIGURE 7.4   Graph of federal budget deficit

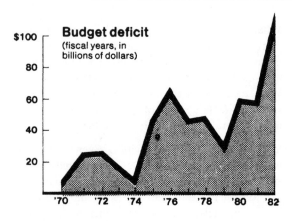

Source: Office of Management and Budget

FIGURE 7.5 Percentage of time spent in various activities this past Saturday and Sunday by members of our group

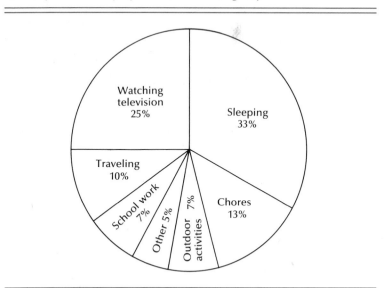

ple to follow. They allow a teacher easily to combine a current events lesson with the development of interpretation skills.

By introducing children gradually to charts and graphs, a teacher allows them first to gain competence in handling small, simple sets of data. They can be introduced to more difficult examples gradually, rather than being overwhelmed at the outset. Teachers can help provide natural experiences by incorporating tables, charts, and graphs into all of their lessons where these figures help explain a point.

Processing Information from Pictures. Some of the most common and interesting teaching materials in the social studies are pictures or pictorial print materials. Students generally enjoy them and the mass media make them easily and inexpensively available to us. The Sunday *New York Times Magazine,* for example, has outstanding pictorial material in both its articles and advertisements. A standby of teachers for years, *National Geographic,* is a continuous source of material on different countries and peoples.

Research data also suggest that learning through imagery, such as pictures, often is easier than through other forms.[4] For primary-grade children especially, pictorial materials are a very good way to present social studies subject matter. Such visual material can be used in individual lessons or units or on bulletin boards to spark interest in a topic.

Several media books describe the types of picture that are available and how they may be used in the classroom. The National Council for the Social Studies publication, *Reach for a Picture,* by Leonard Kenworthy is one such useful, brief guide.[5] In planning for teaching you may want to begin saving different types of pictures from magazines and other sources and to file them for future reference. Although many commercial sets of pictures are available and are especially designed for elementary classes, they are often quite expensive.

Types of Pictures. It would be impossible to categorize all of the pictures that could be used in the social studies. Many, such as a picture of a mountain or the Washington Monument, appear to be self-explanatory and *informational*. Others, such as Figure 7.6 *tell a story* or help students see relationships. Still others are more *open-ended*, permitting different viewers to read many interpretations of what is being communicated. These pictures provide springboards for discussion. Still other photos are *expressive;* they portray human emotions or arouse them in the viewer. Shots of starving people, war ravaged areas, and little children are examples of expressive pictures.

FIGURE 7.6   Using pictures to show relationships

Things change.   **43**

Source: McGraw-Hill Social Studies, *Looking at Me, Teacher's Manual* (New York: McGraw-Hill, 1983), p. 84. Reprinted by permission.

Discussing Pictures. In handling the discussion of open-ended and expressive pictures, the following steps are suggested:

1. Encourage the children to make inferences about what is happening through a question such as, What is happening in this picture? Allow the children some time to study the picture and to think about it. Encourage expansion on short answers and diversity in responses by questions such as, Do you see anything else in the picture? and Can anyone else tell me what he or she thinks is happening in this picture?
2. If people are included in the picture, focus on their feelings and intentions. Ask questions such as, How do you think the person is feeling? and What do you think the person is thinking about?
3. Relate the picture to events in the children's lives. Raise questions such as Does this remind you of anything in your own lives? or Does this make you think of anyone you know?
4. Summarize or draw conclusions from the discussion. If a problem was suggested in the picture, elicit some solutions and discuss the pros and cons of each. Questions such as the following may be helpful: How could we label this picture? What was this picture about? What will happen now?

Chronological Skills: Using Timelines and Time Charts

Apart from research and analysis tools, students also require some skills in relating how people, places, and things are oriented in time. Adults are familiar with and comfortable in using time concepts such as *a long time ago, recently, in the past,* and *infinity.* Children, on the other hand, often find them confusing and difficult to use in comparing historical events. For first graders a ''long time ago'' may mean when they were born. Distinguishing that time period from the one when the European explorers set sail across the Atlantic is difficult for a young child.

Developing a Concept of Time

In each society the larger culture and the individual's immediate subculture shapes both the ways in which we understand time and the ways in which we respond to its passage. Thus a New Yorker from Manhattan may characterize the pace of life in rural Georgia as ''slow.'' A very young child's concept of time involves understanding which items or events came first and which came last. It also includes a sense of what typically happens as the result of the passage of units we call hours, days, weeks, months, or years.

For older students the concept includes understanding the interrelationship of events and individuals over a temporal period. At this point students are acquiring a sense of what is meant by a unit of time such as a century. Eventually children come to understand the abstractness and arbitrariness of all units of time, whether they be measured in nanoseconds (billionths of a second) or some new standard.

Learning to tell time, although initially confusing to some youngsters, is a simpler task than developing concepts of time. Learning to read a clock's or watch's output is rather a process of decoding information and associating certain readings with particular events. The advent of digital time telling has further simplified the process. Digital output tells the child exactly what is meant, often including the appropriate A.M. or P.M. designation.

Activities Using Timelines and Charts

Timelines and charts provide a simple system for ordering and comparing events. A timeline can be as basic as the one shown in Figure 7.7, or a teacher and student may add as much detail as is desired. In making and using timelines and charts students themselves should be allowed to sort data and do the actual construction. The process of organizing and ordering data in sequence, comparing and contrasting events, is crucial to developing chronological skills.

Time charts are similar to other charts but are used to organize information in some time sequence. Often some extended research may be required in order to collect and order the material for the chart. Timelines and charts may be combined with other material such as maps to clarify and summarize data (See Figure 7.8).

In introducing timelines and charts to young children teachers might ask parents to assist in activities similar to the following. Construct a simple time line that shows when the student was born and includes events such as:

birth of a brother or sister

arrival of a pet

acquiring a special toy such as a bicycle

moving to your current address

learning to walk

Older students might be given lists of events and asked to organize them along a timeline. Consider, for example, the following list: the beginning of the Civil War, the Spanish-American War, the amendment requiring the direct election of senators, the amendment requiring women's suffrage, the United States' entrance into World War II, President Kennedy's sending of troops to Vietnam, and man first walks on the moon. Data covering periods ranging from a day to many cen-

FIGURE 7.7   Simple timeline of some major Civil War battles

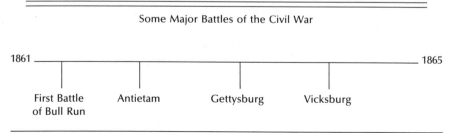

Some Major Battles of the Civil War

1861 — First Battle of Bull Run — Antietam — Gettysburg — Vicksburg — 1865

FIGURE 7.8   Timeline related to spatial information

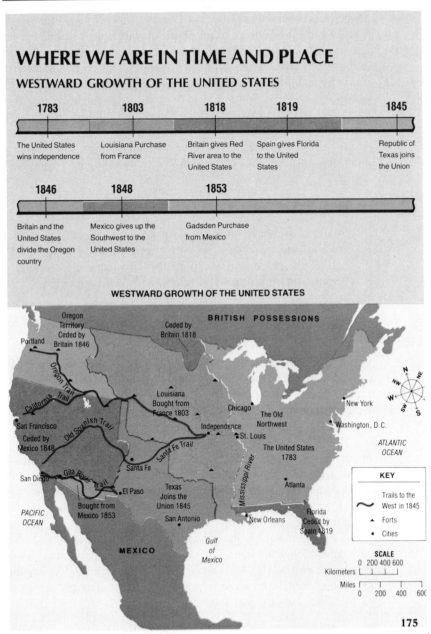

Source: Peter Martorella et al. *Elementary Social Studies.* Copyright 1983. McGraw-Hill Book Company. Reprinted by permission.

turies can be ordered by students, working individually or in groups, along time-lines.

Three-Dimensional Timelines and Charts. Timelines and charts also can be *three-dimensional*. For example, on a simple clothes hanger mobile events may be represented by drawings, pictures from magazines, or artwork. The representations of the events are attached by string or yarn to the hanger in the correct chronological order and with the appropriate dates. Any unit of time may be used — a day, a decade, a century. Some themes or subjects that might be used for timeline mobiles are Constitutional amendments, major inventions, and changes in transportation.

A three-dimensional timeline to help intermediate and middle-grade students order their own histories is the lifeline activity in Figure 7.9.

EXERCISE 7.3   Lifeline Activity

Select a group of five to seven students, grades 2–8 and do the lifeline activity in the text with them. Identify the grade level and briefly describe and evaluate the results of the activity. Include copies of the students' lifelines with your report.

Spatial Skills: Using Maps and Globes

Competent citizens must be able to locate themselves and others in space and to travel about successfully. They also need to become more aware of the significant spatial objects in their environment and to understand how our spatial view of the world shapes many of our social perspectives. *Maps* and *globes* are two of the common tools for developing and applying spatial skills.

However, these tools, which have proven so useful to social scientists, are highly abstract models. A globe is an abstract model of the earth. In turn, maps are models or representations of portions of a globe. Initially, when maps and globes are first encountered by children, they are difficult to comprehend.

Maps and globes do not look to a child at all like that which they are supposed to represent. Elements such as "imaginary lines," which do not exist in reality but are clearly visible on maps and globes, are confusing. Boundary lines, latitude and longitude lines, and the equator, for example, have no concrete referents in the real world. Moreover, many of the maps and globes that are used in classrooms contain far more information than the average elementary student (or teacher) can understand or use.

Guidelines for Developing Spatial Skills

The development of spatial skills, as of social studies skills, should be an ongoing and systematic process at all grade levels. Further, activities and text materials

FIGURE 7.9   Three-dimensional timeline activity

LIFELINE TIMELINE ACTIVITY

Materials List

Roll of transparent tape for each group

Large box of crayons for each group

Pile of 3″ x 5″ blank cards for each group

Pile of colored construction paper for each group

Felt-tipped colored pens for each group

6′ piece of string or yarn for each child

Pair of scissors for each child

Pencil or pen for each child

Procedures

Organize the children arbitrarily into groups of five in an area where they will have plenty of room to spread out with their materials. A floor area may be a good place. Give directions such as these:

Will each of you hold up your pieces of string (or yarn) like this? [Demonstrate by stretching out your arms with one end of the string in the left hand and the other in your right.] This is your lifeline. One end is the beginning and the other is the end of your life. You are to put on your lifeline all of the things you can think of that have been or are important in your life. You can draw pictures of the important things, or cut out things that show them. [If the children are old enough, they also may be encouraged to write on the pieces.] After you decide on the important things and make them, put them on your life-lines with tape or in some other way. Put the *first* important thing that ever happened to you *first* on the tape. [And so on.] *You may include anything you like and show it in any way you like.* Use and share any of the materials you have in your group.

Once each child is started, try to refrain from helping too much to avoid structuring student responses. As they complete their lifelines, children should be paired off to share them, describing and explaining each event. When each pair finishes, create a new pair until each child has finished and has had an opportunity to share with at least two others. Finally, let the children hang their lifelines around the room or on lines strung up and then to move about to examine all those which they have not seen.

Source: Adapted from an activity in *Man: A Course of Study* (MACOS), produced by Education Development Center, Cambridge, Mass.

should reinforce and expand skills that children have acquired in previous learning experiences and in earlier grades.

One way to accomplish this is to list skills that will be addressed across the elementary and middle-school curriculum. Here is such a list:

Guidelines for Developing Map and Globe Skills

Primary Grades

Using three-dimensional objects such as blocks, toys, and dolls to represent the relative spatial locations of objects.

Constructing simple maps to represent objects in space.

Reading and using home, school, street, and neighborhood maps.

Reading and using picture maps.

Identifying and using the globe as a model of the earth.

Identifying and using maps to represent some portion(s) of the earth.

Distinguishing between a map and a globe.

Identifying familiar cities, states, regions, and countries.

Identifying relative size and position of spatial objects.

Identifying boundaries.

Interpreting pictures and colors as symbols on maps and globes.

Distinguishing between land and water masses.

Tracing routes.

Using basic map keys.

Using cardinal directional words to identify locations.

Calculating relative distance.

Using simple grids to locate spatial objects.

Using simple maps and globes to answer questions and solve problems.

Intermediate and Middle Grades

Using an atlas.

Using a compass to determine North, South, East, West, and intermediate points.

Identifying and comparing map projections.

Identifying and comparing distortions in different map projections.

Identifying the four seasons, day, year, night, and day as a function of the earth's rotation and its position relative to the sun.

Identifying great circle routes.

Identifying meridians.

Using the equator to determine location.

Using latitude and longitude to determine location.

Using latitude to infer climate.

Using longitude to infer time differences.

Constructing maps using scale and detail.

Comparing maps of different scales.

Reading and using basic information from travel maps.

Reading and using many types of maps, such as climate region, population distribution, landform, elevation, resources, and economic activity maps.

Using several types of maps and globes to answer questions and solve problems.

Several other guidelines exist for spatial skills in the elementary and middle school grades. Jarolimek, for example, has identified nineteen skills for the primary grades and twenty-eight for the intermediate and upper grades.[6] Similar basic reference guides are provided in the Thirty-Third Yearbook of the National Council for the Social Studies, *Skill Development in the Social Studies,*[7] the Fortieth Yearbook, *Focus on Geography: Key Concepts and Teaching Strategies,*[8] and the report by Rice and Cobb, *What Can Children Learn in Geography?*[9] As we suggested in Chapter 2, all such guidelines, including the one in this text, should be used flexibly by teachers.

Introducing Maps

Since maps and globes are the primary tools for teaching spatial skills, it is important that children be properly introduced to them. The initial stages of instruction in using maps and globes should concentrate on immediate, concrete referents. Therefore a child's first maps should be of his or her immediate environment, such as the school classroom, the home, and areas bordering each.

Barbara Bartz has recommended that a child's first map of the United States should be created in the form of a huge jigsaw puzzle with large, thick pieces so that a child can hold it, walk on it, and observe it from different perspectives.[10] She suggests further that maps used with children should meet the three basic criteria of *simplicity, visibility,* and *usefulness of information.* Maps for instruction with children should contain only as much information as is needed, should be easily seen and examined, and should contain information that children can apply in some way to their daily lives.

Varieties of Maps. Students also should be introduced to the wide range of maps that exist. Children should discover early that although one type of map or globe can answer spatial questions, other types will be needed for different questions. Besides the traditional questions of How do I get from here to there? or Where is a place located? maps can help answer questions such as Where are concentrations of minorities and ethnic groups in the United States? or What are the most promising areas to locate new major league baseball franchises? Some different types of maps are shown in Figures 7.8, and 7.11–7.12.

As children begin to explore different types of maps, they may be introduced to the central spatial concepts. These include *map symbols, scale,* and *cardinal directions.*

Symbols and Scale. One of the prerequisites for using any map properly is some understanding of the language used or how to "read" a map. Symbols and scale are two important elements of map communication which children need to learn fairly early. Even a simple map may employ a symbol, a boundary line, and some form of scale, if only 1:1.

Once the basic concept of map symbol has been learned, students gradually can be introduced to the symbols commonly used on maps and to the meaning of colors used, such as blue to represent water. The inches-to-miles or centimeters-to-kilometers scale commonly found on road maps can be introduced when they are first used.

0   10

Scale: One inch equals two miles

When symbols and scale are presented in this fashion, students have a better chance of understanding that they may be created arbitrarily, but that some standardization ultimately makes communication easier. When map makers agree on a common symbol for railroad tracks, for example, our task of reading a map is made easier.

Cardinal Directions. Part of the language of spatial communication generally is the use of cardinal directions: north, south, east, and west. These are highly abstract and complex concepts for students to learn. Cardinal directions (points of the compass) often are confusing both to students and teachers.

There are some basic strategies that teachers can use to help students gradually acquire these difficult concepts. These including frequently using natural landmarks and classroom locations as reference points. Scavenger hunts in which students follow directional instructions such as "Go to the north side of the school building for your next instructions" can be used. Calling attention to the position of the sun and its relative locations throughout each day and to the use of directions on maps will also help.

In teaching students about cardinal directions teachers must be careful that children do not come to regard labeled points as *absolute* cardinal points. Some students, for example, will mistakenly infer that north, east, west, and south are specific points in space rather than directions. They must come to understand that, for instance, north is not always "up," moving to your right will not always be going east, and the like.

Using a Compass. Ultimately, learning the concept of a compass and how it functions will be central to students' understanding of cardinal directions. An inexpensive compass for each student should be available for activities and ongoing reference in the classroom. Children should begin by experimenting with locating objects within the classroom and the school grounds using the compass. They then can move to assessing the relative locations of spatial points in their community such as their homes, city hall, a playground.

Map and Globe Activities and Materials

In the primary grades children can begin to map the most immediately concrete object they know, themselves, through *body maps*. These are outlines of the children's bodies drawn on large sheets of paper. An example of this type of activity is given in the sample lesson in Figure 7.10.

Later, students can transfer the general principle of mapping — creating a model of some object or place on the earth, as seen from a bird's eye view — to other familiar objects in their classroom, school, home, or neighborhood. In addition to

FIGURE 7.10 Mapping activity for young children

MAKING A BODY MAP

General objectives

Observe an outline description of self — one general and basic way to identify personal characteristics. Observe how outlines can provide only a limited description of something; other data are required for a more complete and accurate description. Introduce a basic notion of a map.

Materials

Large sheets of paper for each member of the class or a large roll of paper approximately 4 feet wide.

Commentary

A body map provides a concrete representation of one aspect of self for a child. It is used here to build on the earlier discussion of physical vs. behavioral dimensions of self. The child is led to discover simple mapping and its limitations, namely that it omits many characteristics of an item. He or she experiences the utility of being able to describe something through only an outline map of it, and also the loss of detail when we look no further than the shape of an item.

Suggested procedures/questions

Introduce the activity by a comment such as, "We are going to make body maps today. We are going to discover one way of looking at ourselves." Be sure that a large area on the floor has been cleared or that a large flat section of a wall is available. You may have children lie on the floor or stand against the wall to be traced by you. If you feel that some of the students can do the job capably, let them help you later. In either event, be sure to tape down the corners of the section of paper with which you are working. One suggested strategy is to do four students at a time. If you wish you can have the students hold hands and create a series of linked maps. As you complete a map, write the name of the student in the foot.

Since this sequence of activities will take several days, you may wish to stop at this point. The next steps are to have the children cut out their maps and hang them around the room or on a string clothesline. After the children have done this, have them discuss the following types of questions: "In what ways are all of the maps alike?" In what ways are the maps different?" "What kinds of things about each of us do the maps show?" "What kinds of things about each of us do the maps leave out?"

At a later point you may wish to have the children add characteristics to their maps through coloring or painting. In concluding this activity, take some time to discuss the point emphasized under the second objective.

---

commercially produced items, teacher-made materials such as toys and blocks may be used in mapping activities for building cities and the like.

Introducing Globes. Unlike maps, globes give children a *three-dimensional* model of our planet. In essence a globe is like many of the toy models with which students are already familiar. Kenworthy has suggested, for example, "In introducing globes and maps, it may be useful to start with other 'models,' showing how dolls represent real people, and how miniature airplanes represent real airplanes."[11]

Globes allow students easily to compare sizes, locations, and shapes of all places on the earth. Children can see the relationships between all of the land masses and bodies of water on the earth and begin to develop a sense of the relative distances between major places on the earth. If there is a *relief* globe available, students can even feel elevated areas of the earth such as the Rocky Mountains.

Jarolimek observes, "If the globe is in the classroom, it will provoke curiosity and a desire to know more about it and how to use it."[12] He suggests that teachers use the globe frequently when teaching social studies and other subjects. Students, for example, might locate where people they learn about live.

Globes are usually available in eight- and twelve-inch sizes for individual desk use, sixteen-inch and larger ones are available for group instruction. Michaelis has suggested that lightweight plastic, raised relief globes that clearly show the land and water features of the earth be used in the primary grades.[13] Later, he adds, other globes with additional details, such as colors, may be introduced.

Using Maps and Globes in Problem Solving. One of the most natural and functional ways to integrate maps and globes continuously into social studies teaching is to use them to answer real questions that students have or to solve interesting problems a teacher has created. With a map like the one in Figure 7.11, for example, students could be asked to pretend that they were presidential candidates trying to gain the most votes in the electoral college, thereby winning the election.

For the purpose of the exercise, they are to try to win while getting the elec-

FIGURE 7.11 Number of votes in the Electoral College by state

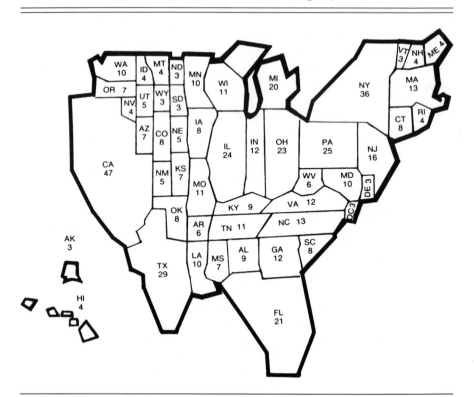

toral votes of the *smallest* number of states possible. How many states will be needed? Which are they? Which states' votes seem to be the least significant in the electoral college? What conclusions or generalizations can be drawn about possible campaign strategies?

A different spatially related problem-solving activity is presented in Figure 7.12, the Dublinville School Problem. The activity involves a few spatial variables — population distribution, transportation, location, and boundaries — and asks students to try to solve the same type of difficult problem that many school boards face. How should the problem of overcrowding be resolved?

Travel Maps. Travel maps also may be used for problem solving. A class may be asked to plan and chart a trip to a distant city, indicating routes, landmarks, cities to be visited, relative distances, and the like. Different groups may work on the same trips, and then compare their itineraries.

For older children simple travel maps are a fine way to advance their spatial understanding and to demonstrate that maps have important functions. Using a collection of travel maps from different cities, states, provinces, counties, and countries heightens student interest. It also increases their awareness of how travel maps around the world have been standardized to a large extent.

That is, no matter where we wish to travel on earth by land, on foot or on a road, the maps that help us generally have the same basic elements. A travel map of Venice, Italy, for example, while containing foreign names, has basically the same features as a travel map of San Francisco.

EXERCISE 7.4   Developing a Mapping Activity

Develop an activity for engaging children in mapping some spatial area within their immediate environment. Follow the guidelines and suggestions in the text. Field test the activity with a group of five to seven students for whom it is appropriate. Indicate the school and grade level of the students, provide copies of their maps, and describe and evaluate the results.

Sources of Travel Maps. Although road maps are sold in book and map stores, they also are available from some gasoline stations. Tourist bureaus of most states also distribute free state maps. Write to the tourist bureau in which you are interested at the state capital. Some foreign consulates and embassies provide road maps both of the country and of each of the major cities within the country. Addresses for writing to them are generally available in reference works such as *The New York Times Almanac* or the New York City (Manhattan borough) telephone directory.

Sources of Other Maps and Globes. Apart from travel maps, a wealth of commercial map and globe materials of every description are available in various price ranges. A cross-sectional sample follows:

FIGURE 7.12   Dublinville's school problem — where will the kids go?

Dublinville Township has four elementary schools: Farley Glen, Jamesville, Fort Williams, and Sandtown. These are shown in the map. Students who live within the dotted lines shown on the map go to the school that is in their area. This plan for school attendance usually has worked fairly well in the past.

But this year there is a problem in the Jamesville school area. There are now twenty-eight classes of students in the area, but Jamesville has only twenty-six classrooms. There is not time to build new classrooms at Jamesville. Where will the kids go to school?

Fort Williams School does not have any extra space. Sandtown and Farley Glen schools do have extra space and could take the students from Jamesville. But the parents in the Jamesville area do not want their children sent all the way to Farley Glen, the closest school.

It might be possible to increase the number of students in each classroom at Jamesville. Nobody, though, seems to like the idea. It also might be possible to change the size and location (boundary) of each school area. Doing this would mean that students who had gone to one school for several years would now have to go to a new one. Changing school areas is a lot of work, and they might have to be changed again next year if one area gets more children. Some parents and the school board are not in favor of changing the size and location of the school areas.

"I'm just not sure what we are going to do with the two extra classes of students," the School Board President has said.

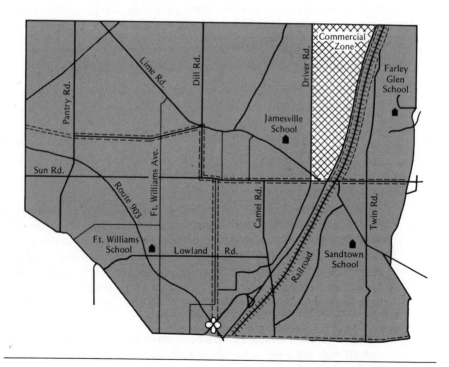

National Geographic Picture Atlas of Our Fifty States. Washington, D.C.: National Geographic Society.

Brown, Dale, and Bacon, Phillip. *Where and Why.* A. J. Nystrom.

Making Inferences from Maps. St. Louis, Mo.: Milliken.

Finding Our Way with Maps and Globes. Burbank, Calif.: Walt Disney Educational Media Co.

First Steps with Maps and Globes. Chicago: Rand McNally.

Action Map. Chicago: Dennoyer-Geppert.

State and Local Studies series. Graphic Learning Corporation, P.O. Box 13829, Tallahassee, FL.

Types of Maps Published by Government Agencies. Superintendent of Documents, U.S. Government Printing Office, North Capitol and H Streets, NW, Washington, DC 20402.

An extensive list of sources of inexpensive maps and aerial photos has been developed by Robert Thomas and his colleagues, and appears in the text, *New Perspectives on Geographic Education.*[14]

Research, Chronological, and Spatial Tools of the Future

Just as the list of research, chronological, and spatial tools that were adequate and useful to our ancestors had to be modified to prepare today's citizens for a global space age, so will our lists need to be updated. Particularly as we enter the era of widespread and easily accessible data bases, inexpensive microcomputers, and proliferating video storage devices, competent citizens increasingly will need to acquire new skills or learn to transfer old ones. Information dissemination and processing increasingly is being transformed.

Electronic Card Catalogs

Many university libraries are now switching to electronic card catalogs. These use interactive computer terminals to locate and indicate the availability of books in the collections of a single university, its branches, or even among a consortia of institutions. Gradually libraries using such systems will phase out the sets of drawers that most readers learned to use as a basic research tool. The children who enter school in 1985 very likely will attend a college or university that no longer has the card catalog they learn to use in the elementary grades.

Preparing for the Future and the Present

When skills are no longer functional, however useful and important they once may have been, they need to be replaced by those which will best prepare citizens for the present and the future. The citizens of the twenty-first century will need to learn research, chronological, and spatial skills that prepare them for the new technological era they are entering.

Notes

1. Peter H. Martorella, *Concept Learning in the Social Studies: Models for Structuring Curriculum* (Scranton, Pa.: INTEXT, 1971), pp. 114–115.
2. Wendy Sleicher, a student at Temple University and an elementary teacher, suggested some of these sources.
3. Mason L. Weems, *The Life of George Washington* (Philadelphia: Joseph Allen, 1832), pp. 11, 14.
4. See, for example, Jerome S. Bruner, *Beyond the Information Given* (New York: W. W. Norton, 1973); Robert Somer, *The Mind's Eye* (New York: Dell, 1978); and J. R. Levin and Others, "The Keyword Method in the Classroom. How to Remember the States and Their Capitals," *Elementary School Journal* 80 (1980): 185–191.
5. Leonard S. Kenworthy, *Reach for a Picture,* How To Do It Series (Washington, D.C.: National Council for the Social Studies, 1977).
6. John Jarolimek, *Social Studies in Elementary Education,* 6th ed. (New York: Macmillan, 1982), pp. 282–284.
7. Helen McCracken Carpenter, ed., *Skill Development in Social Studies,* 33rd Yearbook (Washington, D.C.: National Council for the Social Studies, 1963), pp. 148–170; 310–327.
8. Phillip Bacon, ed., *Focus on Geography: Key Concepts and Strategies,* 40th Yearbook (Washington, D.C.: National Council for the Social Studies, 1970).
9. Marion J. Rice and Russell L. Cobb, *What Can Children Learn in Geography? A Review of Research* (Boulder, Colo.: ERIC Clearing House for Social Studies/Social Sciences, 1978).
10. Barbara Bartz, "Maps in the Classroom," in *The Social Sciences and Geographic Education: A Reader,* ed. John M. Ball et al. (New York: John Wiley, 1971), pp. 99–100.
11. Leonard S. Kenworthy, *Social Studies for the Eighties in Elementary and Middle Schools,* 3rd ed. (New York: John Wiley, 1981), p. 145.
12. Jarolimek, *Social Studies in Elementary Education,* pp. 267–268.
13. John U. Michaelis, *Social Studies for Children in a Democracy,* 6th ed. (Englewood Cliffs, N.J.: Prentice-Hall, 1976), pp. 410–411.
14. Robert N. Thomas et al., "Teaching Geography Through Field and Archival Methods," *New Perspectives on Geographic Education,* ed. Gary A. Manson and Merrill K. Ridd (Dubuque, Iowa: Kendall/Hunt, 1977), pp. 179–188.

Suggested Readings

Anderson, Charlotte C., and Winston, Barbara J. "Acquiring Information by Asking Questions, Using Maps and Graphs, and Making Direct Observations," in *Developing Decision-Making Skills.* 47th Yearbook, ed. Dana G. Kurfman. Washington, D.C.: National Council for the Social Studies, 1977, pp. 71–106.

Bacon, Phillip, ed., *Focus on Geography: Key Concepts and Strategies.* 40th Yearbook. Washington, D.C.: National Council for the Social Studies, 1970.

Ball, John M., et al., eds. *The Social Sciences and Geographic Education: A Reader.* New York: John Wiley, 1971.

Carpenter, Helen McCracken, ed. *Skill Development in Social Studies,* 33rd Yearbook. Washington, D.C.: National Council for the Social Studies, 1963.

Jarolimek, John. *Social Studies in Elementary Education,* 6th ed. New York: Macmillan, 1982, Chapter 10.

Manson, Gary A., and Ridd, Merrill K., eds. *New Perspectives on Geographic Education.* Dubuque, Iowa: Kendall/Hunt, 1977.

Preston, Ralph C., and Herman, Wayne. *Teaching Social Studies in the Elementary School.* 5th ed. New York: Holt, Rinehart and Winston, 1981, Chapters 21–22.

Rice, Marion J., and Russell L. Cobb. *What Can Children Learn in Geography? A Review of Research.* Boulder, Colo.: ERIC Clearing House for Social Studies/Social Sciences, 1978.

Ryan, Frank, and Arthur Ellis. *Instructional Implications of Inquiry.* Englewood Cliffs, N.J.: Prentice-Hall, 1974.

PART FOUR

Developing Concerned Citizens

8

Teaching for Social Concern

In every society, even the most restrictive, citizens have both rights and responsibilities. Typically, these define the rules we must observe in our daily relations with others and with society as a whole. In our personal activities they set the boundaries for our aspirations, dreams, and expectations from life. They also establish the general framework for our system of beliefs, attitudes, and values, and our code of morality. Ultimately, they also shape to some extent our social decisions and the related actions we take.

The system of rights and responsibilities we assume as a member of our society influences even our notions of appropriate social behavior. It guides which actions we come to regard as courageous or cowardly, outspoken or conforming, concerned or apathetic, lawful or illegal, controversial or indisputable, right or wrong, desirable or undesirable, and a host of other notions.

In Parts II and III of the text, we have explored two of the three dimensions of the effective citizen, reflection and competence. We turn now to the third, *concern*. We are members of a pluralistic democratic society and an increasingly interdependent world. Our knowledge and skills must be guided by our feelings and concerns for others and the common social good as well as by our personal needs and aspirations.

In this chapter we will examine the nature of *citizenship in a democratic society* and the characteristics of *the concerned citizen* who must function within that social and political world. We also will examine three of the fundamental areas in which teachers may contribute to the development of concerned citizens: (1) understanding and supporting our *right of freedom of speech;* (2) understanding and becoming involved in *contemporary affairs and social issues;* and (3) *balancing national and global perspectives.*

In Chapter 9 we will discuss dealing with beliefs, attitudes, values, and ethical concerns in the classroom. These inevitably intersect with the three themes of this chapter.

Citizenship in a Democratic Society

In the setting in which an individual develops, its norms often seem quite natural. One child may grow up in an environment where mutual support and trust of others is the norm. Another child may learn that active participation in the political process, free spirited disputation over social issues, and respect for the dignity of all human beings regardless of their views, sex, color, life styles, socioeconomic status, race, religion, ethnic group, or sexual preferences are desirable norms.

Time, events, and experiences may modify these perspectives on the larger social world, perhaps dramatically. However, our early social development provides us with our first social commitments and expectations about our rights and responsibilities in society. Equally important, it establishes standards to assess our own and others' social behavior.

The Rights and Responsibilities of Citizens

Our society, which we characterize as *democratic,* has established in its Constitution fundamental rights to which all of its citizens are entitled. These rights define both the character of our society and the latitude of each citizen to shape his or her own destiny. In its inception the Constitution was a radical document, born of an illegal but successful insurrection of citizens against their government and forged from the compromises of different political and social philosophies. With its small but significant revisions the Constitution today, along with the force of law that derives from almost two centuries of judicial interpretations of its meaning and intent, serves as the basic statement of our rights as citizens.

Our Rights as Citizens. The *bill* or list of some of those most fundamental of rights was not enumerated in the original Constitution. Thomas Jefferson, among others, forcefully argued that these rights could not be inferred or taken for granted, that they might be glossed over by future generations. The argument won out, and his wisdom is embodied in the first ten changes that were quickly made in the Constitution, the Bill of Rights. It is a simple, clear, and profound set of statements of some of our basic rights as citizens. Helping young citizens to understand its meaning and significance for the character of our society is important in developing citizenship education.

Consider just a few of the major rights that are constitutionally guaranteed and that all American citizens today inherit as their birthright.

> Congress shall make no law respecting an establishment of religion, or prohibiting the free exercise thereof; or abridging the freedom of speech or of the press; or the right of the people peaceably to assemble, and to petition the government for a redress of grievances. [First Amendment]
>
> The right of the people to be secure in their persons, houses, papers, and

effects, against unreasonable searches and seizures, shall not be violated; . . . [Fourth Amendment]

In all criminal prosecutions, the accused shall enjoy the right to a speedy and public trial, by an impartial jury of the state and district wherein the crime shall have been committed, . . . [Sixth Amendment]

Young citizens should learn that some rights were considered at the time to be excessive; they might be exercised imprudently by citizens new to democracy. All in some way were controversial in their day, and their interpretations remain so. Above all, they should know that the *majority* of Americans originally were intentionally denied rights embodied in the Constitution. Several generations and amendments were required to bring all citizens under its legal protection.

EXERCISE 8.1 Defining "Democracy"

The word *democracy* is used in many ways in our society. Trace the term back to its original meaning in early Greece. Compare that meaning with the varieties of meanings the term has today. You may wish to consult introductory texts in political science or reference works.

When you feel you have a good grasp of the term in its current uses, develop a definition of democracy that could be easily understood by elementary students.

Our Responsibilities as Citizens. What we regard today as democracy, both as a form of government and as a way of life, is, of course, a much broader construct than a statement of our rights or privileges. Children must understand that it also includes all citizens' *responsibilities* to maintain, support, and make responsive the governmental and social system that our Revolution, statement of independence, and Constitution spawned.

The combined exercise of our rights and responsibilities must be the concern of all citizens in a democracy. One investigator who studied childrens' understanding of domestic rights concluded that most children already have some idea of the nature of a right by the third grade.[1] Melton suggests that the curriculum could meaningfully incorporate a study of rights as early as that level.[2]

EXERCISE 8.2 The Rights of Citizens

Review the Constitution in its entirety, including all amendments. Make a list organized into two columns: one of the rights that are specified and one indicating where in the Constitution they appear.

The Concerned Citizen

Individuals who exercise fully and effectively their rights and responsibilities as members of society we will call *concerned* citizens. Concerned citizens are aware of and responsive to the larger social world around them. They also are willing to make commitments and to take action on matters of social concern.

Characteristics of Concerned Citizens

In sum the concerned citizen is socially *aware, responsive, committed,* and *active.* These four characteristics are summarized in Table 8.1.

Central to functioning as a concerned citizen in a democratic society is the right of freedom of speech. This right enables us to share views openly in public and through the media. It allows us not only to become aware of ideas, events, and issues, but also to become responsive and committed to them, and finally to act on them — all without fear of governmental reprisals.

The Right of Freedom of Speech

One of the most significant of Americans' rights is their First Amendment right of freedom of speech and of the press. This traditionally has meant that citizens expect to be able to say generally whatever is on their minds about whomever they please, no matter what the position or station in life of the person being discussed. Every day on some radio or television station or in a letter to the editor, an average American unburdens himself or herself of some views on just about any subject or individual.

Forms of Freedom of Speech

Our Constitutional freedom to state our point of view has been interpreted broadly by the courts, and has been extended to a variety of forms of communication. Consider the case of Ruby Laverne Code of Seattle, Washington. Arrested at a tavern where she was performing as a topless waitress and convicted of indecent exposure, she appealed her case to the Superior Court. It overturned her conviction on the grounds that her dancing was a form of communication covered by the First Amendment. In ruling in her favor, the court stated:

> Miss Code is a go-go dancer with five years of experience, and therefore I believe that she can be classified as a professional dancer. Topless go-go dancing is communication, although the court and other people may not like the message. Miss Code has the right to communicate through her dancing.

Our freedom to express our point of view is one of the most precious of those we inherit as citizens, and the courts have often given us wide latitude in exercising it. Although most of us appreciate the personal freedom this special right allows us, we sometimes have difficulty accepting the *reciprocal responsibility* that accompanies the right.

TABLE 8.1   The characteristics of the concerned citizen

The concerned citizen is:

Aware

Being aware in this context involves knowing about the social world beyond one's home and community. It includes identifying significant social issues at the local, regional, national, and international levels. Further, it involves analyzing our rights and responsibilities, and examining citizens' beliefs, attitudes, values, and ethics.

Responsive

Being responsive moves one beyond identifying and understanding elements. It involves exploring controversy and taking positions on issues. It requires ethical decisions, determining what is the right thing to do in a situation. Being responsive also may involve establishing personal priorities with respect to values and issues.

Committed

Commitment fundamentally involves choosing from among the social issues one has identified, those about which one plans to do something. It is deciding to do more than examine or learn about an item; it is then developing some course of action to carry out one's intentions.

Active

We act when we carry through on a commitment to do something we have decided is important. Doing what we have decided is right is a form of action, as is altering some behavior that we have determined is inappropriate. Personal action which is appropriate to our age, talents, and resources may take many forms. For example, it may be as basic as wearing a button that reads, "Vote for Susie Super."

Tolerance and Openmindedness

The flip-side of the coin of freedom of speech is the responsibility to let others express their point of view in their way. It involves the cultivation of reason and the protection of the right of others to offer divergent arguments.

Although some individuals may swim against the tide of conformity both in their views and in their expression and although their ideas may even offend our basic sensibilities, that does not detract from their right and our responsibility. It is *our* right, not theirs, alone that we safeguard.

Understanding Others' Points of View.   To genuinely understand a point of view that differs radically from our own, we first must decide that we are willing to hear it out fully. We must also consider the probability that there is more than one valid point of view or that a right or wrong answer does not exist. Further, and most important, we must be willing to consider the hypothesis that the other person's position, and not ours, may be the *correct* one.

Being *tolerant* and *open-minded* with respect to others' right to freedom of speech refers to the range of points of view we are willing to consider. One who is willing to consider any view, no matter how repugnant it may appear at the outset, is at the *left* end of the continuum of tolerance and openmindedness shown in Figure 8.1. Someone who is willing to listen only to ideas that are similar to his or her own may be said to be at the the *right* end of the continuum.

Guidelines for Discussing Freedom of Speech

As students begin to exchange ideas freely in social studies discussions, they should formally consider the principle of freedom of speech. It is central to all other freedoms in our society, and especially for young citizens its importance and implications need to be emphasized. Here are some of the points about freedom of speech that teachers should stress:

1. It is a special right that historically has distinguished our nation from many others. Without this right, our life and our society would be much different.
2. It is a right that Americans continually have had to safeguard since the founding of the Republic. Inevitably some individuals and groups in our society have objected to the content of someone's point of view, the way in which it was expressed, or even their nonexpression of a view, when one was expected.
3. The right would be meaningless for most citizens if it did not also entail the responsibility to entertain the views of others or to let them exercise the right as well.
4. Part of the vitality of a society in which freedom of speech is championed and protected by law is that diverse opinions freely expressed and widely circulated may give rise to innovations and improvements in society, to name but a few of the effects.
5. Within our right of free speech, we may seriously entertain divergent points of view — even those with which we strongly disagree — without subscribing to, being sympathetic with, or planning to act on the ideas expressed.

Contemporary Affairs and Social Issues

It's Friday. Time for current events!

Too often a certain day — usually the first or last of the week — is set aside in classrooms for "current events." This practice gives students the impression that contemporary affairs are not a vital part of everyday life. Rather, they are viewed as just another special subject — like art and music — that is scheduled into the curriculum once a week.

Figure 8.1 Levels of tolerance and openmindedness.

High Level   Low Level

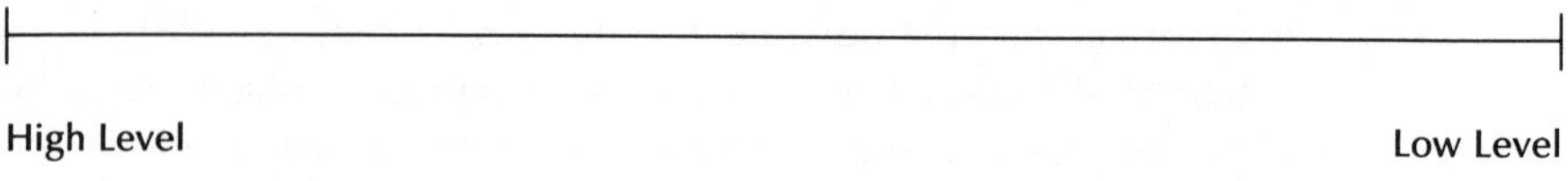

There is the danger too that young children will begin to associate certain days of the week with special events. For example, one little boy looking at our national calender thought it was a strange coincidence that so many important events and birthdays happened to occur on a *Monday*.

Our children live in a society that is inundated with information on contemporary affairs through the mass media. No matter where one lives in the United States, one can get a dose of news in the morning, at noon, at dinnertime, and toward bedtime. Cable television and many radio stations even offer news around the clock. The various print media similarly afford us many easy opportunities to learn about contemporary affairs at the local, state, national, and global levels.

Contemporary Affairs and Young Children

''But they're too young to be exposed to all of that stuff.'' Does that sound familiar? Educators sometimes argue that young children should be sheltered from or at least not alerted to many of the unpleasant events that often dominate the news.

If such a position were ever tenable, and it is debatable that it was, television and a highly mobile society have made it impossible to hold. From their earliest years American children have had the rest of the world, including outer space, brought to their cribs. In one evening, they can encounter poverty, violence, killing, intolerance, injustice, hatred, deception, dishonesty — to name but a few ills in the world that a typical evening of television may present.

As teachers we cannot and should not try to shield children from the world they must confront as citizens. We should try to help them begin to make some sense from the swarm of news and often confusing social phenomena around them.

Carol Seefeldt recommends that children begin to examine contemporary affairs by seeing themselves as makers of news, by creating news stories based on their own experiences. She suggests that teachers begin by writing a short story on the board and reading it to children. Students then would be encouraged to dictate a short event from their own experience.

> The experience of contributing to the news story and of sharing news items and events helps children to understand the concept of news. Many young children, when first introduced to news, believe that in order to have news they must first have something new, like a new car, toy, or shoes, in order to contribute. As events or items of interest that have happened or will occur are shared, children develop an awareness of the concept of news. Many kindergarten children will begin to (1) pick out words they know from the story on the board, (2) speculate about what the news may be for the day, (3) offer additional news for the teacher to include on the board, or (4) ask the adult to read it to them before sharing time.
>
> Show and tell, characterized by squirming, restless children who are waiting for their turns, can become a dismal failure with young children. Children simply do not have the ability to sit and listen as each child takes a turn. Nor does every child have something important or interesting to share every day. Rather than the usual show and tell, teachers can have a news-sharing session. Children can be

encouraged to share personal news or news items they have found in the local paper or in news magazines, thus reinforcing the concept of news events.[3]

Activities for Discussing Contemporary Affairs

Contemporary affairs need to be incorporated naturally and regularly into the social studies curriculum. First-grade children studying about families, for example, could be introduced to small contemporary cases and pictures, reflecting current problems and life styles. Children can be encouraged on an ongoing basis to bring to class or place on a special bulletin board pictures and articles about events that especially interest or puzzle them. Similarly, in introducing each new unit or lesson, a teacher may encourage the class to identify materials or share information from the news that relates to the subject matter under study.

Periodically a teacher may assess how well students are attending to contemporary events by conducting a simulated newscast in which the class is divided into four "news desks." These are the local, state, national, and international "desks," which are to prepare the evening's report of events at these levels. After brainstorming, each group can select a newscaster to report the news. The class can then analyze the results for inaccuracies, interrelationships, and omissions.

Making Contemporary Affairs Discussions Timely. When contemporary events have special significance for the local community, nation, or world, they also should be allowed to take precedence over the regularly scheduled subject matter. On the day after the presidential elections, as a simple example, children ought to discuss at their level of understanding what occurred and the implications. If a teacher does not live in the community where he or she teaches, it is important to read the local paper regularly in order to identify significant local events and issues.

Guidelines for Developing Contemporary Affairs Activities

The following list contains general guidelines for developing contemporary affairs activities. It suggests both ways the social studies program can contribute to young citizens' understanding and utilization of our rich national resource of current information and goals for the activities. Contemporary affairs activities should:

1. Demonstrate the links between the events that swirl about us and our lives.
2. Separate the factual dimensions of contemporary affairs from opinions and biases.
3. Develop selectivity in seeking out information and issues that are significant.
4. Develop a broad framework for viewing and linking contemporary affairs, from the local, to the regional, to the state, to the national, to the international level.
5. Identify ways to get more and comparative information on topics.
6. Identify *issues* among general accounts of events.
7. Illustrate examples of controversies and constructive ways to resolve them.
8. Encourage students to take positions on important issues and identify courses of action.
9. Illustrate what is meant by a "point of view" and identify alternative ones on an issue.

10. Distinguish between trivial and significant news.
11. Develop a functional concept of "news."
12. Identify alternative sources of information for contemporary affairs, and some ways to gauge the relative merits of each.
13. Illustrate what is meant by an "issue" and how it is related to a controversy.
14. Develop the principle that citizens should respond to and reflect on contemporary affairs, rather than passively observe them.
15. Support and demonstrate the general principle that contemporary affairs are an ongoing, vital part of daily life and the social studies curriculum.
16. Demonstrate that all citizens can and should be participants in events, as well as concerned spectators.

Using Newspapers and Print Materials

Some of the major sources of information for contemporary affairs are newspapers and other printed materials. Many printed materials for adults actually are written at a very low reading level and contain several instructive visual and chart materials. However, their intelligent use requires some understanding of how newspapers select, construct, often bias and distort, and feature stories.

National and International News. Many newspapers often feature local or "colorful" news at the expense of national and international affairs. Among the major exceptions are *The New York Times* and *The Washington Post*. The Sunday edition of *The New York Times,* which is sold throughout the United States in most major cities, is an especially useful reference source for teachers.

Student Versions of Newspapers. Some publishers also have produced versions of weekly newspapers for elementary and middle-grade students at each grade level. Among these are two series that have been in existence for several years: the *My Weekly Reader* and *Current Events* series produced by Xerox Publications, Education Center, Columbus, Ohio 43216 and the *Scholastic News* and *Junior Scholastic* series produced by Scholastic Classroom Magazines, Box 644, Lyndhurst, NJ 07071-9985. Although these are especially adapted for students and include materials that attempt to be both objective and interesting, they, of necessity, have some of the same limitations as other printed materials.

Reading Levels and Printed Materials. Printed materials present special problems for use in contemporary affairs discussions, both because of their structure and their reading levels. The print media does not operate under the same constraints and traditions as radio and television, and their objectives are often different in disseminating news. We will consider the issues related to printed materials in more detail in Chapter 11 under the discussion of reading abilities.

Social Issues

Examining contemporary affairs inevitably leads students into social issues. The term social issue is used loosely in the social studies. It refers to anything from a social crisis — which might be local, regional, state, national, or global — to an item of controversy.[4]

The Nature of Social Issues. For classroom applications, a social issue will be any problem that is solvable and affects a sizeable group of people. It is social rather than personal, since it deals with many individuals. Every social issue involves a problem in the sense that it calls for alternative hypotheses to resolve it. Once it is resolved to the satisfaction of most of those involved, it ceases to be an issue.

These are somewhat subjective criteria, and they leave teachers with wide latitude to select topics for discussion and analysis. They permit teachers to include topics for investigation which may be largely of local or regional import, such as rampant corruption in the state legislature. Social issues change over time, as old ones no longer affect large numbers of people, and as new social phenomena arise. What we symbolize as the high tech revolution, for example, is a phenomenon of only the last decade. It has spawned a major social issue revolving around people versus machines, and what the work force of the twenty-first century will be like.

Social Issue Topics. Some other social issues that exist today either in our nation or the world at large are:

environmental pollution	religious freedom
world hunger and starvation	wars and armed conflicts
equitable treatment for the elderly	nuclear armament
availability of energy	crime
equitable treatment for ethnic groups	human rights
distribution of the world's resources	unemployment
racial equity	sex equity

Sources of Materials on Social Issues. In addition to those sources already mentioned, many local and national civic and public interest groups provide free or inexpensive materials and assistance to teachers on social issues. A few of these are the League of Women Voters, The American Civil Liberties Union, the American Friends Service, the National Council of Churches, and the Anti-Defamation League. The Public Affairs Committee, Inc., 381 Park Avenue South, New York, NY 10016 has an ongoing program to produce brief, inexpensive pamphlets on a wide range of timely social issues. The National Council for the Social Studies also issues periodical publications on selected social issues.

Social Consciousness and Social Action

Citizens of any age exhibit consciousness of social issues when they decide there is something in their society that requires some personal attention. Social consciousness may be directed toward those things which can be easily changed with minimal effect on society, or toward those which require complex changes that will have far-reaching consequences. It can be developed early in children. A kindergarten child, for example, who recognizes that the playground has too much litter on it displays one level of social consciousness.

Jarolimek advises,

> To be socially active does not mean that young children have to be concerned with the great social issues of our time. But they can and should be involved in experiences that bridge the gap between what is learned in school and the real world in which they live. They can and should practice skills and apply knowledge that prepares them for intelligent and responsible involvement in social affairs and the society of which they are a part.[5]

More than anything else, social consciousness involves an awareness that it is both a right and a responsibility of citizens to identify and work to redress some social ills. In a democracy, each citizen is relatively free to select areas and levels of issues to address, but all should be involved. In developing concerned citizens teachers have the responsibility to encourage youngsters of all ages to act on their social concerns. This involves helping them to recognize and respond to areas of social need. These areas should be within the students' realm of understanding, experience, and interests, and should be compatible with their parents' wishes.

Social Action Projects. Some social action projects that elementary youngsters have developed follow. A middle-school group formed a club to help the elderly in a neighborhood by doing jobs such as yard work and running errands. A second-grade class identified a dangerous damaged sidewalk in their community and petitioned the city council to do something about it. One group raised food donations for the needy. Some students collected books throughout the neighborhood for the local library's used-book sale. An upper-grade group offered free baby-sitting services to families on election day.[6]

Some other ideas for projects might be helping to raise funds for a family in distress; volunteering to clean up a littered area; visiting shut-ins who want company; reading to a blind person; and putting on a school play for a group in a nursing home. With older children, the challenge is to assist them in identifying more complex issues to correspond to their growing skills.

Freedom of Choice. Social consciousness is *not* developed by telling students which social ills to address and how they should be resolved. Alan Griffin reminded us over a quarter of a century ago: "*Unless the public believes that teachers are actually conducting open inquiry, rather than peddling their own preference, either the curriculum or the teacher's freedom as a citizen is almost sure to be adversely affected.*"[7]

Although schools — public schools, at least — should not try to dictate the *objects* of social consciousness to students and parents, they should attempt to develop it in students. At any age students should be offered a variety of social issues to consider. Children need opportunities to explore issues on their own, consistent with their skills and with the support that their parents or parent surrogates offer.

The general message that a child should derive from activities that encourage social consciousness is this: "Through citizenship, we receive a number of privileges as our birthright. At the same time, we also inherit the reciprocal responsibility to make some continuing contribution to our society." In order for a society to prosper and improve, citizens must in some way give, as well as receive. Children who internalize this simple message early in life become involved, contributing citizens, who look beyond their immediate personal needs to national goals.

EXERCISE 8.3   Social Consciousness Activities for Students

Create two lists of possible activities similar to those described earlier that would encourage social consciousness in children. Develop one list of five or more activities for grades K–2; one for 3–5; and another for 6–8. Give a title to each of the activities and describe specifically how students would undertake it. Also indicate the preparation and followup discussions that should accompany each activity.

Controversial Issues

Social issues frequently generate controversy in an open society. This form of public argument or debate is one sign that our democratic system is functioning properly. Societies that are not open, have little tolerance for different points of view, or have rigidly circumscribed rights have little controversy. Such societies punish those who create controversy and also attempt in other ways to suppress and irradicate it.

Not every controversy can be resolved to everyone's satisfaction. Consider the heated debate still surrounding the nature of the universe's origin. However, the rights and privileges we share as citizens provide us with the tools to resolve or debate controversial issues peacefully and constructively.

Controversy in a Democracy. Controversy is a normal part of life in a democracy, and young citizens should be exposed to it early in a form appropriate to their level of maturity and experiences. Children need to accept controversy as dimension of democracy, rather than always seeking to avoid it. There are times in every responsible citizen's life, regardless of age, when he or she creates controversy.

The opportunities for controversy result naturally from the normal exercise of our rights and responsibilities. We do not have to seek them out. Acts as simple as identifying someone publicly as our friend, renting our house to whomever we wish, buying a car made in another country, or even contracting certain diseases can involve us in controversy.

Guidelines for Discussing Controversial Issues

Leonard Kenworthy has suggested several guidelines for handling discussions of controversial issues. He suggests that teachers adopt ground rules at the outset regarding matters such as avoiding name-calling and monopolizing of discussions. Further, teachers should ensure that all positions have an equal hearing, that appropriate resource materials are available, and that students separate facts from opinions in the discussion.[8]

Invariably in the discussion of controversial issues students wish to know what the teacher thinks. For a teacher always to suggest that he or she has *no* opinion would be silly or dishonest. It also is likely to puzzle students. If it is important for them to try to develop a position on the issue, why hasn't the teacher done so?

Teachers have several options when such a question arises. They may state their position at that point; suggest that they have a tentative position, but would like to hear all of the students' arguments before making a final decision; or indicate that they have a position, but would rather not state it until the discussion is finished and students have come to their own decisions. When the teacher really has no opinion because of the nature of the issue, he or she should share this fact and the reasons.

It is important for students to understand that in a controversy the positions of those in authority, including the teacher, are not necesssarily the best or the correct ones. Moreover, in many controversies authority figures (and often "authorities" on the subject of the controversy) take competing positions. The most prudent course for all citizens is to seek out all points of view, to consider the facts, to come to a tentative conclusion, and to keep an open mind to new arguments.

Balancing National and Global Education

While dealing with contemporary affairs and social issues, every society to some extent promotes *nationalism* or a spirit of putting the interests of one nation above those of others. The slogan, "Buy American," for example, represents an appeal to nationalism. Sincere appeals to individuals' patriotism, such as a request to "Pledge allegiance . . ." in schools, are another example.

In its positive aspects, nationalism provides the citizens of a country with a sense of belonging to a larger community and of sharing in a tradition. Although each citizen has a *personal* (family, ethnic, religious, or racial) tradition, we also share a *national* tradition, composed of many disparate elements. Though only a few Americans, for example, set foot on the moon, we as a nation identified with their experience, took pride in the national accomplishment, and were willing to shoulder a portion of the economic burden to underwrite their achievement. Nationalism also can be a cohesive force that binds citizens together, that encourages citizens to work cooperatively, to contribute to the next generation's welfare, and, if necessary, to be willing to sacrifice their lives for the common good.

Nationalism can be a force for great good when it motivates citizens to achieve goals that will benefit everyone. When it builds unity at the expense of hatred and distrust of other nations, world security is endangered. Similarly, when nationalism encourages aggression toward nations or groups of people who are different from us or when it deliberately excludes some members of a society to the advantage of the majority, it is a negative force.

There is always a balance to be struck with nationalism. Promoted to excess, it can lead a nation to an exaggerated sense of superiority, as occurred in Germany during the reign of Hitler. It also can contribute to the escalation of disputes into wars. Perhaps most significant, extreme nationalism creates barriers to greater understanding across cultures and reduces the opportunities for peoples of all nations to work together to improve the common lot of humankind.

National Education

National education requires that we understand the rich and diverse traditions within our country, as well as our rights and responsibilities as citizens. In a democracy such as ours it also requires that each of us learns how to participate effectively in the process of governing and improving our nation. It also requires that we have the courage to assess in a balanced fashion our national achievements and tragedies, our strengths and our faults.

Global Education

Global education, the National Council for the Social Studies has stated,

> refers to efforts to cultivate in young people a perspective of the world which emphasizes the interconnections among cultures, species, and the planet. The purpose of global education is to develop in youth the knowledge, skills, and attitudes needed to live effectively in a world possessing limited natural resources and characterized by ethnic diversity, cultural pluralism, and increasing interdependence.[9]

Global education includes learning how other peoples, particularly those least like us, view the world and our nation. At a minimum, global education requires that we understand the role of our nation in the world and how our destiny is intertwined with those of other nations. To underscore this last point, Donald Morris has used the analogy of the earth as a giant spaceship hurtling through space on which the citizens of all nations are passengers in separate sections.

> Just for a moment, imagine that you are a first-class passenger on a huge spaceship with thousands of passengers travelling through space at a speed of 66,000 mph. You discover that the craft's environmental system is faulty. Passengers in some sections are actually dying due to the emission of poisonous gases into their oxygen supply. Furthermore, you learn that there is a serious shortage of provisions — food supplies are rapidly diminishing and the water supply, thought pre-

viously to be more than adequate, is rapidly becoming polluted due to fouling from breakdowns in the craft's waste and propulsion systems.

To complicate matters even more, in the economy sections where passengers are crowded together under the most difficult of situations it is reported that many are seriously ill. The ship's medical officers are able to help only a fraction of the sick and medicines are in short supply.

Mutinies have been reported, and although some of the crew and passengers are engaged in serious conflict in one of the compartments it is hoped that this conflict is being contained successfully; however, there is widespread fear as to what may happen if it cannot be contained or resolved within that compartment.

The spacecraft has been designed with an overall destruct system, the controls of which have been carefully guarded. Unfortunately the number of technologists who have gained access to the destruct system has increased, and all of the crew and passengers have become uneasy due to evidences of mental instability in some of those gaining such access.

We could go on, but the point is: what would you do put in such a position? Now that you have "imagined" this situation, are you ready to face reality? You are on such a spaceship right now — Spaceship Earth![10]

In developing global awareness in students, teachers should try to show how our behavior as a nation affects and is affected by the rest of the world. An example of how this may be done is provided in Figure 8.2, which describes a les-

FIGURE 8.2   Portion of an activity on global interdependence

FINAL SESSIONS

Earth as a Spaceship and Earth as a System

Final sessions pulled together the seemingly disconnected insights transferring the "living in a spaceship" identification to "living on spaceship earth."

A transparency illustrating a real environment was projected and children were asked to identify the essentials of any environment for staying alive. This was a simple transfer of the learning in the spaceship lesson. Another transparency illustrating the earth as a composite of several systems — air, water, land, etc., — was projected and children discussed the interdependence of these systems. One by one each system was removed from the earth to see if the earth could exist as a total system. As will be noted from the dialog, their answers were astonishingly revealing in terms of how much learning input they had stored up, ready for this kind of reasoning and inquiry.

Following this large group discussion, the children were given experimental materials to

work with in small groups. A raised relief map of the world, a baster, and some clear water were the beginning. The children "rained" on the world and watched the water flow from mountain top, to stream, to river, to lake, to bigger river, to ocean. They watched water flow from the Pacific and meet the Atlantic. They *saw* the connected water system of the world. A second step using an eye dropper (to slow down the process somewhat for observation purposes) and polluted water (white tempera diluted) involved the children in polluting the water system of the world.

They tried polluting just one small isolated stream and observed how eventually, using enough polluted liquid, this polluted stream reached everywhere. Even if it flowed down the Mississippi, the pollution eventually reached the Amazon, or the Nile.

The next experiment used a constellation globe (which has a clear plastic earth inside a large clear plastic globe) and a miniature fire extinguisher. The same concept regarding the world's air system was illustrated as children tried to pol-
(Figure continues on following page.)

FIGURE 8.2   Continued

lute the air in only one part of the world. The experiment quite vividly illustrated the point as the outer globe filled completely with the small blast of "polluted air." The enthusiasm of the children as well as the kinds of discussion that were generated after these experiments revealed that a tremendous amount of sound learning was occurring in the classroom.

DIALOG

Lessons — Earth as a Spaceship and Earth as a System

Teacher: Let's just take away all the plant life on earth, the trees, the grass, the plants. They're all gone. What might happen?

First pupil: We need the trees and plants for food.

Second: No we don't. We still have animals and fish, so we can have plenty of meat and milk. That's all we need.

Third: But some of the animals live on plants. What will happen to them?

Fourth: They would die. And eventually we would all die.

Fifth: Also the plants and trees have roots. They hold the soil and rocks. Pretty soon the land would all wash away.

Sixth: Besides, a lot of animals and birds use trees and bushes for protection from the rain and snow.

Seventh: And if the land gets all washed away, where would the animals live?

Eighth: What about the air? Green plants turn carbon dioxide into oxygen. (A long and thorough explanation ensued as this youngster proudly revealed his science knowledge.) We would use up all the air.

Ninth: You can't take the plant life away. It's important.

Tenth: Yes, we need it to survive.

Teacher: All right, we'll leave the plants. Let's try using up all the mineral resources in the world. No iron ore left, no oil, or coal, no copper, and so on.

First: But we use a lot of iron — like in buildings.

Second: And we make steel from iron for lots of things.

Third: Yes, like bridges and cars. How would we get around?

Fourth: And airplanes and ships.

Fifth: What would happen to trade? We couldn't ship anything and people couldn't send us things from other countries.

Sixth: And what would happen to the stores? They have to have stuff to sell. And nearly everything is made of iron or steel or rubber or stuff like that.

Seventh: No it isn't. We have lots of plastic.

Eighth: Well, my father has a plant and they make all kinds of iron bolts. What would he do if there wasn't any iron left?

Ninth: Lots of people would lose their jobs.

Tenth: And there wouldn't be any trucks to drive. What would the truck drivers do?

Eleventh: How would we keep warm in the winter if we didn't have coal or oil?

Twelfth: Pretty soon we would burn up all the trees for fuel.

Thirteenth: We wouldn't even have a place to live.

Fourteenth: There wouldn't be any telephones.

Fifteenth: Or schools.

Chorus: Hurray.

Everybody: (Laughter) . . .

Source: Peggy Herring, "Experimental Program," *New Dimensions* 4 (1970), p. 81. Reprinted by permission.

son for third to fifth graders. The lesson is the final one in a series built on the spaceship analogy.

EXERCISE 8.4   The Interdependence of Nations

Consider how your own community or some segment of it is linked with other nations. How is it dependent on other countries? How are they dependent on your community?

Establish the ties that industries and organizations within the community have with other parts of the world. Make a list of all of the goods, services, human exchanges, and the like that come *into* your community from the rest of the world. Then construct a similar list showing the resources going *from* the community to the rest of the world.

Global Education and the Study of Other Countries

Teachers often are overwhelmed by the sheer volume of data that are available for some countries — Canada, and the larger European countries, for instance. For other nations, however, the problem is to obtain sufficient up-to-date information in a form that can be used by teacher and students alike. Many developing countries, such as Chad or the Mongolian People's Republic, may be difficult to study in the classroom because so little related material is available in this country.

Sources of Information. For years, the *National Geographic* has been a current reference source for teachers and students. It treats in conversational style countries that are often glossed over in texts or ignored by the mass media. A counterpart for children in the intermediate grades, *World,* is now available also. The Center for International and Area Studies (Brigham Young University, Box 61, Provo, UT 84602), among its many global education publications, produces a series of inexpensive four-page briefings on each country of the world. Global Perspectives in Education, Inc. (218 East 18 Street, New York, NY 10003), also produces materials for the intermediate and middle-school grades.

Some materials also are made available inexpensively or free of charge through a country's embassy. A list of the names and addresses of embassies located in the United States is available in many almanacs, for example, *The New York Times Encyclopedia Almanac.* Many international agencies also offer materials free or at a nominal charge. UNICEF's Information Center on Children's Cultures and UNESCO's Division of Education for International Understanding (331 East 38th Street, New York, NY 10016) are two examples.

Approaches to the Study of Other Countries. In studying other countries one can organize subject matter and materials in several ways to help students compare

---

EXERCISE 8.5   Universal Human Rights

Examine the United Nations *Declaration of the Rights of the Child* shown in Figure 8.3. Summarize each of the ten principles in simple language that fourth-grade children can understand. Organize a set of questions for a discussion with youngsters relating to the principles.

Select a group of five to seven children aged eight to ten and discuss the rights with them. Tape record the discussion, and analyze the students' reactions and comments.

---

characteristics of nations and develop generalizations. A basic approach is to select a few significant structural characteristics of each country to focus on. These should be central to an understanding of (1) how the country is organized politically and geographically, (2) what its people are like, (3) what makes it similar to other nations and what makes it unique, and (4) how it is related to the rest of the world.

A Sample Approach. One pattern for use with intermediate and middle-grade students in studying a country employs *institutional analysis.* Major institutions are used as the organizing themes for activities and lessons. In each country studied the unit of analysis and some related sample questions would be:

The family structure. How is it organized? Whom does it include? How does it vary throughout the country? What role does each family member have? How does the family of today differ from that of the past? What values does the family promote and support?

The economy. How do most of the people support themselves? What types of trade exist? How is wealth distributed? How are goods and services distributed? What is the relative standard of living? What is the division between agriculture and industry? What resources (including natural resources) does the country have?

The government. Which people are considered citizens? How are the people governed? To what extent are citizens allowed to participate in the political process? How are laws made and enforced? What rights and responsibilities do citizens have?

Education. How is the basic process of educating the young handled? Who is educated and which levels of education are open to all? What are individuals educated to do? What is the major source of information about the society for most people?

Social Activities. What are some of the major forms of recreation? What are some of the major holidays or festivals? What are some of the games that children like to play or some of the toys they enjoy?

FIGURE 8.3   International declaration of children's rights

DECLARATION OF THE RIGHTS OF THE CHILD

Preamble

Whereas the peoples of the United Nations have, in the Charter, reaffirmed their faith in fundamental human rights, and in the dignity and worth of the human person, and have determined to promote social progress and better standards of life in larger freedom,

Whereas the United Nations has, in the Universal Declaration of Human Rights, proclaimed that everyone is entitled to all the rights and freedoms set forth therein, without distinction of any kind, such as race, color, sex, language, religion, political or other opinion, national or social origin, property, birth or other status,

Whereas the child, by reason of his physical and mental immaturity, needs special safeguards and care, including appropriate legal protection, before as well as after birth,

Whereas the need for such special safeguards has been stated in the Geneva Declaration of the Rights of the Child of 1924, and recognized in the Universal Declaration of Human Rights and in the statutes of specialized agencies and international organizations concerned with the welfare of children,

Whereas mankind owes to the child the best it has to give,

Now therefore,

The General Assembly

Proclaims this Declaration of the Rights of the Child to the end that he may have a happy childhood and enjoy for his own good and for the good of society the rights and freedoms herein set forth, and calls upon parents, upon men and women as individuals and upon voluntary organizations, local authorities and national governments to recognize these rights and strive for their observance by legislative and other measures progressively taken in accordance with the following principles:

Principle 1

The child shall enjoy all the rights set forth in this Declaration. All children, without any exception whatsoever, shall be entitled to these rights, without distinction or discrimination on account of race, color, sex, language, religion, political or other opinion, national or social origin, property, birth or other status, whether of himself or of his family.

Principle 2

The child shall enjoy special protection, and shall be given opportunities and facilities, by law and by other means, to enable him to develop physically, mentally, morally, spiritually and socially in a healthy and normal manner and in conditions of freedom and dignity. In the enactment of laws for this purpose the best interests of the child shall be the paramount consideration.

Principle 3

The child shall be entitled from his birth to a name and a nationality.

Principle 4

The child shall enjoy the benefits of social security. He shall be entitled to grow and develop in health; to this end special care and protection shall be provided both to him and to his mother, including adequate pre-natal and post-natal care. The child shall have the right to adequate nutrition, housing, recreation and medical services.

Principle 5

The child who is physically, mentally or socially handicapped shall be given the special treatment, education and care required by his particular condition.

Principle 6

The child, for the full and harmonious development of his personality, needs love and understanding. He shall, wherever possible, grow up in the care and under the responsibility of his parents, and in any case in an atmosphere of affection and of moral and material security; a child of tender years shall not, save in exceptional circumstances, be separated from his mother. Society and the public authorities shall have the duty to extend particular care to children without a family and to those without adequate means of support. Payment of state and other assistance toward the maintenance of children of large families is desirable.

(Figure continues on following page.)

FIGURE 8.3   Continued

Principle 7

The child is entitled to receive education, which shall be free and compulsory, at least in the elementary stages. He shall be given an education which will promote his general culture, and enable him on a basis of equal opportunity to develop his abilities, his individual judgment, and his sense of moral and social responsibility, and to become a useful member of society.

The best interests of the child shall be the guiding principle of those responsible for his education and guidance; that responsibility lies in the first place with his parents.

The child shall have full opportunity for play and recreation, which should be directed to the same purposes as education; society and the public authorities shall endeavor to promote the enjoyment of this right.

Principle 8

The child shall in all circumstances be among the first to receive protection and relief.

Principle 9

The child shall be protected against all forms of neglect, cruelty and exploitation. He shall not be the subject of traffic, in any form.

The child shall not be admitted to employment before an appropriate minimum age; he shall in no case be caused or permitted to engage in any occupation or employment which would prejudice his health or education, or interfere with his physical, mental or moral development.

Principle 10

The child shall be protected from practices which may foster racial, religious and any other form of discrimination. He shall be brought up in a spirit of understanding, tolerance, friendship among peoples, peace and universal brotherhood and in full consciousness that his energy and talents should be devoted to the services of his fellow men.

Source: United Nations General Assembly resolution 1386 (XIV). Reprinted by permission.

Religious Practices. Which religions and practices exist, and which are dominant? To what extent does freedom of religion exist? How are the religions related to the daily lives of the citizens?

Relating a Country to the Rest of the World. Apart from an in-depth comparison of a country's major institutions, questions like these might be used to relate each country to the rest of the world.

Where is the country? How would you locate it and how would you describe its location?

How would you describe the people of the country? Why would you use that description?

How would you describe the physical features of the country? To which other geographical area would you compare it?

How is it like some of the other countries you have studied (specify)? How is it different? How is it similar to and different from the United States?

What are some of the ways (Country *A*) and (Country *B*) are related? (For example, Japan and the United States trade products, have similar governments, etc. Repeat for as many countries as significant relationships can be identified.)

> **EXERCISE 8.6   Creating Research Folders on Countries**
>
> Identify four *developing* countries, and create a *Research Folder* for each. Collect and organize pictures, articles, and materials that can be used as background by a teacher or as subject matter by students. For each country begin your search for material by contacting the appropriate embassy and some international agencies.

National Stereotypes. In studying a country students should not get the impression that uniformity exists among all of the people within it. Such impressions lead to *stereotypes*. We know that *all* Americans are not like New Yorkers, but our teaching may fail to generalize the same point to other nations. All French are not like Parisians, and not all Italians are fond of cuisine with tomato sauce.

Study of other nations also should avoid what Leonard Kenworthy calls the "cute approach." He notes that teachers often seize on what they perceive to be the colorful aspects of a country, although these are not really representative of customs throughout the country or are isolated cases from history (e.g., wooden shoes and windmills in Holland).[11] Suppose, for example, a teacher in another country were to approach the study of the United States with a group of eleven-year olds by focusing upon the Amish and their buggies, Old Williamsburg, Hollywood, and the image of the old Wild West.

The syndrome of "strange lands and funny people" is a related pitfall. Unlike the "cute approach," this one isolates for study or special attention what children are likely to perceive as bizarre. When teachers highlight out of proportion to the rest of the subject matter such features of a country as exotic rituals, unusual wild animals, deviant social practices, and isolated events, they leave children with the impression that a country is a "strange place" or has "funny people."

Sensitivity to Differences. As we suggested earlier, tolerance and openmindedness go beyond willingness to consider divergent arguments and solutions. They also include sensitivity to different cultural and subcultural practices, styles of dress, foods, and general life styles. Children need to learn to suspend judgment on something — not labeling it "good" just because they like it or it is familiar or compares favorably with their own culture. Leonard Kenworthy warns us,

> As readers and as travelers, many of us go around the world equipped with American yardsticks. We tend to judge others by our standards and values. For example, we rate the people of various nations as to how closely they adhere to our standards of cleanliness, or we judge them by our fetish for punctuality.
>
> When studying other nations, we ought to try to understand their values, and at least appreciate the areas of life in which they excel.[12]

There is no easy or quick way for a child from one cultural setting to truly get inside of another and to evaluate it fairly on its own terms. This requires, among other capabilities, that of *empathy* which normally does not appear in children until the intermediate grades. However, children can begin to learn, even in the primary grades, the basic principles of tolerance of differences and receptivity to new ideas and customs.

National and Global Education in a Nuclear Age

For the future of the world, both national and global education demand that we understand the dimensions of a potential nuclear holocaust and how nations can avert it. Students must know that no nation can afford to make nuclear attack a potential instrument of national policy. They also should understand that all nations must cooperate in mutual self-interest to outlaw all instruments of world destruction on earth and in space.

There need be no conflict between national and global education. They are complementary rather than competing needs. Reflective, competent, and concerned citizens need a balanced program of both to function effectively in an increasingly interdependent world and a nuclear age.

Notes

1. G. B. Melton, "Children's Concept of Their Rights," *Journal of Clinical Child Psychology* 36 (1980): 186–190.
2. Ibid.
3. Carol Seefeldt, *Social Studies for the Preschool-Primary Child* (Columbus, Ohio: Charles E. Merrill, 1977), p. 183.
4. See, for example, the criteria for a social issue used in Pearl M. Olner, *Teaching Elementary Social Studies* (New York: Harcourt Brace Jovanovich, 1976), pp. 152–153.
5. John Jarolimek, *Social Studies in Elementary Education*, 6th ed. (New York: Macmillan, 1982), p. 342.
6. Ibid., pp. 342–343.
7. Alan Griffin, "The Teacher As Citizen," in *The Sociology of Education*, ed. Robert Bell (Homewood, Ill.: Dorsey Press, 1962), pp. 348–349.
8. Leonard S. Kenworthy, *Social Studies for the Eighties in Elementary and Middle Schools* (New York: John Wiley, 1981), p. 189.
9. National Council for the Social Studies, "Position Statement on Global Education," *Social Education* 46 (January 1982): 36–37.
10. Donald Morris, "Teaching about Spaceship Earth," *New Dimensions* 4 (1970): 71.
11. Kenworthy, *Social Studies for the Eighties*, pp. 464–465.
12. Ibid., p. 465.

Suggested Readings

Anderson, Carrel M. "Will Schools Educate People for Global Understanding and Responsibility," *Phi Delta Kappan* 61 (October 1979): 110–111.

Anderson, Lee F. *Schooling and Citizenship in a Global Age* (Bloomington, Ind.: Social Studies Development Center, Indiana University, 1979).

Branson, M. S., and Purta, J. T., eds. *International Human Rights, Society, and the Schools,* Bulletin No. 68 (Washington, D.C.: National Council for the Social Studies, 1982).

Cox, C. Benjamin. *The Censorship Game and How To Play It,* Bulletin 50. Washington, D.C.: National Council for the Social Studies, 1977.

Hepburn, Mary, ed. *Democratic Education in Schools and Classrooms,* Bulletin 70. Washington, D.C.: National Council for the Social Studies, 1983.

Jarolimek, John. *Social Studies in Elementary Education.* 6th ed. (New York: Macmillan, 1982), Chapters 7 and 8.

Kenworthy, Leonard S. *Social Studies for the Eighties in Elementary and Middle Schools* (New York: John Wiley, 1981), Chapters 20 and 21.

King, Edith W. *The World: Context for Teaching in the Elementary School* (Dubuque, Iowa: W. C. Brown, 1971).

Morris, Donald H. "Teaching Global Interdependence in Elementary Schools: Old Concept — New Crisis," *Social Education* 38 (November–December 1974): 672–677.

Olner, Pearl M. "Putting Compassion and Caring into Social Studies Classrooms," *Social Education* 47 (April 1983): 273–276.

Remy, Richard C., et al. *International Learning and International Education in a Global Age* (Washington, D.C.: National Council for the Social Studies, 1975).

"Teaching about Controversial Issues," *ERIC Keeping UP* (Fall 1983).

Torney, J. F., et al. *Civic Education in Ten Countries: International Studies in Evaluation, VI* (New York: John Wiley, 1975).

9

Analyzing Attitudes, Values, and Ethics

Elementary schools present an excellent educational environment for developing concerned citizens. Since they are relatively small and often closely knit social units, all phases of the school's policies and programs, including the social studies curriculum, can contribute to this dimension of citizenship education.

Although the issues and goals of developing concerned citizens extend beyond any curriculum, the social studies program can contribute in a number of ways. Several already have been suggested in Chapter 8. Here we will consider a cross-section of principles and teaching strategies for helping young citizens to develop social concern through *an examination of their own and others' social beliefs, attitudes, values, and ethical frameworks.*

To make and act on serious commitments, concerned citizens need well-grounded and factually based systems of beliefs, attitudes, and values. In a democracy they need to have a clear understanding of others' points of view as well. Since much of a citizen's role involves deciding what is the right and the wrong thing to do in life, students also need help in developing a sound ethical framework.

Examining Beliefs, Attitudes, and Values

Each of us holds to some set of beliefs, attitudes, and values — all of which are related. Often people who have similar sets band together and become allies in some common cause or interest. On the basis of common beliefs, attitudes, and values, they join organizations such as hobby clubs, political parties, armies, churches and synagogues, and secret societies, to name but a few. People also become friends on a similar basis.

Conflicting Beliefs, Attitudes, and Values

By the same token *different* beliefs, attitudes, and values can divide us. Throughout history wars, inquisitions, killings, bombings, and holocausts have resulted from nations', groups', and individuals' inability to tolerate differences in others. In less extreme cases, the failure to understand or to consider objectively the implications of differences in others' beliefs, attitudes, and values can breed suspicion, fear, and hatred. In the case of nations, it can make the majority of citizens insensitive to the rights of minorities. It also can increase tensions between people; reduce social, economic, and political interaction; and hasten the outbreak of conflicts.

The Nature of Beliefs

We all hold thousands of beliefs, some important, some trivial, some objectively verifiable, and some not. Consider the following beliefs.

"All deserts are hot."

"Women live longer than men."

"If you walk under an upright ladder, harm will befall you."

"The study of astrology is a way to predict your future."

"God is a woman."

A belief may be defined as *any assertion an individual makes that he or she regards as true.* Not all beliefs are actually true or qualify as a fact, of course. It is only necessary for someone to think, feel, or act as if their assertions are true for them to be beliefs. Beliefs are the building blocks of our attitudes and our values.

Belief Systems. The total of our beliefs may be regarded as a *belief system.* Throughout our lives our belief systems typically undergo many changes as evidence gives us reason to cast aside old beliefs and acquire new ones. Some beliefs die hard, no matter how strong the evidence that casts doubt on them. If our belief system is receptive to change, it is regarded as an *open* one. Those systems which resist change may be characterized as *closed.*

The Nature of Attitudes

Attitudes are closely related to beliefs. They are *clusters of related beliefs that express our likes and dislikes, general feelings, and opinions about some individual, group, object, or event.* We can have attitudes toward all sorts of items — desserts, women, Catholics, wars, the economy, or even toward nonexistent entities, such as unicorns. Beliefs and attitudes come from our parents, the mass media, the texts we read, our teachers, and our peers — in short, from many sources and personal experiences.

The Nature of Values

For over a decade a vast body of educational literature has developed dealing with the subject called at different times *values, valuing,* or *values clarification.* Not surprisingly, many definitions and applications of the term have come into use as a result.

We will consider first a working definition of values. James Shaver and William Strong have provided a clear and useful synthesis of several authors' works, and we will draw on their conclusions.[1] *Values are the standards or criteria we use in making judgments about whether something is positive or negative, good or bad, pleasing or displeasing.* Our standard, for example, for determining whether an individual's behavior toward others is good or bad derives in part from our value of politeness.

Core Values. People share many basic or core values according to Milton Rokeach. Among them are:[2]

independence	freedom	wisdom
courageousness	salvation	pleasure
social recognition	self-respect	honesty
cleanliness	happiness	true friendship
helpfulness	equality	broadmindedness
cheerfulness	mature love	responsibility

Value Judgments

In contrast to the values themselves, *value judgments* are the actual assertions or claims we make on the basis of our values. From our values of honesty, equality, and wisdom, for example, we make value judgments when we say, write, or think statements such as: ''Tom is an honest person''; ''Gay teachers are entitled to the same rights as heterosexual ones''; or ''What America needs are more public libraries.''

Often more than one value drives a value judgment. Thus, our values of wisdom and equality may lead us to the judgment that all poor children should receive a free college education paid by the federal government. Value judgments are expressions or applications of our values, and both are closely related to our beliefs and attitudes. The characteristics of the four are summarized in Table 9.1.

Strategies for Attitude and Value Analysis

In practice, teaching strategies often combine objectives relating to beliefs, attitudes, and values. Teaching materials and texts similarly lump them together under headings such as ''values education.'' Since beliefs, attitudes, and values all are interrelated, a teaching strategy that focuses on one invariably affects the others.

Suppose, for example, I engage students in an activity in which they examine seriously at some length factual information related to their attitudes toward minorities. Their related value of *equality* ultimately is likely to be affected in some way. Similarly, any value judgment we make, such as ''All individuals should be

TABLE 9.1 Comparison of beliefs, attitudes, values, and value judgments

Beliefs	Any assertions an individual makes that he or she regards as true.
Attitudes	Clusters of related beliefs that express one's likes and dislikes, general feelings, and opinions about some individual, group, object, or event.
Values	The standards or criteria we use in making judgments about whether something is positive or negative, good or bad, pleasing or displeasing.
Value judgments	The actual assertions or claims we make on the basis of our values.

treated equally under the law'' is but one form of a belief statement. The practical import of these interrelationships for classroom instruction is that objectives directed toward any one of them automatically involves the others to some extent.

Analysis of Attitudes Toward Self

One of the most fundamental sets of attitudes that all students wrestle with is that which relates to *self*. One's attitude or set of beliefs related to one's self is most commonly referred to as one's *self-concept*. A person forms a self-concept in part by organizing and filtering what he or she perceives as the attitudes and reactions of many others toward him or her.

Self-Concept. The teacher who tells a little girl, "You certainly do a fine job when you are given an assignment," contributes to her attitude towards her self as a responsible, conscientious person. At the same time, she has to balance the teacher's view with that of her angry parent who asks, "Can't you ever do what you are told?" Consider the following insight into the self-concept of Elisa. What views of others toward her has she internalized?

> Who Am I? Me the only girl in the world that is the way I am. Me. I'm a child that hopes for love and happiness in the future or someday. I'm a child of 11½ years old. My name is Elisa. Inside of my heart or body I feel lonely and empty. I feel like nothing nobody never pays attention to me. Everybody in my family thinks that I'm stupid. They don't care about me not even my mother.[3]

Activities. Activities that encourage students to reflect on their views toward self can be used to introduce the examination of attitudes and values. Some examples of activities that may be used are sentence completions, fantasy exercises, and self statements.

Sentence Completions. A simple way to encourage students to verbalize and discuss aspects of self is through the use of open-ended sentences. These allow children freedom to express some of their positive and negative attitudes without fear of sanctions. Older children may be asked to write out the responses, whereas younger ones and nonreaders may be asked to respond verbally. In either case, some time should be provided for students to listen to each others' views, as well as to state their own.

Here are some examples of open-ended sentences:

1. The person I am most like is _____.
2. The person I would most like to be is _____.
3. Some of the things that make me happy are _____.
4. Some of the things that make me angry are _____.
5. Besides being an American, I am _____.

Fantasy. A quick review of the best-seller list, some of the top television programs, and the top money making films reveals that Americans of all ages love fantasy. Make believe is not only for children, and it is not only just for fun. It can be a highly effective vehicle for learning. Through fantasy students can often express beliefs and attitudes they are otherwise reluctant to discuss.

An example of the use of fantasy is the activity in Figure 9.1. It offers a playful, concrete way for children to express attitudes toward self and others, and to vent emotions. Fantasy animals serve as the vehicles for the attitudes and emotions.

Self Statements. There are many ways to help children take stock of their positive qualities and share with the teacher areas of special concern. Self statements are effective ways to do this but they require sensitivity on the part of the teacher to safeguard the privacy of students and their parents. Teachers must also recognize

FIGURE 9.1 Animal fantasy activity

Give each child three sheets of blank paper. Ask each child to write his or her first name in the lower right hand corner of one sheet. On the second sheet, instruct the children to write the first name of someone they love or like very much in the same location. (At this point, you may wish to establish the ground rule that class members cannot be used for this exercise.) Repeat the process for the third sheet, using as the object someone disliked very much. (Repeat the ground rule, if used.)

When the class is finished, ask everyone to do two things. First, draw an *animal* to represent each of the three people whose names were written on the sheets. Crayons, pencils, or color pens may be used, but emphasize that this is not a drawing exercise. The children should not be concerned if their "animals" do not much resemble the real ones. Second, instruct the children to write on each sheet one or two words that best describe the animal.

When everyone is finished, the results should be shared in some systematic fashion. Comparisons should begin with each category ("self" first, "loved one" next, and so on). The drawings as well as the adjectives should be shared. Students should be encouraged to discuss their feelings about the exercise and their own personal discoveries.

the limitations of their professional training in dealing with children who have histories of serious emotional problems. For some children, extended self-analysis can be traumatic and require special professional supervision and counsel.

Let us look at two types of self-statement activity that are appropriate for all youngsters, if handled as described.

"I Like . . ." Cards. In the first activity all of the students in a class complete an open-ended sentence anonymously on blank cards. The teacher writes on the chalk board the sentence, "I like myself because _____." Students are then asked to complete it on their blank cards. They are not to put their names on the cards, and they are not to show or tell anyone what they have written.

FIGURE 9.2   Self-attitude activity

MY BODY

Look at the items below and next to them put the number of the statement that best describes how you feel.

Statements: 1. I really wish I could change it.
2. I don't like it, but I can live with it.
3. I am satisfied.
4. I consider myself to be really lucky.

_____ Hair	_____ Fingernails
_____ Face color	_____ Shape of body
_____ Appetite	_____ Arms
_____ Hands	_____ Eyes
_____ Amount of hair over my body	_____ Skin
_____ Nose	_____ Lips
_____ Fingers	_____ Legs
_____ Stomach and waist	_____ Teeth
_____ Energy	_____ Feet
_____ Back	_____ Sleep habits
_____ Ears	_____ Health
_____ Chin	_____ Posture
_____ Neck	_____ Weight
_____ Shape of head	_____ Forehead
_____ Height	_____ Face

When the students have finished, all cards should be collected face down, shuffled, and then read aloud to the class *without comments or requests for clarification*. This activity may be repeated several times during the year. A variation is for the teacher to type all of the student responses on a single sheet of paper, which is then publicly displayed.

"My Body" Sheets. An element of self understanding for students in the elementary grades is their interest in their bodies and the physical changes that they undergo. Exercises and activities similar to the "my body" sheet shown in Figure 9.2 allow children to reflect systematically and privately on the physical dimensions of their self-concepts. Exercises such as these also give the teacher a record of each child's concerns and sensitivities. The teacher may wish to counsel and work with children who have many number 1 and number 2 responses.

Analysis of General Attitudes

What is your attitude toward marriage? More specifically, what is your attitude toward marriage between people of different religions? How about between different races? How do your attitudes compare with those of others? Are peoples' attitudes changing?

These are the sorts of questions considered in general attitude analysis. Consider the series of questions just raised and your private responses.

In 1983 a Gallup Poll was conducted concerning Americans' attitudes toward interracial and interfaith marriages. It repeated a survey that had been conducted at three earlier periods. The conclusion drawn was that religious and racial prejudice was declining. Some of the factual data that supported the poll's generalization are shown in Table 9.2.

Selecting Topics for Discussing Comparative Attitudes. There are many categories of other attitudes from which teachers can select according to their own backgrounds and levels of expertise, the maturity and interests of their students, and the scope and sequence of the curriculum.

Sample Topics. A few areas in which attitudes might be examined are as follows:

equality of the sexes	taxes
the economy	clothing styles
mass media	poverty
the family	professional sports
careers	our community or neighborhood
the environment	different racial groups
war	different religious groups
national defense	different cultural groups
nuclear weapons	other countries
school	education
handicapped people	sick people

divorce

exploration of space

the Vietnam War

the police

busing

racial quotas

In matching topics for attitude analysis with the scope and sequence of the curriculum, a teacher might develop a list of related attitudes similar to this one, which was used for the primary grades (Refer to Chapter 1 for scope and sequence.):

Grade 1. Self, types of family groupings, the home, school, class activities, classmates

Grade 2. Self, the local neighborhood, groups within the neighborhood, ideal communities, forms of recreation, the police, class activities

Grade 3. Self, selected communities around the United States and the world, cities, rural areas, suburbs, careers, equality between the sexes, the environment, mass media

TABLE 9.2 Americans' attitudes toward interfaith and interracial marriages

	Marriage between whites and nonwhites		
Date	*Approve*	*Disapprove*	*No opinion*
1983	43%	50%	7%
1978	36%	54%	10%
1972	29%	60%	11%
1968	20%	72%	8%

	Marriage between Catholics and Protestants		
Date	*Approve*	*Disapprove*	*No opinion*
1983	79%	10%	11%
1978	73%	13%	14%
1972	72%	13%	15%
1968	68%	22%	15%

	Marriage between Jews and non-Jews		
Date	*Approve*	*Disapprove*	*No opinion*
1983	77%	10%	13%
1978	69%	14%	17%
1972	67%	14%	19%
1968	59%	21%	20%

Source: Gallup Poll, 1983, Los Angeles Times Service.

EXERCISE 9.1   Examining Economic Attitudes

Following is a set of beliefs that represents the attitude toward economic matters of one Adam Smyth-Keynes. Place an A next to those with which you agree and a D next to those with which you disagree.

If possible, form a discussion group of five to seven people and compare your positions. In the course of your discussion, consider whether Adam Smyth-Keynes has any inconsistencies in his beliefs. Are there any in yours?

1. One of the most important motivating forces in human beings is the search for economic self-gain.
2. Government should have only minimal control over the economy.
3. Whatever benefits business benefits everyone.
4. Everyone should work for what he or she gets; it demoralizes people to get something for nothing.
5. It is the responsibility of the federal government to keep the economy growing at a steady rate.
6. One of the greatest threats to the economic security of this country is the rising national debt.
7. Labor should always have the right to organize, bargain collectively, and strike, if necessary.
8. Any business that cannot make a profit without government aid should be allowed to go bankrupt.
9. In terms of stimulating the economy, it makes no difference whether the government spends our taxes on "guns" (military and national defense) or on "butter" (domestic projects).
10. Poverty actually creates many jobs for some professionals (for example, social workers) whose function it is to aid the poor.
11. Because of subsidies, tax breaks, and other governmental favors, the rich get richer and the poor get poorer.
12. Most people on welfare could be self-supporting if they really wanted to be.
13. High tariffs protect local jobs and keep wages high.
14. Sales and excise taxes are preferable to graduated income taxes.
15. Poverty ensures that most of society's "dirty work" or undesirable jobs get done, since such work is often the only means of survival for the poor.

Some activities that can be used for any attitude objects include *attitude surveys* and *inventories* and *attitude scales*.

Attitude Surveys and Inventories. Attitudes may be examined, compared, and discussed through the presentation of survey results. The Gallup Poll in Table 9.2 is one example. Attitude inventories, such as the one shown in Exercise 9.1, are another. Students can often examine and clarify their own beliefs and attitudes easiest by examining someone else's.

An attitude inventory can be a composite of beliefs from many sources organized as an individual position. It also may include quoted statements or ones the teacher has created. Depending on the topic and the students' capabilities, they may be able to organize their own surveys, and collect and analyze the results.

Attitude Scaling. The work of C. S. Osgood and his associates with the *semantic differential* technique offers teachers a useful tool for analyzing general attitudes.[4] The technique employs sets of scales or rating sheets through which an individual's attitude toward any object — person, event, experience, and the like — can be assessed. The scales are easy to construct, use, and score.

Individual or group scores can be compared with those of other groups, such as a class or series of classes in a school, or with the position taken in a text or in the mass media. The semantic differential technique can be used either to analyze and compare attitudes or to *measure* the effects of a unit of instruction. This latter application will be discussed in Chapter 10.

Constructing Attitude Scales. A scale is constructed by first identifying some attitude object — for example, school, my neighborhood, war, Abraham Lincoln, abortion, divorce, Indians. Along with the object are selected pairs of adjectives that express opposites — for example, happy–sad, rich–poor, good–bad. Any set of adjectives that is related to the attitude object being analyzed may be used. Any number of pairs may be used, but five to fifteen would probably be most useful.

EXERCISE 9.2   Developing an Attitude Inventory

Select some area in which attitudes might be analyzed. Use one of the twenty-eight topics listed earlier in the chapter or one of your own choosing. Develop an attitude inventory similar to the one shown in Exercise 9.1 and related to the topic you have selected. The attitude inventory should be appropriate for children in grades 4–6.

Osgood and his associates developed a basic set of pairs that are applicable to many topics.[5] Some of these pairs and listed on the following page.

good–bad	valuable–worthless
nice–awful	kind–cruel
beautiful–ugly	happy–sad
sweet–sour	bitter–sweet
honest–dishonest	pleasant–unpleasant
fair–unfair	

Using an Attitude Scale. The scale requires a student to rate an attitude object along a continuum. Seven blanks are provided along the continuum. In the initial stage a simple attitude scale would appear as shown in Figure 9.3.

Scoring a Completed Attitude Scale. When the scale has been completed, one can obtain a total score for easy comparisons and arrive at an overall rating that is primarily positive or primarily negative. Each point on the continuum is assigned a number from 1 to 7, with the space next to the *positive* adjective, for example, "nice," being assigned the number 7. The space next to the opposing *negative* adjective, "awful," is assigned the number 1. The spaces in between are numbered accordingly as shown here.

Since the scale in Figure 9.3 has ten pairs, the highest possible score is 70, which would indicate an extremely *positive* attitude toward politicians. The lowest possible score is 10, which would indicate an extremely *negative* attitude. A score of 40 would suggest a moderate view. A composite or class score representing the average attitude within the group can be obtained by summing the score for each pair of adjectives, and then dividing the total by the number of respondents.

FIGURE 9.3 An attitude scale

Politicians

Happy	I___I___I___I___I___I___I___I	Sad
Honest	I___I___I___I___I___I___I___I	Dishonest
Poor	I___I___I___I___I___I___I___I	Rich
Dumb	I___I___I___I___I___I___I___I	Smart
Kind	I___I___I___I___I___I___I___I	Cruel
Bad	I___I___I___I___I___I___I___I	Good
Nice	I___I___I___I___I___I___I___I	Awful
Fair	I___I___I___I___I___I___I___I	Unfair
Lazy	I___I___I___I___I___I___I___I	Hard Working
Alert	I___I___I___I___I___I___I___I	Dull

EXERCISE 9.3   Developing an Attitude Scale

Select *four* topics, two for the primary grades and two for the intermediate grades, and develop four attitude scales similar to the one in Figure 9.3. Then select a class at any appropriate grade level to field test *one*.

Value Analysis

Closely related to attitudes are our *values*. In dealing with values, both in the formal and the informal curriculum of the schools, educators often swing to one of two extremes. They may try to inculcate values that seem reasonable, inoffensive, or sanctioned by the local community and society at large. Or they may encourage the point of view that all values are relative, that one set of standards for making judgments about whether something is good or bad is as good as another.

Dealing with Values in Public Schools.   Neither is a tenable position for dealing with values in a public school in a democratic and pluralistic society. As we suggested in Chapters 1 and 8, our pluralistic society supports many competing sets of values as legitimate. Value conflicts abound in our society and in our personal lives. We must choose between virtue and pleasure, being honest and hurting someone's feelings, obeying a law or our conscience, and countless other competing values.

Students need to learn that value conflicts cannot be avoided and that they seldom occur in the form of choices between good and evil, right and wrong. Rather, they are occasions for decision making between two or more positive choices. Although obedience may be a better choice than honesty in one case, honesty may be wiser in another. Reflective thought is the best guide to making the most prudent choice. In this respect, helping students recognize and grapple with value conflicts is similar to engaging them in the sorts of problem solving activities discussed in Chapter 5.

Nations also must resolve value conflicts and make choices. No nation could long survive without a system for judging the importance of values in a given situation. *Nations cannot act as if all values are relative.* Among other things, they must make value judgments about waging wars or negotiating for peace, choosing allies, and allocating national resources.

We do students a disservice in schools if we suggest to them that learning values either by rote or arbitrarily is appropriate. The alternative approach is to aid students in analyzing both the values they hold and the bases for them. This includes comparing existing values and priorities with competing sets and examining the implications of value judgments. It also involves considering the discrepancies between what they assert as values and what values are reflected in their decisions and actions.

Values and Rules. At some point in the social studies curriculum, we also need to clarify for students the distinction between *rules* and values. Rules that schools and other institutions establish and enforce imply certain values such as honesty, punctuality, cleanliness, politeness, and obedience. As individuals, however, we can elect to observe the rules without internalizing the values of those who created them.

Often in society there is practical merit in following rules without necessarily adopting the values that undergird them. As a routine matter of health maintenance and disease control, for instance, we may support a school's policies on student cleanliness. At the same time we personally may assign a low priority to this value or even disagree with the value judgments of those who enforce the rules on cleanliness.

It is equally important, however, for all citizens periodically to reexamine the bases for many of the seemingly arbitrary rules they are asked to obey and the values that underlie those rules. Throughout our nation's history, beginning with the American Revolution, courageous individuals have continued to challenge arbitrary and unjust rules to the betterment of society.

Strategies for Analyzing Values. We will now examine three basic teaching strategies for analyzing values: identifying value judgments, establishing value hierarchies, and examining another's values.

Identifying Value Judgments. One of the first steps in analyzing values is to recognize assertions that reflect value judgments. As we suggested earlier, value judgments are statements that reflect our values.

Kennedy was one of our best presidents.

Tommy is not a nice person.

The Soviets are warmongers.

You ought to be in pictures.

That was the worst plate of spaghetti I have ever eaten.

Contrast these value assertions with statements of fact, such as "Columbus is in Ohio" and "Ronald Reagan was elected president." Value judgments may be positive or negative and they may be directed at any object. They apply the basic standards by which we judge things to some individual, group, event, or item. It is as if our values were held up to some object and each value rated against some criterion. Beginning in the intermediate grades, students can be asked to find instances of value judgments in their textbooks and newspaper articles.

Establishing Value Hierarchies. Which value in life is the most important to you? Which is the least important? Developing value hierarchies, determining what is higher and what is lower in our system of values, helps make us more aware of our priorities and concerns. When we compare our value preferences with those of others, we also gain a broader understanding of how others view the world.

Value hierarchies can be approached directly by giving children a list of value terms and asking them to organize the terms from most important to least important. Suppose we consider this set of values: wisdom, freedom, national security, material comforts, equality, family security, and salvation. All of these are important values, but which do you regard as the *most* important? Record your choice at the *left* end of the following continuum. Arrange the remaining values in the order of your choice. Ask a friend to complete the same sorting process, and then compare your choices. Any set and number of values may be used, although the larger the number the more difficult the task.

Most important   Least important

Another way to use hierarchies is to develop brief value decision sheets similar to the one shown in Figure 9.4. These call for students to *translate* their value hierarchies into decisions about relative importance.

A value decision sheet presents some realistic situation, then calls for some decision about priorities in actions. Each action reflects a value; for example, in Figure 9.4 the value of *equality* is represented by the statement, "All people should be treated equally."

FIGURE 9.4   Value decision sheet

BUILDING A NEW CITY

A new community is being planned. Everything in the community is new. All the decisions about how the community will be built must be carefully planned: where the people will live, shop, work, go to school, practice their religion, and have fun.

Below are some things the planners will have to think about. Put a 1 in front of the thing that you feel is the most important one for the planners to think about. Put a 2 in front of the next most important thing. Continue until you have numbered all of the items from 1 to 7.

_____ People should be free to buy or build a house any place they like.

_____ There should be lots of churches and temples built.

_____ There should be plenty of schools, libraries, and colleges so that everyone can learn.

_____ There should be a large police department.

_____ People should have lots of things to do that they really enjoy.

_____ All people should be treated equally.

_____ There should be jobs for everyone who wants them.

Examining Others' Values. Truly internalizing others' values requires us to see and experience life as they do. Activities such as "Making a Historical Diary" (See Figure 9.5) can help children in the intermediate grades try to capture another's frame of reference. Role playing and simulations are excellent techniques to

FIGURE 9.5 Making a historical diary

Imagine that you are a boy or girl living in some important historical period, and are keeping a diary. For example, suppose you were a child during the Great Depression. Pick any day you think was special during the period. Write a page in your diary telling what your day was like. Describe some things that happened around you and how you felt about them.

use across the grades for helping children to understand the values of others. We will discuss these techniques in detail later in this chapter.

In earlier chapters we indicated that young children do not normally begin to exhibit *empathic* behavior until the intermediate grades. Even young children, however, can be exposed to values different than their own, and be helped to understand them. Children's literature is an important vehicle for introducing students to differing value systems and significant value issues.

EXERCISE 9.4 Constructing a Value Decision Sheet

Construct two value decision sheets similar to the one shown in Figure 9.4. Use any topic you wish and create one sheet to be used with a primary grade and one with an intermediate grade.

Values and Children's Literature

The rich assortment of books available for children of all ages can be used to introduce children in an engaging and meaningful way to values that otherwise might seem strange. Such books also can present familiar value themes in an arresting way that provokes thinking. An example is Norma Klein's, *Girls Can Be Anything* (New York: E. P. Dutton, 1973), which introduces primary children to the principle of sex equity.

Sources of Children's Literature

Among the sources that are especially useful for identifying appropriate lists of books are the following:

Books with Interracial Themes
Council on Interracial Books for Children
9 East 40th Street
New York, NY 10016

Nonsexist Books
The Feminist Press
State University of New York College at Old Westbury
Box 334
Old Westbury, NY 11568

Notable Trade Books in the Social Studies
National Council for the Social Studies
3501 Newark Street, N.W.
Washington, DC 20016 (New list published annually)

Distinguished Children's Literature
Newberry Medal and Caldecott Medal books
American Library Association
50 East Huron
Chicago, IL 60611 (New awards annually)

EXERCISE 9.6   Locating Value Issues in Children's Literature

Identify six books, three suitable for the primary grades and three for the intermediate/middle grades that focus on values and seem to be especially interesting. List the author, title, publisher, and copyright date for each. Briefly describe the plot of each book, the age it is appropriate for, its interest, and the values it illustrates. Also include a sample quotation and page reference from each book to illustrate its treatment of values.

Establishing an Ethical Framework

Attitudes and values, whether they appear in literature, classroom activities, or real life, eventually intersect with basic moral issues. Moral issues require us to make decisions about what should be done. Morality involves matters of right and wrong.

What is proper? What is just? What is the fair thing to do? Our moral principles or *ethics* guide us in answering basic questions such as these as they recur throughout our lives. The network of beliefs, attitudes, and values within our ethical framework is pressed into action whenever we confront a dilemma concerning what is the right thing to do.

Moral Codes

Initially many of us derive our moral codes from our parents or our parent surrogates. They point the way to what is right and wrong behavior. In some form they reward us when we respond correctly, and rebuke us when we err. As children, we learn early on a host of moral do's and don't's in this fashion.

If we never progress beyond this stage of imitation and repetition our ethical framework does not develop. Our morality will be largely a matter of acting out patterns of responses that we learned long ago and that have been refined and reinforced over the years.

On the other hand, if our family provides no clear direction for our moral progress, we may face life without an ethical compass to guide us in our decisions. We are likely to skip from situation to situation doing what seems prudent at the time. What is right becomes a matter of what is expedient. Each moral decision bears little relationship to the last one or to the next one. If nothing happens to change our behavior, we will remain ethically rootless.

Moral Education in Public Schools

Between the two extreme patterns of moral education lies an alternative for public schools in a democracy. In Chapter 2 we considered one approach to moral education that was based on Lawrence Kohlberg's developmental theory. Apart from its emphasis on stages, it suggested a strategy for encouraging moral growth. Although several researchers and other educators have raised fundamental questions about many aspects of Kohlberg's theory,[6] the general instructional strategems derived from the theories can help children develop an ethical framework.

Teaching Strategies. Kohlberg and others — most notably Donald Oliver, Fred Newman and James Shaver[7] — have advocated that teachers provide ample opportunities for children to discuss and debate moral issues at their level of understanding. This approach assumes neither that any prescribed or consensual set of answers to moral issues is satisfactory nor that all courses of action are equally good. For example, honesty may *not* be the best policy when your country is at war and the lives of several thousand innocent people depend on your lie to save them. Similarly, one *can* morally condemn a Hitler or a Stalin for slaughtering millions of people, even though they had the nominal support of their people and they made no pretensions about their objectives. Determining what is the *right* course of action, especially in a complex, rapidly changing world, involves more than looking to tradition or to personal benefits, a group, or a nation for a decision.

Moral Dilemmas. Teaching strategies that employ this approach to moral development focus on *moral dilemmas*. By taking a stand on moral issues and then discussing the reasons for that stand, students of all ages begin to develop an ethical framework grounded in reason. Moral dilemmas have always been the stuff of great dramas and the exciting issues of history.

Consider the moral predicament of Herbert Hoover. As president, he was caught in a terrible dilemma. He believed earnestly that it would be a bad policy for the federal government to give direct help to needy people. Doing that, he believed, would ruin their character, and ultimately cause them to look to their government for solutions to their problems, instead of trying to solve most of them by themselves. At the same time, he saw that the old ways of government were not working, or at least not quickly enough to help many people. All around him he saw the economy collapsing and the poor being crushed.

What should he do? Should he radically change the role of the federal government and intervene directly to help millions of people? By his standards, this action would corrupt the character of the people. It also would violate his principles on the appropriate role of the government in citizens' lives.

Should he stick to his guns and let the economic problems run their course? This would preserve for the long run the system that, by his standards, had always served the country well. However, it would also prolong the acute misery of most Americans. Moreover, it might turn the nation against democracy and capitalism.

We all know which horn of the dilemma Hoover seized, and historians and politicians have debated his moral decision for decades. Although history and current affairs are filled with moral dilemmas, fictitious cases are also suitable for framing important moral issues.

Consider another moral dilemma, which little Willie Doit faces. He once broke his arm climbing a high wall and his mother and father made him promise never again to climb in high places without their permission. One day on his way home from school, Willie sees a small boy who somehow has climbed a tall tree. The little boy is crying because he now is frightened of the height, and is too scared to come down.

There is no one else in sight. Willie is sure the little boy is going to fall to the pavement, because he is so scared. If no one helps the little boy right away he may be seriously injured. What should Willie do? Should he obey his parents or help the little boy?

Guidelines for Constructing Moral Dilemmas. Constructing a moral dilemma involves the following considerations:

1. The issue should offer students only *two* choices for a decision: Should *A* or should *B* be done?
2. The issue should be appropriate for the students' age and interest level.
3. There should not be only one reasonable or conventionally accepted response to the dilemma. Both choices should be likely to attract some support within the class. If there is no difference of opinion at the outset, it will be difficult to generate discussion.
4. The dilemma must involve justice or fairness. Right or wrong in this case should not mean factually correct or incorrect.
5. All the material to be used to present the dilemma, whether written, oral, or visual, should be clear. The focus should be on the dilemma and on the students' decisions.

Guidelines for Presenting and Discussing Moral Dilemmas. In presenting and discussing a dilemma, you may want to use the following procedures:

1. Present the dilemma to students in the form of a handout statement, an oral reading, a role-play scenario, maps, or other media formats.
2. Allow the students to take a position on the issue raised in the dilemma. If the students are prepared, organize them into discussion groups for this purpose. Be sure that in each group both positions on the issue are represented at the outset.

3. Use a series of probe questions to follow up the dilemma. When convergence on one point of view appears, raise questions that force consideration of the other. Act as a "devil's advocate" to argue whatever position is currently not popular.
4. Keep the focus on the dilemma. It is important to keep students' attention on the issue they are trying to decide. If necessary, arbitrarily eliminate options that might draw students off the hard choice to be made. For example, in the case of Willie Doit, students often suggest that he run home and ask his parents to save the child. To deflect this line of argument a teacher could say simply, "There is no time."
5. Encourage the students to try to put themselves in the shoes of all the characters in the dilemma.

Sample Moral Dilemma Activity. A dilemma and related probe question that are suitable for intermediate-grade children is provided in Figure 9.6 on page 218. It is taken from some materials used by Lawrence Kohlberg and his associates.

EXERCISE 9.6   Creating Moral Dilemmas for Children

Identify a moral dilemma and a grade level for which it is appropriate. Construct the dilemma in a story form similar to the examples given in the text. Also develop probe questions to guide children's discussion of the dilemma. Use the questions in Figure 9.6 as a guide.

Role Playing and Simulation Techniques

Role playing and simulation can be used effectively for many types of social studies objectives. They are especially useful, however, for developing social concern. They often make consideration of beliefs, attitudes, and values easier for both teacher and students. Both techniques involve a gamelike atmosphere and both get students to step outside of their usual perspective. Children usually enjoy them, and when used skillfully (and with *debriefing* or discussion afterwards), they can be an important springboard to further learning.

The Nature of Role Playing

What is the difference between role playing and putting on a play? Although there are similar elements in both activities, including the taking of parts, there are fundamental differences in both structure and function. A play depends on structure throughout; structure is provided by the cast of characters and the basic plot and settings, but most importantly by its script or complete story line. The ultimate outcome, as well as how each role is to be performed, is scripted in advance. Role playing may be considered to have the following sequences and characteristics.

1. *Role interpretation.* One accepts a role and invests it with whatever interpretation he or she chooses.
2. *Action interpretation.* The dialog, pantomime, or actions related to the role taken are created by the player.
3. *Interaction.* There are at least two participants interacting in some way in the framework of the role-play episode.
4. *Reality commitment.* Players agree to take their roles seriously and portray them accordingly.

Role-play enactments may begin with a simple story, problem situation, or scenario and may employ props if desired. Drama (frequently high drama!) is a mainstay of role playing and accounts for much of its appeal to children, but it

FIGURE 9.6 Moral dilemma activity

Gladys has waited all week to go to the movies. On Saturday, her parents give her some money so she can see a special movie in town that will only be there one day. When Gladys gets to the movie theatre, there is already a long line with many children waiting to buy tickets. Gladys takes a place at the end of the line.

All of a sudden, a big wind blows the money out of Gladys' hand. Gladys leaves the line to pick up her money. When she gets back, there are lots more people in line and a new girl named Mary has taken her place. Gladys tells Mary that she had that place and asks Mary to let her back in line. If Mary does not let Gladys in line, Gladys will have to go to the end of the line and there may not be enough tickets left and she won't get a chance to see the movie.

1. Should Mary let Gladys back into the line?
2. Why do you think that is what Mary should do?

Probe Questions:

3. Does it make a difference if Mary doesn't know why Gladys left the line?
4. How does Mary know whether or not Gladys is telling the truth?
5. Why is telling the truth important?
6. Gladys comes back and tells Mary that she left the line to chase after her ticket money which the wind blew out of her hand. Would you let Gladys in line if you were Mary? Why?
7. If Mary is Gladys' friend, should that make a difference? Why?
8. Suppose that instead of the wind blowing the money out of Gladys' hand, Gladys decided to leave the line to get an ice cream cone. If that is what happened, should Mary let Gladys in line when she comes back?
9. What's the difference between leaving the line to get some ice cream and leaving the line to chase some money?

Source: Lawrence Kohlberg et al. "Moral Judgment Interview." Unpublished paper. (Cambridge, Mass.: Harvard University, no date).

should never be allowed to overshadow or supplant the objectives of the activity. Role playing is a *vehicle,* not an end in instruction.

The Value of Role Playing

Some of the possible values of role playing are as follows. It allows one to:

1. *Test alternative behavior patterns.* By exploring different role behaviors in an enactment, children get an opportunity to test out what might be the alternative consequences.
2. *Prepare to cope with actual or potential problems.* In preparing to deal with a problem situation by acting out possible roles, a student acquires more confidence in his or her ability to handle it.
3. *Empathize with another.* Taking the role of another allows one to "walk a mile in his/her moccasins," and better understand his or her perspective.
4. *Deal with an issue directly and openly.* The transfer of an issue or common concern that may be sensitive to a public forum permits class members to take positions without having to defend them as personal ones.
5. *Seek explanations.* Many actions or social events may seem puzzling, particularly to children, if one cannot visualize how a continuous chain of events occurred. The role-play enactment often concretizes abstractions and, through action, injects meaning into otherwise ambiguous causal relationships. A role-play enactment of some of the problems that older people in our society encounter, for example, is probably a strong way to sensitize children to this important social problem.
6. *Demonstrate knowledge in alternative ways.* Students who have difficulty in expressing themselves in either writing or speaking, or those who merely are reluctant to participate in class discussions, often seem to find role playing an acceptable way to share their knowledge.
7. *Test self-expression.* A student who is reluctant to express thoughts and feelings has a nonthreatening forum in which to test them before actually identifying with them personally.

Conducting Role-Playing Activities

Successful role-playing activities require advance planning, and attention to how the stages are to unfold. Teachers need to be prepared for the honest emotions that may emerge when students become immersed in a role. Beyond the dramatic enactment lie the important stages of setting up, discussing, and internalizing the insights gained during the enactments.

Role-playing activities can be broken into five stages:

1. initiation and direction
2. describing the scenario
3. assigning roles
4. enactment
5. debriefing

Initiation and Direction. Every role-play activity begins with some problem that the class or the teacher has identified. Teachers should choose less controversial or sensitive topics until children become accustomed to the procedures. As students become experienced and comfortable with the technique, they can move on to more urgent concerns.

Before moving on to the enactment, the class should be "warmed up" for dramatic activity. Simple pantomime scenes or one-sentence scenarios can serve this purpose. Once the class is psychologically prepared, the role play itself can be set up.

Describing the Scenario. The problem to be discussed should be related in some way to the children's lives so that they see its importance. The actual problem episode that is to trigger the role playing may be presented orally, pictorially, or in writing. A simple story problem may be some variation of an incident such as the following: Sarah pushes Tyrone out of line in the cafeteria. Ms. Wharton sees Sarah and comes rushing up to her.

Assigning Roles. Role assignment needs to be approached cautiously to avoid both the appearance of type casting and the inclusion of any really reluctant actors. Using volunteers or drawing by lots eliminates the suggestion of type casting, but it may involve students who cannot function effectively in the roles assigned. Often the teacher may want to select students who are most likely to give the greatest validity to the roles identified and hence present the problem-solution alternatives most effectively. In either event, assignment requires sensitivity and some experimentation to ensure a productive enactment.

Once assigned, all participants (including audience participants) should be briefed on the role they are to play. In most cases this will be an oral briefing. However, role-profile cards such as the one shown here may be supplied and referred to during the role play if necessary.

> *Betty Ann:* Everyone in this class seems to like you. You are considered to be the smartest one in the class. Most children like to have you on their team when choosing up sides for games. You enjoy school and the work you do there.

Audience participants have equivalent, although temporarily passive, roles. They may be asked to assess whether the roles assigned appear to be enacted genuinely, to think of alternative ways of playing roles, to focus on specific actors and to try to identify vicariously with them, to determine what the issue and roles are (when not shared with them), and to play other roles assigned not in advance but during enactment.

Enactment. A quick briefing with the characters before the role play begins can establish how they plan to enact their roles. Although they may actually revise them or find them inappropriate once the role play unfolds, reviewing their initial actions will help the children clarify their procedures.

During the enactment, it is important to remind both the actors and the audience to use the names of the characters in the role-play situation. This step focuses attention on behaviors and reinforces the fact that the individual class members themselves are not the objects of analysis. Similarly it may frequently be necessary to remind the actors to stay in role, that is, to deal with situations and events as their characters would. Children have a tendency, in humorous or anxiety-producing situations, to stop the role play and respond to the events as spectators. Gentle prodding to them and to the audience participants who may become noisy or distracting early in the role-play activity helps establish the ground rules.

Debriefing. The debriefing period should immediately follow the enactment. The characters should be allowed to share any feelings they had during the role-play and possibly to ask and answer questions from the audience. At some point an exploration of alternative ways of handling the characters' roles should occur. If participants are willing, they can be asked to reenact the role play in different ways. The subsequent discussion can focus on which approaches seemed the most effective and why.

The debriefing session may take many forms depending on the issue, the age of the group, and its experience with role playing. This phase is a crucial and integral part of role playing and requires the greatest attention and guidance on the teacher's part to ensure productive results.

Role Playing and Puppetry

One interesting way to introduce even very young children to role playing is through the use of puppets. The teacher can use them to reenact and dramatize historical events and social issues, and to demonstrate social phenomena such as customs and rules. Since puppets are perceived by children as toys, they can often be used to encourage very shy or reticent students to participate in role playing. Children of all ages and even adults usually enjoy working with puppets.

Sources of Puppets. Many companies provide commercial puppets for use in school activities. A major reference for the names and addresses of suppliers, as well as for books and ideas relating to puppet activities, is Tamara Hunt and Nancy Renfro's *Puppetry and Early Childhood Education,* edited by Ann W. Scwalb (Austin, Tex.: Renfro Studios, 1981). However, commercial puppets are often quite expensive, and those made by teachers and students are usually more appropriate for the specific characters to be used in role-playing scenarios.

Simple paper plates on a stick, finger, mitten, and mitt puppets, such as those shown in Figure 9.7, are inexpensive and easy to create. Step-by-step directions for constructing these and other types of puppet can be found in the Hunt and Renfro reference.

Scenarios for Role Playing with Puppets. Some simple problem scenarios for role playing by children follow. Students can also be encouraged to suggest incidents.

1. Suzanne and Bruce both always want to sit in the chair closest to the television set. So do their mother and father, but they never get to. The scene

FIGURE 9.7 Types of teacher- and student-made puppets

Paper-Plate Rod Puppets and Masks

MATERIALS

Paper plate; skewer or cardboard tube for rod control; paper features.

PROCEDURE

Tape rod control onto back of paper plate. Children can make their own features or use those in early part of this chapter to glue onto the plate. By cutting out eye holes, puppets can be converted into masks.

Mitt Puppets

MATERIALS

Two pieces of 8 by 9-inch paper bag, mural paper or fabric; trim.

PROCEDURE

Make a master pattern on lightweight cardboard of mitt puppet for children to trace on desired materials; cut out.

Run a thin line of glue around border edges of one body piece, but leave bottom edge unglued.

Lay second body piece over glued edge of bottom piece; press flat and dry thoroughly. (Pieces may also be stapled or sewn together.)

Create features and costumes with crayons, marker pens, scrap fabric and trims.

Paper Bag Puppets (Flap Mouth)

MATERIALS

Small or medium sized paper bag; paper features; assorted fabric scraps.

PROCEDURE

Children may make their own features for paper bag puppets or cut out and color the basic features illustrated in the earlier part of this chapter.

Provide assorted scrap fabric and coloring medium to decorate the bags; the bag surfaces lend themselves well to gluing and painting activities.

To operate, place fingers inside flap of bag as shown; move up and down.

Policeperson

Farmer

hand position

Pilgrim

Source: Tamara Hunt and Nancy Renfro, *Puppetry and Early Childhood Education* (Austin, Tex.: Nancy Renfro Studios, 1982), pp. 162, 165, 168. Reprinted by permission.

starts with Bruce and Suzanne fighting over who is going to get to sit in the chair.

2. Timmy has just turned seven years old and he thinks he should get an allowance to spend as he pleases. His father thinks that he is too young to have an allowance and that if he gets one he will just spend it on lots of silly things like bubble gum cards. His mother thinks an allowance is O.K. but that it should be saved for when Timmy goes to college. Timmy doesn't agree with either his father or mother. The scene begins with Timmy's parents telling him how they feel.

The Nature of Simulations

Closely related to role playing is simulation. Often called *simulation games,* simulations are any gamelike activities designed to provide lifelike problem-solving experiences. The elements of a simulation represent more or less accurately some phenomenon in the real world. These characteristics distinguish it from a simple game such as Bingo or Spell Down, in which there are rules and some goal, but no representation of real social events.

Simulations in Society. Simulations are used extensively outside of schools. In the automobile industry, for example, they are used to study the effects of wind on models in order to design fuel-efficient cars. In the space program they help to prepare astronauts for conditions that they will encounter in space. In the classroom simulations similarly allow us to study and better understand the "real thing" by experiencing it under somewhat artificial but more manageable conditions. In Chapter 13 some computer simulations will be discussed.

The Value of Simulations

Simulations share many of the advantages of role playing. Some actually incorporate role-playing elements. For example, students might experience the law-making process by playing the roles of legislators. A major asset of simulations is that they enable many students to relate easily to and become highly interested in a problem they might not otherwise take very seriously. Furthermore, they allow students to assume some control over their own learning and to be less dependent on the teacher.

Both a strength and a limitation of simulations is that they permit study of a *simplified* representation of some reality. All simulations limit the number of variables they present to players; otherwise they would be too complicated. In a simulation of Congress, for example, not all of the lawmakers' actual considerations could be included and weighed. In this sense, simulations make the study of a problem easier to understand, but they also distort it somewhat.

Commercially Prepared Simulations

In addition to their own simulations, teachers have several commercially prepared and teacher-constructed versions already available on a variety of topics. Most of these have been designed for secondary students; those for the elementary and middle-school grades are almost all for grade 4 and above.

A major reference source for a list and descriptions of several simulations is Robert E. Horn, and Anne Cleaves, eds., *The Guide to Simulation/Games for Education and Training,* 4th Ed. (Beverly Hills, Ca.: Sage, 1980). Sharon Pray Muir also has produced a brief selective list and description of many simulations designed for elementary and middle schools.[8] Among the simulations she included are the following, with a brief explanation of each added:

Balance of Power (Four imaginary nations try to keep the peace)

Design (Analyzing the varieties of American housing)

Dig (Hands-on archeological dig identifying a former civilization)

Ecopolis (Solving ecological problems)

Equality (Students represent ethnic groups in an imaginary city)

Rafa', Rafa' (Understanding new and different cultural groups)

World (Insight into how nations develop and become embroiled in conflicts)

EXERCISE 9.8   Field-testing a Simulation Game

Locate a simulation game appropriate for an elementary or middle-school grade. Consult your local library or instructional materials center for a copy. Read the instructions carefully and develop discussion questions for use in debriefing after the game.

Field test the simulation with an elementary or middle-school class. Write a brief evaluation of simulation. Also use your experience to develop a set of guidelines and problems to avoid in future use.

Guidelines for Conducting Simulation Activities

Several fine texts cover in some detail the rather involved processes in constructing an effective simulation. Among them are Alice Kaplan Gordon, *Games for Growth* (Chicago: SRA, 1970) and Samuel Livingston and Clarice Stoll, *Simulation Games: An Introduction for the Social Studies Teacher* (New York: Free Press, 1973).

Most of the extended discussions of the procedures in developing simulations include steps like these:

1. Define the problem or issue the simulation is to represent.
2. State the objectives of the simulation as narrowly and clearly as possible.
3. Specify the actors or parts that are to be played.
4. Spell out in some detail the roles that the players are to assume or what they are to achieve.
5. Indicate the resources and the constraints or rules that exist for the players.
6. Specify the decision-making mechanisms or how the simulation is to operate.

7. Develop a trial version of the simulation, and field test it.
8. On the basis of the test, modify the simulation and retest it until all "bugs" have been eliminated.

To use simulations effectively one can follow the same guidelines suggested earlier for role playing. Again, the *debriefing* period is a crucial and integral phase. In establishing a time frame for the use of simulations, one must set aside a sufficient block of time to discuss student insights and reactions. It is important in this discussion period also to relate the simulated events to ones within students' experiences.

Notes

1. James P. Shaver and William Strong, *Facing Value Decisions: Rationale-Building for Teachers* (Belmont, Calif.: Wadsworth, 1976), pp. 15–17.
2. Milton Rokeach, *The Nature of Human Values* (New York: Free Press, 1973), pp. 27–31.
3. Caroline Mirthes, *Can't You Hear Me Talking to You?* (New York: Bantam, 1971), p. 2.
4. Charles Osgood et al., *The Measurement of Meaning* (Urbana, Ill.: University of Illinois Press, 1967).
5. Ibid.
6. See, for example, W. Kurtines and E. B. Grief, "The Development of Moral Thought: Review and Evaluation of Kohlberg's Approach," *Psychological Bulletin* 81 (1974): 453–470; James Rest, "Developmental Psychology as a Guide to Value Education: A Review of 'Kohlbergian' Programs," *Review of Educational Research* 44 (1974): 241–259; and R. S. Peters, "A Reply to Kohlberg: Why doesn't Lawrence Kohlberg do his homework?," *Phi Delta Kappan* 56 (1975): 678.
7. See Donald W. Oliver and James P. Shaver, *Teaching Public Issues in the High School* (Boston: Houghton Mifflin, 1966); and Fred M. Newmann and Donald W. Oliver, *Clarifying Public Controversy: An Approach to Teaching Social Studies* (Boston: Little, Brown, 1970).
8. Sharon P. Muir, "Simulation Games for Elementary Social Studies," *Social Education* 44 (January 1980): 35–39.

Suggested Readings

Bem, Daryl. *Beliefs, Attitudes, and Human Affairs* (Belmont, Calif.: Brooks/Cole, 1970).

Fraenkel, Jack R. *Helping Students to Think and Value*. 2nd ed. (Englewood Cliffs, N.J.: Prentice-Hall, 1980), Chapter 5.

Galbraith, Ronald E., and Jones, Thomas M. *Moral Reasoning: A Teaching Handbook for Adapting Kohlberg to the Classroom* (Anoka, Minn.: Greenhaven Press, 1976).

Gordon, Alice Kaplan. *Games for Growth* (Chicago: SRA, 1970).

Hersh, Richard E., et al. *Models of Moral Education: An Appraisal* (New York: Longman, 1980).

Martorella, Peter H., ed. *Social Studies Strategies: Theory into Practice* (New York: Harper and Row, 1976), Part III.

Purpel, David, and Ryan, Kevin, eds. *Moral Education . . . It Comes with the Territory* (Berkeley, Calif.: McCutchan, 1976).

Raths, Louis E., et al. *Values and Teaching: Working with Values in the Classroom.* 2nd ed. (Columbus, Ohio: Charles E. Merrill, 1978).

Reimer, Joseph, et al. *Promoting Moral Growth: From Piaget to Kohlberg.* 2nd ed. (New York: Longman, 1983).

Rokeach, Milton. *Beliefs, Attitudes and Values: A Theory of Organization and Change* (San Francisco: Jossey-Bass, 1968).

Shaftel, Fannie R., and Shaftel, George. *Role Playing in the Curriculum.* 2nd ed. (Englewood Cliffs, N.J.: Prentice-Hall, 1982).

Shaver, James P., and Strong, William. *Facing Value Decisions: Rationale-building for Teachers* (Belmont, Calif.: Wadsworth, 1976).

Triandis, Harry C. *Attitude and Attitude Change* (New York: John Wiley, 1971).

PART FIVE

Creating an Effective Instructional Climate

10

Evaluating Reflection, Competence, and Concern

Tests, grades, measurement, standards, evaluation — these are the grist of controversy in education. Schools today are under considerable pressure from society to validate in some way their effect on children. Increasingly they are being asked to demonstrate objectively what information children have learned after a year or after twelve or thirteen years of instruction.

Schools are also expected to provide approximate indications of how their students' learning compares with their classmates and other students across the country (and often the world). As an illustration of the level of societal concern, there has been renewed and successful pressure on all levels of schools, including elementary and middle schools, to retain children in a grade, if they have not reached certain levels of achievement.

The Evaluation Controversy

On one side of the debate are those who argue that higher standards, more objective measurement practices, more rigorous evaluation, and tougher grading are needed in schools from the early grades through the universities. Those on the other side would counter that tests and grades shift the focus in education from learning for its own sake to competition for grades. They would add that evaluation only emphasizes the gap between good and poor students, that measurement or standards alone do not improve instruction or motivate students to succeed, and that the concern for better evaluation ignores the problem of getting all students to realize their full potential. Both sides, however, would agree on the importance of evaluating students' progress in some way.[1]

We cannot resolve the debate in a text of this sort. Teachers and administrators must address these issues in a practical way that is responsive to parents' and community members' concerns and also provides leadership and education. Educators must be able to provide reasonable and clear answers to parent's questions such as, "What did *my* child, not the class, learn in social studies this year?" They also must take the time to educate the total school community — at parent nights, during school board meetings, through school and local papers, in community meetings, and wherever the opportunity presents itself — to dispel the mystique and nonsense surrounding matters such as test results and alleged declining standards in American public schools.

Tests, grades, measurement, standards, and evaluation are all a part of our schools, but some elements play a greater role at one level than another. How do they differ and how do they function in social studies instruction? We will consider how the classroom teacher can more effectively and objectively evaluate student progress.

Developing a Framework for Evaluation

Evaluation can be viewed fundamentally as a way of making a decision based on organized data. The dictionary definition of the term is what often makes us as educators so uncomfortable with evaluating *someone:* "to determine or judge the value or worth of." Most people probably would prefer to avoid such a responsibility. However, educators, parents, and society in general wish to have some objective indicators of our schools' success. Students, more basically, wish to know "How am I doing?"

Grades, Measurement, and Standards

Grades are one of the shorthand ways of communicating the results of an evaluation. "Steve got an A on social studies" means that someone evaluated Steve's achievements in social studies and decided that they were exceptional. One need not have used a grade to communicate the evaluation; a sentence or paragraph, placement within a group, or other means could have served the same purpose. Grades often are used because they are easy to record and communicate, and they are often easy to compare. Above all, grades can be reduced to mathematical terms. This means that evaluations from different subjects may be lumped together and used to form a single evaluation — for example, "Sue was a 3.5 student in the middle school."

In contrast to grades, *measurement* is a way to collect data on which we base evaluation. It refers to any systematic data collection, including paper-and-pencil devices, such as *tests,* and more simple techniques, such as keeping track of the number of times a student asks a question in social studies.

Standards are related to both measurement and evaluation. They are the criteria for making judgments. They determine what should be placed on a test, how carefully something should be measured, and the like.

The Evaluation Process

Suppose a teacher, Mr. Halpern, has begun to evaluate his students' progress toward the objectives he has established. He decides that the following measures are appropriate:

scores from teacher-made tests

anecdotal records of class interaction

checklists of group participation skills

ratings on individual projects

ratings on oral reports

scores from a standardized test

checklists of written assignments

Mr. Halpern's next decision concerns the *weight* or percentage of the total evaluation that will be assigned to each measure. After some thought, he concludes that each indicator should be weighted as shown in the pie chart in Figure 10.1.

He has decided that ratings of individual projects will receive the greatest weight, because a great deal of class time during the evaluation period was spent on them. Further, they were designed specifically to address many of the unit objectives.

FIGURE 10.1   A sample evaluation framework

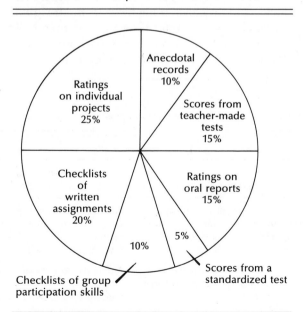

Conversely, a standardized test received little weight, since only one was given and it dealt with only a few objectives. The sizes of the remaining five pieces were determined on a similar basis. If Mr. Halpern had deemed it appropriate, all of the pieces could have been equal.

Evaluation and Instructional Objectives. In making his evaluation decisions, Mr. Halpern looked to the goals and specific instructional objectives he had established for the social studies program. The seven elements of his evaluation framework address all aspects of the program which he considered to be important. They also take into account those areas in which the class had spent most of its time during the evaluation period, and which all members of his class had been informed were significant.

Using an Evaluation Grid. An evaluation grid sometimes is useful for determining whether all goals and objectives have been reflected in the evaluation framework and in which ways. It involves listing in one column all of the instructional objectives the teacher considers to have been important. In the next column are ways in which student achievement of the objectives are to be measured, such as written assignments or oral reports. A portion of an evaluation grid is shown in Table 10.1.

EXERCISE 10.1   Developing an Evaluation Grid

Locate a teacher's guide for a social studies basal text, any grade level. Identify five objectives from the guide, and develop an evaluation grid similar to the one shown in Table 10.1. Describe specifically what sorts of materials and items will be included in the various measures for each objective.

TABLE 10.1   A sample evaluation grid

Evaluation grid	
Important objectives	*How achievement of the objectives will be measured*
1. Identify major ethnic groups within the United States and some of the traditions associated with them.	Ratings on an oral report Checklists related to written assignments A teacher-made test
2. Learn research techniques associated with locating information from written materials.	Anecdotal records of individual student work Student logs of work done

Subjective and Objective Aspects of Evaluation

An evaluation pie chart similar to the one shown in Figure 10.1 allows a teacher to separate in some measure subjective and objective aspects of evaluation. Determining the weight of each element in the evaluation is a *subjective* process. It involves a value judgment both that certain elements will make up the evaluation and that each will be weighted in a particular way. Even individual tests, whether they require students to select or create answers, begin with a subjective judgment by the teacher: what will be included on the test to represent which instructional objectives, and what will be left out?

After the subjective stage of evaluation decisions come the more *objective* steps in the evaluation process. Although Mr. Halpern, for example, wished to include a place in his evaluation framework for his students' classroom interactions, he wished to keep that element in perspective. He did not want it to color his overall evaluation judgment.

Consider one of Mr. Halpern's students, Melanie Eager. She always has her hand up in social studies discussions, asks good questions, and listens attentively to Mr. Halpern's and other students' points. In sum, she is outstanding in classroom interaction. However, as indicated in Figure 10.1, Mr. Halpern has decided in advance that this aspect of his evaluation will be one-fifth of the total. Through reference to his evaluation pie, he has an objective way of keeping Melanie's outstanding achievements in *one* area in perspective.

Norm-Referenced and Criterion-Referenced Testing

Testing over the past half-century has assumed a large role in our society. It is safe to say that a child who enters a public school in the United States will take dozens of tests of every size and description before he or she graduates. College and the world of work likely will present yet another battery of tests for the student to take. For better or worse, tests and testing probably will dog students throughout at least the early part of their lives and occupational careers.

The Use and Misuse of Tests

Although testing can aid the teacher in evaluation, it is often used out of proportion to its usefulness or appropriateness. Tests, especially paper-and-pencil tests, are occasionally used when other tools would be more appropriate. It seems obvious to us, for example, that if we wished to discover whether a student were an exceptional artist, we would not ask him or her to take a paper-and-pencil test on art. Rather we probably would have a qualified artist judge the student's artwork. So it is with many aspects of achievement in the social studies. If we wish to evaluate how well students can use data to solve a problem or to determine how effectively they apply techniques of research, student productions or projects probably are more appropriate than a test.

Using Norm-Referenced and Criterion-Referenced Tests

The two basic types of tests that teachers employ in teaching social studies are called *norm-referenced* and *criterion-referenced* tests. Norm-referenced tests allow teachers *to compare their students' performance with the norms or results obtained from the performance of a sample group of other students on the same test.* They provide answers to a question such as, How does the performance of my fifth-grade students compare with that of other fifth graders?

Criterion-referenced tests allow teachers *to compare the performance of their students against some standard of what they should know.* They provide answers to a question such as, How does the performance of my fifth-grade students compare with the criterion of what they are expected to know or demonstrate? An example of a criterion would be: Given a series of historical passages depicting a problem to be solved, in 75 percent of the cases a student will be able to develop at least two plausible hypotheses to account for the problems. To develop large-scale criterion-referenced tests school districts often contract with major test publishers to develop suitable materials for the school's curriculum. An example of a criterion-referenced item developed for an eighth-grade test by the Instructional Objectives Exchange is shown in Figure 10.2, along with a general description of the objective that the item measures.[2]

As Lindheim points out, one cannot tell whether a test is criterion-referenced or norm-referenced merely by looking at the items, since they often appear the same.[3] To differentiate them, it is necessary to examine the test specifications and the general background information related to the test. This type of information usually is provided in a separate test manual, which includes any special instructions for administering the test.

The National Assessment of Education Progress

In 1969 a consortium of states embarked on a national project called the National Assessment of Educational Progress (NAEP), which continues today.[4] NAEP employs criterion-referenced testing procedures to measure student growth in ten areas, including social studies. Samples of students from across the United States have been included in the ongoing project, and findings have been reported for the following age groups: 9, 13, 17, young adults. Tests are repeated on a cyclical basis, and results are made available to the general public. A sample item from an NAEP Social Studies Test is shown in Figure 10.3.

Standardized Tests

Measures commonly called "standardized" are examples of *norm-referenced* tests, since they provide national norms. There are also standardized sets of instructions for administering the tests to ensure uniform test-taking procedures. Usually, the items on a standardized test have been refined over time. Three types of questions have been eliminated through field tests and trials: (1) those which are poorly worded or ambiguous, (2) those which most students answer correctly, and (3) those which most students answer incorrectly.

FIGURE 10.2   Sample criterion-referenced test item

**ILLUSTRATIVE TEST SPECIFICATIONS SOCIAL STUDIES: GRADE EIGHT
UNDERSTANDING OUR RELATIONSHIP WITH THE ENVIRONMENT**

General Description

The student will read a description of a natural event or a change in a human activity that has an impact on the natural or human environment. The student will then select from four environmental effects the one effect which is most likely to result from the given event or activity.

Sample Item

Directions: Read the descriptions in the boxes below. Choose the most likely result of the event or activity described. Mark the letter of the correct answer on your answer sheet.

> *Mountain Fork is a small town on the banks of Silver Creek. The citizens of Mountain Fork have decided to outlaw driving on Sundays in their town. Only emergency vehicles will be allowed to operate.*

Which one of the following will most likely happen because of this change in activities?

A. There will be more smoke and haze in Mountain Fork on Sundays. (opposite effect)

B. Less gasoline and oil will be used in Mountain Fork. (correct)

C. Fewer wild animals will live near Mountain Fork. (unrelated occurrence)

D. The water in Silver Creek will become dirtier. (unrelated occurrence)

Source: Elaine Lindheim, "Improving Testing in the Social Studies," in *Criterion-Referenced Testing for the Social Studies,* ed., Paul L. Williams and Jerry R. Moore (Washington, DC.: National Council for the Social Studies, 1980), pp. 32–33.

A classroom teacher should realize that the subject matter contained in standardized tests *may not correspond at all to what is being studied in any individual classroom.* This may occur since the tests are designed for use across the United States and because the subject matter being studied at a given grade level may vary from district to district. In using and interpreting the results of standardized tests, teachers should consider carefully whether the knowledge it measures matches that which the classroom social studies program provides. Unless a clear match exists, the standardized test is useful merely as a general *diagnostic* tool. It reveals what students know and do not know generally, rather than evaluating or assessing an instructional program's effectiveness.

Standardized Tests Differentiate Students. Typical standardized tests for elementary students are designed to differentiate among student populations; that is, they produce a distribution of students who score in the high, middle, and low ranges. Thus on such standardized tests there will always be some students who

FIGURE 10.3 Sample item from the National Assessment of Educational Progress (NAEP) test.

Sample Test Item No. 2.

2. On the map below, four areas of the world are screened in gray. Each outlined area contains a small oval. Fill in the oval inside the area where Spanish is the most commonly spoken language.

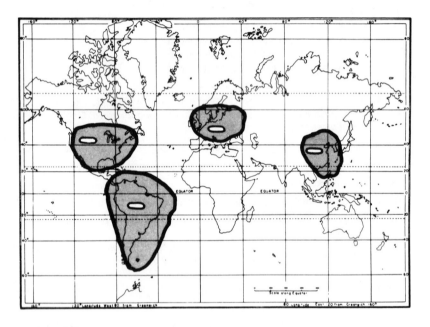

○ **I don't know.**

Source: NAEP, Demonstration Package, no date.

score "low," since items most students answer correctly are deleted or revised in new versions of the test.

As a case in point, reflect on a standardized test that many readers have taken, the Scholastic Aptitude Test (SAT). It is possible that everyone at some time could obtain a score of 800 (the top score) on both the Verbal and Quantitative sections of the test. In practice, however, the test clearly differentiates among students. This fact is used by colleges and universities, who are among the major groups interested in such scores, to help them select which students they will admit. For those colleges who have three to ten applications for every admission space, the test identifies a pool of 5 to 10 percent of all eligible students. If the majority of test takers should begin to score 800, the test would be changed, since it would no longer effectively differentiate among students.

Sources of Standardized Tests for Elementary and Middle Schools

A major source of information on all of the standardized tests currently available, including those in social studies, is the *Mental Measurement Yearbook*, published periodically by Oscar Buros. It is available in most college libraries and contains information such as a description of a test, places it can be purchased, and one or more critiques of its strengths and weaknesses. A special volume abstracts from a recent yearbook information relating specifically to social studies tests:

> Oscar Buros, ed., *Social Studies Tests and Reviews*. Highland Park, N.J.: Gryphon Press, 1975.

Some of the major standardized tests that schools typically administer to elementary and middle-school students are as follows:[5]

> *Iowa Tests of Basic Skills*, Social Studies Supplement, Riverside Publishers.
>
> *Metropolitan Achievement Tests: Social Studies Test*, The Psychological Corporation.
>
> *Primary Social Studies Test*, Houghton Mifflin Publishers.
>
> *Sequential Tests of Educational Progress. Social Studies* (STEP), Addison-Wesley.
>
> *SRA Achievement Series, Social Studies Subtest*, Science Research Associates.
>
> *Stanford Achievement Test, Social Studies Subtest*, The Psychological Corporation.

EXERCISE 10.2   Analysis of a Social Studies Standardized Test

Examine one of the standardized tests available for social studies at any grade level. Note its name, the publisher, the copyright date, and the grade level. Also obtain the following information, if available:

1. How were the national norms obtained, how many students were involved, and how are they described?
2. What different *forms* of question does it use (e.g., multiple choice, matching)?
3. What topics or subjects in social studies does it include?
4. How many of the questions can *you* answer?

Mastery Learning

Reflect for a moment on the typical pattern of decisions leading up to evaluations in elementary and middle schools. Objectives are set and instruction is provided to meet them over a period of time, frequently one-fourth of a school year or nine weeks. At the end of the period, student progress is evaluated with a variety of tools such as the ones we have described.

The results usually look something like this: some students are ahead of the rest, some lag behind, and most will lump around the same place in achievement. This pattern then is translated into a set of grades or rating that differentiates students along some continuum. It is assumed that this distribution of student achievement is reasonable and normal.

At the end of the school year, the set of periodic evaluations we have just described are summed and averaged somehow. Some students are given a final evaluation in each subject area as "superior" or A or "average" or C, and so on. The next year the students move on and begin again with a new learning agenda.

Mastery of Objectives

Envision an alternative approach. Specific objectives again are laid out for students, but with the criterion for *mastery* of them clearly established and with the understanding that all objectives are achievable by all students. Rather than having an arbitrary time period within which students are to progress toward achievement of objectives, they are allowed to take as much time as is needed to master one objective before moving on to the next. Evaluation consists of verifying that a student has achieved an acceptable level of mastery of the established objectives. Since *all* students are expected to achieve mastery at some point, there is no differentiation or grouping of A or C students.

Providing Learning Alternatives

All students are expected to move to the acceptable level of mastery, but it is assumed that some will take more time than others. When students encounter difficulties on the first try at mastery, alternative instructional techniques are provided. Just as in the conventional classroom approach, some students learn faster than the norm and some learn slower. At any given time and for any particular objective, each student may be at a different point enroute to mastery.

Mastery learning uses a criterion-referenced, rather than a norm-referenced, basis for evaluation. It requires explicit objectives and criteria for mastery and procedures for accommodating wide variations in the amount of time students will need. It works most effectively for topical areas that lend themselves to these requirements. Mastery learning is both an instructional approach and a system of evaluation. When the appropriate conditions for its implementation exist, it is an effective and comprehensive form of individualized instruction.

Mastery Learning and Instructional Time

In sum mastery learning assumes that if time or instruction is not held constant for all students and if instructional alternatives are provided when students encounter learning difficulties, all but a few students can master the objectives.[6] In fact John Carroll, an early proponent of mastery learning, has written:

> The amount of time that a student needs to learn a given task under optimal learning conditions is, in the author's opinion, a reflection of some basic characteristic or characteristics of the student that may be called "aptitude." Why pupils vary in the amount of time they need for a given learning task is not known; variations in aptitude are, in the author's opinion, simply a given for the educator to deal with in the best possible way.[7]

Teacher-Made Tests

Teacher-made tests are measurement tools that a teacher devises to assist in evaluating student achievement. Such tools are appropriate for use in a specific classroom. Although teachers often share the ideas in them, such tests usually cannot be transferred to other classes without modifications.

Teacher-made tests often include features and items like those in norm-referenced and criterion-referenced tests. They include *essay* questions and so-called *objective* items. They differ primarily in their uses and in the procedures used to develop them.

Teacher-Made Tests for Young Children

Teachers in the primary grades are understandably less likely to construct tests than their intermediate or middle-school counterparts, but appropriate tests can be developed for use at all levels. Young children and nonreaders can be given oral tests, for example, where they are asked to draw a line through the picture of the correct choice in a set of alternative answers.

Tests for young children should rely heavily on visual, rather than verbal materials. Teachers can use materials such as pictures, filmstrip frames, slides, and even hand-drawn figures. Similarly, children may be asked to respond with a drawing rather than in writing.

Constructing Teacher-Made Tests

Several specialized books, pamphlets, and guidelines exist to help teachers construct their own tests.[8] Once a teacher has determined through the use of a device such as the evaluation grid described earlier that student progress toward certain objectives can best be measured by a teacher-made test, several choices exist. These generally are lumped under "essay" and "objective" items.

Writing Essay Test Items. Essay questions are an especially effective way to measure students' ability to organize, analyze, apply, synthesize, and evaluate information in their own way. They give students with the freedom to think broadly and to express themselves in different ways. However, they are more difficult to measure objectively, can cover only a few objectives in a short period of time, take a long time to score, and allow students to digress. Sometimes they also penalize the child who has trouble expressing himself or herself.

Translating concrete objects and ideas into abstract answers in an essay is a cognitive task that is related both to development and to language facility. Young children and those for whom English is a second language often have more difficulty in putting something in their own words than in selecting, identifying, applying, or demonstrating correct answers from among alternatives.

General Guidelines. Two basic guidelines for constructing well-designed essay questions are:

1. Use clear, specific, and simple language.

   Yes: "Describe two major ways in which urban and rural neighborhoods differ."

   No: "Elaborate briefly on the distinctions between the urban and rural ethos."

2. Limit the scope of the question and the expected answer as much as possible.

   Yes: "Identify three significant ways in which America's involvement in the Vietnam War was different from its participation in World War II."

   No: "How was the Vietnam War different from World War II?"

Before presenting the question to students, the teacher should make a model answer that lists the major points or items, or the type of discussion the teacher will accept as correct, partially correct, or satisfactory.[9] A sample model answer that allows a student considerable freedom in framing an answer follows.

Question: Defend *or* argue against the following statement: *Capitalism is the best economic system in the world.*

Give reasons for the stand you take and use examples to support your argument.

Model Answer: Either position, pro or con, is acceptable. Cite reasons for your argument and use examples from history to help substantiate your claims. Answers should include:

1. At least four clear and distinct reasons
2. At least one example for each reason

Partial credit will be given for answers which have less than four reasons and four examples.

Writing Objective Test Items. *Objective* refers to how responses to a question may be graded, not to the question itself. As we suggested earlier, deciding to include one item instead of another on a test to represent learning is a *subjective*

EXERCISE 10.3   Constructing an Essay Question

Assume you are teaching a fifth-grade class studying American history. Pick any specific topic that you wish within that general subject, and construct a well-designed essay question and a model answer.

---

judgment. Witness the little boy who protested that he was really knowledgeable in social studies despite his terrible objective test scores. His only defense for the poor test scores was, "Teacher never asks any questions about anything I studied and learned."

Objective test items are easy to grade quickly, they are not susceptible to teacher bias in scoring, they permit many objectives to be addressed in a short time, and they do not penalize students who are not verbal. However, they encourage guessing, are often more difficult and time-consuming to construct than essay questions, and give students no opportunity to demonstrate divergent thinking.

Types of Objective Test Items. Types of objective test items most appropriate for use in the social studies are *multiple-choice, alternative response,* and *matching.* There are many variations of each form, and several comprehensive texts are offered in the Suggested Reading as guides. A fourth form, *completion* or *fill-in-the-blank* also exists. However, its use in social studies usually causes problems. Clear items are difficult to construct and a student can often respond with many reasonable answers, besides the correct one. For example, consider this poorly constructed question:

_____ _____ was the author of the _____ of _____.

The item was used by a teacher who expected the four answers, "Thomas," "Jefferson," "Declaration," and "Independence." Think, however, of all the plausible alternative sets of answers, including "John," "Steinbeck," "Grapes," and "Wrath."

An example of each of the three types of items, multiple-choice, alternative response, and matching, is given below, followed by some guidelines on the writing of the item.

MULTIPLE CHOICE QUESTIONS

The smallest of the fifty states in terms of land area is which of the following?

a. Wyoming
b. Delaware
c. West Virginia
d. Rhode Island

Some Guidelines for Writing Multiple-Choice Items:

○ ○ The stem (the first part) should state the question or issue.

○ ○ All the choices should be plausible, related, and approximately the same length.

○ ○ Use four options, and avoid use of "All of the above" and "None of the above," which often are confusing to students.

○ ○ The stem should be stated in a positive form, avoiding the use of terms such as "not" and "never."

○ ○ Organize the stem around one idea only.

ALTERNATIVE RESPONSE QUESTIONS

All the statements below deal with the map you have been given. If the statement is true according to the map, circle the T next to it. If it is false, circle the F.

T   F   The country has a large city near a port.

T   F   There are mountains in the country.

T   F   It is probably very cold there.

Some Guidelines for Writing Alternative-Response Items:

○ ○ Each statement should include a *single* point or issue.

○ ○ Avoid statements designed to "trick" or mislead students if they do not read carefully.

○ ○ Avoid terms such as "always," "never," "all," "generally," "occasionally," and "every," which signal the correct answer.

MATCHING QUESTIONS

Look at the two sets of items below. The set on the left lists cities, and the one on the right gives states. In front of the set of cities is a blank space. Write in each space the letter of the state that belongs with the city.

_____ Milwaukee   a. Ohio

_____ Pittsburgh   b. California

_____ Cleveland   c. Wisconsin

_____ Boise   d. Pennsylvania

_____ San Francisco   e. Idaho

f. Texas

g. Minnesota

h. Maine

Some Guidelines for Writing Matching Items:

○ ○ The items in each column should be related.

○ ○ The directions should state clearly what the student is to do and any special limitations on the use of choices (e.g., whether items can be used more than once).

○ ○ Generally there should be more choices than can be matched.

○ ○ The order of the items in each set of choices should be either alphabetical or random.

○ ○ The number of items in the shorter column should be less than ten so students will not waste time searching through long lists.

EXERCISE 10.4   Constructing Objective Test Questions

Assume you are teaching an intermediate grade or middle-school class studying American history. Pick any specific topics that you wish within that general subject, and construct two well-designed objective questions, one multiple-choices and one requiring matching.

Measuring Reflection, Competence, and Concern

We suggested in Chapter 1 that in social studies our ultimate goal is the development of reflective, competent, and concerned citizens. The evaluation system we devise, correspondingly, should tap each of these three dimensions. Moreover, our objectives and our programs should guide the character of our evaluation system, rather than the reverse. We conduct evaluations to determine the relative effectiveness of significant components of our instructional program and to validate student achievement, not for their own sake.

In the preceding sections, we have considered some strategies for developing a general framework for evaluation and for using a repertoire of *testing* tools. Many of these tools now are readily available to teachers since many current basal social studies textbook programs provide sample test items. Even when an item may not be satisfactory, it may provide a sample test format for constructing one's own test items.

We turn now to how some evaluation tools may be applied to social studies objectives related to reflection, competence, and concern. Since tests are often not the best tool for assessing achievements in certain areas, we shall also look at others. Among these are anecdotal records, checklists, and rating scales.

Anecdotal Records, Checklists, and Rating Scales

Anecdotal records are brief, written vignettes that note the date, context, and description of a student's behavior. They may focus on any subject, such as an incident illustrating a student's growth in social skills.

Checklists appear in many forms, and are inventories of which learning tasks have been completed or what level of competency has been achieved. They are a simple way of recording which objectives a student has satisfied. They may be completed by the teacher or the student and are especially useful for "either/or" objectives: either the student achieved the objective or not.

Rating scales, which were introduced in Chapter 9 as a way to *diagnose* student attitudes, come in many different forms. If used cautiously, rating scales also can provide data for evaluation. Unlike checklists, rating scales can measure the *degree* of progress. For example, a teacher may assess whether a student has demonstrated considerable or minimal growth in an area, rather than merely checking "has made progress" or "has not made progress."

Assessing Reflection

We have characterized the reflective citizen as one who knows a body of facts, concepts, and generalizations about the organization, understanding, and development of individuals, groups, and societies. Reflective citizens also understand the processes of hypothesis formation, problem solving and decision making. Students' achievement of instructional objectives related to each of these characteristics can be measured in a variety of ways.

All forms of tests, if their content is directly related to program objectives, are appropriate to measure gains in knowledge and in the ability to identify and state hypotheses. Rating scales, checklists, and anecdotal records are especially helpful for verifying progress in developing problem-solving and decision-making abilities. These may be used in conjunction with observations of students' class participation, projects, and library activities, and with analysis of written assignments.

Let us look at some items that may be constructed to measure reflection. Along with each item is the characteristic it attempts to measure.

CONCEPT IDENTIFICATION

Item: Test Question
Which of the pictures below shows an island?

(a)   (b)   (c)   (d)

GENERALIZATION LEARNING

Item: Test Question
You will see a series of slides that go with the questions on your sheets. The number of the slide will be the same as the number of the question. For example, slide 1 goes with question 1. After the slide is shown, circle the answer on your sheet.

Which of the following statements best summarizes what slide 1 shows?

a. Unemployment increases as inflation decreases.
b. Unemployment decreases as inflation decreases.
c. Unemployment increases as inflation increases.
d. Unemployment and inflation are not related.

HYPOTHESIS FORMATION

Item: Test Question
Look carefully at the large picture taped to the front chalkboard to answer this question.
Circle the sentence that explains why the child is crying in the picture.

a. She can't find her toy.
b. Her mother has spanked her.
c. Her toy is broken.
d. She is lost.

Assessing Competence

We described competent citizens as having a repertoire of skills. Paper-and-pencil tests and many standardized tests often measure such skills, especially spatial skills. As with many skills in life, however, some social studies skills can best be demonstrated through *performance*. Suppose, for example, a teacher is interested in discovering whether students understand how to use maps. A scavenger hunt that requires the use of a map may be a more realistic measure than a written test. Checklists and rating scales are especially useful for assessing skills, particularly social skills.

Some measurement items that may be constructed to assess competence are shown below, along with the characteristic the item measures.

PROCESSING AND INTERPRETING DATA

Item: Test Question

Sample Test Item No. 1.

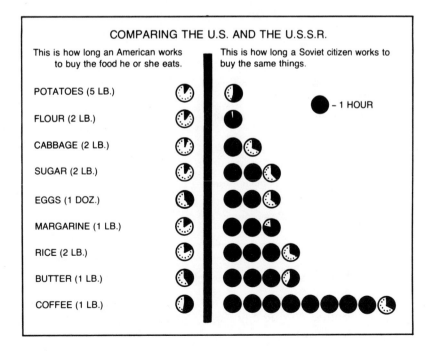

1. According to the graph above, which one of the following statements is TRUE?
   - ○ Russians eat more cabbage than Americans.
   - ○ Russians work more hours per day than Americans.
   - ○ More coffee is grown in Russia than in the United States.
   - ● Russians work approximately 6 times longer to buy a dozen eggs than Americans work.
   - ○ I don't know.

Source: NAEP, Demonstration Booklet, no date.

IDENTIFYING AND USING REFERENCE SOURCES

Item: Checklist of Reference Skills

A checklist similar to the following one could be constructed for a group working together or for an entire class. When a student has demonstrated the skill satisfactorily, a check is made next to the student's name.

Reference sources checklist

	Mary	Bill	Tara	Fred	Jo
1. Uses picture captions and titles to organize information	——	——	——	——	——
2. Uses glossaries and dictionaries to identify word meaning	——	——	——	——	——
3. Uses dictionaries as aids to pronunciation	——	——	——	——	——
4. Uses a variety of reference works	——	——	——	——	——
5. Uses an atlas	——	——	——	——	——
6. Uses the telephone directory and the Yellow Pages as sources of information	——	——	——	——	——
7. Uses an index to locate information	——	——	——	——	——
8. Uses newspapers and magazines as sources of information	——	——	——	——	——
9. Writes letters to obtain information	——	——	——	——	——
10. Identifies people as sources of information	——	——	——	——	——

EXERCISE 10.5   Constructing a Checklist

Develop a checklist for assessing whether students have acquired *chronology skills* (e.g., making timelines) for the social studies.

GROUP PARTICIPATION

Item: Rating Sheet for Group Participation
Each student working within a group would be
rated on each of the characteristics on the sheet.

Group Participation Rating Sheet

Student's Name _____ Date

Group Members _____

Date Group Formed _____

Each of the characteristics of group participation will be rated as follows:

5 = Consistently Exhibited   2 = Seldom Exhibited

4 = Frequently Exhibited   1 = Not Exhibited

3 = Occasionally Exhibited

Characteristics	*Ratings*
1. Accepts ideas of others	_____
2. Initiates ideas	_____
3. Gives opinions	_____
4. Is task oriented	_____
5. Helps others	_____
6. Seeks information	_____
7. Encourages others to contribute	_____
8. Works well with all members	_____
9. Raises provocative questions	_____
10. Listens to others	_____
11. Disagrees in a constructive fashion	_____
12. Makes an overall positive contribution to the group	_____
Total Rating	_____

Additional Comments: _____

EXERCISE 10.6   Constructing a Rating Sheet

Develop a rating sheet similar to the one in the text for use in evaluating a student research project.

Assessing Concern

We have characterized concerned citizens as those who have an awareness of their rights and responsibilities, a sense of social conciousness, and a firm basis for deciding what is right and wrong. They also have learned how to identify and analyze issues and to suspend judgment on alternate beliefs, attitudes, values, customs, and cultures.

In assessing progress toward objectives in this area, teachers should look primarily to devices such as checklists, anecdotal records, and rating scales. As we saw in Chapter 9 instruments such as attitude scales and value inventories can also be valuable as diagnostic tools to be used *prior* to the study of a topic.

Some measurement items for dimensions of concern follow. Along with each example, the characteristic the item measures is indicated.

EXAMINING ALTERNATIVE ATTITUDES

Item: Work Assignment

At the completion of the reading and discussion of a chapter in their text, students are asked to complete the assignment sheet.

Assignment Sheet[10]

From our study and discussion of the colonial period, what can you say were the attitudes of these different groups towards their experiences? List as many things as you can for each group. Then try to put yourself in the shoes of the English, the Africans, and the Indians, and offer some reasons *why* they might have felt this way.

How the English Felt   Why They Felt This Way

_____   _____

_____   _____

_____   _____

How the Africans Felt   Why They Felt This Way

_____   _____

_____   _____

_____   _____

How the Indians Felt   Why They Felt This Way

_____   _____

_____   _____

_____   _____

OPENMINDEDNESS AND TOLERANCE

Item: Anecdotal Record

Over a nine-week period a teacher compiled anecdotal records of students' behavior relating to openmindedness and tolerance. On a small card related behaviors were recorded, along with the date and the context of each behavior. A sample card follows.

Samantha Wilcox — 12/3

Overheard several students talking during their free period about a TV show that had a gay character. One student made a disparaging remark about gays. Samantha chided him, and defended people's rights to be different and not be ridiculed. After she spoke, the other students didn't contest her point, and then dropped the subject.

DEVELOPING SENSITIVITY TO ALTERNATE POINTS OF VIEW

Item: Checklist on Student Sensitivity to Alternate Points of View

A checklist similar to the following one could be constructed for a group working together or for an entire class. If a student has demonstrated the behavior a check is made next to his or her name.

Checklist of student behaviors related to sensitivity for alternate points of view

	Tod	Abe	Jean	Rea
1. Is open to new ideas.	___	___	___	___
2. Listens while others speak.	___	___	___	___
3. Is willing to change his/her mind.	___	___	___	___
4. Does not ridicule other's ideas.	___	___	___	___
5. Does not engage in name-calling.	___	___	___	___
6. Does not reject those who disagree.	___	___	___	___
7. Supports other's rights to speak.	___	___	___	___
8. Is curious about ideas different from his/her own.	___	___	___	___

Notes

1. *Testing, Teaching and Learning: Report of a Conference on Research on Testing* (Washington, D.C.: National Institute of Education, 1979), Part I.
2. Elaine Lindheim, "Improving Testing in the Social Studies: Specifying Outcomes," in *Criterion Referenced Testing for the Social Studies.* Paul L. Williams and Jerry R. Moore, Bulletin No. 64 (Washington, D.C.: National Council for the Social Studies, 1980), pp. 32–33.
3. Ibid., p. 27.
4. Ronald K. Hambleton and Robert A. Simon, "NAEP Social Studies and Citizenship Exercises and Their Usefulness for Improving Instruction," in *Criterion Referenced Testing for the Social Studies.* Paul L. Williams and Jerry R. Moore, Bulletin No. 64 (Washington, D.C.: National Council for the Social Studies, 1980), pp. 47–63.
5. Richard L. Needham, "A Brief Bibliography of Social Studies Tests," in *Criterion Referenced Testing for the Social Studies.* Paul L. Williams and Jerry R. Moore, eds., Bulletin No. 64 (Washington, D.C.: National Council for the Social Studies, 1980), pp. 84–88.
6. Benjamin S. Bloom, "Learning for Mastery," in *Mastery Learning: Theory and Practice,* ed. James H. Block (New York: Holt, Rinehart and Winston, 1971), pp. 47–63.
7. John B. Carroll, "Problems of Measurement Related to the Concept of Learning for Mastery," in *Mastery Learning: Theory and Practice,* ed. James H. Block (New York: Holt, Rinehart and Winston, 1971), pp. 31–32.
8. See, for example, the set of materials produced by the Educational Testing Service and entitled, *The Evaluation and Advisory Series.* These are made available free of charge by wrting to ETS Information Services Division, Princeton, NJ 08541.
9. Terry D. TenBrink, "Evaluation," in *Classroom Teaching Skills,* 2nd ed., James M. Cooper et al. (Lexington, Mass.: D. C. Heath, 1982), p. 381.
10. Adapted from Norman E. Wallen, *Getting Together with People* (Reading, Mass.: Addison-Wesley, 1974), p. 37.

Suggested Readings

Block, James H., ed. *Mastery Learning: Theory and Practice.* New York: Holt, Rinehart and Winston, 1971.

Bloom, Benjamin S., Hastings, J. Thomas, and Madaus, George F. *Handbook on Formative and Summative Evaluation of Student Learning.* New York: McGraw-Hill, 1971.

Fraenkel, Jack R. *Helping Students Think and Value: Strategies for Teaching Social Studies,* 2nd ed. Englewood Cliffs, N.J.: Prentice-Hall, 1980, Chapters 6 and 7.

Massialas, Byron G., and Hurst, Joseph B. *Social Studies in a New Era: The Elementary School as a Laboratory.* New York: Longman, 1978, Chapter 11.

Oliner, Pearl M. *Teaching Elementary Social Studies: A Rational and Humanistic Approach.* New York: Harcourt Brace Jovanovich, 1976, Chapter 9.

Popham, W. James. *Criterion-Referenced Measurement.* Englewood Cliffs, N.J.: Prentice-Hall, 1978.

TenBrink, Terry D. "Evaluation," in *Classroom Teaching Skills.* 2nd ed. James M. Cooper et al. Lexington, Mass.: D. C. Heath, 1982, pp. 363–403.

Thomas, R. Murray, and Brubaker, Dale L., eds. *Teaching Elementary Social Studies: Readings*. Belmont, Calif.: Wadsworth, 1972, Part 4.

Tuckman, Bruce W. *Measuring Educational Outcomes: Fundamentals of Testing*. New York: Harcourt Brace Jovanovich, 1975.

Williams, Paul L., and Moore, Jerry R., eds. *Criterion Referenced Testing for the Social Studies*. Bulletin No. 64. Washington, D.C.: National Council for the Social Studies, 1980.

11

Improving Communication in the Classroom

No two classrooms are alike. Each has a unique identity created from the people who inhabit it, the activities they pursue there, and the ways they physically transform it. When an observer says that a particular classroom is cold or warm, dismal or cheerful, exciting or dull, its particular identity is being revealed.

Many elements combine to create a classroom's environment. Seldom can one teacher or even a trained observer discover all of the elements that make up its identity. Learning a few basic things about them and how they affect the quality of life within a classroom, however, can have an effect on instruction in social studies, as well as that in other subject areas. In this chapter we will focus on key factors that influence the patterns of communication and the effectiveness of instruction within a classroom.

The Classroom as a Medium of Communication

Examine the room designs in Figure 11.1. How are the rooms similar and different? How are the designs of the rooms likely to influence patterns of student and teacher interactions? In which classroom would you prefer to teach and why?

The Uses of Classroom Space

By attending to the organization of space within an area we can see much about the kinds of activities that are likely to be encouraged and discouraged within it. For example, the dynamics of a party in a room filled with chairs for guests will be different from one where there is no seating. For a similar reason, schools abandoned seats bolted to the floor when they wished to provide for more flexible groupings of students.

The ways in which teachers and students organize their classroom area will

253

FIGURE 11.1 Three classroom designs

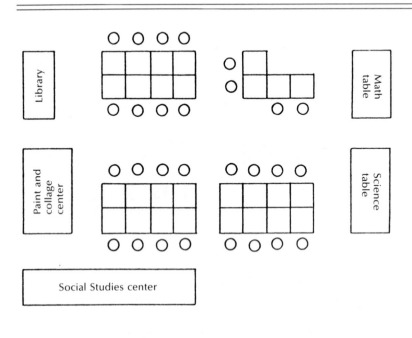

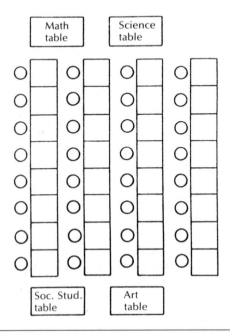

FIGURE 11.1 Continued

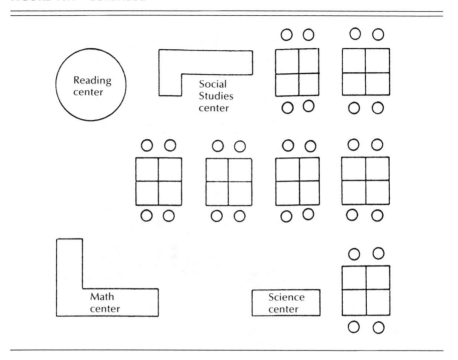

either facilitate or impede their mutual objectives. Dorothy Hennings points out that students quickly recognize the implications of the placement of certain objects, such as the teacher's desk; the arrangement of their own desks (rows, tables, clusters); and the presence or absence of private areas (listening and conversation booths, play areas).[1] Some classroom designs are perceived as restricting or promoting freedom, encouraging or discouraging conversation, promoting independence or dependence on the teacher. Similarly, when pleasant facilities — including comfortable chairs, cushions, and lighting — are provided for certain activities or subjects, students understand that these activities are important or valued by the teacher. An attractive social studies center, where students can move about, encourages use.

Space and Verbal Interaction within a Classroom

The respective physical locations of the teacher and students during discussions and lessons can also affect verbal interaction. Classroom observations have suggested that an area of "silence" exists in many classrooms. This section approximates the shape of area *B* in Figure 11.2.[2] Students who are located in this area are less likely to get the teacher's attention than students in the rest of the room.

FIGURE 11.2   Area *B* — the "area of silence" in classrooms

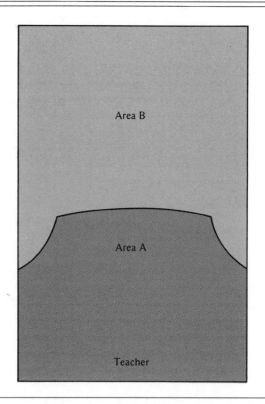

EXERCISE 11.1   Spatial Organization of Classrooms

Visit a primary and an intermediate classroom. Draw a map of each (referring to Chapter 7), locating all of the desks, facilities within the room, materials areas, centers, assorted work areas, and social studies materials. Label each map by grade and place the names of each item or area somewhere on the map; you may use a legend.

After constructing the maps, draw a third, showing *your* idea of how a classroom (at any grade level) should be organized spatially. Add any necessary explanations. Discuss how your design for a classroom reflects your ideas about teaching.

The Varieties of Teacher Communication

Many dimensions of teacher behavior besides classroom organization are part of the classroom communication system. Foremost among them are teachers' and students' *nonverbal* and *verbal* communication during instruction.

Nonverbal Communication

Although teachers' use of space and arrangement of objects is a form of nonverbal communication to students, the most dynamic form of expression includes posture and body movements. Consider the following case. A young man who is a substitute teacher enters a school for the first time. He pauses for just a moment outside of a fifth-grade class to which he has suddenly been assigned. School has already started. Children in the class are laughing and talking loudly; a few are yelling and tossing objects around. Three boys are running around the room.

The teacher strides briskly to the front of the room with shoulders erect and a blank expression on his face. He faces the class from in front of the teacher's desk, and, still expressionless, without saying a word takes off his jacket and rolls up his sleeves. Making eye contact with the three standing boys and motioning them to sit down with two quick stabs of his finger, the teacher at the same time scans the class.

Not a word has passed yet between the teacher and the students, but already he has communicated a great deal to the children. Whatever one thinks of his nonverbal messages, they were clearly and deliberately sent and were received by the entire class: The students' behavior was inappropriate. The teacher is in charge. He is aware of everything happening in the room. He is serious. It is time to get down to the business of learning.

Contrast this teacher's intentional use of nonverbal communication with that of another described by Robert Koch. The second teacher appears to be unaware of the nonverbal messages she is sending.

> When Miss R. entered her room, she looked confused. This emotional climate was created by an uncertain gait, a bewildered facial expression, and she watched the floor as though she might stumble. She ignored the noisy class and they her. They went on talking.
>
> She sat at her desk, fumbled with books, laid them aside, reached for them again, found passages and marked these with hastily torn slips of paper.
>
> Suddenly she looked up as though aware for the first time that others were about, picked out a single student, glared, and threatened to send him to the principal. The class was silent just a moment, then ignored her and resumed making noise. The one student heeded her admonition. Evidently they had learned that she would carry out her threats, but only to the one addressed.
>
> She began her lesson. She knew her subject, but sounded bored. Nonverbal cues were clearly communicated by her facial expression, her monotone, and her stance. Her class responded appropriately with yawns.

She paid good attention to any single student working at the board, but ignored the group as if they weren't there.

She did not smile, stand near or touch anyone, or meet gazes with eye contact.

The children, as though testing the limits, grew noisier, walked about, punched each other, ignored the lesson.[3]

Just as teachers need to be conscious of the nature and effects of their verbal messages, so they must be aware of messages sent by their facial expressions, body posture and movements, and gestures. Learning to control and use these selectively and clearly will ensure that students receive the message we wish to send. It also prevents confusion and misunderstandings, as occur when a teacher says "That's an interesting opinion," while scowling.

Verbal Communication

One of our most important and frequently used tools in teaching is our voice. It can convey pleasure, excitement, sorrow, sadness, apprehension, surprise, and many other emotions that enhance our instruction and provide variety. Surprisingly, teachers seldom exploit all of the potential of this teaching device.

Voices come naturally in all types, of course, from mellow, confident, and reassuring ones to dull, monotonous, and shrill types. In large measure, however, we can control the quality of our voices with practice and feedback.

Besides the tone or quality of our voices the content of the communication is, of course, important. A considerable amount of research over the past quarter-century has documented the verbal interaction patterns that typically occur between teachers and students. Over a hundred systems now exist for categorizing or coding the verbal statements that occur in classrooms. One relatively simple system developed by Robert Bales, for example, uses twelve categories, such as "gives suggestions" or "asks for information."[4] Observations of a teacher's verbal behavior over a period of time provide a profile of typical interaction patterns within his or her classroom.

Much of the communication between teacher and students consists of *questions* and *answers*. More often than not, according to research, teachers initiate the questions, read them from texts, or assign them in writing to students. The questions teachers use, as their voices, are important tools for inducing learning. They too can be dull or provocative, stifling or exciting.

Developing Effective Questioning Techniques

Questions are the verbal trigger of reflective thinking. Both the *type* and the *sequencing* of questions can significantly affect the level of interaction and thinking that emerges within a class. An effective set of questions communicates clearly what is requested and focuses attention on the important objectives of a lesson or activity. It also allows all students to participate in a discussion, moves thinking along systematically, and generates new information.

EXERCISE 11.2   Developing a Teaching Voice

Identify a teacher whom you feel uses his or her voice especially effectively in teaching. Ask the teacher for permission to tape record approximately a ten- to fifteen-minute segment of instruction during which he or she will be talking a great deal.

Analyze the recording by identifying the various ways in which the teacher uses his or her voice. Then try to imitate the techniques in your own five- to ten-minute tape recording (in which you teach either a real or an imaginary class).

Patterns of Effective Questioning

Some aspects of effective questioning, such as clarity in phrasing, apply to all questions. However, no *type* of question or set of questions is suitable for all instructional objectives. Some questions are useful for stimulating a broad base of discussion; others are helpful in determining what students have learned. Still others are powerful inducements to creative thinking. Effective questioning requires that teachers select from a repertoire of tested strategies and principles those most likely to achieve objectives.

We will consider four ways to develop effective patterns of questioning: (1) providing sufficient time for answering questions, (2) developing a basic question script for lessons, (3) sequencing questions from easy to more complex, and (4) avoiding poorly stated questions.

Use of Time in Questioning. A frequently overlooked dimension of effective questioning is what has been called *wait-time*. Wait-time occurs between the asking of a question and the point at which an answer is expected. When it is short, a teacher expects an answer immediately. If one is not forthcoming, the teacher may restate the question, rephrase it, ask a new one, or provide the answer. A long wait-time may be five seconds or longer.

Average Wait-Time in Questioning. The pioneering research of Mary Budd Rowe demonstrated that teachers had an average wait-time of only *one second* for a question.[5] Rowe discovered that if a teacher prolonged the average wait-time to five seconds or longer, the length of students' responses increased. Conversely, short wait-time produced short answers.

She also discovered that teachers who learned to use silence found that children who ordinarily said little began to start talking and to offer new ideas. The teachers themselves, as they extended their wait-time, also began to include more variety in their questions. Rowe summed up the basic findings of her research in this fashion:

> When wait-time is very short, students tend to give very short answers or they are more prone to say, "I don't know." In addition, their answers often

come with a question mark in the tone, as if to say, "Is that what you want?" But if you increase the wait-time, especially the period after a child has made a response, you are more likely to get whole sentences, and the confidence as expressed by tone is higher. Another bonus that results from increased wait-time is the appearance of speculative thinking (e.g., "It might be the water," . . . "but it could be too many plants.") and the use of arguments based on evidence. If the wait-time is prolonged an average of five seconds or more, young children shift from teacher-centered show-and-tell kinds of behavior to child-child comparing of differences.[6]

EXERCISE 11.3   Assessing Wait-Time in Questioning

Select a topic in social studies and a grade level, and develop a short lesson with a set of questions. Identify a class to which the lesson may be taught, then teach it and record the discussion. At the conclusion isolate each instance of questioning and determine the wait-time. On a sheet of paper list all of the questions you raised and next to them the amount of wait-time that followed.

Question Scripts. Another way to increase the incidence of effective questions is to use a question script. A question script is a basic set of questions that have been organized in advance for use in a lesson or activity. Unlike spontaneous questions, these are a few — usually three to five — well-organized, and especially important. They may be supplemented by spontaneous ones.

Question scripts require a teacher to consider the role of questions in a lesson and to devote some care to their development. The presence of a script ensures that several well-thought-out and carefully phrased questions will be used to guide the development of a lesson or activity as well as students' thinking.

Sequencing Questions. Increasing wait-time and creating question scripts are important initial steps in developing effective questioning techniques. Another important strategy is learning to *sequence questions from less complex to more complex.* This helps to build a logical progression of thought in students and to move them from lower to higher levels of thinking. In the taxonomies of objectives developed by Benjamin Bloom and his associates and discussed earlier in Chapter 3 sample questions are provided for all levels of thought.

Although it is obviously desirable to have all students thinking at the highest levels possible, most need to move gradually from a lower to a higher level. Getting students to operate at higher levels of thinking thus becomes a matter of *moving* them up one level at a time. The moving occurs through a sequence of questions from simple to more complex.

For example, suppose you and I have just viewed the film *War and Peace* together. At the conclusion we begin to discuss it. My initial question is, "Do you remember the names of all the major characters?"

From that discussion opener we progress to "Which parts did you enjoy the most?" and "Why?" Toward the middle of the discussion I inquire, "Did this film remind you of any others you have ever seen? In which ways?" We conclude our discussion with "What was the meaning of that film?"

Compare that sequence of questions with a similar discussion. In this scenario you and I again emerge after seeing *War and Peace,* and I ask at the outset, "How would you sum up the film [of three hours or more] in a sentence?"

In the first case, the sequence of questions has helped me organize my thoughts for the final question, which requires a high level of thinking. The same type of question, when it occurs at the *beginning* of the second discussion, is difficult to deal with. Furthermore, even if I could respond to it at the outset, my answer is likely to be more thoughtful and more complete after I have had an opportunity to order and compare the information from the film and to listen to your recollections and insights.

The Taba Questioning Strategies. Hilda Taba and her associates developed, researched, and refined a series of strategies for social studies questioning. These involved a sequence of questions designed to raise children's levels of thinking.[7] Two of the strategies are considered here. Each includes a set of core questions to be asked in exactly the sequence indicated. Each questioning strategy also is designed to achieve limited objectives.

The first questioning strategy is designed to achieve one of three broad objectives. It attempts to (1) encourage all students in a class to participate in a discussion, (2) to determine what students know and do not know about a topic before they study it, or (3) to assess what students have learned as a result of experiences or study related to a topic. This strategy uses three sequenced questions, an *opening* question, a *grouping* question, and a *labeling* question. The Northwest Regional Laboratory has developed training materials based on the Taba strategies, and the following guidelines are adapted from its work.[8]

In a classroom the Taba model might be applied as indicated in this hypothetical situation. Mr. Walker wishes to find out what his class of third graders has learned about neighborhoods. He begins by asking, "What would you expect to find in a neighborhood?"

He accepts all responses without any verbal or nonverbal criticisms and lists all answers on the board. When Suzie volunteered the response "an elephant" and the entire class tittered, Mr. Walker stifled the urge to frown and instructed the class that there were no right or wrong answers since the question asked what each person would expect to find. When he was satisfied that there were no more questions, he asked the class to look over the list of responses on the board numbered 1 to 35.

Opening Question

Examples	*Function of Question*
What comes to mind when you hear the word *freedom?* What did you see in the film? What do you think of when George Washington is mentioned?	Calls for recollection of information. Allows all students to participate in the discussion on an equal footing.

Grouping Question

Look over our list of items. Are there any that could be grouped together? Why did you group them in that way? Are there any things on the board that could be grouped together? Why did you put those items together?	Requires students to organize information on the basis of similarities and differences that they perceive, and to provide a rationale for their classifications.

Labeling Groups

Let's look at group *A*. Can you think of a one- or two-word label or name for it?	To summarize and further refine thinking.

Then he asked, "Are there any items on the board that could be grouped together?" His class quickly responded, and they came up with six groups, A, B, C, D, E, and F. After items were grouped together, Mr. Walker placed a letter of the alphabet next to the items to represent each group and asked the person who suggested the grouping to explain why he had done so. Whatever rationale was given was accepted, and whenever a grouping was challenged or an addition suggested the author of the categorizing was allowed to decide whether additions or revisions should be made. Anyone, however, was free to suggest his or her own grouping.

Finally, the authors of the groupings were asked to provide a name for each cluster. The students were then asked if they thought any of the six categories could be combined. Suggestions were offered and the authors of the categories agreed, so that four final categories remained.

A second Taba questioning strategy uses a sequence of questions to get students to draw conclusions and generalizations from data.[9] It also employs three core questions: an *opening* question, an *interpretive* question, and a *capstone* question. Again, several supporting questions are used as needed to clarify and summarize points and to keep the discussion on target.

Opening Question

Example	*Function of Question*
What did you see on the field trip?	Calls for recollection of information. Allows all students to participate in the discussion on an equal footing.
What did we learn about the Navaho?	

Interpretive Question

What differences did you notice between two people?	Get students to draw relationships between data being considered, to compare and contrast information.
How did Jefferson feel about the issue that was different from how Hamilton felt?	

Capstone Question

What conclusion could we draw from our investigation?	Asks student to form a conclusion, a summary, or a generalization.
From our study, what can you say about families?	

An application of this questioning strategy is illustrated in the first-grade Addison-Wesley basal text series, *Teacher's Guide for People in Neighborhoods,* shown in Figure 11.3.

EXERCISE 11.4   Applying Questioning Techniques

Select a grade level and a topic for a social studies lesson. Develop a set of questions for the lesson, applying either of the two Taba strategies. Construct the core questions first, and then develop supplemental questions (e.g., for clarification that you anticipate needing in a discussion). Arrange these two sets of questions separately on a sheet.

Avoiding Poorly Stated Questions. Besides providing insufficient wait time, lacking a question script, and not properly sequencing questions, there is yet another way teachers' questioning strategies can go astray. Improperly worded questions are a major source of problems both for teachers and students, since they do not accomplish the teacher's purpose and cause confusion for students. Questions that are ambiguous, call for a yes or no answer, are slanted, or require students to guess what the teacher wants for an answer all should be avoided. Several such questions are illustrated in the book, *Teacher's Guide: Justice in Urban America Series*. The following examples are adapted from that work.[10]

Type of Question	Example	Reason to Avoid It
Yes-No	Does Iran manufacture automobiles?	Produces no discussion and encourages guessing
Ambiguous	What happened in the Civil War?	Confusing and unclear; students are not sure what the teacher wants
Leading	Don't you really think Kennedy was a great President?	Tells students what teacher seems to want to hear
Slanted	Why is America the greatest country in the world?	Promotes a point of view in the question

FIGURE 11.3.   Application of Taba questioning strategy

Activity 10: Have the children look at the picture on page 64. Ask:

1. What do you see in this picture?
2. Why do you suppose the tracks for this electric train are built above the streets? Read the caption to the children and tell them that the buildings in the Loop are offices, banks, big stores, theaters, and restaurants.
3. What people do you suppose use the trains to go to downtown Chicago?
4. How is this part of Chicago different from Vicki's neighborhood? (If the children do not recall what Vicki's neighborhood looks like, have them look at the pictures on pages 24–26 to note the low buildings, yards, etc.)
5. How is the downtown part of Chicago important to Mrs. Winters? To Vicki? (If necessary, continue questioning until the children relate the downtown area to Mrs. Winters' work and shopping and to the proposed Christmas trip for Vicki.)

Typical Responses:
Mr. and Mrs. Winter had to leave their own neighborhoods to work. Some neighborhoods have more kinds of stores, so people go there to shop.

Different neighborhoods have different kinds of things in them so people go there to get what they need.

Source: Teacher's Guide for People in Neighborhoods, a text in the Addison-Wesley Taba Program in Social Studies, Menlo Park, Calif., 1972, p. T77.

Managing the Classroom Environment

"I really like these children and I think they like me, but I just can't seem to get them to behave."

Perhaps one of the overriding concerns of beginning teachers is whether they will be able to manage their classes effectively. A class that is out of control and bent on unproductive or destructive pursuits is an ugly and demoralizing sight. It is much more so when one is the center of it and is responsible for redirecting it into constructive learning activities. The feeling one has is of complete powerlessness and incompetence.

In such a classroom communication is garbled and coated with tension. No effective instruction can occur in the midst of a maelstrom, nor can children have any sense of stability and security. Classroom management, therefore, merits at least brief attention in our discussion of social studies instruction. Often books and articles on management give tips on how to be successful in the classroom. These range from maxims such as "Don't smile before Christmas" to case studies of success.

The limitation of trying to adopt such practices wholesale is that one overlooks the need for a rationale for what one wishes to do. Learning to use an eclectic set of management techniques without some notion of *why* they are to be used eventually creates problems. When a specific action becomes ineffective, the teacher will not know what went wrong and which adjustments to make.

Student Expectations for Classroom Management

Each teacher has some expectations of what the behavior of his or her students should be. Some teachers will accept a high level of noise and a great deal of student movement, whereas others will not. Students in the elementary grades generally adjust quickly each year to a new teacher's expectations.

Students also have expectations about the behavior of a teacher. These include both how the teacher should treat them and what the teacher should do to manage the general classroom environment. Among other things, they relate to how teachers should establish and maintain rules and policies. Successful classroom management always involves sensitivity to students' expectations about teacher behavior.

Consider the actions of a new teacher, as related by Mario Fantini and Gerald Weinstein, and her obliviousness to students' expectations of her behavior.

> *Teacher:* Hello (embarrassed laugh) . . . I guess we're all in here together and . . . um . . . I wonder why . . . we are in here. . . . What we're doing here . . . um . . . Perhaps we should begin so we can talk to each other by telling everybody our names. I'm Mary Miller and you are . . .
>
> *Bill:* Bill Brown.
>
> *Teacher:* Bill Brown? And you are . . . (Prolonged pause)
>
> *Jane:* Oh . . . um . . . Jane. Jane Williams.

Teacher: Jane Williams? And you are . . . ?

Bob: Who'm I?

Teacher: Yes.

Bob: Bob.

Teacher: Bob? Now Bill, do you know Bob . . . did you know each other before? And . . . Jane — is that right?

Jane: Um-hmmmmmmmmm.

Teacher: Did you know each other?

Bob: Naw . . . I don't know them.

Teacher: You don't know them? I guess you're going to get to know them, and I guess we're all going to get to know each other. If you remember my name, like I try to remember yours. . . . I-I'll try pretty hard . . . I'm pretty dumb on names . . . (Class doesn't seem to be listening) Well, I think . . . we're all here together . . .

Bill: Can I get a drink?

Teacher: Um — wait a second to discuss that.

Bill: Well, can't I get a drink and not discuss it?

Teacher: I think maybe it might be a little more fun if we all talked about it.

Bill: (with exaggerated desperation) I'm thirsty.

Teacher: You're thirsty? Do you (hesitantly) . . . are there any rules in this school about drinks and stuff?

Jane: Don't you know the rules? (Teacher suffers ridicule from students because she doesn't know rules)

Teacher: Wha . . . Wh-who is the school for? Who makes the rules for you?

Jane: The principal.

Teacher: Why does he make them?

Bill: I'll be right back.

Teacher: O.K. (Bill leaves)[11]

Larry Cuban, in writing of his experiences in working in inner-city schools, suggests that gaining students' respect and understanding students' perspectives on teacher behavior is crucial at the outset of the school year.

> Students, for example, expect a teacher to lay down rules, hand out texts, demand silence, and assign homework — in short to run a tight ship. These expectations don't preclude students testing the limits of the teacher's ability to enforce the rules; it is part of the early trading off that marks the struggle between teacher and class. If the teacher uses the techniques of control satisfactorily while simultaneously proving to children that he can teach, the class will settle into a routine comfortable to them. But, if the teacher cannot conform to their expectations or has strong doubts about his use of authority, then clever minds click, strategies change, and tactics shift.[12]

EXERCISE 11.5 Teacher Expectations of Student Behavior

Take a blank sheet of paper and draw a horizontal line through the middle to form two boxes. In the top box write the heading "Well-Behaved Students." In the bottom box write "Badly Behaved Students."

List in each of the boxes the behaviors you feel correspond to each type of student. Which of the positive behaviors are the most important to you? Why? Which of the negative behaviors would disturb you the most? Why? As a teacher how would you reward or reinforce the positive behaviors and reduce or eliminate the negative ones?

Characteristics of Well-Managed Classrooms

What do teachers who have well-managed classrooms do to achieve their results? Jacob Kounin conducted a major research project over a decade ago to answer this question, and his findings remain the most systematic information we have on the subject.[13] Kounin concluded that it was possible to isolate specific teacher behaviors that led to managerial success in the classroom. "These techniques of classroom management," he wrote, "apply to the group and not merely to individual children. They are techniques of creating an effective classroom ecology and learning milieu. One might note that none of them necessitates punitiveness or restrictiveness."[14]

Kounin found that teachers who had a *high* degree of work involvement and a *low* degree of misbehavior in their classrooms demonstrated consistently characteristics that he labeled and described as follows:[15]

1. *Withitness:* Communicating that one knows what is going on in the classroom.
2. *Overlapping:* Being able to attend to two issues simultaneously.
3. *Smoothness:* Managing physical movement from one activity to another without jerkiness, distractions, or temporary halts.
4. *Momentum:* Keeping physical activities moving at an appropriate pace.
5. *Group alerting:* Degree to which the teacher attempts to involve nonreciting children in the recitation task.
6. *Accountability:* Extent to which children are held responsible for the tasks during recitations.
7. *Valence:* Making statements that point out that an activity has something special to it.
8. *Challenge arousal:* Making statements that draw attention to the challenge in a task.
9. *Seatwork variety:* Planning varied work activities for children at their seats.
10. *Challenge:* Intellectual challenge in seatwork.

Withitness and *overlapping* require teachers to give evidence that they actually know what is happening in the classroom at all times, even when their backs are to the class.

Smoothness and *momentum* refer to ease and quickness of transitions from one activity to another. They require moving children to a new area or task with clear directions, without interruptions or returns to the previous activity, and without getting bogged down on a topic.

Group alerting includes teacher behavior that attempts to involve all the children — at least, psychologically — in the instructional task. It is characterized by statements such as, "Suppose we all think about the answer. Whom shall I call?"

Accountability requires the teacher to follow through on requests made of students. An example of an accountability statement is "I will walk around the room to see which hypothesis you have written down."

Valence and *challenge arousal* behaviors include those through which teachers attempt to build up the positive features of an activity, to present students with a problem, or to pique their curiosity.

Seatwork variety and *challenge* both relate to provisions for interesting, meaningful, and thought-provoking assignments.

Behavioral and Humanistic Approaches
to Classroom Management

In recent years several texts on classroom management have been written, many of which promote either a *behavioral* or a *humanistic* approach to classroom management.[16] Both approaches include techniques that can be useful if teachers understand the principles behind each of the theories.

A behavioral or behavior modification approach stresses specification of classroom and school rules and desired patterns of behavior. It requires the systematic application of reinforcement or rewards when children exhibit desired behavior. Humanistic approaches vary, but they all deal with the *whole* individual rather than isolated behaviors and they involve the individual in attempting to identify solutions to problems.

Behavioral Techniques. As an example of some useful behavioral techniques consider the following guidelines, adapted from the work of Wesley Becker and his associates.[17]

1. Planning of activities should take into account the fact that not all children will finish at the same time. To provide for this phenomenon, a secondary *desirable* activity should be given as an outlet for the children when their primary assignment is completed.
2. There should be clear and systematic reminders as to what each child should be doing or is to do next. This process may be accomplished through such

devices as color-coded name tags and yarn necklaces, signs, blackboard messages, individual folders, check-out stations, and turn-in boxes.

3. A day-to-day routine that is consistent should be established. Completing one task then signals that the next should begin.
4. Motivation is built into the instructional program when the completion of one assignment is automatically rewarded by the beginning of a new desired activity. Finishing an assigned activity means that a child gets to do something that is pleasing to him or her.
5. Periodically, the instructional program should include a change of pace. This might be in the order or type of activities.

Humanistic Techniques. William Glasser in *Schools without Failure* offers some basic humanistic techniques for addressing behavioral problems. He suggests a five-step approach to behavioral problems:[18]

1. Show the student that you care about him or her.
2. Have the student identify the problem and admit to it.
3. Help the student make value judgments about the misbehavior.
4. Help the student identify the consequences of the misbehavior, if necessary and appropriate.
5. Work with students to establish a plan to alter the misbehavior.

Assessing the Quality of Classroom Interaction

Unlike many other professionals, elementary teachers spend most of their working day apart from their colleagues. What they do and say in their classroom interactions with students and what happens as a result largely go unobserved. This phenomenon makes it difficult for teachers to receive the feedback that most on-the-job professionals do. Feedback results when the behavior, comments, or sanctions of others suggest to us that we should continue or change our behavior. It can be either positive or negative.

A physician, for example, receives such feedback when the local hospital bars her from performing operations and her nurse informs her that all of her patients have canceled their appointments. It occurs more subtly when fellow workers seek out our advice on professional matters and choose us as partners on projects. A simple ''That was a great lesson'' or ''They didn't seem to understand the questions'' provides us with feedback on our teaching.

Continuous Feedback on Classroom Communications

Teachers should recognize the need for instituting techniques for feedback on an ongoing basis, not only when a problem appears to exist. Since feedback can be positive as well as negative, it can reinforce and encourage us when we are functioning effectively. It also may surprise us when, against our own negative impressions, objective feedback suggests that things are working well.

Although teachers often do work alone, they may employ a number of feedback techniques either alone or with the cooperation of the students or other professionals, to ascertain the quality of human interaction within the classroom. These may focus on specific points such as the effectiveness of questioning techniques, or on more general areas such as student perceptions of the total classroom environment, the patterns of interaction within a classroom, and nonverbal communication.

Feedback on Questioning Techniques

As we suggested earlier, the value of a question depends on several factors, including what objective the question or question set was trying to satisfy and when the question was asked. Gathering feedback on questioning begins when one decides which behaviors are to be analyzed — for example, wait-time, the sequence of questions, or the avoidance of poorly stated questions.

Over the course of several lessons, questioning sessions can be recorded, either on audio or video tape. The questioning techniques then may be evaluated by comparing the actual results with the guidelines outlined in the earlier section. A more general form of evaluation could focus solely on such basic elements of questioning as:

Clarity of questions: length, loudness, ambiguities, use of strange words, peculiar sentence structure, grammar, and speech.

Question building blocks: extent to which each new question seems to build on the answers to the old one.

Relation to lesson objectives: extent to which the questions help achieve or detract from the lesson's objectives.

Thought-provoking qualities: Do the questions merely establish what students already have learned or do they stimulate new thinking?

Interest appeal: Do the questions spark curiosity or interest in the topic?

Answer followup: How are incorrect and correct answers handled?

Feedback on Student Perceptions of the Classroom Environment

Student perceptions of what is happening in a classroom, including the quality of the human interactions, are an important source of feedback. What students perceive may or may not be accurate, but it should be taken into account. Social scientists have long realized that what individuals perceive to be reality sometimes is more important than the reality itself. Sometimes student feedback may lead a teacher to alter the conditions within the classroom, and at other times it may suggest that students' perceptions need to be changed.

Various simple diagnostic techniques are available for assessing students' general feelings about their classroom. One such device is an evaluation thermometer, shown in Figure 11.4, which can be used with even very young children. The emotion charts in Chapter 7 are also effective with primary students.

Older children may complete — anonymously — simple questionnaires sim-

FIGURE 11.4 Evaluation thermometer

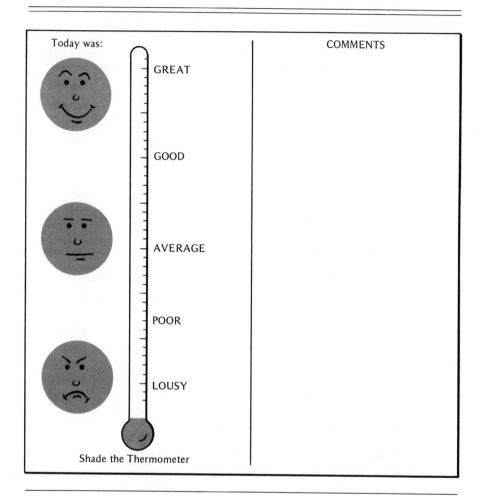

ilar to those in Figures 11.5 and 11.6. Students often respond to such requests quite candidly. As an option, a teacher may even wish to share the results of such questionnaires with the class, particularly if discrepancies exist. Suppose, for example, most of the class perceived that the others did *not* like the class, while indicating that they personally *did* like it. The class could be asked to discuss why most liked the class but didn't realize that their neighbors did as well.

Feedback on Patterns of Verbal Interaction

It is also possible objectively to assess the general patterns of *verbal* interaction, particularly those between the teacher and students. This type of feedback reveals, among other things, which students are called on most frequently. It reveals how

FIGURE 11.5 Questionnaire concerning classroom environment: student's perception

Directions: Indicate how *you* feel about the characteristics of this class; that is, place an X under the heading that you feel best describes the class. Do *not* put your name on this sheet, since your responses will be kept anonymous.

	Strongly agree	Agree	Sometimes yes, sometimes no	Not often	Never
1. There is an adequate level of discussion in our class sessions.					
2. Class members are putting as much effort into their class work as they should.					
3. The class would be a lot better if one or two individuals were not here.					
4. Class sessions are generally enjoyable.					
5. Class members are generally very friendly and pleasant toward one another.					

teachers respond to student comments and requests, how much time students spend talking and how much time the teacher does, and how teachers verbally reward and punish students.

Feedback on Patterns of Nonverbal Interaction

Social scientists and educators have devised systems for categorizing teachers' *nonverbal* behavior in the classroom as they have for verbal interactions. Through more awareness of and conscious control over our nonverbal messages, we can improve communication within a classroom and even shift some of the verbal communication load. A teacher can often gain feedback merely by becoming conscious of body posture, facial gestures, and muscle tension.

Role-Playing Techniques. Other feedback techniques include role playing with a friend or colleague who focuses strictly on the nonverbal messages we are sending, and provides us with a list of them. Self-study before a full-sized mirror, focusing on our facial expressions, posture, use and locations of our hands, movements of our head, and the like while we mimic a teaching session can also begin to give us a better profile of our nonverbal behavior.

Videotaping Class Sessions. Probably the most effective technique involves the use of videotapes. When the sound has been turned off, and if a few frames of

FIGURE 11.6 Questionnaire concerning classroom environment: student's perceptions of others' views

Directions: Indicate what you think *other members* of the class would say about the char- acteristics of this class; that is, place an X under the heading that you feel best describes what the *other* class members would indicate. Do *not* put your name on this sheet, since your responses are to be anonymous.

	Most would strongly agree	Most would agree	Most would say sometimes	Most would say not often	Most would say never
1. There is an adequate level of discussion in our class sessions.					
2. Class members are putting as much effort into their class work as they should.					
3. The class would be a lot bet- ter if one or two individuals were not here.					
4. Class sessions are generally enjoyable.					
5. Class members are generally very friendly and pleasant toward one another.					

tape can be replayed easily, both the nonverbal behavior and its effects on students can be easily and objectively analyzed. By replaying the tape one can concentrate on a single aspect of nonverbal behavior, such as eye contact, and then to move to another aspect.

EXERCISE 11.6   Self-Observation of Nonverbal Behavior

Arrange to videotape yourself teaching a social studies lesson. From the taped results, select a fifteen-minute segment, turn off the sound, and analyze your nonverbal teaching behavior. For the analysis, divide a sheet of paper into two columns. Label the left one "Nonverbal Behaviors," and list distinct behaviors in the order in which they occurred. In the right column, list the cor- responding reactions of the students under the heading, "Stu- dent Responses."

Communicating with Parents and Other Community Members

Today's elementary teacher is expected to be able to communicate with parents about their children's program of studies. As other members of the school community increasingly become involved with the schools, they too wish to be well informed. The net effect is that teachers today need to understand how to enlist the cooperation of parents, parent surrogates, and other community members better than their earlier counterparts did. This process often involves publicizing the activities of the school, preparing informational materials and programs, engaging in public dialog, and inviting the community to aid and observe in classrooms.

Anticipating Parent Concerns

"Whatever happened to history and geography?" some parent is likely to want to know. "Why don't the kids know all of the names of the presidents in order anymore?" another may wonder.

Since many aspects of the social studies program that contemporary elementary students will study differ considerably from that which their parents encountered when they were in school, teachers need to anticipate some parent apprehension. All of us, parents included, have an image of social studies that is often based on our own past experiences as students. When the school curriculum does not reflect our image, we naturally are puzzled.

Alerting Parents to New Social Studies Activities. Alerting parents in clear, simple, but noncondescending language through a flyer or a letter is one way to forestall concern about a new program, approach, set of materials, or requirements. This is also a way directly to enlist the aid of parents in achieving objectives or ensuring that students complete out-of-school assignments. Parents also might be invited to sit in on class activities or to examine curricular materials.

Accommodating Working Parents and Single-Parent Families

In the typical American family today the mother, as well as the father works. The number of single-parent families is increasing, and it is estimated that approximately half of the children born in 1982 will live in a single-parent home sometime before they graduate from high school.[19] The United States Bureau of the Census estimates that about one in five American children is currently living in such a family. In many two-parent families, one of the parents has more than one job. Many other such statistics about the modern American family have important implications for schools and how they relate to parents.

Although some parents are available to participate in school activities and conferences during the school's normal operating hours, roughly 8:30–4:00, increasingly more are not. One of the ways that schools and teachers are attempting to accommodate this new life style is increased use of telephone reports, mailings, and evening activities.

Involving Parents in the School

Events such as "back-to-school night" or what some children call "meet-the-creature [teacher] night" are an important way both of involving parents in the life of the school and of communicating the nature of their children's educational program. For a new teacher, it is especially important that a well-thought-out program be developed for such occasions, since few such opportunities to communicate directly with parents exist. The impressions that many parents receive of the teacher, the classroom, and the school are often the ones that stay with them throughout the year.

Communicating Social Studies Activities. For such occasions, experienced teachers often attempt to make the classroom especially festive and to provide visible illustrations of all of the children's work, such as a social studies project. Materials and texts are prominently displayed, and signs identifying items may be attached. Duplicated sheets explaining various programs or a typical daily schedule may be distributed as well.

Some other activities that teachers have used are:

1. Showing slides of typical classroom scenes, of activities, or of special class events.
2. Providing an overview, with charts and transparencies, of the year's social studies work, along with a question-and-answer period.
3. Having members of the class report on different phases of the social studies program.
4. Involving parents in some sample activities similar to the ones that the children have done — for example, a problem-solving activity in social studies.
5. Collecting questions from parents beforehand and organizing discussions around them.
6. Introducing and explaining new programs, materials, units, activities, or procedures.

Although parents should be encouraged to share honestly any concerns they have, such events should not be occasions to discuss in detail individual student cases. A separate conference can be arranged for this purpose.

EXERCISE 11.7   Attending and Observing at School Functions

Attend a back-to-school night or similar parent function and visit two classrooms, one a primary class and the other an intermediate/middle-school class. Describe in detail how each of the teachers prepared the classrooms for the occasion. Also describe the nature of the evening program prepared by each teacher. If possible, discuss with each of the teachers their further ideas about conducting such programs.

Involving the Community in the School

One way in which the community can be united with the school is through children's social action projects, which we discussed in Chapter 8. As children become contributors to the community under the sponsorship of the school, community members can better appreciate their responsibility to support and encourage local schools.

Using the Local Paper. Many elementary schools also reach out to the community through the local newspaper. Some intermediate grade and middle school children actually have written columns on a regular basis, reporting on school life, student achievements, and important events. Some teachers and administrators regularly contact the local press to publicize school events through pictures and short reports. Community newspapers are often very cooperative in publishing all such material, since community readers are generally eager to learn about their schools.

EXERCISE 11.8   Observing a Local School Board Meeting

Attend a regularly scheduled local school board meeting, and record the events. Obtain a copy of the agenda at the meeting, and evaluate the evening's proceedings. Note any formal actions taken by the board, and keep a log of the amount of time spent on each agenda item.

Attending School Board Meetings. Local school board meetings sometimes can also be used as a forum to publicize school and classroom activities. In smaller communities, where board agendas are not overfilled, there are often opportunities for children to participate in programs. At least, it is usually possible for a teacher briefly to publicize some special classroom activity or project in which community members might be interested.

Notes

1. Dorothy G. Hennings, *Mastering Classroom Communications* (Pacific Palisades, Calif.: Goodyear, 1975), p. 173.
2. Anita E. Simon and E. Gil Boyer, eds. *Mirrors for Behavior. III: An Anthology of Observation Instruments* (Wyncote, Pa.: Communication Materials Center, 1974), p. 61.
3. Robert Koch, "Nonverbal Observables," in *Teaching: Vantage Points for Study,* 2nd ed., ed. R. T. Hyman (Philadelphia: J. B. Lippincott, 1974), pp. 428–429.
4. Robert F. Bales, "Categories for Interaction Process Analysis System," in *Mirrors for Behavior. III: An Anthology of Observation Instruments,* ed. Anita E. Simon and E. Gil Boyer (Wyncote, Pa.: Communication Materials Center, 1974), p. 159.

5. Mary Budd Rowe, "Science, Silence and Sanctions," *Science and Children* (March 1969): 11.

6. Ibid., p. 12.

7. Hilda Taba, *Teaching Strategies and Cognitive Functioning in Elementary School Children,* Cooperative Research Project No. 2404 (Washington, D.C.: United States Office of Education, 1969).

8. John A. McCollum and Rose M. Davis, *Trainer's Manual: Development of Higher Level Thinking Abilities,* rev. ed. (Portland, Ore.: Northwest Regional Educational Laboratory, 1969), pp. 160–161.

9. Ibid., pp. 245–247.

10. *Teacher's Guide: Justice in Urban America Series* (Boston: Houghton Mifflin, 1970), p. 22.

11. Mario D. Fantini and Gerald Weinstein, *The Disadvantaged: Challenge to Education* (New York: Harper and Row, 1968), pp. 316–317.

12. Larry Cuban, *To Make a Difference: Teaching in the Inner City* (Free Press, 1970), pp. 170–171.

13. Jacob S. Kounin, *Discipline and Group Management in Classrooms* (New York: Holt, Rinehart and Winston, 1970).

14. Ibid., p. 144.

15. Ibid., pp. 143–144.

16. See a summary of the findings and an extensive list of major works on the topic in Wilford A. Weber, "Classroom Management," *Classroom Teaching Skills,* 2nd ed. James M. Cooper et al. (Lexington, Mass.: D. C. Heath, 1982), pp. 279–361.

17. Wesley A. Becker et al., *Teaching: A Course in Applied Psychology* (Chicago: Science Research Associates, 1971), pp. 176–177.

18. William Glasser, *Schools without Failure* (New York: Harper and Row, 1961).

19. Robert D. Allers, "Children from Single-Parent Homes," *Today's Education* 71 (First Annual Edition 1982): 68.

Suggested Readings

Bloom, Benjamin. *Taxonomy of Educational Objectives: The Cognitive Domain: The Classification of Educational Goals, Cognitive Domain.* New York: David McKay, 1956.

Carin, Arthur A., and Sund, Robert B. *Developing Questioning Techniques.* Columbus, Ohio: Charles E. Merrill, 1971.

Charles, C. M. *Elementary Classroom Management.* New York: Longman, 1983.

Cuban, Larry. *To Make a Difference: Teaching in the Inner City.* New York: Free Press, 1970.

Curwin, Richard L., and Fuhrmann, Barbara S. *Discover Your Teaching Self: Humanistic Approaches to Effective Teaching.* Englewood Cliffs, N.J.: Prentice-Hall, 1975.

Goffman, Erving. *Presentation of Self in Everyday Life.* New York: Anchor Books, 1959.

Hall, Edward B. *The Hidden Dimension.* New York: Doubleday, 1966.

Hennings, Dorothy G. *Mastering Classroom Communications.* Pacific Palisades, Calif.: Goodyear, 1975.

Kounin, Jacob S. *Discipline and Group Management in Classrooms.* 2nd ed. New York: Holt, Rinehart and Winston, 1982.

Taba, Hilda. *Teaching Strategies and Cognitive Functioning in Elementary School Children,* Cooperative Research Project No. 2404. Washington, D.C.: United States Office of Education, 1969.

Weber, Wilford A. ''Classroom Management,'' *Classroom Teaching Skills.* 2nd ed. James M. Cooper et al. Lexington, Mass.: D. C. Heath, 1982, pp. 279–361.

12

Provisions for
Special Students

Each of us is unique. Because each of us is special, each has certain talents and capabilities and also limitations. Some aspects of these characteristics are inherited and some are learned and developed over time. We have both psychological and biological differences.

In a democracy a public educational system should be sensitive to the special qualities of *all* students and attempt to provide them with equal opportunities for development. It should capitalize on their strengths and help compensate for their limitations. Above all, equal opportunities in an educational setting should mean providing children who are lumped into categories — such as gifted, culturally different, less able, and handicapped — with learning experiences appropriate for their capabilities and directed toward common goals and objectives.

In this chapter we shall consider first how to deal with fundamental differences that affect learning under the topic of *individualized instruction*. Then we shall examine some ways teachers can respond to individual student needs.

Individualized Instruction

In its simplest form *individualized instruction is making provision for differences among learners*. There are many differences in students, of course, and it would be impossible for one teacher to consider all of them for any given learning task. Teachers typically select some differences they regard as especially significant to recognize in the instructional program. They then consider the available resources and begin to develop strategies and materials for instruction.

Individual Differences among Students

Some differences, such as slightly reduced visual acuity, are easy to address and involve only modest adjustments in classroom practices. Others may require major reorganization of the classroom or even of an educational system. For example, it is widely accepted that all children enter kindergarten or the first grade at approximately the same chronological age. Recognizing that developmentally children differ widely in the ages at which they are ready to begin formal learning would challenge this common practice. It would require fundamental changes in both legal statutes and school admission policies.

Types of Student Differences. Some differences among students that have been used in the past as a basis for individualizing instruction include the following:

reading abilities

developmental capabilities

hearing problems

motivational levels

physical settings
   preferred for learning

amounts of time needed
   to complete a task

learning styles

background and prior learning

thinking styles

cultural experiences

achievements

sight problems

interests

interpersonal skills

ages

attention spans

Responding to Student Differences. Whatever the nature of the differences among students, when teachers select some to address, they are engaging in individualized instruction. The long list of possible differences accounts, in part, for the existence of so many instructional approaches in education, all of which are characterized as "individualized." No single system of individualization could take into account simultaneously all of the ways individuals differ that are significant for learning. Each system considers only one or at best, several differences.

Forms of Individualized Instruction. In practice teachers often combine several instructional approaches in responding to student differences. For example, a teacher may provide alternative sets of social studies materials at varying reading levels as a way of responding to differences in students' *reading abilities.* The teacher also may locate student assignments based on the reading material in a learning center to allow students to proceed at their own pace.

Some of the other approaches that teachers have used to accommodate student differences are nongraded classes, ability-grouped classes, open classrooms, programmed instruction, computer-assisted instruction, and learning packets. In some cases the students may decide what is to be learned or how it is to be learned, whereas in others they control only the pace of learning.[1] Among the approaches the most widely used at the elementary level are probably *learning centers.*

Learning Centers

Learning or activity centers often are associated with open classroom settings, but they can be incorporated into any pattern of organizing instruction. They are a flexible form of individualization because they can accommodate provisions for many types of differences: interests, rates of learning, reading levels, prior learning, learning styles, cognitive styles, attention spans, and interpersonal skills among others.

In this approach one or more social studies centers are designated and attractively displayed within the classroom. A center should have provisions for either individuals or small groups to work there. The types of materials might include:

Multimedia Materials

Listening post with multiple sets of headphones

Filmstrip projector with screen

Record or tape player for use with listening post

8mm projector

Microcomputer and peripherals

Videotape machine

Slide projector

Collections of photographs and pictures

Globe and maps

Dioramas

Tapes, records, films, filmstrips, 8mm film loops, slides, computer software, and videocassettes

Study prints

Simulation games

Artifacts

Compasses

Posters

Print Materials

Magazines and newspapers

Historical fiction works

Nonfiction and biographical information books

Reproductions of historical documents

Timelines

Teacher-made files

Study kits

Reference works

Activity sheets and cards

Cartoons

Charts, graphs, and tables

Travel folders

Catalogs

Implementing Learning Centers. Generally a center will focus on a single theme and provide several options for exploring it. Any of the topics discussed in Chapter 3 in the section on units and in Chapter 8 under social issues or similar ones would be suitable for center themes. The contents and subjects of centers should be changed periodically, and students may be encouraged to participate in the creation and development of a center. The spatial design of a classroom organized around learning centers is shown in Figure 12.1.

Several books are available that provide detailed instruction on how to construct centers and develop materials and related activities. These are listed in the Suggested Readings at the end of the chapter. The following case study reported by Joan Ferry, at the time of the account a fifth-grade teacher, illustrates how a center may be managed and *correlated and integrated* with other instructional approaches.[2]

A Sample Learning Center. Ferry relates how a team of three teachers and eighty-one fifth-graders incorporated centers into a unit of study that included the economics topics, "The Costs of Production, "Supply and Demand," and "Paying the Price" (relative costs of items). Each teacher was responsible for one of the topics, and taught each of the classes over three sessions for a total of approximately three hours. After the teacher sessions, community members representing different careers addressed all three classes and focused on topics such as costs of production and distribution, the credit economy, profit, competition, goods and services, supply and demand, buying and selling techniques, raw materials, and monopolies.

In discussing the planning for the unit Ferry relates,

> Class trips have been planned as a part of the unit. Some trips have already been taken in order to schedule them all before the close of school. The rest of the trips will be taken during the economics unit. Some involve all the fifth graders, while at other times students will choose one trip of three, thereby allowing three separate groups to visit three separate places simultaneously.
>
> At least three math classes will also be devoted to studying a mathematical aspect of economics. Each teacher will teach his or her math class decimals, percent, interest, and budgeting incomes. Math problems will be devised that are based on these concepts. The problems will focus on the kinds of economical choices a fifth grader faces in his daily living. The relationship of everyday economics to the mathematical problems presented will be emphasized.

FIGURE 12.1 Classroom organized around learning centers

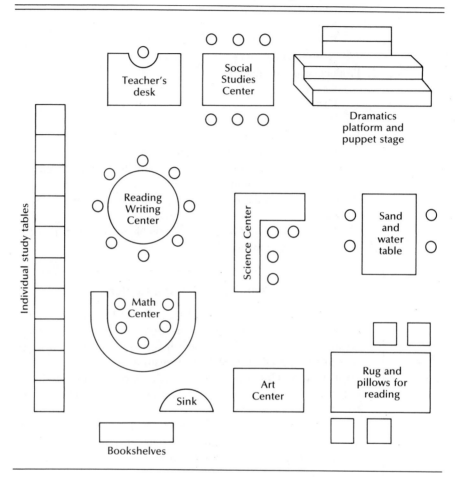

After the above activities have started, the learning centers . . . will be used by our fifth graders. Many of the centers are intended to reinforce ideas already presented, whereas others will attempt to present new ideas. Still other centers will provide opportunities for interested students to study aspects which are indirectly related to economics.

Each child will have his or her own 5" × 8" card listing all the centers. Each card will indicate which centers are mandatory for the student and which ones are recommended. A student may work, however, at any other center he or she desires, provided he or she has fulfilled the required work.[3]

Over forty activities were developed for the center covering the unit's subject matter. Some titles of activities directions and materials that were provided in the center are as follows:

1. What would you buy?
   Directions
   Magazines
   Example
   Activity assignment
2. Products and consumers
   Directions
   Poster
   Worksheet
3. Finding out about chocolate
   List of workers involved in production
   Worksheet to be used in conjunction with book provided
   Instructions for drawing
4. What happened to these items before you bought them?
   Directions
   Box containing nail, soda can, cotton blouse, knitted hat, and leather wallet
   Activity assignment

Exercise 12.1   Planning a Learning Center

Organize a group of two or three. Refer to Chapter 8 and select a topic from the list of social issues presented there or identify another one in which you are interested. Identify a grade level or population of students for whom a learning center would be appropriate. Consult several basic texts dealing with learning centers, including those in the Suggested Readings, if available, for ideas and suggestions.

Develop a multimedia center built around the theme you have selected. Include enough materials and activities for approximately two to three weeks of work.

Learning Contracts. Occasionally, in conjunction with learning centers, teachers require students to make a learning contract. This is a simple way to clarify for students their objectives in the center and to help them learn to establish reasonable deadlines and work schedules. Contracts also help teachers with the managerial problems of operating centers with many students working at different rates.

There is no set format for a contract, but typically one spells out such matters as what a student agrees to do in a center, what resources will be used and in which ways, and when each phase of the activity has been completed. An example of a learning contract and how it is used in conjunction with a learning center is given in Figure 12.2. The illustration also includes a simple record-keeping sheet that may be used to keep track of all the students working in the center.[4]

FIGURE 12.2   A learning center activity with a learning contract

Contract

for

The American Revolution
Learning Center

I_____ , Contract to complete the
following activities in the American Revolution Learning Center:

1. Complete the *black* colored activity card.
2. Choose one *blue* colored activity card and complete it.
3. Have a conference with my teacher to go over the *blue* activity.
4. Choose one *red* colored activity card and complete it.
5. Have a conference with my teacher to go over my *red* activity.

Student's name_____

Teacher's name_____

Date_____

Figure continues on following page

FIGURE 12.2 Continued

AMERICAN REVOLUTION CENTER

There are three groups of learning alternatives for this center. Alternative 1 (written in *black*) is designed to provide a common base of information for all students. The *blue* activities are intended to expose the student to a literary or audiovisual interpretation of one aspect or personality of the Revolution. They require some written output from the student. The *red* activities are the least structured. In carrying out these activities, the student must locate his or her own resource materials and develop a personalized expression of his or her knowledge.

Instructions

This learning center is about the American Revolution. Before beginning work at the center, you should read about the Revolution in your social studies book and take part in class discussions about the Revolution. When you come to the center.

1. Do alternative 1 (written in *black*).

2. Choose one *blue* learning alternative from the activity task cards. When you have finished it, have a conference with your teacher.

3. Choose one *red* alternative from the task card file and carry it out. When you have finished it, have a conference with your teacher.

4. If you have time, choose one of the enrichment packages and work through it, *or* design your own enrichment activity and carry it out after consultation with your teacher.

5. Place all written work in your individual record-keeping folder.

From *One at a Time All at Once* by Jack E. Blackburn and W. Conrad Powell. Copyright © 1976 by Scott, Foresman and Company. Reprinted by permission.

Record-keeping Sheet for
The American Revolution Learning Center

Students' Names	Black Activity Completed	Blue Activity Completed	Teacher Conference	Red Activity Completed	Teacher Conference

THIS CARD IS FROM ONE AT A TIME   © 1976 GOODYEAR PUBLISHING COMPANY INC

Attending to Reading Differences

We hear of high school graduates who cannot read and about high percentages of illiterate adults among our national population. At the same time, our elementary schools without exception across the nation spend more time at every grade on reading as a subject than on any other one in the curriculum. It is not unusual even for schools to devote three times as much of a school day to reading than to other subjects such as social studies. If time devoted to a subject were the sole criterion of learning, children in our elementary schools should learn reading better than any other subject.

Why then do so many young Americans have reading problems? The reasons for our national reading problem have become the object of serious social controversy in the United States.

The individual differences in the levels at which children read in the elementary level are often vast. They become even more pronounced in the intermediate and middle-school grades than in the primary ones. This phenomenon is an especially serious obstacle to learning in the social studies where much of the subject matter in schools typically is in written form. Printed media, such as basal texts and newspapers, put students with poor reading abilities at a disadvantage.

Aiding Students in Reading Newspapers and Basal Texts

As we suggested in Chapter 8, newspapers — whether they are local ones or those prepared especially for students — are a special forum of information in the social studies. They offer students a wealth of data on contemporary affairs, and help bridge the gap between the real world and the world of the school curriculum. To interpret and process the information they contain properly, however, most students — even good readers — need assistance.

Basal texts, although they have been carefully shaped with a particular student audience in mind, have some of the same problems as newspapers, and require the same aids for effective reading. Basal texts are frequently associated with a particular reading level that has been identified by using one or more of the popular formulas. Given the range of reading abilities in a classroom, teachers quickly discover that many students have some problems in effectively reading the textbook designed for the ''average student.''

Some of the important tasks with which students will need practice in effectively reading newspapers and basal texts are the following:

1. *Separating headlines from the substance of an article.* This involves a recognition that a headline is usually someone's (frequently not the author's) *interpretation* or *value judgment* about what the article says.
2. *Becoming familiar with common colloquialisms, metaphors, acronyms, and cryptic expressions.* This requires identifying, categorizing, and explaining such expressions as ''Kennedy was eyeball to eyeball with the Soviets, and they blinked.''

3. *Identifying new concepts in stories, and dismantling sentences packed with difficult concepts.* Students need to break apart difficult sentences like this one, which appeared in a student version of a newspaper: ''Marco Polo surely absorbed from that imperial myth a sense of self-assurance and a vision of Venice's 'manifest destiny' that fortified and complemented a pragmatic education in business.''

4. *Making lists of new and difficult words and specialized vocabulary.* This helps students to review items they have learned.

5. *Summarizing in a sentence or a paragraph the gist of an article.* This practice helps students improve comprehension and test understanding.

6. *Comparing different accounts of the same event.* This helps students to understand the interpretative aspects of reporting and to separate fact from opinion.

7. *Learning to read charts, graphs, tables, pictures, and cartoons.* It is especially important that children begin to decode the meaning in such media, since they frequently are used as a shorthand way to communicate complex ideas or data.

8. *Identifying practical and interesting items of information.* Students need to see papers not only as entertainment or general information vehicles, but also as ways to answer useful questions such as, How can I locate a job?

9. *Learning to pronounce strange and difficult terms.* An important psychological component of understanding the strange aspects of our life is knowing how to describe them verbally.

10. *Being able to detect bias.* This involves recognizing how an author slants an article through the use of value-laden terms and one-sided arguments.

11. *Recognizing cause-and-effect relationships.* Students need to recognize primary actors and events and how they are linked in an article or story.

12. *Identifying the big idea in a story.* This ability involves separating the important points from the colorful but nonessential ones.

13. *Using context clues to understand points.* Learning to do this permits an individual to go beyond vocabulary limitations and to use what is known to guess about what is unknown.

14. *Applying material read to old and new experiences.* This involves making reading more than an intellectual exercise, and reinforcing its utilitarian aspects.

15. *Recognizing how information is categorized and organized.* Papers and most print materials such as basal texts have a pattern of classifying and organizing the material they contain. This includes, for example, identifying the sections of papers and what is usually presented there, as well as locating the listing of contents.

Using Tables of Contents, Glossaries, Indexes, Appendixes, and Chapter Headings.

Texts designed for students differ considerably from a typical fiction or nonfiction book. They contain several features that effective readers quickly learn to use to gain information. Taking some time at the beginning of the year to introduce the components of the text, such as the table of contents, the index, the structure of each chapter, and the appendixes and glossary, can aid students in their reading. Periodic exercises designed to get students to use these features of texts can reinforce the initial lesson.

Measures of Readability

Text publishers and teachers alike need objective means of measuring the difficulty of reading materials. Over thirty such measures exist, and they are useful within their limitations. They provide a standard for comparing materials that is usually based on two aspects of writing style: sentence length and word difficulty. They also offer a *probability estimate* — whether a set of social studies materials is likely to be easy or difficult for a given student to process.

Limitations of Measures of Readability. Such formulas, however, often miss some of the complexity associated with reading in an area like social studies. Such subjects involve many specialized concepts, many complex visual materials that must be processed (such as maps and tables), and many abstract associations. Professionals who deal with severe reading difficulties in students realize that assessing individuals' actual reading capabilities and limitations is far more complex than assigning scores.[5]

In spite of the limitations of reading measures, however, they can serve as basic tools to help identify appropriate reading materials in social studies. They can reveal whether supplementary or basal materials are likely to present students with serious reading problems. Two of the most commonly used measures are the *Fry readability formula* and the *cloze procedure.*

The Fry Readability Formula. One of the easiest reading formulas to use is that named after Edward Fry.[6] It also correlates highly with other similar formulas, for example, the Dale-Schall and the Flesch ones. It involves a graph similar to that in Figure 12.3 and the counting of syllables and average number of sentences in representative hundred-word passages from reading material. Averages are calculated to the nearest tenth of a sentence.

Identifying Approximate Reading Level of Material. To find the approximate grade level of the reading material, one reads across the top of the graph until one locates the line with the correct number of syllables. One reads along the side of the graph to find the line that corresponds to the sentence length. The point at which the two lines meet will fall within the range of the approximate grade level of the material.

FIGURE 12.3   Fry readability formula

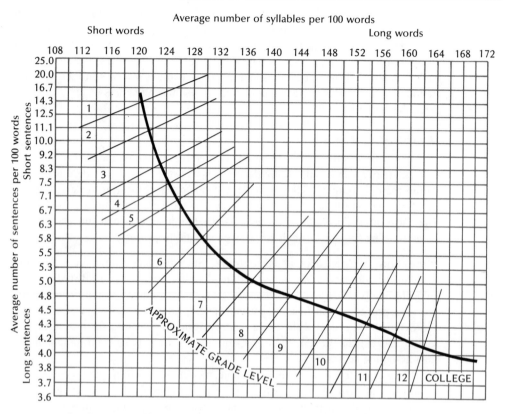

Source: Edward Fry, "A Readability Formula That Saves Time," *Journal of Reading*, 2 (April 1968), p. 577.

Consider a hypothetical basal textbook. We select passages of 100 words at random from somewhere near the front and the back of the text. We also pick two other passages at random from other locations in the text. The results of our tedious syllable and sentence tallies are shown in Table 12.1.

The Cloze Procedure. A totally different approach to assessing the appropriateness of reading materials requires a student to supply missing words in a sample passage from the material. The technique, called the *cloze procedure*, has several variations, but the essence is that every *fifth* word of a passage is omitted, blanked out, or hidden from a student.[7] Lines are inserted where the missing words go. The student then reads and supplies as many missing words as possible. A sample passage of *exactly* 250 words representative of the complete text should be selected. If the reading levels vary considerably throughout the text, several 250 word passages should be used.

TABLE 12.1   Reading level from Fry graph: fourth grade

Hundred-word passages	Number of syllables	Number of sentences
First	112	7.3
Second	132	10.0
Third	127	9.5
Fourth	141	11.1
Total	512	37.9
Average	128	9.2

Sample Reading Passage. A portion of a prepared passage for a student test would look something like this:

> Many communities were started _____ the oceans. Some people _____ make a living there _____ fishing. Others could farm _____ cut down trees. Ships _____ sail to and from _____ community. A community where _____ come and go is _____ port. The ships could _____ people in and take _____ out. The ship could _____ in things people need _____ live. They could carry _____ many goods to be _____. So the community could _____ in touch with many _____. [Portion of a 250 word passage]

The passage with the missing words supplied is:

> Many communities were started near the oceans. Some people could make a living there by fishing. Others could farm or cut down trees. Ships could sail to and from the community. A community where ships come and go is a port. The ships could bring people in and take them out. The ship could bring in things people need to live. They could carry away many goods to be sold. So the community could be in touch with many lands.[8]

Identifying Difficulty Level of Reading Material. Students are asked to insert the missing words, although misspellings are acceptable; no time limits are set. If the student can supply approximately 50 percent or more of the correct words, the passage is considered to be not too difficult to read. Although the test and the procedures may seem to be arbitrary, if not invalid, they appear in practice to produce results similar to more complex analyses of reading levels.

Reading Pictures

Teachers have always been great collectors of pictures of all sorts. Old magazines and newspapers, as well as commercially prepared materials, are treasure troves

---

EXERCISE 12.2   Applying Measures of Readability

Locate a basal social studies text that is used for any grade level in a local elementary or middle school to which you have access. Using the directions in the preceding sections assess the readability of the text using both the Fry graph and the cloze procedure. Use portions of the same passages for both measures to permit some comparisons. In using the cloze procedure, have several students, identified as being average or "on-grade" readers by their teacher, fill in the missing words to see if the results differ. Analyze and evaluate the results of your assessments.

---

of visual materials that can be used for lessons. They also can be used as subject matter in the same manner as written material. A variety of pictures and visual materials — including paintings, photos, slides, drawings, dioramas, transparencies — are available for teaching social studies. Pictures that children themselves draw, color, paint, or photograph, and collages that they create are also rich sources of material for discussion. A child's picture can reflect feelings, as well as thoughts, and serve as a medium of communication. In order for students to use visual data effectively, however, they need to understand how to *read* pictures.

Techniques for Reading Pictures and Other Visual Material. Reading visual material effectively requires some of the same techniques that print reading does. It involves more than merely perceiving what is visually present. In reading visual materials viewers try to answer a series of questions. These include identifying which data the picture presents (What is presented?), distinguishing whether it represents fact or fiction (Is this an actual or recreated version of reality?), relating the data to other information (What bearing does this have on what is known already?), and summarizing the data (What would be an appropriate title or caption for the item?).

Reading Expressive and Informational Pictures. An *expressive* picture is one that portrays people, events, or problems in ways that evoke emotional responses and are subject to different interpretations. Pictures like these — whether they show the sun setting over the Grand Canyon or a survivor of a concentration camp — have as their primary objective the generation of emotional responses from viewers. Examples of curricular materials that provide such pictures are series of multiracial children portraying a variety of moods, produced by the David Cook Company, and the series of materials developed by Fannie and George Shaftel and produced by Holt, Rinehart and Winston:

Words and Action: Role-Playing Photo-Problems for Young Children

Role-Playing in Action: Role-Playing and Discussion Photographs for Elementary Social Studies

Values in Action: Role-Playing Problem-Situations for the Intermediate Grades

Such pictures may be contrasted with *informational* ones, which are designed to communicate specific facts. Both types are used in social studies instruction, although informational pictures are most commonly found in text materials. Students need to have experiences with both types, and to be able to recognize the differences between them. An inexpensive pamphlet, available from the National Council for the Social Studies, lists several sources of both expressive and informational pictures: Leonard S. Kenworthy, *Reach for a Picture* (How To Do It Series 2, No. 3, 1977).

Cognitive Styles and Learning Styles

Although we learn and think in some of the same ways, each of us has a preferred pattern or style of acquiring new information. If left to our own devices, each of us would think and learn in distinct ways. We can characterize two of our basic tendencies as our *cognitive* (or thinking) *style* and our *learning style*.

Our cognitive style refers to the *pattern we typically follow in solving problems, thinking, and generally processing information.* Individuals may vary their cognitive styles from one situation to another, but one usually is dominant. Learning style refers to *our conscious set of preferences about the conditions under which we like to learn something.* Our learning style, unlike our cognitive style, may vary from task to task and may include any conditions that influence how we learn. These include factors such as the temperature or ambience within a classroom, our mood, our physical state, and the sounds around us.

Cognitive and Learning Styles and Individualized Instruction

Attending to students' dominant cognitive and learning styles is one of the ways for teachers to recognize and respond to individual differences. It involves providing alternative ways and conditions under which to approach an assignment or solve problems. Rather than offering students options in assignments, it provides alternative ways for doing the same assignment. Teachers try to find the best match between the learning environment and the styles of individual students.

Types of Cognitive Styles

Over twenty systems for classifying cognitive styles have been devised.[9] Several of them are complex, and would be difficult to apply to individualized instruction in the usual classroom setting. One approach that has been widely used is based on the work of Herman Witkin and his associates at the Educational Testing Service in Princeton, New Jersey.

Field-Dependent and Field-Independent Cognitive Styles. Witkin and his team of investigators identified two basic cognitive styles, which they labeled *field-dependent* and *field-independent*.[10] Some of the salient comparative characteristics of each type are summarized here:

Field-Independent Individuals:

Can deal effectively with unstructured problems

Are task oriented

Are less concerned with social interaction

Field-Dependent Individuals:

Are better at remembering information that has social content

Prefer group activities

Prefer highly structured tasks and activities

Matching Instruction to Cognitive Styles

Teachers who wish to provide for differences in cognitive styles among students can offer them choices between structured (dependent) and unstructured (independent) assignments. Similarly, they could offer guidelines for activities in both open-ended (independent) and detailed (dependent) forms. They could ensure that alternatives in instructional strategies are available such as discovery (independent) and expository (dependent) approaches. They could also offer choices between working independently or in groups on tasks.

More detailed information on the characteristics of the two types of cognitive style is available, as well as paper-and-pencil measures, which are easy to use and score. A test, which is available in several forms for elementary, middle-school, and even very young and nonreading children, is known as the *Embedded Figures Test.* It is available from Consulting Psychologists Press, 577 College Avenue, Palo Alto, CA 94306.

Types of Learning Styles

Any teacher can create his or her own system for assessing and providing for learning style differences, although several approaches have been formalized by others. Dunn, Dunn, and Price, among others, have created paper-and-pencil inventories in which students indicate their preferences for the conditions under which they engage in activities and learning.[11] The authors organize preferences into five categories, which they label *environmental, sociological, emotional, physical,* and *psychological.*[12] These include preferences such as whether students like sound or quiet, whether they like to eat while doing some task, whether they prefer to remain stationary or move about the classroom, and whether they like to work alone or with others.

Matching Instruction to Learning Styles

A simple approach to using learning style differences to individualize instruction is to consider which conditions in the classroom or school environment are under the teacher's control. The next step is to decide for which of the conditions it is practical or productive to provide students with options in social studies instruction. Further, the subjects, topics, or units for which options are to be included should be identified. The final two steps are to survey student preferences concerning these options, and to provide them.

Although it might be ideal to begin with a survey of students' preferences and to suggest all possible conditions that influence learning, classroom life invariably requires compromises. It may not be reasonable or possible, for example, to offer students the options of very cool or very warm assignment areas. If the school is crowded and its heat is controlled by an aging, erratic boiler, temperature options are not likely to be under the teacher's control.

EXERCISE 12.3   Assessing Learning Style Profiles

Analyze the conditions under which you seem to learn best, including the physical setting, the times of the day, your physical and psychological conditions, the general environment, and the ways you prefer to approach a task. After you have completed this analysis, organize the observations into a list grouped under several headings. This is your learning style profile.

Using this personal profile, interview an elementary-grade student to assess his or her profile. Take each of your items and ask the student which he or she considers to be important, to what extent, and why. Write up all of your observations and conclusions formally.

Sex Equity and Equal Treatment for All Students

Over the past decade many studies have demonstrated that sex equity is a serious issue in our society. Qualified women in the work force, for example, often are paid less, promoted less often, and hold fewer top-level managerial positions than their male counterparts.

Inequalities by gender are visible even in education. Although women make up a disproportionate share of the professional staff in elementary schools, as an illustration, only a few are principals. The number of female superintendents across the entire United States, although increasing, would make up a small elite club.

A large part of sex inequalities results from the perceptions about gender that we encourage and reinforce in our society and specifically in the mass media, the home, and the school. When we teach children either directly or indirectly that certain roles, occupations, and goals are reserved for or more appropriate for one sex than another, we engage in *sex stereotyping*. This may occur through the materials, activities, practices, models, and experiences we provide in our classrooms.

Monitoring Sex-Stereotyping Behavior

Roberta Woolever has developed a checklist of twenty questions for teachers to monitor their own sex-stereotyped behavior. Some of these are summarized in the following list, along with others.[13]

1. Do you organize classroom activities by sex?
2. Do boys and girls have an equal chance to do all classroom chores?
3. Do you use nonstereotyped supplemental materials and pictures?
4. Do you show and discuss both males and females in nontraditional occupational roles?
5. Do you call attention to sex stereotyping in the mass media and gender exclusion in certain areas of society? (See sample activity in Figure 12.4.)
6. Do you avoid having different expectations for male and for female students based on sex stereotypes?
7. Do you encourage students to discuss their questions and concerns about gender identification and related issues?
8. Do you support all children's rights to identify with whatever sex roles they and their parents choose?
9. Do you have adequate knowledge of real and fictional differences between sexes?
10. Does the language you use and encourage students to use reflect nonsexist vocabulary?

Equity for All Children

Sex equity is, of course, only one dimension of the larger issue of equal treatment for all students. Regardless of their race, religion, ethnic group, cultural group, beliefs, intellectual capabilities, or gender, all students deserve an equal chance to learn and succeed. In a pluralistic society children often arrive at the school door with an assortment of languages, a variety of religious beliefs, intellectual abilities that vary, physical and psychological impediments, and differing ethnic traditions, customs, and racial backgrounds. At each school, of course, the range of the diversity that students represent will vary. In a homogeneous community there is likely to be less than in one where a polyglot of families reside.

Teachers have the difficult responsibility of trying to ensure that the diversity students bring to the classroom enriches rather than impedes all students' learning. This is a complex task, especially for a beginning teacher and especially in classes where great diversity exists. The very students who require the most tolerance, sensitivity, and understanding are often the most taxing. Some schools have special professionals, such as aides and special education teachers, to ease a teacher's burden, but many do not.

Equity and Teacher Expectations. Exercising the responsibility to treat all children equitably begins with suspending judgment initially on what can be expected of each child with respect to classroom performance, learning, behavior, background, and aspirations. When a teacher's *expectations* are that a particular child will be industrious, bright, and well-behaved, and will bring rich experiences and high learning ideals to the classroom, these views *positively* affect the teacher's behavior toward the student. By contrast, if the teacher's expectations result from the way students are labeled — for example, slow-learner, Hispanic, working-class, or lazy — the teacher's behavior toward them may be influenced *negatively*.

FIGURE 12.4   Classroom activity related to gender stereotyping

MAGAZINE/NEWSPAPER SCAVENGER HUNT

Objective:
To learn about people in the news and heighten awareness of stereotyping and gender exclusion in certain roles.

Time:
30–45 minutes

Materials:

> newspapers and magazines (variety)
>
> scissors
>
> paste
>
> 20×24 newsprint (1 sheet per team)
>
> list of items to find (1 copy per team)

Playing:

1. Divide class into teams of 4.
2. Distribute materials to each team. Set time limit and begin.
3. Teams search through newspaper and magazines, finding items listed.
4. Items are cut out and pasted to large newsprint sheet.

Winner:
First team to find all items, or most items, when time runs out.

Follow Up:
Display each team's product.
   Discuss: Why was it difficult (or impossible) to find some items? Why was it easy to find some items?

SAMPLE ITEMS

(Sex-equity Content — Intermediate Level)

Directions to Students:
Search through the magazines and newspapers you have been given. Find the pictures listed below; then cut them out and paste them to your large sheet of paper. Work as a team. Identify the names of people where possible.*

1. Female world leader
2. Female United States Senator
3. Female United States Representative
4. Female sports figure
5. Female executive
6. Male cooking

FIGURE 12.4 Continued

7. Male interacting with children
8. Male doing housework
9. Female doing housework
10. Male world leader
11. Male United States Senator
12. Male United States Representative

   *Note to teacher: You may want to award bonus points for identifications.

   Source: Sarah M. Butzin, "Learning Experiences to Promote Sex Equity," *Social Education* 46 (January 1982): 51. Reprinted by permission.

Teachers should not overlook actual student behavior, however. The real problems of students who manifest antisocial behavior in class and who have serious learning deficiencies, for example, cannot be dismissed as simply a result of teacher expectations. Equity of opportunity for all students means that teachers try consistently not to prejudge any student on the basis of a label. It means also that students are encouraged to act toward each other in this fashion. Finally, it refers to fair and consistent treatment of all students and to objective maintenance and enforcement of clear standards of work, achievement, and behavior.

Mainstreaming the Handicapped

In recent years society has devoted increasing attention to the special needs of its handicapped citizens, and to how opportunities provided to other Americans could be extended to them. For example, federal, state, and local laws have been passed to expand access to public facilities by requirements for provisions such as ramps at sidewalks or Braille instructions in elevators. Many other changes have been effected voluntarily by businesses and institutions, once they became aware of the needs of the handicapped.

Public Law 94-142

Schools also were affected by governmental statutes and regulations. The most significant of these was the federal "Education for All Handicapped Children Act," usually referred to as PL 94-142. It stated in effect that if any school system in the United States wished to receive special federal funding, it had to make provisions by 1980 for "free, appropriate, public education." This was to be for all handicapped children between the ages of three and twenty-one, regardless of impairments or handicaps. Handicaps, as the term is used in practice, include:

deafness   orthopedic impairment
hearing impairment   emotionally disturbed

blindness   learning disabilities
visual impairment   health impairment
mental retardation

A Least Restrictive Educational Environment. One of the significant provisions of the law for elementary teachers was that handicapped children must be educated with nonhandicapped ones to the maximum extent possible and in the "least restrictive" educational environment. What this last provision means, in practice, has been the subject of considerable debate. Many different implementations of the provision exist in schools across the nation. School practices associated with this provision are referred to as *mainstreaming* the handicapped; that is, bringing them into the mainstream of public education by placing them in regular classrooms for at least part of their education.

An assumption of PL 94-142 is that handicapped children will advance socially, psychologically, and educationally when they are not isolated from other children. They will be better prepared for the realities of the world if they have to function in normal environments. For nonhandicapped children, experiences with handicapped children also should help break down stereotypes and negative attitudes toward them.

In many schools some handicapped children *always* have been mainstreamed. Children in wheelchairs, with poor eyesight, hearing problems, and assorted psychological disorders, for example, were assimilated into many classrooms long before legislation required it. What PL 94-142 attempted, among other things, was to increase both the types and numbers of handicapped children to be mainstreamed. It also sought to establish the legal right of all students to such education, whether the schools wished to provide it or not.

We should realize that the "least restricted environment" provision of PL 94-142 required neither that all handicapped children be placed in regular classrooms nor that all aspects of their education occur there. However, it did place on school districts the burden of proof that some part of handicapped students' education cannot take place in a regular classroom or that some students cannot be educated at all in a regular setting. The basic social intent of PL 94-142 was to bring all handicapped individuals, as much as is possible, fully into the mainstream of society, including its schools.

An Individualized Educational Program (IEP)

In addition to the sections already mentioned, PL 94-142 contains one requiring the development for each student of an individualized educational program (IEP). An IEP is a written plan specifying a student's present level of educational performance, the educational program to be provided for the child, and the criteria that will be used to measure progress. The child's parent and the child, where appropriate, are to be involved in the development of an IEP. The elementary teacher also may be involved in a conference. An IEP may take any form, but by law it must include the components indicated.

Many states have developed sample formats for use by local school districts. A completed first page of an IEP for a child who is learning disabled, and who is placed in a regular fourth-grade class is shown in Figure 12.5. For 150 minutes a week she is taken from her regular classroom and receives special instruction in the school's instructional resource room.

Individual districts, however, generally may construct their own formats, and many variations exist throughout the country. Because of the enormous amount of clerical work and time involved in the physical preparation of IEPs for a large district, some schools use computers to expedite the process.

Strategies for Mainstreaming in the Social Studies

There are several strategies for facilitating mainstreaming in general, including that for social studies. Most of the discussion on individualized instruction applies to students whose differences are their particular handicaps. Some ways of adapting the physical environment of the classroom to accommodate various handicaps are provided in the work, *What's the Difference: Teaching Positive Attitudes toward People with Disabilities,* a collection of classroom activities by Ellen Barnes and her associates.[14] Here are some examples:

For hearing-impaired people:	*use visual clues/signs in classroom, maps of the building, etc.
	*seat child to face speaker(s), the teacher and other children.
	*write on board or on paper directions for activities.
For visually impaired people:	*maintain consistent room arrangement.
	*remove barriers so that walking is easy.
	*have Braille labels on materials.
	*use auditory cues.
	*seat near board.
	*tape record lessons.
For physically handicapped people:	*have open spaces for wheelchairs and crutches.
	*keep activities on one level.
	*exercise facilities, like chin-up bars.
For active children:	*create learning centers that require movement and allow excess energy to be expended.
	*have some space which is contained and low stimulus.

Howard Sanford offers several strategies and guidelines for adapting social studies activities in a mainstreamed classroom. Among his ideas are these two:

[For students with memory problems] The teacher should emphasize key points through outlining activities . . . and compiling picture vocabulary and word files.

[For students with visual problems] A number of geographic aids — including Braille atlases; relief maps of a molded plastic texture; dissected maps of continents and countries; relief globes and mileage scales; large type outline maps; and land-form models featuring three-dimensional tactile maps which illustrate and teach geographic concepts — are available.[15]

Sources of Materials. For students with visual and hearing difficulties several agencies provide special social studies media materials such as *captioned* films and filmstrips and audio recordings of texts on a loan basis. Many community agencies offer the use of these materials. They may also be secured from the following organizations:

American Foundation for the Blind
15 West 16th Street
New York, NY 10011

Americation Printing House for the Blind
1839 Frankfurt Avenue
Louisville, KY 40206

Captioned Films for the Deaf
Special Office for Materials Distribution
Indiana University
Audiovisual Center
Bloomington, IN 47401

EXERCISE 12.4   Examining an Individualized Educational Program (IEP)

Arrange with a local elementary school to examine the IEPs of several students. Compare the format used with the one shown in this text, and examine the information provided for each student. Identify the extent to which the students are placed completely in a regular classroom setting. Note particularly whether any provisions for social studies programs are included. Briefly summarize your findings and evaluate them.

Nurturing the Gifted

The gifted are one of our nation's most valuable natural resources. They enrich and enlighten our world through their contributions to literature and the visual and performing arts. They produce our scientific breakthroughs and new technologies. Our societal problem solvers, national leaders, and diplomats come from their ranks. The Congress in 1978, as it passed the *Gifted and Talented Children's Act,* as-

FIGURE 12.5 Sample portion of a completed IEP

INDIVIDUALIZED EDUCATION PROGRAM PLAN

Student's Name: Rachel Lawrence

Birth Date: October 5, 1967

Present Date: February 1, 1977

Grade/Program: Grade 4

Teacher(s): Mrs. Matson

School: Hope Elementary School

Primary Assignment(s):	Date Started	Expected Duration of Services	Special Media or Materials
Regular Education 4th Grade and resource room attendance (3 times per week, 50 min. each time.)	4-15-77	Until June, 1978	Talking books, tape recorder
Physical Education			

Rachel is working easily in all areas of the 4th grade, both socially and academically, except for her deficits in reading. The resource room, through on-going diagnostic-prescriptive procedures, will attempt to strengthen her reading skills sufficiently to enable her to remain in the regular class environment at least 50% of the time.

Extent to which the child will Participate in Regular Education

Services:

Bus Transportation	4-15-77	on-going

IEP Planning Meeting Participants:

    Name

*Local Education Agency Representative: Mr. Donald Klein

*Parent, Guardian or Surrogate Parent: Mrs. Kathleen Lawrence

    Student:

    *Teacher(s):   Mrs. Gray

    **Evaluator(s):   Mr. Robert Smith

    Other(s):

Dates for review and/or revision of the Individualized Education Program Plan: January 31, 1978

Person responsible for the maintenance and implementation of the IEP plan: Building Principal — Mr. Bell

* Must attend. If the parent, guardian or surrogate parent does not attend, documentation of attempts to gain their participation should be attached.

**Must attend if the student is newly identified as exceptional.

Source: Pennsylvania Department of Education, Bureau of Special Education.

serted boldly, "The nation's greatest resource for solving national problems in areas of national concern is its gifted and talented children."

In a host of ways these gifted and talented individuals are an important national resource. Whether we nurture and use wisely this resource depends in great measure on what special provisions our educational systems make.

Society's Perspective on the Gifted

American society historically has existed in a state of tension concerning the gifted student. One school of thought maintains that the gifted are an elite who are well qualified to look out for themselves without any special help. Schools filled with average students and those with special problems, this view continues, should focus their limited resources on the majority, not the gifted minority.

At the same time our society promotes the notion of excellence and the ideal that each individual should strive to achieve all that his or her abilities allow. Schools are alternately chided and prodded when they ignore this societal goal. We exhort our schools to help in the competition to produce exceptional individuals who will keep our nation in the forefront of the world in areas like technology, industrial productivity, space, peace-keeping, human rights, and standards of living. When we seem to fall behind, as in the 1950s in the space race with the Soviets, we initiate national crash programs and offer special incentives to stimulate the education of talented individuals.

The Gifted

Who are the gifted? Definitions vary considerably, but most of them include some combination of the following characteristics:[16]

special academic aptitudes

general intellectual abilities

creativity

artistic abilities

leadership abilities

psychomotor abilities

Some states and local school districts have created operational meanings for those characteristics which they use to define gifted students — for example, a score of 130 or above on an individual I.Q. test as a measure of general intellectual ability. These procedures often come under attack on the grounds that they favor students reared in the mainstream culture.[17] As an alternative, there have been attempts to provide culture-free instruments to identify giftedness in students with cultural backgrounds different from that of the majority of students. The System of Multicultural Pluralistic Assessment (SOMPA) is an example of one such approach.[18]

Approaches to Gifted Education

Schools that provide for the special needs of gifted usually employ some variation of three organizational approaches. One is to group students by ability. For example, students judged to be gifted in social studies might be placed together, either by grades or across several grades. A variation is to place all students designated as gifted together for all subjects.

A second approach is to keep students within a regular classroom setting, but to provide *enriched* learning experiences in one or more subjects. Enrichment may be provided within the regular classroom or through "pull-out" programs, in which gifted students are taken from their classrooms to special programs one or more times a week.

The third approach emphasizes *accelerating* students' progress. Either through special in-class activities or other special programs, students advance as rapidly as they can through the study of a subject. When a "grade" of subject matter has been mastered, a student advances to the next grade. A gifted student under the accelerated approach might complete, for example, three years of the social studies program in a single year.

EXERCISE 12.5 Identifying School Provisions for the Gifted

Arrange to visit a local elementary or middle school to determine what provisions they make for gifted students. Identify the procedures the school uses (1) to determine which students are gifted, (2) to locate gifted culturally different and minority students, and (3) to provide special programs for the gifted. Organize your findings into a brief report, and then add your reactions and comments.

Social Studies Strategies

We will focus on students who have exceptional intellectual and thinking abilities in social studies. Some of the more common symptoms of this dimension of giftedness in children are given in the following sections.

Special Capabilities of Gifted Students for Social Studies Learning. Signs of exceptional intellectual and thinking abilities in social studies include the following.

With respect to *verbal ability,* the child exhibits:

1. a high level of language development
2. a vast store of information
3. advanced comprehension
4. facility in speaking and expressing complex ideas

FIGURE 12.6 Plan for a mentorship activity, including record-keeping procedures

Figure 2. A Finalized Plan for a Community-Based "Mentor-Directed Enrichment Project."

Mentor's Name ___Jeannie G.___   **Pupil's Name** ___Grania M.___

Project Topic ___Sealing: Right or Wrong?___

Project Meeting Time ___Friday Afternoons 1:00–3:00 or longer___

Phase	Week #	Learning Activities (Including Resources)	Related Learning Outcomes
Phase I Planning Proposal	1.	(a) Mentor writes up proposed project in his or her area of expertise (b) University instructor and enrichment teacher use proposal to match mentor to an interested pupil	(a) Preparing for first meeting with pupil
Phase II Agreeing on Finalized Project Plan	2.	(a) Introduce proposal and topic (b) Find out what Grania knows about seals and sealing, and what her attitudes are (can change project plan if necessary) (c) Prepare questionnaire for next week's interview, and role-play an interview using tape recorder (d) Make "thank you" card	(a) Increasing intrinsic motivation (b) Planning an enrichment project (c) Posing answerable questions (d) Interviewing skills (e) Practicing courtesy
Phase III Carrying Out the Project Plan	3.	(a) Visit Vancouver Aquarium to observe seals (b) Interview (tape record) seal trainer discussing what seals are like (c) Take slides of seals; sketch them	(a) Observation skills (b) Interviewing skills and confidence (c) Background knowledge about seals (d) Artistic skills
	4.	(a) At school, Grania decides which sketches, slides, and information are to be used in her presentation (b) Read materials on seals and compare to observations made at aquarium	(a) Decision-making and organization skills (b) Comparing and contrasting
	5.	(a) Assess project thus far (review) (b) Prepare and rehearse questions for next week's interview with Gordon Rogers (a "pro-sealer" from Newfoundland) and the following week's interview with someone from the Greenpeace organization (anti-sealing)	(a) Grania has greater voice in preparing questions (b) Brainstorming imaginative questions
	6.	(a) Interview Gordon Rogers (b) Obtain leads to other pro-sealing sources	(a) Gain a "pro-sealer's" point of view firsthand (b) Refine interviewing skills
	7.	(a) Interview spokesperson from the Greenpeace organization (b) Obtain leads to other anti-sealing resources (c) Obtain materials to be used in presentation (including visuals)	(a) Gain an anti-sealing point of view firsthand (b) Refine interviewing skills

Phase IV **Completing and Presenting the Project**	8. (a) Organize the material to be used in the class presentation (b) Mount Grania's sketches (c) Mould clay seals; paint them (d) Prepare posters to display pro and con information obtained	(a) Decision-making and organization skills (b) Lettering posters (neatness)
	9. (a) Role-play the class presentation (mentor demonstrates; pupil practices) (b) Objectively present both pro and con information to allow class members to decide for themselves if sealing is right or wrong	(a) Speaking skills and self-confidence (b) Objective reporting of controversial information
	10. (a) Pupil gives class presentation and answers questions about what she liked best about her project, and so forth	(a) Public speaking skills (b) Thinking "on one's feet" while answering questions

(Figure continues on following page.)

FIGURE 12.6 Continued

Figure 3. Mentor's Weekly Report.

Mentor ___Jeannie___ **Pupil** ___Grania___ **Meeting #** ___5___

Project Topic ___Sealing: Right or Wrong?___

Starting Time ___1:00 p.m.___ **Finishing Time** ___4:00 p.m.___

1. State what your pupil did today and how it is related to his or her final enrichment project product.
Today Grania and I got a pro-sealing view by interviewing Gordon Rogers, who hails from Newfoundland. He provided us with insight into the sealing industry and with some excellent background material (books, ideas to pursue). The interview raised some questions in our minds, which will help us to present our project in that we want our audience to decide the issue themselves. We will merely present the facts that we have gleaned. We now have a more rounded view of the question we are investigating; we've had a real glimpse into the life of the seal hunter. We will use Rogers' information to present the pro-sealing case to our audience.

2. Describe two main specific learning outcomes your pupil demonstrated today. (That is, briefly describe specific thinking skills, social skills, performance skills, and so forth.)
Grania herself noted her improvement in interviewing: there were no false starts as there had been with the seal trainer at the aquarium. She seemed more comfortable and sure of herself and so. I was pleased to see Grania remain after the interview to talk to Rogers and give him some information regarding our project. I know this was a feat for her because she is normally shy with strangers and usually turns to me to provide information. This demonstrated her overcoming shyness and proved her enthusiasm for the project.

3. Describe how you and/or your pupil used specific resources (human, nonhuman, community, and so forth). How effectively?
Rogers proved to be a veritable well of information. I was impressed with how Grania "filled out" the questions she asked with follow-up queries. Rogers also suggested some books to read, and suggested that we interview a Federal Fisheries officer (an excellent plan, I say). We certainly got the maximum from today's interview.

4. Describe the specific instruction methods (exposition, discovery, modeling, role playing, and so forth) that you used today. How effectively?
Discovery: By my remaining mute, Grania was put into a position where she had to speak to Rogers on her own. I was pleased to see that she warmed to her subject and grew confident. Questioning: I "quizzed" Grania about sealing on the bus ride to and from the interview, making sure that I included "higher level" questions for her to ponder and answer orally. In both these ways her enthusiasm for the project was maximized.

5. Describe specific motivation and/or discipline techniques that you used today (such as assertiveness, reality therapy, behavior modification, and so forth). How effectively?
Fortunately, merely setting up the interview between Grania and Rogers proved motivating: Rogers was knowledgeable and enthusiastic and transmitted this to Grania. I simply had to bring up some of the points that he had raised and Grania responded most enthusiastically. Made my job easy—but proved effective!

6. Describe three specific things you learned from today's mentoring experience.
   a. Shyness vanishes as a child is motivated and "gets into" a project. This should be applied to the classroom.
   b. A friendly discussion fosters learning better than a structured question-and-answer period. The prepared questions facilitated a flowing discussion.
   c. Allowing the child to discover things about herself by herself should be a definite aim in mentoring. Grania was pleased with her newly found talent in relating to others.

7. Briefly indicate next week's plans regarding each of the following:
   a. What will your pupil do (visit, make something, and so forth)?
   We hope to conduct a telephone interview with the Federal Fisheries officer and a personal interview with a Greenpeace officer. We will also be molding seals from baker's clay, mounting Grania's pictures, and viewing our slides. Hopefully, we will get around to planning our display and reviewing the tapes for the presentation.
   b. What resources will be needed?
      ● tape recorder
      ● baker's clay
      ● mounting cardboard
      ● viewer

   Note: Did you have any problems for which you need my assistance?
   Not yet . . . thank you!

Source: William A. Gray, "Mentor-Assisted Enrichment Projects for the Gifted and Talented," *Educational Leadership* 40 (November 1982): 19–20. Reprinted by permission.

5. many and often original questions
6. unusual curiosity and originality in questions
7. ability to engage in sustained, meaningful, give-and-take discussions
8. an exceptional memory

With respect to the *written work,* the child exhibits:

1. an unusual capacity for processing information
2. a special knack for seeing unusual or less obvious relationships among data
3. a pattern of consistently generating original ideas and solutions
4. unusual examples of cause-and-effect relationships, logical predictions, and frequent use of abstractions
5. an unusual ability to accurately synthesize large bodies of information
6. the capacity to use with ease a number of different reference materials in solving problems and testing hypotheses
7. advanced reading ability
8. unusual ability to understand alternative points of view

Instructional Strategies. Among the ways in which special social studies programs for the gifted have been provided are:

Using Alternative Materials at Advanced Reading Levels. Example: Eighth-grade and above materials on American history to supplement or replace normal fifth-grade American history text and program.

Exclusively Using Discovery Approaches and Simulations and Role-Playing Techniques. Example: Substituting the usual narrative expository study of a topic with a series of discovery lessons and simulation and role-playing activities that are open-ended and require consideration of alternatives and problem solving.

Using a Special, Alternative Curriculum. Example: Substituting a year's course of study in geography, economics, or anthropology for the standard basal text in the first grade.

Employing Mentors Specializing or Working in Areas Related to the Social Studies Curriculum. Example: Having a student conduct a project to obtain data regarding the ethics of seal hunting. Figure 12.6 shows how one mentor program was organized and monitored.

Emphasizing Problem-Solving Assignments and Activities. Example: Reorganize the second-grade curriculum around a series of learning centers that contain problem-solving tasks.

Focusing on Research as Conducted by Social Scientists. Example: Organizing several units around the use and analysis of primary and secondary source materials.

Studying Cutting-Edge Issues and Developments. Example: Spending the entire sixth-grade year examining the state of current computer technology and the microprocessor revolution, how different countries have been affected by it, what the projections for the future indicate, and developing scenarios of the ways in which the world of the future will be different due to the computer.

Using of Student Projects. Example: As an alternative to studying about communities in the basal text, students design carry out, and evaluate with teacher assistance a series of projects to better understand their local community.

Notes

1. James A. Kulick, "Individualized Systems of Instruction," in *The Encyclopedia of Educational Research,* 5th ed., Harold E. Mitzel, ed. (New York: Macmillan, 1982).
2. Joan Ferry, "Social Studies Learning Centers for a Fifth Grade," Unpublished paper, Perkasie School District, Bucks County, Pa., no date.
3. Ibid.
4. Jack E. Blackburn and W. Conrad Powell, *One at a Time All at Once: The Creative Teacher's Guide to Individualized Instruction without Anarchy* (Pacific Palisades, Calif.: Goodyear, 1976), pp. 86–88.
5. Alvin Gronowski and Morton Botel, "Background for a New Syntactic Complexity Formula," *The Reading Teacher* 28 (October 1974): 31–35.
6. Edward Fry, "A Readability Formula that Saves Time," *Journal of Reading* 2 (April 1968): 577.
7. John Bormuth, "The Cloze Readability Procedure," *Elementary English* 45 (April 1968): 429–436.
8. Leonard Martelli et al. *Going Places: Teacher's Edition, Level 2* (New York: McGraw-Hill, 1983), p. 132.
9. J. E. Robinson and J. L. Gray, "Cognitive Style as a Variable in School Learning," *Journal of Educational Psychology* 66 (1974): 793–799.
10. Herman A. Witkin et al., "Field-Dependent and Field-Independent Cognitive Styles," *Review of Educational Research* 47 (1977): 1–64.
11. Rita Dunn et al., *Learning Style Inventory* (Price Systems, Box 3271, Lawrence, KS 66044, no date).
12. Rita Dunn et al., "Identifying Individual Learning Styles," in *Student Learning Styles: Diagnosing and Prescribing Programs* (Reston, Va.: National Association of Secondary School Principals, 1979), pp. 39–54.
13. Roberta Woolever, "Affirmative Action in the Classroom: What Would It Mean?" *Social Education* 44 (January 1982): 47–48.
14. Ellen Barnes et al., *What's the Difference: Teaching Positive Attitudes toward People with Disabilities* (Syracuse, N.Y.: Human Policy Press, 1978), p. 14.
15. Howard Sanford, "Organizing and Presenting Social Studies Content in a Main-streamed Class," in *Mainstreaming in the Social Studies,* Bulletin 62, John G. Herlihy and Myra T. Herlihy, eds. (Washington, D.C.: National Council for the Social Studies, 1980), p. 48.
16. S. Marland, *Education of the Gifted and Talented,* Report of the Congress of the United States by the United States Commissioner of Education (Washington, D.C.: U.S. Government Printing Office, 1972).

17. E. Paul Torrance, "Ways of Discovering Gifted Black Children," in *Educational Planning for the Gifted: Overcoming Cultural, Geographical, and Socioeconomic Barriers,* ed. Alexinia Y. Baldwin et al. (Reston, Va.: The Council for Exceptional Children, 1978), p. 30.
18. Jane R. Mercer and June F. Lewis, "Using the System of Multicultural Pluralistic Assessment (SOMPA) to Identify the Gifted Minority Child," in *Educational Planning for the Gifted: Overcoming Cultural, Geographical, and Socioeconomic Barriers,* ed. Alexinia Y. Baldwin et al. (Reston, Va.: The Council for Exceptional Children, 1978), pp. 7–13.

Suggested Readings

Baldwin, Alexinia Y., et al., eds. *Educational Planning for the Gifted: Overcoming Cultural, Geographical, and Socioeconomic Barriers.* Reston, Va.: The Council for Exceptional Children, 1978.

Barnes, Ellen, et al. *What's the Difference: Teaching Positive Attitudes toward People with Disabilities.* Syracuse, NY: Human Policy Press, 1978.

Blackburn, Jack E., and Powell, W. Conrad. *One at a Time All at Once: The Creative Teacher's Guide to Individualized Instruction without Anarchy.* Pacific Palisades, Calif.: Goodyear, 1976.

Clark, Barbara. *Growing up Gifted.* 2nd ed. Columbus, Ohio: Charles E. Merrill, 1983.

Dell, Helen D. *Individualizing Instruction: Materials and Classroom Procedures.* Chicago: Science Research Associates, 1972.

Herlihy, John G., and Herlihy, Myra T., eds. *Mainstreaming in the Social Studies,* Bulletin 62. Washington, D.C.: National Council for the Social Studies, 1980.

Jetter, Jan, ed. *Approaches to Individualized Education.* Alexandria, Va.: Association for Supervision and Curriculum Development, 1980.

Joyce, William, ed. "Mainstreaming: The Least Restrictive Environment," *Social Education* 43 (January 1979): 57–68.

Kenworthy, Leonard S. "Reach for a Picture," *How to Do It Series,* Series 2, No. 3. Washington, D.C.: National Council for the Social Studies, 1977.

Laycock, Frank. *Gifted Children.* Glenview, Ill.: Scott, Foresman, 1979.

Learning Objectives for Individualized Instruction: Social Science. Sunnyvale, Calif.: Westinghouse Learning Press, 1975.

Lunstrum, John P. "Reading in the Social Studies," in *Developing Decision-Making Skills,* 47th Yearbook, ed. Dana G. Kurfman. Washington, D.C.: National Council for the Social Studies, 1977, pp. 109–139.

Mahony, Joseph E. "Improving Reading Skills in the Social Studies," *How to Do It Series,* Series 2, No. 1. Washington, D.C.: National Council for the Social Studies, 1977.

Ochoa, Anna S., and Shuster, Susan K. *Social Studies in the Mainstreamed Classroom.* Boulder, Colo.: ERIC Clearinghouse for the Social Studies/Social Sciences Education, 1980.

Reilly, Mary Ellen. "Eliminating Sexism: A Challenge to Education," *Social Education* 43 (April 1979): 312–316.

Renzulli, Joseph. *The Enrichment Triad Model: A Guide for Developing Defensible Programs for the Gifted and Talented.* Mansfield Center, Conn.: Creative Learning Press, 1977.

Rose, Shirley E. "The Gifted Student and Social Studies Teaching," *The Social Studies* 69 (March/April 1978): 43–49.

Scott, Kathryn P., ed. "Sex Equity in the Elementary School," *Social Education* 46 (January 1982): 44–57

Student Learning Styles: Diagnosing and Prescribing Programs. Reston, Va.: National Association of Secondary School Principals, 1979.

Thomas, John I. *Learning Centers: Opening up the Classroom.* Boston: Holbrook Press, 1975.

Turnbull, Ann P., and Schulz, Jane B. *Mainstreaming Handicapped Students: A Guide for the Classroom Teacher.* Boston: Allyn and Bacon, 1979.

Witkin, Herman A., et al. "Field-Dependent and Field-Independent Cognitive Styles," *Review of Educational Research* 47 (1977): 1–64.

13

Discovering and Implementing New Resources and Technologies

We return to the theme with which we began. The social studies curriculum evolved as a response to society's concern that young citizens be properly prepared for their civic responsibilities. Schools were entrusted with this charge because other institutions within society, such as the family, were perceived to be inadequate for the task.

This perspective originated in an era when only a few children attended elementary school, and where even fewer went on to the secondary schools. Only a handful of students, mostly from families of means, attended colleges and universities. It also was a period in which mass communication was in its infancy, and personal communication was limited by our restricted transportation network and highway system. Students typically remained in the same area where they were born or raised. Parents, themselves, often had attended school for only a few years. Moreover, technology was not a major force in our society, and it was a stranger to the educational process.

Toward Social Studies in the Twenty-First Century

As we approach the twenty-first century, social studies is on the threshold of a new era. We are a far different nation today than that which first commissioned our public school system and gave rise to the early social studies curriculum. Over 35 million youngsters today receive compulsory schooling; a large percentage of them will attend institutions of higher education.

These students can avail themselves of one of the world's finest free public library systems, one that provides a rich assortment of informational sources. Resources include large collections of print materials; videotapes, audiotapes, and films; computer software, and access to data bases all over the United States. The extensive network of public and commercial mass media also provides an abundance of free or inexpensive social information. Technology in general today is a driving force in our society, and it has the potential to be an important ally of the school's educational programs.

Today's students also are the beneficiaries of accessible transportation systems, which have spawned a transient generation. Like their parents, these students are likely to change their residences several times during their lives and to move about the nation frequently. On the average, they will be raised by parents who are well schooled, have much more leisure time to devote to their children than their ancestors, and are concerned and involved with all facets of their children's schooling.

In sum, today's children have access to a rich, informal educational system that exists *outside* of the school. The formal social studies curriculum of the classroom is but one dimension of the broad social studies program available in society at large. Resources abound for aiding in the development of reflective, competent, and concerned citizens. In the twenty-first century these resources will be even greater. The challenge for teachers is to identify those which are readily available in each community and to harness them to the objectives of the social studies curriculum.

Identifying Resources and Trends for Contemporary Social Studies Programs

Today's teacher has access to a cornucopia of resources for making social studies programs effective and vital. Not the least of these is the extensive network across the United States of colleges and universities, teacher centers, and local and state educational agencies. From the multitude of resources available, beginning teachers especially need to identify those which will aid them in their daily teaching. They also need to locate resources that will keep them abreast of new developments within the field and informed about contemporary issues and social trends.

Organizational Resources

To aid teachers in their search are professional organizations that focus exclusively on the social studies. The following organizations produce materials and make them available to social studies teachers on an ongoing basis:

The National Council for the Social Studies
3501 Newark Street, N.W.
Washington, DC 20016

National Council for Geographic Education
Department of Geography
University of Houston
Houston, TX 77004

The Social Science Education Consortium
855 Broadway
Boulder, CO 80302

Educational Resources Information Center (ERIC)
Clearinghouse for Social
Studies/Social Science Education
855 Broadway
Boulder, CO 80302

Many other organizations provide similar services, even though their overall focus is broader than the social studies curriculum. The Anti-Defamation League of B'nai B'rith, 315 Lexington Avenue, New York, NY 10016, is one. It has branch offices in twenty-six major cities to provide assistance to teachers.

Commercial Resources

Some private, commercial companies also provide specialized catalogs of instructional materials for each subject area. One of the largest for the field of social studies is the Social Studies School Service, 10,000 Culver Boulevard, Culver City, CA 90230. Organizations that evaluate sets of instructional materials also offer their independent evaluations to teachers. One such service, which has evaluated several social studies texts and programs, is the Educational Products Information Exchange (EPIE) Institute, Teachers College, Columbia University, New York, NY 10027.

For the rest of the chapter we will focus on two other important types of resource available to teachers: community and technological resources. The first is more traditional and is a connection to the past. The second represents the link to the twenty-first century.

The Community as a Resource

Every school has a rich resource at its doorstep — the community in which it resides. Probably one of the least tapped resources for social studies teaching is the wealth of material that generally is available within every community. Local organizations and businesses will often cooperate with teachers in arranging field trips, guest speakers, information, and assistance. Public agencies such as police and fire departments sometimes have special programs and speakers they will provide to schools. Individuals, likewise are generally eager to offer their assistance to local elementary schools.

Community Resource Persons

One elementary school, for example, discovered that a local resident was an author of children's books, and invited her to the school to explain how she developed her ideas and did her writing. Another school regularly invited elderly residents to tell and show what the community had been like before the children were born. Other typical uses of community resource persons include having individuals who represent different careers report on what they do; having persons work with students as mentors (described in Chapter 12); having individuals report to a class on their trips to special places; and drawing on community members who have specialized advice on selected topics.

Field Work and Field Trips

In addition to bringing the community to the school, students can be taken into the field. Armstrong and Savage observe:

> the community can be the *laboratory* the learner uses to study data, make decisions, and test decisions against other data. . . . The 'concreteness' and the 'real worldliness' of features of the local community are likely to stimulate a higher degree of personal commitment and enthusiasm for social studies than can be anticipated when books, films, and other simulators of reality are used.[1]

Some examples of community *sites* for field visits are: farms, museums, supermarkets, bakeries, construction sites, factories, television studios, waterfronts, military bases, and archeological excavations.

Field Work. Social scientists refer to information that is gathered on site rather than through texts and other such materials as *field work*. Field work is often used to *generate or test hypotheses in problem solving* or to provide *clear examples in concept learning*. Students, as well as social scientists, can be involved in many types of field work in their communities. It encourages active, concrete, "hands-on" learning.

Field Trips. Elementary teachers often use the term *field trips* to refer to students' visits to field sites. Although the term is in common usage, there are several problems with its connotations. It often suggests a holiday from class work or a tourist-type spectator activity. Field work should be a pleasant change-of-pace activity for children, but it should also be treated as an *integral* part of their school instruction, rather than as a diversion.

A trip to the field does not of itself imply field work or even a meaningful activity. In field work students in some way act on what they observe or experience. They do this by relating their experiences in the field to other information they have studied or are studying, and then reflecting on the connections.

Relating the School to the Real World. Field work can be used to demonstrate the tie between things students (and all of us) take for granted, such as processed food, automobiles, and housing, and the means of their production. It has been argued, for example, that many children no longer realize that the cows and fields of wheat they see have any connection with the milk and bread in their meals. Field experiences can help students understand the connectedness of all elements of our society. They also can help develop a greater appreciation of what different individuals in our society contribute to the common good.

Translating a Field Trip into Field Work

In ensuring that a field trip results in productive field work, teachers might view the planning process in three stages — before the trip, during the trip, and following the trip — as the following guidelines suggest.

Guidelines for Fieldwork

Before the Trip

1. Establish clear and specific objectives for the trip. Plan to share these with the students either before or after the trip, as appropriate to your instructional strategy.
2. View the trip as a *means* rather than an end. Consider such issues as how time will be used, and how variety in experiences will be provided. This is an especially important consideration for very young children.
3. Be sure you are familiar with the major features of the site you will visit. Identify those features of the field trip which will interest children and reflect *action* (people doing things).
4. Make a list of those features of the site you plan to discuss and emphasize during the trip. Then make some notes on the types of comments and questions you plan to raise concerning them.
5. If possible, obtain pictures, written information, slides, and the like to introduce the site to be visited. In preparing for the visit focus on special features you wish students to notice. If appropriate provide them with a sheet of points to consider during the visit. If they are to engage in an activity, be sure to indicate what they are expected to do and not to do. When appropriate also provide them with structured observation sheets to be completed during the trip.
6. Develop a checklist of all the procedural, administrative details that need to be arranged, such as confirmation of visitation date, bus plans, parental permissions, provisions for meals or snacks (if any), restroom facilities, safety precautions (if necessary), special student dress (if needed), and the like. Organize a simple file system, as well, for collecting all forms or funds required from students and parents.

During the Trip

7. Focus students' attention on those features of the trip which are most important. Have them observe and record, where appropriate, answers to questions such as:

"What things did I see?"

"Which people did I see, and what were they doing?"

"How did _____ get done? Which people were involved? What materials were used?"

8. Whenever possible, engage students in some activity during the visit, such as picking vegetables while at a farm. When this is not possible raise related questions, as well as answer them.
9. Take pictures or slides, if possible, to use in discussing important aspects of the trip during the followup.
10. Make brief notes on what seemed to interest and bore students, and on important questions that were asked. Note also any points you would like to call attention to during the followup discussion.

Following the Trip

11. Allow students to offer their open-ended impressions of what they learned from the trip, what they enjoyed most from it, and what they did not like and why.
12. Review your notes (item 10), and discuss important points, referring to any pictures or slides (item 9).
13. Review (or identify) the objectives for the trip, and relate the experiences to previous learning.
14. Engage the students in additional followup activities.
15. While the procedural and substantive features of the trip are still fresh in your mind, construct a file card similar to the one shown in Figure 13.1 for future reference.

Computers and Software as Resources in the Social Studies

Technology is making more and more resources of the community available to the schools.[2] Teachers' newest tools are technological ones. They are just beginning to have a dramatic effect on our schools and instructional programs.

Using Technology and Media

Traditional technological aids such as overhead projectors, film projectors, and media such as transparencies and films will continue to be a mainstay of classrooms. In-

FIGURE 13.1   Sample field trip data sheet

	Field trip data sheet
Theme or Objectives of Trip:	How a modern factory works; assembly line procedure; demonstration of computer components
Place:	Widgit Computer Works
Address:	1000 Futura Boulevard Silicon Valley, CA 10000
Telephone Number:	100/999-1000
Contact Person:	Steve Jobs
Grade Levels for Which Trip is Appropriate	4–8
Summary of Main Features of Trip and General Comments:	Students are shown a videotape of all of the plant's operations (twenty minutes). Tour of all facilities covers the parts that are used in constructing microcomputers, as well as the assembly operations. Students are allowed to ask all workers questions during the tour. At the end of the tour students are allowed to work at assembled microcomputers in a special room for as long as they wished. Tour itself, without any questions, probably takes an hour. The company provided snacks for the children.
Overall rating of Trip:	One of the best we have ever taken!
Suggestions for Future Visits by Other Classes:	It would be helpful to students to have a general discussion before the trip concerning their perceptions and stereotypes of factories.

creasingly, however, they will share a role with two newer technological tools, *microcomputers* and *video recorders and players*. In the rest of the chapter we will focus on these two electronic aids, which can enrich and reshape our instructional practices in the social studies.

The Micro Revolution

Unlike most other educational innovations, what has been characterized as the "micro revolution" has a good chance to survive, expand, and dramatically alter the shape and character of our schools, teaching practices, and curriculum. This marvel of the high tech era is the first major electronic innovation that has been pushed from society to the schools, from parent and student to teacher and principal. The driving force of the revolution is a new and inexpensive ($25.00 and up) computer of desk-top size that is called a *micro* or *personal* computer to distinguish it from its larger and older counterparts.

Microcomputers as Instructional Aids

Across the United States many educators are just beginning to experience the excitement that the use of computers, especially *micro*computers can inject into their instruction. Microcomputers or personal computers have the capacity to handle several variables seemingly simultaneously; they can provide immediate feedback on answers; they can retrieve quickly large stores of information. Moreover, they have infinite "patience."

With appropriate software, a microcomputer can perform such instructional operations as:

1. Address a student on a personal basis, referring periodically to individual characteristics.
2. Tell a student how well he or she performed on some instructional task.
3. Always say positive things or make positive suggestions, no matter how poorly a student performs.
4. Provide a different set of exercises to each student within a group.
5. Encourage a student to stay working at a task.
6. Keep accurate records of a student's activities, progress, and amount of time spent on various tasks.
7. Repeat directions and instructions as many times as an individual requires in order to learn something.
8. Entertain through the use of animation, sounds, and unexpected statements.
9. Encourage cooperative behavior and discourage competition among students by emphasizing criterion-referenced evaluation (see Chapter 10).

In short, microcomputers can become important electronic allies with teachers in the pursuit of social studies objectives. These technological tools already have demonstrated that they can capture student interest, provide instructional variety, and can serve as springboards to initiate study of a unit, among many other uses. Teachers need to become more aware of the scope and dimensions of the micro revolution, and its ramifications for all areas of formal education, including the social studies curriculum. The acquisition of such knowledge is frequently called "computer literacy."

Computer Literacy

The term *computer literacy,* as it applies to teachers and students, has been the subject of much debate within the field of computer education.[3] No definition is commonly accepted, although there are similarities among the several contending notions. At the least the term implies some awareness of the nature and applications of computers. At most it implies a proficiency in one or more computer languages and in their several dialects.

It has a broader meaning than the ability to operate microcomputers and programs already prepared and a narrower connotation than training as a computer programmer. It also suggests the capacity to *create* with a computer, as well as to solve problems. Computer literate individuals can use microcomputers to solve real problems they have identified. Morusund has suggested that a working definition of computer literacy is "a knowledge of the capabilities, limitations, applications, and possible effects of computers."[4]

Six dimensions of computer literacy for teachers of social studies are suggested. They involve knowledge of the following:

1. basic sources of information
2. the process of communicating with microcomputers
3. hardware components
4. software and courseware
5. microcomputer applications in the social studies
6. social implications of microcomputers

Basic Sources of Information

There is a rapidly developing body of literature related to the microcomputer hardware and software industries and their applications. Not surprisingly, much of it is in the form of periodicals. Since developments in these areas are occurring at a dizzying speed, journals are the most timely and effective print vehicle for conveying information.

Many are devoted to a specific brand of microcomputer, for example, *Antic* for Atari users and *PC World* for IBM PC users. Some are primarily concerned with software, and still others attempt to be all-purpose journals. A sample of some of those all-purpose periodicals that are not very technical and which should be of general interest to educators follows:

Creative Computing	*Compute!*
Classroom Computer Learning	*Infoworld*
Popular Computing	*Electronic Learning*

Periodicals such as these give teachers the most up-to-date data on new products and developments, and reviews of microcomputer software and hardware.

One of the more comprehensive sources of information on microcomputers and related materials is the *Directory of Educational Computing Resources*, distributed annually by the publishers of *Classroom Computer Learning,* 19 Davis Drive, Belmont, CA 94002. It includes information such as the following:

software sources

hardware sources

computer associations

regional and national sources of teacher assistance

calendar of national and regional conferences

Communicating with Microcomputers

To communicate at all, humans and microcomputers require an interpreter. We would prefer to use our native language to communicate. The computer, on the other hand, understands only its own language, essentially sets of commands to turn sequences of electrical switches on and off.

Through our learning a language such as BASIC, which the interpreter included with the computer understands, communication is possible. An understanding of this process and an awareness of the nature and capabilities of various languages for communication with microcomputers (for example, PILOT, Pascal, FORTRAN, Ada, Logo, Forth, COBOL, BASIC) provides some insight into the strengths and limitations of computers as instructional and managerial tools.

Programming and Communication. Computer literacy programs for teachers frequently overemphasize learning to *program* microcomputers, usually in a language such as BASIC, PILOT or Logo. Apart from those who wish to teach students how to program, *neither today's generation of teachers nor the future one will ever have to learn to be programmers in order to communicate with or use microcomputers effectively in the classroom.* Peter McWilliams, who has written widely about computers, points out, for example, that "Learning BASIC, like learning any language is something some people take to and some people don't. It is unnecessary to the successful operation of a computer, and has nothing to do with the goal of computer literacy."[5] In sum, whether a teacher enjoys or is very successful at or understands programming is unrelated to effective use of microcomputers for instructional purposes.

Some firsthand experience in trying to communicate with a computer, however, is essential to appreciate the limitations of computers in communication. They require a high degree of literalness in what we tell them, and they have a very low tolerance for deviations from established communication rules. If a student types the sentence "The airpl ane flies in the sky," you know perfectly well what he or she is saying. You read *six* words, not seven, realizing that the space bar on the typewriter accidentally was hit, inserting a space between the letters l and a. The computer is not so tolerant, however. The presence or absence of a single space in violation of some syntactical rule, for example, may create a communications breakdown with a computer. A computer understands the command, PRINT "Hello" but will balk at the request, PRIN T "Hello" because of the space between the N and T.

Computer Languages. BASIC is the most common language today for communicating with microcomputers. A second language, which resembles BASIC and is popular for teaching students to do simple programming, is PILOT. All popular microcomputers have their own *dialects* of these two languages. That is, there is a version of BASIC for an Apple, one for the TRS-80, and so on. All the dialects are similar, but each is sufficiently different so that one make of computer cannot understand another's dialect.

Logo. A language that has become increasingly popular in schools, especially for use with very young children, is Logo.[6] Among its appealing features for children are that it permits objects to be drawn on the screen easily. Also, even a child can begin to write short programs with it after only a few instructions. Its advocates maintain that it also promotes logical, structured thought and that it encourages creativity.

With Logo lines can be drawn from a point on the screen by giving instructions to an imaginary figure called a *turtle*. An example of a simple Logo program for drawing a figure is shown in Figure 13.2. It is written in the dialect called MIT Logo for an Apple II. Below the program a brief explanation is provided. Contrast the style with that of BASIC, as shown in Figure 13.3, later in the chapter.

Hardware Components

As I type this chapter, several pieces of computer *hardware* are visible before me. There is a *monitor* on which this writing is being displayed, a set of *disk drives,* a *printer,* and a detachable *keyboard.* The actual *microprocessor* or thumbnail-sized electronic chip that makes all of the microcomputer activities possible is not visible.

Computer Peripherals. Besides basic microcomputer hardware systems such as the one described here, there are several additional components or *peripherals* that may be attached to them for performing other functions. Among the peripherals are the following:

Machines that will read coded cards or answer sheets for test scoring and analyses.

Light pens and transparent television/monitor touch-screen overlays that permit responses to questions to be entered directly through contact with the screen rather than through keyboard entries.

Graphics tablets on which drawings such as maps may be entered directly into an instructional program through a sketch on a special tablet.

Voice synthesizers and recognition components whose capabilities permit spoken commands or hard-word-pronunciation enhancements to programs.

Modems that allow easy communication between computers of all sizes, such as between a microcomputer and a large data-base computer.

Videotape and videodisc machines that can add limitless amounts of visual material to instruction, under the control of either the teacher or the student.

Software and Courseware

All of the applications of microcomputers to social studies instruction involve sets of communications or instructions to the computer to perform certain tasks. These

FIGURE 13.2   Sample of a short program written in Logo

```
   To Triangle

ST

REPEAT 3 [FD 10 RT 120]

HT

   END


   TO PATTERN

   REPEAT 6 [TRIANGLE RT 60]

   END
```

The meanings of the instructions are as follows:

1. Set up a drawing procedure to be called "TRIANGLE" (TO TRIANGLE).

2. Make the drawing of the lines visible or "show the turtle" (ST).

3. Do the following three times: draw a line forward 10 units and turn right 120 degrees (REPEAT 3 [FD 10 RT 120]).

4. This is the end of the procedure called "TRIANGLE" (END).

5. Set up a new procedure called "PATTERN" (TO PATTERN).

6. Do the following six times: carry out the procedure called "TRIANGLE" and turn right 60 degrees (REPEAT 6 [TRIANGLE RT 60]).

7. This is the end of the procedure called "PATTERN" (END).

The instructions to the microcomputer in Logo produce drawings similar to these:

communications in the special languages we have considered constitute the *programs* of instructions or the *software,* which gives purpose and direction to the hardware. *Courseware* has a broader meaning than software. It is software that includes teacher plans, supporting student activities, or some systematic combination of media.

Availability.   In order to select software and courseware for instructional use in the social studies, teachers first need to identify where materials are available. Since educational software development is still in its infancy, many sources are still unknown to teachers. Currently, four basic sources of materials exist:

1. Materials that are not copyrighted and are available at cost or for a nominal fee.
2. Programs published in journals and books for copying and adaptation to different systems.
3. Self-produced programs.
4. Commercially produced materials.

Collections of Educational Software.   Three of the larger collections of software materials that are not copyrighted and that are distributed at cost or may have a handling charge are maintained by the following organizations.

Softswap
San Mateo County Office of Education
333 Main Street
Redwood City, CA 94065

Apple Avocation Alliance
721 Pike Street
Cheyenne, WY 82009

Commodore Systems Division
487 Devon Park Drive
Wayne, PA 19087

The third set of materials is distributed through Commodore dealers throughout the United States, and includes programs in history and geography. Many other informal systems for sharing software, some through telephone hookups of microcomputers, are developing across the United States.

Materials that are not copyrighted or are self-made tend to be a mixed bag. The creation of exceptional software is a time-consuming, complex task requiring individuals skilled in programming and in the capabilities of various hardware systems. Consequently, when individuals are able to develop such materials, they often decide to market them commercially.

Evaluating Software. Not all commercial software is exceptional, however, and teachers need to examine *all* software as critically as they do traditional print materials and media. They need to become conversant with the capabilities and limitations of existing software, and to learn how to evaluate such materials objectively. A useful set of criteria and a simple easy-to-use evaluation format, *Evaluator's Guide for Microcomputer-Based Instructional Materials,* has been developed by the International Council for Computers in Education, University of Oregon, Eugene, OR, 97403.

In the past it has been difficult for teachers even to obtain examination or review copies of commercial software from publishers, who feared, with some justification, that expensive software would be *copied* and then returned.[7] There are signs that this policy is changing. Increasingly, publishers are developing strategies to safeguard against copying and to expedite reviewing. Several major companies, such as Scholastic, Inc., now allow educators to examine materials and then return them within thirty days.

The Compatibility Issue. Since the finest of hardware systems are useless for instruction without some software, either commercially or individually produced, it is often suggested that educators seek the software they need before purchasing hardware. This common suggestion results in part from the fact that software designed for one hardware system, say an Apple IIe, will not operate on another such as an Atari 800XL. There are signs that this compatibility issue will be resolved in the future, but for now it is a major consideration in selecting software.

Matching Hardware and Software. When the school already has purchased computer systems, educators need to be certain that software will function properly with the available hardware. In determining whether software will operate on the school's microcomputer system, educators need to ask at least three questions:

1. For which type and model of computer is it designed (Apple IIe, TRS-80, Model III, etc.)?
2. How much memory must our computer system have to operate the software?
3. Besides the microcomputer and television or monitor, what other peripherals, are necessary in order to use the software fully (e.g., one or more disk drives, printer)?

Microcomputer Applications in the Social Studies

As an instructional tool, computers can help the teacher achieve more adequately, efficiently, or economically various objectives laid out in the curriculum. In this role computers are used, as are other tools, only when needed for an appropriate educational task. Personal computers serve as electronic extensions of the teacher, much like an overhead projector. The instructional aim is not to use the computer, but rather to accomplish some curricular objective for which the computer is a suitable tool.

The information educators receive today concerning how microcomputers and software can aid them in teaching social studies is not likely to satisfy them, though it should whet their appetites. The major problem is not the number or quality of materials, although this is certainly a serious one. It is the limited extent to which software and courseware seriously address the total scope and sequence of the typical social studies curriculum.

An assortment of programs with individual lessons, exercises, and activities — some of them stimulating and thought provoking — do exist for most popular microcomputers. However, there is little software available to address the wide range of objectives associated with the scope and sequence of a typical K–12 social studies curriculum. The findings from two recent general surveys of software available for the social studies underscore this point.[8]

The Current Status of Software Applications. If we consider the framework for the social studies curriculum that has been developed throughout this text, several generalizations are possible concerning the software available in social studies at the elementary level.

1. Materials are not equally distributed among the three dimensions of the social studies curriculum: reflection, competence, and concern. Few materials address in any systematic way the dimension of social *concern*.
2. Although several programs exist to teach students to develop and test hypotheses, to generalize, to engage in problem solving, and to develop research, analysis, spatial, and social skills, most are designed to teach specific sets of *facts*.

3. Among the social sciences, history, political science, economics, and geography are dominant.
4. No materials exist to teach specific concepts.
5. Even the most unimaginative of programs provide some individualization of instruction.

The future task of developing successful, comprehensive K–12 social studies software will require the joint efforts of educators, subject matter specialists, and computer personnel. This should occur in much the same way that teams of specialists have combined to produce quality curriculum products in the print media. Ultimately, unless the software produced meets a substantial number of significant curricular objectives, social studies educators are not likely to regard personal computers as important tools.

Sample Software for the Social Studies. In spite of the limitations of existing software, there are several ways in which the current generation of microcomputers and software can enhance social studies instruction or ease the burdens of teachers. A complete listing of all social studies software currently available for elementary and middle-school students is beyond the scope of this text. We will discuss a few programs briefly, however, to illustrate the variety of objectives that existing software can address.

Processing and Interpreting Data. The computer is an ideal tool for areas of the social studies that involve data retrieval, analysis, organization, and processing.[9] Organization of data into such forms as tables, pie charts, and bar graphs for easy visualization is often a useful way to summarize large bodies of statistical data. Several commercial programs make this transformation an easy task, and produce attractive color displays very quickly. Examples of well-designed programs that allow students easily to process and translate raw data into forms such as pie graphs, bar graphs, and charts are *Graph It* by Atari and *Data-Plot* from Muse Software.

Communication Skills. A variety of word processing programs have been developed to encourage students to write reports or do projects. Basically, word processing programs take some of the tedium out of writing and rewriting. They also make corrections easy, and they encourage editing and experimentation.[10]

For example, this book was written using a word processing program called *Wordstar* and a spelling program called *Correct It*. Together they allowed me to move around sentences and paragraphs quickly, to add new items up to the last minute without having to retype the entire document or even a whole page, to experiment with words and phrases without a great deal of rewriting, to ignore technical typing issues (such as margin size, page length, or line endings), and to check the spelling of *each* word used in a matter of minutes.

One of the easiest word processing programs to use as we go to press is *Bank Street Writer*, produced both by Broderbund Software and Scholastic, Inc. It was designed for children and is appropriate for use in the intermediate and middle-school grades. Several similar programs are being marketed or are under development.

Group Participation Skills. Any instructor who has observed students in a programming class working on microcomputers will attest to the spontaneous, task-oriented, cooperative social behavior that often arises when a student needs help. As one researcher has noted, "I have seen more collaborative, cooperative, problem-solving among kids who are doing program activities together than anywhere else in schools." [11]

Computer simulations are excellent vehicles for improving group participation skills. Although simulations often assume only one user per computer, anecdotal data suggest that they seem to encourage cooperative behavior when a small group is assigned to the game. One of the early social studies simulations, and still one of the most interesting, is *Oregon Trail,* developed by the Minnesota Educational Computing Consortium (MECC). It presents the series of decisions that pioneers in a wagon train have to make as they cross the United States. The simulation is both an effective learning device and a catalyst for cooperative behavior when played by a group. Newer simulations, such as *President-Elect,* illustrate the power of personal computers to predict rapidly the effects of a number of variables on an event such as an election.

Facts. Probably more computer materials exist to teach facts (such as names of capitals and states or countries or provinces, lists of presidents, collections of dates, names of continents and oceans) than to fulfill any other objective. Many of these programs are classified as "drill and practice," since they emphasize memorization through repetition. The worst are merely electronic workbooks. The most interesting of these programs employ graphics, audio instructions, and immediate feedback on responses and percentages of correct answers. Some of the best designed and most colorful of these are *Atlas of Canada* and *European Countries and Capitals* by Atari and the *Exploring America* series by Eye Gate Media.

The fundamental programming structure of this type of instructional material, apart from the inclusion of graphics, often is simple. Designing a small program to teach such material is a suitable project for social studies teachers who are interested in experimenting with hands-on programming in BASIC. Some teachers enjoy constructing such programs and have become proficient at creating their own computer-based activities.

Figure 13.3 shows a very simple program that requires very little programming ability and time to construct, and that uses humor to stimulate interest in a general area.

Concepts. Although no computer materials currently exist to teach social studies concepts, computers have the capacity to handle the task more effectively than any other instructional tool. [12] In essence materials for teaching concepts with a microcomputer follow the guidelines discussed in Chapter 4.

The programs *Moptown Parade* and *Moptown Hotel,* produced by The Learn-

FIGURE 13.3 Sample microcomputer program

10   INPUT "What's your name"; Y$

20   INPUT "Who's your favorite president"; F$

30   INPUT "Choose just one word that says something about what you would like to do to the president"; V$

40   PRINT "I'm going to tell you a story about "; F$

50   PRINT "Once upon a time, President "; F$

60   PRINT "Had a young admirer named "; Y$

70   PRINT Y$; " wished to "; V$; " "; F$

80   PRINT "Interestingly, "; F$; " also wanted to "; V$; " "; Y$

90   PRINT "Will "; Y$; " " V$; " "; F$

100   PRINT "Will "; F$; " "; V$; " "; Y$

110   PRINT "The world awaits the outcome of the meeting between "; Y$; " and "; F$

A sample run of the program might look like the following (responses a student might type in are in parentheses)

> What's your name? (Jake)
>
> Who's your favorite president, Jake? (Franklin Pierce)
>
> Choose just one word that says something about what you would like to do to the president? (tickle)
>
> I'm going to tell you a story about Franklin Pierce
>
> Once upon a time, President Franklin Pierce
>
> Had a young admirer named Jake
>
> Jake wished to tickle Franklin Pierce
>
> Interestingly, Franklin Pierce also wanted to tickle Jake
>
> Will Jake tickle Franklin Pierce
>
> Will Franklin Pierce tickle Jake
>
> The world awaits the outcome of the meeting between Jake and Franklin Pierce

ing Company for young children, helps develop more efficient concept learning strategies in general. Also, Project ComICon (Computers to Individualize Concept Learning), supported by the Atari Institute and directed by the author at Temple University, currently is developing prototype materials to illustrate how teachers may design their own computer programs to teach any concepts.

Problem Solving. Several computer simulation games have been designed to encourage problem solving and cooperative behavior while pursuing geography, history, political science, anthropology, economics, and sociology subject-matter topics.

One of the more detailed and colorful sets of simulation materials for students in the intermediate and middle school grades is *The Search Series* by McGraw-Hill. It includes five topics that range from an ancient navigator expedition to an archeological dig. Another example is the *Snooper Troops* series developed by Spinnaker Software Inc., which develops deductive logic skills and problem solving in children in the intermediate and middle grades. For preschool and primary children, *Gertrude's Secret* and *Rocky's Boots* by The Learning Company are designed to achieve the same objectives.

Management of Classroom Tasks. Besides aiding teachers with instructional tasks, microcomputers can help teachers manage some of their general professional responsibilities.[13] For example, they can aid in:

preparing written materials

general record keeping

filing records and general information

testing and test scoring

assessing the reading levels of materials

Commercial programs exist to assist in all of these tasks, and some have even been published in journals for copying. A few are *Finding Readability Levels* by Sunburst Communications to assess reading levels, *Grade Book Disk* by Southeastern Educational Software to keep class records and student averages, and *PFS:File* by Software Publishing Corporation to develop and retrieve files easily.

EXERCISE 13.2   Examining Social Studies Software

Examine a software program for social studies that is appropriate for a student in the elementary or middle grades. Analyze the strengths and weaknesses of the program, and then identify two instructional objectives the material attempts to achieve.

Social Implications of Microcomputers. The political, social, and economic consequences of the micro revolution, as well as its fascinating history and geographical dispersion, should be the province of the social studies class. The rapid growth of data banks and computer networking and the ease with which proprietary materials may be copied have created serious ethical and legal issues, which students need to address just as they should consider other urgent contemporary value questions.

Social Issues. Just a few of the topics that may be examined are:

How each of us feels about the rise of computers

The role that computers can and should play in our society

The fears and anxieties that computers produce in many people

The real and imagined potential of computers for dehumanization

What a computerized society of the future will be like

The Video Revolution and the Social Studies

For learning theory one of the important limitations of most computer-based instruction is its heavy reliance on *abstract* or *verbal* teaching. As we discussed in Chapter 2, the use of *imagery* or visual material, in contrast to abstractions, both enlivens social studies instruction and makes it easier for most students to understand. Whatever its other instructional assets, the current generation of microcomputer hardware and software is restricted in terms of what it can offer *visually* for social studies educators. Compared to the imagery available in other forms — such as still pictures, slides, paintings, films, and filmstrips — the visual representation offered by the current state of advanced computer graphics is primitive.

The recent revolution in video technology promises to provide educators with convenient and inexpensive new electronic tools for producing and using visual material. Both *videocassette* and *videodisc* technologies continue to improve in performance and convenience, and to decrease in price. Low-cost versions of both are currently in the $300.00–$400.00 range, and many schools now own both types of machines. In addition, teachers increasingly are purchasing them for their combined personal and professional use.

Videodiscs

Videodiscs are vinyl discs that resemble long-playing records. They have the capability to store over 50,000 frames of images or information. One way to think of them is as a book with over 50,000 pages, any one of which can be viewed instantly with no sorting. Because of its capability for quickly retrieving visual material and for providing high-quality images, among other features which videotape technology does not currently provide, it is being used in several projects that are developing educational materials.

Unlike videotape recorders, however, disc players do not permit teachers to create their own materials. The production of discs is a complex and expensive process for small-scale or individual production.[14] It requires special equipment and technical assistance. Furthermore, once the discs have been produced, they cannot be altered. To date, only a few discs are available for school use, although this may change in the near future.

Videocassettes

The new generation of videocassette recorders with freeze-frame, fast-forward capabilities, and portability, along with companion video cameras have opened up several possibilities for the social studies curriculum. Using these technological resources, teachers can create video data tailored to the needs and interests of their students rather than relying on commercially produced materials. Students learning about norms, for example, could be given visual illustrations from their own social groups, as well as from groups in other social strata and cultures. With a video camera, a videotape recorder, and some imagination teachers can create a limitless store of individualized instructional materials.

Classroom Applications of Teacher-Made Video Materials

Teachers who have access to a portable video recorder and a video camera have a rich variety of possible uses for these tools in social studies instruction. R. Murray Thomas has provided an excellent list of examples of how teachers have used these media effectively in instruction.[15] Some of his suggestions for applications are as follows:

> previewing an activity
>
> bringing outside experiences into the classroom
>
> evaluating a student presentation
>
> aiding absentees
>
> informing parents

Previewing an Activity. Thomas offers the example of an intermediate-grade teacher who each year introduced project assignments by showing the new class what previous students had accomplished.

> To show what kind of projects have been popular in the past and to show the quality of work that can result, she presents to this year's group a videotape picturing projects from the two previous years. The scenes include projects in the form of products — such as maps, model villages, dolls dressed in native costumes, scrapbooks containing pictures and drawings — and in the form of activities — such as an illustrated talk to the class, a dance, and a dramatic scene.[16]

Bringing Outside Experiences into the Classroom. Thomas suggests that teachers might record special events that occur in the community, such as fairs and festivals. Also public events, school board meetings, and other special public meetings could be taped. Some communities today routinely tape such events for the public cable channel.

Evaluating Presentations. Often it is helpful to a student who has made a presentation to have a visual record of the event for evaluation. In conjunction with rating sheets, such as those discussed in Chapter 10, teacher and students can identify on the videotape specific behaviors that resulted in the rating.

Aiding Absentees. Often during some local epidemic or protracted student illness, Thomas points out, students who are ill lose out on some special classroom event. This might be a play, a series of student reports, a guest speaker, or the like. A video record of the event could be viewed when the child was well.

Informing Parents. Thomas tells how a kindergarten teacher used class videotapes in a novel way during parents' visiting night.

> She showed two videotapes, one made the previous fall and one the week before the meeting. The purpose was to show the progress the children had made in working and playing well together, taking responsibility, speaking before a group of classmates, trying out new activities, and mastering physical skills.[17]

EXERCISE 13.3   Classroom Applications of Teacher-Made Video Materials

Use the five categories of classroom applications of teacher-made video materials discussed in the text as a framework. Under these headings construct your own list of as many different applications relating to the social studies as you can think of.

Sources of Prepared Video Materials

Beyond personal production and television programs many other sources of video material exist. Many commercial producers now provide videocassette materials. Local and regional public libraries increasingly are acquiring video materials that are available for loan.

Some school districts have provisions for making copies of those videotapes which are in the public domain or for which copying rights have been secured. Many regional media centers that traditionally have supplied cooperating school districts with film rentals have developed video collections in recent years. In one state a central distribution center makes available to schools within the county a large collection of video materials, including items that touch on virtually every area of the elementary and middle school social studies curriculum.

An example of such social studies material is a series of twenty-minute tapes entitled *Trade-Offs*. The series, which deals with economic issues and is designed for the intermediate grades, is shown in Figure 13.4. For the small cost of a two-hour tape (less than $10.00) a school or teacher may obtain a *personal* copy of such video material for classroom use.

Interactive Video Systems

Combine the power of microcomputers with the new video technology and what do you get?[18] The result is an *interactive video system*.[19] Such systems permit visual images and audio messages stored on discs or tape to be incorporated into computer-based instruction. In addition to words and graphics on the screen before them, students can hear speech, music, and other sounds, and see any images that

FIGURE 13.4

TRADE-OFFS SERIES

At What Price? (Market Clearing Price)
Choice (Opportunity Cost)
Does It Pay? (Investment in Capital Goods)
Give and Take (Trade-offs Among Goals)
Helping Out (Market Intervention: Increasing Indirect Benefits)
How Could That Happen? (Interdependence of Market Prices)
Innocent Bystanders (Market Intervention: Reducing Indirect Costs)
Learning and Earning (Investment In Human Capital)
Less and More (Increasing Productivity)
Malcolm Decides (Personal Decision Making)
To Buy Or Not To Buy (Buyers and Market Demand)
To Sell Or Not To Sell (Sellers and Market Supply)
We Decide (Social Decision Making)
Why Money? (Voluntary Exchange)
Working Together (Specialization)

can be recorded. These include visual data from sources such as slides, charts, graphs, drawings, and maps.

Interactive video systems also convert television from a passive medium into an interactive one, because the learner not only can select material to be viewed, but also can *re*-view it. An interactive video system provides a microcomputer with an exciting visual peripheral to complement its other capabilities. Interactive video may use one or more screens to provide video and computer output. It offers computer instruction coordinated with some preprogrammed video disc or tape output. More complex systems permit written material, such as a question, to be overlaid directly on the video display.[20]

Combining Microcomputers and Videoplayers

The video portions of the instruction are under the control of the computer. It can stop, advance, freeze a single frame, or show a portion of a tape or a sequence of frames on a disc according to programmed instructions and decisions the student makes. Using the easy editing features of the newer videocassette recorders and portable cameras, teachers can individualize even prerecorded tapes by deleting unwanted segments of tape or sound and by adding special comments, questions, or even new video material. Since the video recorder will move to any spot on the tape, according to the program instructions, there is no need to locate video material in any special order or sequence.

An Example of an Interactive Video System. One example of how such a system might work might be a fifth-grade American history course in which a teacher has a series of videotaped scenes illustrating famous historical sites. The instructor uses the computer to ask questions about the sites and to determine which of them most interests the student. On the basis of the student's answers, certain sequences of video material are shown and the system stops.

Followup questions related to the video segment then appear on the screen. Depending on the student's responses, a review may begin or the student may be presented with new choices of what may be viewed. The system will move back and forth to the appropriate frames on a videotape, show the appropriate sequence of frames, stop, and return the instruction to the computer.

Social Studies Projects Employing Interactive Video Systems

Interactive video systems are just beginning to appear in schools. Their use is likely to increase considerably as teachers become more knowledgeable about the technologies involved and as costs drop. Only a few projects are now producing social studies materials. When they are completed, these three projects will illustrate both tape and disk technologies used in interactive video systems.

Project CENT. Under the aegis of the Lafayette School Corporation in Lafayette, Indiana, Project CENT (Consumer Education and New Technology) is developing consumer economics lessons using the *Trade-Offs* series mentioned earlier.[21] The system allows developers to regulate the pacing and use of videocassette material and to interject questions throughout its play. For example, after viewing some examples of *goods* and *service,* students might be given a list of cases on the monitor, and then asked to identify examples. If necessary, selective portions of taped material could be replayed.

Microcomputer/Videodisc Project. Also dealing with economics, but for high school students, is a project sponsored by MECC.[22] It uses specially created videodiscs to create an interactive instructional system. Unlike Project CENT, the MECC project uses *two* monitors, one for disc output and one for computer output. A student manual is included that directs students' attention to either the monitor showing the visual images or the one that has computer output.

Project ComICon. Unlike the other two projects, Project ComICon as mentioned earlier will demonstrate how instructors may create their own interactive video systems to teach concepts in any subject matter area, including the social studies.

EXERCISE 13.4   Developing a Scenario of the Future

Devise *your* scenario of what the social studies program of the twenty-first century will be like. In an essay of 500 words or less, develop your ideas, along with your supporting rationale.

The Social Studies Classroom of the Future

It is not difficult to extrapolate from the rapid growth of communications and computer technology over the past few years and the changes taking place in our society to form a vision of the social studies classroom of the future. One can prophesy that schools in the twenty-first century will be radically different from the ones we know today.

Instructional Tools of the Future

The fundamental purposes of our schools are not likely to change, but the tools they use most commonly to achieve their ends are likely to be dramatically altered. And with these alterations will come wholesale restructuring of the schools' infrastructures and their curriculum.

It is conceivable, for example, that once extensive specialized information retrieval systems become miniaturized and are available at low cost to every child, our notions of what it means to be "well educated" or "knowledgeable" will be transformed. Access to even the most sophisticated data base is likely to be convenient and inexpensive in the next century.

The Social Studies Curriculum

When this phenomenon occurs, the social studies curriculum K–12 will undergo revisions as well. Many of the skills, factual data, and algorithms we now consider important or essential will be subject to question. The increasing availability and applications of microcomputers will extend the range of the school and its curriculum far beyond any building or set of classrooms. The world will truly become the social studies classroom for students of the twenty-first century.

The Challenge of the Future

The challenge for us as teachers of social studies is both an exciting and a demanding one. We must determine which roles technology and the rich informal educational system beyond the school most appropriately can play in the development of reflective, competent, and concerned citizens.

Notes

1. David G. Armstrong and Tom V. Savage, Jr., "A Framework for Utilizing the Community for Social Learning in Grades 4 to 6," *Social Education* 40 (March 1976): 164.
2. Material in this section is adapted from Peter H. Martorella, "Implications of Microcomputers for Social Studies Teacher Education," in *New Directions in Social Science Teacher Education,* ed. Charles R. Berryman and Marion J. Rice (Athens, Ga.: Department of Social Science Education, 1983), pp. 69–80.
3. See, for example, Beverley Hunter, "Computer Literacy in Grades K–8," *Journal of Educational Technology Systems* (1981–82):59–67; Arthur Luehrmann and Herbert Peckham, *Computer Literacy: A Hands-On Approach, Grades 6–12.* (New York: McGraw-Hill, 1982); Seymour Papert, *Mindstorms.* (New York: Basic Books, 1980);

Robert J. Seidel et al., eds., *Computer Literacy: Issues and Directions for 1985.* (New York: Academic Press, 1982).

4. David Morusund, *School Administrator's Introduction to Instructional Use of Computers.* (LaGrande, Ore.: International Council for Computers in Education, 1980).

5. Peter McWilliams, "Learning BASIC's Basics Is No Longer a Necessity," *Philadelphia Inquirer,* June 19, 1983, Book review section, p. 10.

6. See the following issues of computer journals: *Byte* 7 (August 1982); *Electronic Learning,* 6 (March 1983).

7. L. Letellier, "Copying Software: Crime in the Classroom?" *Electronic Learning* 1 (January/February 1982):42–44; 51–53.

8. Mollie L. Cohen, "Educational Software: A Taste of What's Available for Social Studies," *The Social Studies* (December 1982):1115; Hodges, James O., "A Bibliography of Microcomputer Software for Social Studies Educators: Working Draft," Richmond, Va.: Department of Education, September, 1982.

9. D. K. Rowney, "The Historian and the Computer: A Student of the Past Meets a Machine of the Future," *Byte* 7 (July 1982): 166–167.

10. Peter McWilliams, *The Word Processor Book* (Los Angeles: Prelude Press, 1982).

11. G. W. Bracey, "Computers in Education: What the Research Shows," *Electronic Learning* 2 (November/December 1982): 51–54.

12. See Robert Gagné et al., "Planning and Authoring Computer-Assisted Instruction Lessons," *Educational Technology* 21 (September 1981): 17–29; and Peter H. Martorella, *Concept Learning in the Social Studies: Models for Structuring Curriculum* (Scranton, Pa.: INTEXT, 1971).

13. See, for example, Stanley S. Pogrow, "Microcomputerizing Your Paperwork," *Electronic Learning* 2 (September 1982): 54–59 and Stanley S. Pogrow, "Microcomputerizing Your Paperwork Part II: Scheduling and Attendance Packages," *Electronic Learning* (October 1982): 20–27.

14. Bejar, I. I., "Videodiscs in Education: Integrating the Computer and Communication Technologies," *Byte* 7 (June 1982): 40–47.

15. R. Murray Thomas, and Dale Brubaker, eds., *Teaching Elementary Social Studies: Readings* (Belmont, Calif.: Wadsworth, 1972), pp. 281–289.

16. Ibid., p. 284.

17. Ibid., p. 288.

18. This section is adapted from Peter H. Martorella, "Interactive Video in the Classroom," *Social Education* 47 (May 1983): 325–327.

19. EPIE Institute, *Microcomputer Hardware/Interactive Video Systems* (Stony Brook, N.Y.: EPIE Institute, 1981).

20. Rod Daynes, "The Videodisc Interfacing Primer," *Byte* 7 (June 1982): 48–58.

21. Joanne Troutner, "Technology and Consumer Economics," *Electronic Learning* 1 (January/February 1982): 2, 62.

22. Allen D. Glenn, "Videodiscs and the Social Studies Classroom," *Social Education* 47 (May 1983): 328–330.

Suggested Readings

Armstrong, David A., and Savage, Tom V., Jr. "A Framework for Utilizing the Community for Social Learning in Grades 4 to 6," *Social Education* 40 (March 1976): 164–167.

Burnett, J. Dale. *Logo: An Introduction*. Morris Plains, N.J.: Creative Computing Press, 1982.

Diem, Richard A., ed. "Technology and the Social Studies," Special Issue, *Social Education* 47 (May 1983): 308–343.

Daynes, Rod. "The Videodisc Interfacing Primer," *Byte* 6 (June 1981): 48–59.

Evans, Christopher. *The Micro Millennium*. New York: Washington Square Press, 1979.

EPIE Institute. *Microcomputer Hardware/Interactive Video Systems*. Stony Brook, N.Y.: Epie Institute, 1981.

Fitch, Robert M., and Svengalis, Cordell M. *Futures Unlimited: Teaching about Worlds to Come*, Bulletin 59. Washington, D.C.: National Council for the Social Studies, 1979.

Gagné, Robert, et al. "Planning and Authoring Computer-Assisted Instruction Lessons," *Educational Technology* 21 (September 1981): 17–29.

Goodlad, John I. *A Place Called School: Prospects for the Future*. New York: McGraw-Hill, 1984. Chapter 9.

Gilliom, M. Eugene, et al. *Practical Methods for the Social Studies*. Belmont, Calif.: Wadsworth, 1979, Chapters 5, 6.

Hodges, James O. "A Bibliography of Microcomputer Software for Social Studies Educators: Working Draft." Richmond, Va.: Department of Education, September, 1982.

Lambda Software. *K–12 Course Goals in Computer Education*. Saddle River, N.J.: Lambda Software, P.O. Box LSI, 1982.

Luehrmann, Arthur, and Peckham, Herbert. *Computer Literacy: A Hands-On Approach, Grades 6–12*. New York: McGraw-Hill, 1982.

Metcalf, Fay D., and Downey, Matthew T. *Using Local History in the Classroom*. Nashville, Tenn.: American Association for State and Local History, 1982.

Papert, Seymour. *Mindstorms*. New York: Basic Books, 1980.

Robinson, Sheryl B. "Microcomputer Software and the Social Studies," *ERIC Keeping Up*, December 1982.

Seidel, Robert J. et al., eds. *Computer Literacy: Issues and Directions for 1985*. New York: Academic Press, 1982.

Taylor, Robert P., ed. *The Computer in the School: Tutor, Tool, Tutee*. New York: Teachers College Press, 1980.

Thomas, R. Murray, and Brubaker, Dale, eds. *Teaching Elementary Social Studies: Readings*. Belmont, Calif.: Wadsworth, 1972, Part III.

Troutner, J. "How To Produce an Interactive Video Program," *Electronic Learning* 22 (January 1983): 70–75.

Walter, Russ. *The Secret Guide to Microcomputers*. Vol. I, 11th ed. Boston: Russ Walter Publications, 1984.

Index